# DICKENS AND BENJAMIN

Placing the works of Charles Dickens and Walter Benjamin in conversation with one another, Gillian Piggott argues that the two writers display a shared vision of modernity. Her analysis of their works shows that both writers demonstrate a decreased confidence in the capacity to experience truth or religious meaning in an increasingly materialist world and that both occupy similar positions towards urban modernity and its effect upon experience.

Piggott juxtaposes her exploration of Benjamin's ideas on allegory and messianism with an examination of Dickens's *The Old Curiosity Shop*, arguing that both writers proffer a melancholy vision of a world devoid of space and time for religious experience, a state of affairs they associate with the onset of industrial capitalism. In Benjamin's *The Arcades Project* and Dickens's *Sketches by Boz* and *Tale of Two Cities*, among other works, the authors converge in their hugely influential treatments of the city as a site of perambulation, creativity, memory, and autobiography. At the same time, both authors relate to the vertiginous, mutable, fast-paced nature of city life as involving a concomitant change in the structure of experience, an alteration that can be understood as a reduction in the capacity to experience fully. Piggott's persuasive analyses enable a reading of Dickens as part of a European, particularly a German, tradition of thinkers and writers of industrialization and modernity. For both Dickens and Benjamin, truth appears only in moments of revelation, in fragments of modernity.

# The Nineteenth Century Series
# General Editors' Preface

The aim of the series is to reflect, develop and extend the great burgeoning of interest in the nineteenth century that has been an inevitable feature of recent years, as that former epoch has come more sharply into focus as a locus for our understanding not only of the past but of the contours of our modernity. It centres primarily upon major authors and subjects within Romantic and Victorian literature. It also includes studies of other British writers and issues, where these are matters of current debate: for example, biography and autobiography, journalism, periodical literature, travel writing, book production, gender, non-canonical writing. We are dedicated principally to publishing original monographs and symposia; our policy is to embrace a broad scope in chronology, approach and range of concern, and both to recognize and cut innovatively across such parameters as those suggested by the designations 'Romantic' and 'Victorian'. We welcome new ideas and theories, while valuing traditional scholarship. It is hoped that the world which predates yet so forcibly predicts and engages our own will emerge in parts, in the wider sweep, and in the lively streams of disputation and change that are so manifest an aspect of its intellectual, artistic and social landscape.

Vincent Newey
Joanne Shattock
*University of Leicester*

# Dickens and Benjamin
## Moments of Revelation, Fragments of Modernity

GILLIAN PIGGOTT
*Manchester Metropolitan University, UK.*

ASHGATE

Published by
Ashgate Publishing Limited
Wey Court East
Union Road
Farnham
Surrey, GU9 7PT
England
www.ashgate.com

Ashgate Publishing Company
110 Cherry Street
Suite 3-1
Burlington
VT 05401-3818
USA

**British Library Cataloguing in Publication Data**
Piggott, Gillian.
Dickens and Benjamin: moments of revelation, fragments of modernity. – (The nineteenth century series)
1. Dickens, Charles, 1812–1870 – Political and social views. 2. Benjamin, Walter, 1892–1940 – Political and social views. 3. Civilization, Modern, in literature. 4. City and town life in literature. 5. Comparative literature – English and German. 6. Comparative literature – German and English.
I. Title II. Series
823.8–dc23

**Library of Congress Cataloging-in-Publication Data**
Piggott, Gillian.
Dickens and Benjamin: moments of revelation, fragments of modernity / by Gillian Piggott.
p. cm. (The nineteenth century series)
Includes bibliographical references and index.
1. Dickens, Charles, 1812–1870—Criticism and interpretation. 2. Benjamin, Walter, 1892–1940—Criticism and interpretation. 3. Literature and society. 4. Civilization, Modern, in literature. 5. Materialism in literature. 6. Aesthetics, Comparative. I. Title.

PR4592.S58P54 2012
823'.8—dc23

2012024092

ISBN 9781409422013 (hbk)
ISBN 9781409422020 (ebk – PDF)
ISBN 9781409472131 (ebk – ePUB)

MIX
Paper from responsible sources
FSC® C018575
www.fsc.org

Printed and bound in Great Britain by the MPG Books Group, UK

*For Andrew Jarvis,*
*whose unstinting love and support allowed me to write this book*

# Contents

# List of Figures

# List of Abbreviations

Benjamin's *Gesammelte Schriften* given as *GS* is a reference to Rolf Tiedemann and Hermann Schweppenhäuser (eds.), *Gesammelte Schriften*, 7 vols, with the assistance of Theodor W. Adorno and Gershom Scholem (Frankfurt a.M: Suhrkamp Verlag, 1972–1989).

English translations of Benjamin's works given as *SW*, followed by vol. no., reference Michael W. Jennings and others (eds.), *Walter Benjamin: Selected Writings*, 4 vols (Cambridge, MA; London: The Belknap Press of Harvard University Press, 1996–2003).

English translations of specific essays given as 'Illuminations' reference Hannah Arendt (ed.), *Walter Benjamin: Illuminations*, trans. Harry Zohn (London: Pimlico, 1999).

The English translation of Benjamin's *The Origin of German Tragic Drama* (London: Verso 1977) by John Osborne is abbreviated as *OGTD*.

'The Paris of the Second Empire in Baudelaire' is abbreviated as '2nd Empire'.

'Paris – Capital of the Nineteeth Century' is abbreviated as 'Paris, Capital'.

'On Some Motifs in Baudelaire' is abbreviated as 'Motifs'.

The following additional abbreviations apply:

| | |
|---|---|
| *BH* | *Bleak House* |
| *BR* | *Barnaby Rudge* |
| *C* | *A Christmas Carol* |
| *DC* | *David Copperfield* |
| *DS* | *Dombey and Son* |
| *ED* | *The Mystery of Edwin Drood* |
| *GE* | *Great Expectations* |
| *HM* | *The Haunted Man* |
| *HT* | *Hard Times* |
| *LD* | *Little Dorrit* |
| *MC* | *Martin Chuzzlewit* |
| *NN* | *Nicholas Nickleby* |
| *OCS* | *The Old Curiosity Shop* |
| *OMF* | *Our Mutual Friend* |

| | |
|---|---|
| *OT* | *Oliver Twist* |
| *PP* | *The Pickwick Papers* |
| *SB* | *Sketches by Boz* |
| 'SN' | 'Shy Neighbourhoods' ('The Uncommercial Traveller') |
| 'ST' | 'Shops and Their Tenants' |
| *TTC* | *A Tale of Two Cities* |

# Foreword

Michael Hollington

Gillian Piggott is known to me as an esteemed member of a community of Dickens scholars currently exploring new avenues of approach to England's greatest novelist. It would be a mistake, I think, to suggest that these share any one particular focus or characteristic, but one of the assertions that might safely be made about them is that they tend to look at Dickens, not just as the quintessentially 'English' writer he was felt to be, not without reason, by previous generations, but also as a literary and cultural giant of international and indeed global significance. In the year of the bicentenary of his birth, we are starting to see how much he has meant beyond Britain and the United States – not just in former colonies or other English-speaking parts of the globe, but in other languages and cultures, in Europe, in Asia, and beyond.

I first met Gillian at a Dickens conference in Verona in 2009. There I learnt that she had written a University of Sussex PhD thesis on Dickens and Benjamin (in which of course the present book has its origins) and discovered we shared common interests and a common cause. It had long seemed to me – ever since I read the then newly published *Passagen-Werk* in the 1970s – that Benjamin's work might offer one of the most fertile of the new approaches to Dickens. Over the years since that significant event, and the book's much later appearance in English in the Harvard edition, the two names have been increasingly invoked and linked by critics and theorists of literary and cultural studies, especially in connection with approaches to urban experience. As a kind of litmus test of this process, I observed at an Oslo conference in 2008 devoted to thinking about London and Paris in the nineteenth century that they seemed at times in many minds to be virtually synonymous.

So a book focused specifically on the relationship between the two would appear thoroughly necessary and timely. One reason for this is that the coupling can be based on solid empirical grounds, which is not always the case when rapprochements between writers and theorists are made. I had noticed, way back in my first reading of the *Passagen-Werk* and elsewhere, a number of references to Dickens's novels, and to Chesterton's biography of the writer – obvious signs that Benjamin actually read Dickens. He was not able to do so in English, but he did make close study of several of the novels, as well as of Chesterton's important biographical and critical study, in German and/or French.

He did so, in the early 1930s, for two reasons. The first was his exposure to an essay on Chaplin written in 1928 by the French Surrealist Philippe Soupault. Benjamin wrote a highly appreciative review of it in 1929, in the course of which he underlines Soupault's emphasis on the relation between Chaplin and Dickens and comments that it might lead to 'further reading and investigation'. He did not actually undertake work in this area, however, until a second, more important stimulus – that provided by Adorno's essay on *The Old Curiosity Shop*, first published in Germany 1931.

Like Deleuze later in France, coming to D.H. Lawrence (not then very fashionable in France) as an important source for *l'Anti-Œdipe* as the result of a tip-off from his wife Fanny, Benjamin discovered Dickens (at a time when he was beginning to be widely dismissed in Germany as a mere children's author) through an intermediary, in the shape of his close friend Theodor Wiesengrund Adorno. Adorno came from a comfortable, liberal, anglophile Rhineland family and had been exposed to Dickens from a tender age. Later in the 1930s he would gravitate to Merton College, Oxford (where he introduced the distinguished drama critic John Willett to the work of Benjamin's friend Bertolt Brecht), and later still, to America. So he could read Dickens in English, and thus made an excellent, indeed even authoritative conduit for Benjamin's encounter with the novelist.

Yet at the theoretical level, Adorno's work on *The Old Curiosity Shop* bears unmistakeable signs of strong influence from Benjamin even before the latter had read Dickens. Essentially, his essay stems from Benjamin's thinking about allegory and 'allegoresis' in his *Habilitationsschrift* on the *Origin of German Tragic Drama*, rejected because the jury of examiners found it incomprehensible. Adorno thought he saw in Dickens traces of an allegorical habit of thinking that lay half buried beneath the Romantic privileging of 'symbol'. Benjamin considered this preference questionable, based as he felt it to be on an ersatz theology and philosophy of language which failed to take into proper account the essentially fallen nature of language. Allegory for him had the advantage of accepting the essential division between word and thing – it 'laid bare the device', in the formalist terminology of the period that also decisively influenced Brecht. And Adorno's borrowed contention, that it was still there in *The Old Curiosity Shop* in Dickens's way of treating material objects, naturally enough led Benjamin to want to explore Dickens at first hand.

When I first attempted to read his work, however, I can't say I understood it fully either. Although my 1981 *Dickensian* essay 'Dickens the Flâneur' is sometimes cited as one of the sources for the Benjamin approach to Dickens, I am now of the opinion that I got things wrong there. In particular I did not then perceive the extent to which the idea of the flâneur is for Benjamin a critical and dialectical construct for understanding the Hegelian 'sleep' of modern consumerism that it is the cultural critic's task to try to wake us up from. I gave instead a rather euphoric account of Dickens's habit of pacing city streets in London and Paris – especially in the throes of composition of his great novels – and of observing and physiognomically reading the faces and gestures of the anonymous people he saw around him in the crowd. I understood 'flânerie' too superficially as simply a form of observation.

In subsequent writings on Dickens and the city, I have attempted to correct this misapprehension. But Piggott's book engages with Benjamin at another level entirely. First, in the comprehensive survey it offers of so much of his *œuvre*, scouring even the most difficult of the early texts, and engaging in complex and sophisticated argument in its attempt to fix the relevance of the theory of allegory and language to be found there to Dickens's work. Second, in its clarity, patience and good sense, in its unwillingness to fudge or sing along, karaoke-style, with Benjamin's idiosyncratic method, derived as it is in so many respects from Proust, and thus often highly associative, metaphoric and poetic in nature. And third, in the alertness and acuteness of the readings of Dickens's own writings, especially about the city, that she is able to mount on the basis of her in-depth encounter with Benjamin. Throughout, it is clear that she recognizes in his novels perhaps the most impressive and extensive realization of Baudelaire's dream of 'the miracle of a poetic prose'.

Of course, Piggott's own account of Benjamin has idiosyncratic elements of its own – one wonders how it could be otherwise with this thinker – and may not be equally convincing at every turn. But I'd be surprised if this book didn't become 'incontournable,' as the French say, for anyone in future seeking to think seriously about the possibilities – and limitations? – of the Benjamin approach to Dickens. With entire appropriateness, she plans now to move on to a full-length study of Dickens and Chaplin, working out the task that Benjamin seems to have thought he might take on himself when he made that remark in response to Soupault's essay. It is a linkage that has certainly been studied in the past, but not in the degree of detail and depth that we find exemplified here in the case of Dickens and Benjamin. That book, too, should be well worth waiting for.

# Acknowledgments

There are a number of people to whom I owe an intellectual debt both in the conception and execution of this project. I would like, firstly, to express gratitude to the philosopher who, many years ago, first introduced me to Walter Benjamin's thought with a discussion of what are probably two of the most enigmatic of Benjamin's works, the 'Epistemo-Critical Prologue' of his *Trauerspiel* study, and 'The Concept of Criticism in German Romanticism'. Many thanks to Professor Andrew Benjamin for this baptism of fire, and for a number of others. Warwick University was the exciting crucible wherein the ideas that grew into this project were incubated: Dr Christina Britzolakis and Dr John Rignall, thank you for your interest in the early stages. I owe an enormous debt of thanks to Professor Norman Vance at Sussex University who supervised my PhD on Dickens and Benjamin with the kind of perspicacity, kindness and encouragement one can only dream of in a supervisor. His good-humoured level-headedness was crucial to my progress and is a quality I have tried to emulate in my own dealings with students. Dr Paulina Palmer, thank you for your encouragement, and for the example you provide to us all. Thanks are also due to Professor Michael Hollington, who read my manuscript in various forms and was always generous with his knowledge, his time and with his praise. Thank you Ann Donahue at Ashgate Press, who has been a redoubtable resource of wisdom and patience. Also, many thanks to Kathy Bond Borie at Ashgate for her meticulous editorial work; to Paul McDermott for his energy, his indefatigability in working on the index; and to Mike Fenner for his fine visual representation of Dickens and Benjamin for the front cover. I must also thank a number of colleagues, friends and students at the University of Balamand, Lebanon, who acted as comrades and interlocutors, especially Dr Mike Orr, Karen Wade, Dr Giuseppe Tassone, Dr Andrew Long, Dr John Wall, Mahboubeh Wall, Lana Dabbousy, Sabiha Allouche, Sadika Kebbi and the 'Gothic Girls': Mona Sahyoun, Mayada Masri, Rachelle Askar, Aimee Ayoub, Hind Ayoubi, Angie Murad. You believed in me and your conversations, antics and ideas stimulated me. Um Tarek Mansour and Ghassan, you are simply an inspiration. My 'London friends': Nick Ames, Ann Kooyman Hall, Dawn Chamarette, Louise Pearce, Amena Saleem – you helped because I knew you were there. Sylvia Brooke, I lost you, but you were the one who showed me there is more to life. Thank you so much. I owe you more than I could ever repay. Professor Peter Poellner, thank you for your friendship, your gentleness and for our London walks and conversations.

It only remains for me to thank my dear mother, Gloria, for her kindness and bravery over the years. And Andrew, my rock.

# Introduction

This book explores the possibility that the English novelist Charles Dickens (1812–1870) and the German philosopher Walter Benjamin (1892–1940) share a common vision of modern existence. Bringing together the greatest of nineteenth century writers with one of the twentieth century's most gifted and esoteric thinkers may seem a surprising strategy: but there are fruitful areas of convergence to examine. Benjamin makes the connection with Dickens himself. *The Arcades Project*,[1] his huge file of fragments of material history collated over 13 years, contains 15 entries concerning Charles Dickens.[2] Hence an intertextual coming together of Benjamin with Dickens, on Benjamin's initiative, was the initial spark that grew into this project.

More broadly and importantly, this book argues, both men's works are a complex response to and struggle with the phenomenon of modernity (understood as the socioeconomic, physical, metaphysical and experiential changes brought about by the onset of industrial capitalism and urbanization). Despite their contrasting geographical and historical standpoints and the specificity of their modes of expression,[3] Dickens and Benjamin shared a mutual concern with how consciousness is affected by industrial patterns of time and urban contexts; they wanted to understand the spiritual or religious crisis that resulted from an increasing emphasis upon the material world, material culture, commodities. Their writings included an expression of – or an attempt to work out – how modernity impacted the collective lives of the ordinary people who experienced it. They both, in their idiosyncratic ways, charted modernity – Benjamin in a conscious, formulated way, Dickens within the realms of imaginative fiction. This book argues that their respective accounts of modern experience, which they reflected as well as contributed to, share common ground. Both characterize modern experience as involving a loss, anxiety, a fall; as offering a fragmentary apprehension of knowledge or the breaking up of totalized visions. The evanescent disclosure of truth (or the absolute) is a leitmotif that comes up repeatedly during

[1] 'Das Passagen-Werk', in *GS*, V, 1 and 2; trans. by Howard Eiland and Kevin McLaughlin as *The Arcades Project* (Cambridge, MA; London: Belknap Press of Harvard University Press, 1999), hereafter referred to as *Arcades*. This was Benjamin's magnum opus from 1927–1940.

[2] Sixteen entries, if one counts Benjamin's inclusion of Chesterton's comments upon Victor Hugo taken from Chesterton's *Dickens*. The Dickens entries include a quote from Dickens's 1840–1841 novel, *The Old Curiosity Shop*, and a citation from Dickens's letters. The entries are discussed more fully in Chapter 4.

[3] Benjamin honed his own philosophical style; Dickens wrote narrative fiction. Both men produced articles, too.

the examination of their works. It is, as it were, a refrain within the vision of modernity proffered by Dickens and Benjamin.[4]

It is important to refine what is being said here. It is argued that Dickens and Benjamin responded to a particular historical phenomenon – the rise of industrialization and the metropolis – in ways that bear comparison. This project evolved through an exploration of Benjamin's formulated responses to modernity, which automatically prepared the way to find similar patterns and tendencies in the imagination of Dickens. But the question of influence or a suggestion of causal relationships between the subjects is not at issue. Benjamin's procedure in the *Arcades* was to rip pieces of material culture from their historical contexts and juxtapose them with other earlier or later fragments in a montage that crystallized into a new truth. The methodology of this book is similarly synchronic. It puts to one side the idea that the historical development of Dickens or Benjamin is important in assessing their relationship to each other. This is not in any way to denigrate the importance of socio-historical research in literary scholarship: rather, it is to distinguish this project from such scholarship. The strategy here is a more phenomenological one, which 'brackets off' or suspends the historical context of each writer in the first instance in order to identify particular essences or patterns in the imagination of one writer which resonate with the project of the other. This approach, a simultaneous arrangement of significant elements of Dickens and Benjamin, brings them together in comparison, yielding an analysis which the diachronic perspective would not allow. Once this is done, and the resulting exegesis and analysis have taken place, the significance of the relation between the projects of Dickens and Benjamin, with their differing historical and geographical contexts, will be brought back into play and assessed in the conclusion of this book.

The same applies with respect to relationships between works within each writer's oeuvre. The specificity of Benjamin's fragmentary, allusive style of thinking and writing in any case struggles against the application of any linear narrative upon his body of work. Rather, reading Benjamin often involves a rationale of cherry-picking and bringing together of traces of thought from different essays, a process that brings one closer, tentatively, to a possible 'theory'. In the case of Dickens, the comparative thrust of this book means that what is of interest is how specific qualities in his imagination, manifested in various novels and articles from various periods of his development, can be understood to resonate with Benjamin. His growth as a writer, the relationship of his works to each other, is not of primary importance to this kind of phenomenological enquiry.

On the other hand, if this project requires the temporary suspension of the historical context of the writers, there is a sense in which the historical dimension is always there. It is hardly surprising, for instance, that there are affinities between Dickens and Benjamin when one looks for them, since a major part of Benjamin's

[4] This book suggests that this is a regular theme occurring throughout the body of Benjamin's work. See, for example, his understanding of beauty in art, 'Goethe's Elective Affinities', in *SW*, I, pp. 350–51.

intellectual life was devoted to researching nineteenth-century culture.[5] Benjamin's specific understanding of historiography meant that such communing with the past opened up his own historical present in the twentieth century.[6] His critical thinking on modernity was crystallized through that prolonged engagement. Early and mid nineteenth-century urban culture was an important source of his 'theory' of experience and apperception. His contact with the culture of emerging industrial capitalism – the consequences of which were still being felt – naturally brought him into contact with Dickens's contemporaries and with Dickens himself, whose life and concerns bestrode this period. Dickens, often seen as the quintessence of Englishness, was viewed by Benjamin through a European lens in *The Arcades Project*; he was juxtaposed with Honoré de Balzac (1799–1850), Charles Baudelaire (1821–1867) and Marcel Proust (1871–1922) among hundreds of other figures.

This European view of Dickens is an important aspect of this book, too. Part 1, for instance, which deals with the two writers' respective vision of the religious crisis at the heart of modernity, suggests a possible shared common source of inspiration in seventeenth-century German Baroque culture and late eighteenth-century German Romanticism.

Furthermore, one can hardly ignore that Dickens was a man whose genius reaches far beyond his own time. His monumental achievement was to explore human affairs, politics and morality in a way that elucidates the specificity of the mid-nineteenth century and yet pushed at aesthetic boundaries and opened up intellectual pathways that still resonate today. This continuing relevance must be attributable in part to Dickens's historical moment, his being present at the early stages of industrialization, the fallout of which is still being felt. Critics in Dickens's time and in ours have noticed his talent in speaking to the future. For the great sage John Ruskin, Dickens was 'a pure modernist – a leader of the steam-whistle party par excellence',[7] while Julian Wolfreys believes Dickens's narrative techniques have 'important ramifications for modernist concerns with the city as a fragmentary and mutable space.'[8] Part 2 similarly touches upon Dickens's possible prefiguration of modernist aesthetics.[9] Assessing intellectual affinities across historical boundaries, then, involves the reader of this book in doublethink – an awareness that Dickens and Benjamin are both historical beings who not only express their period in time but have a reach that goes far beyond it; and the need to set that historical dimension aside for the time being.

---

[5] His 13 years of collecting material history for *The Arcades Project* yielded French material primarily, but fragments from other countries, including Germany, England and even Russia, also featured.

[6] Benjamin's historiography in the *Arcades* is fully discussed in Chapter 4.

[7] Philip Collins (ed.), *Dickens: The Critical Heritage* (London: Routledge & Kegan Paul, 1971), p. 443.

[8] *Writing London* (Basingstoke and New York: Palgrave, 1998), p. 12.

[9] 'Modernism' is here understood as a specific set of experimental approaches to writing and art between 1890 and 1940. See Chapter 3, 'Experience and Memory'.

The methodology of this book echoes Benjamin's understanding of historical time: historical insights result from a montage of different historical moments torn from context. It is hoped that, in this project, critical insights will equally result from this approach. If, at the end, it is felt the project has overemphasized the importance of the nineteenth century to Benjamin's ideas; and focused unduly upon the apparent modernity of Dickens's project, it is still a useful contribution to our understanding of Dickens and Benjamin, who have not been explored on quite these terms.[10] This approach puts an interesting pressure on 'the Victorian period' and 'modernity' and re-interrogates their relationship to one another.

That the nineteenth century was so important in the formulation of Benjamin's ideas allows the claim that this book proceeds through a juxtaposing of significant elements and connections in Dickens and Benjamin – rather than being a reading of Benjaminian theory onto Dickens's creative output. This is a creative comparison of the authors' response to modernity. In this sense, the study could be said to resemble the project of those critics who emphasize Dickens's modernity by comparing him with proto-modernist authors who yet had a foot in the nineteenth century: Mark Spilka's *Dickens and Kafka: A Mutual Interpretation* (London: Dennis Dobson, 1963) and Donald Fanger's *Dostoevsky and Romantic Realism*, Harvard Studies in Comparative Literature, 27 (Cambridge, MA: Harvard University Press, 1965). This project, it is suggested, has less in common with scholars who celebrate Dickens's contemporary reach by reading him through poststructuralist and deconstructionist frameworks: John Schad (ed.), *Dickens Refigured: Bodies, Desires and Other Histories* (Manchester and New York: Manchester University Press, 1996); Steven Connor (ed.), *Charles Dickens* (London: Longman, 1996) and John Bowen, *Other Dickens: Pickwick to Chuzzlewit* (Oxford and New York: Oxford University Press, 2000). As fascinating as these latter projects are, the theories with which they tease out new readings of Dickens are not themselves consciously immersed in and derived from an engagement with the culture of former centuries, including Dickens's own – as are Benjamin's 'theories' considered in this book.[11]

Interest in Benjamin and Dickens has gained momentum among Victorianists since this project began, and these contributions must be acknowledged. Three scholars have not conducted a sustained enquiry beyond one chapter

[10] There is surely a book to be written on the significance of the nineteenth century in Benjamin's thought (bearing in mind that Benjamin's historiography would not allow for such an approach). Meanwhile, leading Victorianists have called for greater attention to be paid to Benjamin's *Arcades Project* so that 'Modernity' or 'Modernism' and its relationship to the Victorian period can be further considered (Scott McCracken, 'Random Patterns, Flashes of Insight: Walter Benjamin's Arcades Project', *Journal of Victorian Culture* 7 [Autumn 2002]: pp. 275–86, p. 277).

[11] An exception might be J. Hillis Miller, *Charles Dickens: The World of his Novels* (Cambridge, MA: Harvard University Press, 1958).

or article.[12] Grahame Smith's *Dickens and the Dream of Cinema*, published in 2003, brilliantly uses concepts, insights and vocabulary from Benjamin's later writings on experience to read Dickens in relation to the phenomenon of cinema. Jeremy Tambling's *Going Astray: Dickens and London* (2009) uses Benjamin (and other theorists) to read Dickens's works, life and London itself. In *Excavating Victorians* (2008), Virginia Zimmerman unpacks a number of phrases from Benjamin's 'Theses on the Philosophy of History' to help explore London's philosophical and historical relationship to its ancient past, as represented in *Little Dorrit* and *Our Mutual Friend.* Michael Hollington has written a number of articles using constellations of ideas from Benjamin's Baudelaire material (*The Arcades Project*) and Benjamin's theory of allegory to read Dickens. He began with his groundbreaking 'Dickens the Flâneur' of 1981 and continues to be intrigued by the European light Benjamin's works can throw upon Dickens to this day.[13] His work is undoubtedly an inspiration in this book.

Unlike these other studies, the aim of this book is to tease out and understand the significance, if there is any, of the threads of connection between Dickens and Benjamin. It focuses evenly upon Dickens and Benjamin, investigating two areas of suggested convergence: around the idea that there is a demise in the religious or spiritual dimension of experience in modern existence, and the impact upon experience of urban culture. The further implication is that there are mutual sources of influence in the seventeenth and late eighteenth centuries as well as in the nineteenth century.

In contrast to Grahame Smith's book, this study takes account of ideas in early as well as later Benjamin, examining theories from the 'immanent absolute' in his early theological works to his later theory of 'Erlebnis', and 'Chockerlebnis' (remarkably, terms Smith fails to mention let alone discuss).[14] This establishes Benjamin's body of thought as a substantial presence, making the juxtaposition with Dickens more fruitful. This is not, as Smith puts it, to impose a consistency or identity upon Benjamin's body of work when it lacks it, but to have at hand an intellectual background that generates a deeper understanding of the possible meanings afforded by Benjamin's deliberately open and enigmatic insights and philosophical fragments. Moreover, the breadth of this book's account of Benjamin was requisite to do justice to the affinities and connections with Dickens

---

[12] Theodor W. Adorno, 'Rede uber den Raritätenladen von Charles Dickens', *Frankfurter Zeitung* (April 1931); John Rignall, *Realism and the Strolling Spectator* (London and New York: Routledge, 1992), ch. 5, pp. 62–79; Kevin McLaughlin, *Writing in Parts: Imitation and Exchange in Nineteenth Century Literature* (Stanford, CA: Stanford University Press, 1995), ch. 2, pp. 77–121.

[13] 'Dickens the Flâneur', *The Dickensian* 77 (1981): pp. 77–87.

[14] Two aspects of modern experience described by Benjamin. Full explanations of these terms are found in Part 2, Chapter 3.

that emerged during the course of research; this was important to understanding why there should be an affinity between the two men at all.

In 1931, Theodor W. Adorno wrote his little-known essay on *The Old Curiosity Shop*, 'Rede über den Raritätenladen von Charles Dickens'.[15] This was the first critical combination of Dickens with Benjamin (apart from Benjamin's own). For Adorno's analysis of the 1840–1841 novel was implicitly influenced by Benjamin's theory of allegory, although no mention of Benjamin is made. Part 1 of this book, 'Exquisite Agony: Elements of Messianism and the Baroque in Dickens and Benjamin', offers a more explicit and extensive examination of *The Old Curiosity Shop* in relation to Benjamin's theory of allegory than is found in Adorno's brilliant piece. This examination is divided into two chapters.

Chapter 1 traces the roots of Benjamin's theory of allegory, found in *The Origin of German Tragic Drama* (*Ursprung des deutschen Trauerspiels*), to his encounter with the Kabbalah's mystical language speculations.[16] Taking account of two essays on metaphysics from Benjamin's early period, the chapter suggests that the allegorical gesture bears significant Judaic metaphysical resonances and discusses this in relation to *OCS*. Chapter 2 teases out affinities between the visions of the world depicted by Dickens in *OCS* and that of the German Baroque playwrights in their allegorical drama.[17]

Part 1 suggests that *The Old Curiosity Shop* is Dickens's melancholy meditation upon the spiritual crisis at the heart of the modern, urban world. In Nell's dark environment – a world of decaying matter, objects and physical violence – the religious, transcendent dimension of life is all but obliterated; only sparks, precious and rare moments of revelation are on offer. Much of life is experienced as a messianic yearning for an end to it all, for total redemption. Hence, it is argued, Dickens's allegorical vision shares much in common with Benjamin's image of the modern world, devoid of transcendent and semantic meaning, evoked in the early essays and *OGTD*. A concluding postscript offers possible biographical influences that might point to why this reading of Dickens's novel, as containing elements of the German/Jewish tradition, is so convincing.

Part 2, 'Dickens, Benjamin and the City,' also divided into two chapters, continues to trace the authors' encounters with industrialization and urbanization. Chapter 3 examines how urban rhythms and technology determine a reduction in the quality of experience as delineated by both Benjamin and Dickens.

[15] Adorno's 'Rede über den Raritätenladen von Charles Dickens' is in Adorno's *Gesammelte Schriften*, ed. Gretal Adorno and Rolf Tiedemann, vol. 11, pp. 515–22. English translation by Michael Hollington, *Dickens Quarterly* 6.3 (September 1989): pp. 95–101.

[16] *Ursprung des deutschen Trauerspiels*, revidierte ausgabe besorg von Rolf Tiedemann (Frankfurt a.M: Suhrkamp, 1963) – also in *GS*, I, 1, pp. 205–430; trans. by John Osborne as *The Origin of German Tragic Drama* (London: Verso 1977). The English version is abbreviated as *OGTD* or 'the *Trauerspiel* essay'.

[17] Osborne translates '*Trauerspiel*' as 'tragic drama' – but this is a problematic term, not least because Benjamin spends time in *OGTD* differentiating the *Trauerspiel* from 'tragedy'. This book translates '*Trauerspiel*' as 'mourning play'. See Chapter 1.

Rather than a full assimilation and apprehension of the content of experience, urban consciousness is characterized by depthlessness, shock and repetition. The elliptical appearance of truth, or the attenuated apprehension of it in the urban context echoes the loss of religious apprehension of the absolute, described in Part 1. Both men turn to memory in an attempt to redeem the lost content of experience, and a discussion of Benjamin's essay on Proust and the semi-autobiographical *David Copperfield* is an important feature in this line of enquiry.

Chapter 4 takes the investigation into urban experience further. The importance of the gothic mode as a response to and expression of urban anxiety and epistemological uncertainty comes under discussion, and the roles of the motifs of the flâneur and the crowd in the urban visions of Dickens and Benjamin are juxtaposed. Delving into material on the flâneur revisits some of the material in Michael Hollington's 'Dickens the Flâneur'.[18] But, in contrast to Hollington, this study highlights the unique traits Dickens brings to flânerie, which either take him outside of the concept of 'flâneur' altogether – at least, as it is understood by some critics – or stretch the concept's boundaries to the limit.

This book's focus upon Dickens and the urban must be situated in terms of four other scholars who examine the same area. In F.S. Schwarzbach's *Dickens and the City* (University of London: The Athlone Press, 1979), Dickens's imagery in the novels, his attitudes toward the city and his urban themes are traced back to his biography, to his stated beliefs and experiences in letters and articles. The darkening of Dickens's vision of the city after *Sketches by Boz* can be accounted for by the death of Mary Hogarth, while the novelist's indictment of the industrial city in *Hard Times* must be influenced by his visit to Preston in 1854, argues Schwarzbach. Alexander Welsh's *The City of Dickens* (Oxford: Clarendon, 1971, repr. 1986), discusses the city as an historical phenomenon as well as bringing it to bear as a metaphor within which Dickens's values and purposes are located and examined. Both of these studies clearly contrast with this book in their emphasis upon historico-biographical material as a way into Dickens's fictional world. At times, areas of discussion are raised or judgments reached that are similar to ones touched upon here.[19] Welsh's notion of the metropolis as the 'Earthly City', the obverse of the heavenly city, the site of immanence, poverty, hardship and hard work, where values are honed and expressed has some bearing upon this project. Karl Smith's *Dickens and the Unreal City* (Palgrave Macmillan, 2008) claims that Dickens's city, which he sees as a symbol made up of innumerable components and symbols, dramatizes contemporary religious and secular debates, and is Dickens's way of grappling with religious issues in a more profound way

[18] As already referenced, above.

[19] For instance, an important feature of Dickens's and Benjamin's understanding of modern experience – outlined in Chapter 3 of this book – is an apparent conflation of industrial rhythms or industrialization per se with the city. Schwarzbach observes that in essence, there is little difference between Dickens's notion of the industrial city and the metropolis: p. 145 of *Dickens and the City*.

than through overt statements. This book similarly suggests that the site of modern existence, the city, is indeed where the drama of experience, both spiritual and material, will unfold; but the intellectual journey and the conclusions reached differ from Smith's project.

Finally, Peter Ackroyd has produced three books on Dickens – editing *Dickens' London: An Imaginative Vision* (London: Headline, 1987); and authoring *Dickens* (London: Sinclair-Stevenson, 1990) and *Dickens: Public Life and Private Passion* (BBC Books, 2002). He is also author of *London: The Biography* (London: Vintage, 2001). His approach to historiography and biography is one which blurs the boundaries of fact and fiction, of storytelling and history. One would not expect this technique to have much in common with Benjamin, who strenuously resisted grand narrative history, attempting instead to 'interrupt' the continuum of historical time with a presentation of material fragments. However, especially in the televised adaptations of the two latter projects (*Dickens* and *London*), Ackroyd does show similarities in some areas to *The Arcades Project*, although Benjamin is not mentioned. In his series *Dickens*, broadcast in 2002, for instance, adapted scenes of Dickens's London were montaged simultaneously with footage of present-day London. The scenes were short-lived and dramatic – they punctured the narrative in a shock, imitating a process of memory or insight. This temporal montage technique conjured up the city as haunted by its past characters and lives, both real and imaginary. The city's state of flux, heterogeneity, complexity and energy was a constant – as was its ability to foster inspiration, creativity, self-awareness and reflexivity. Dickens, and Ackroyd himself, were presented as strolling observers of the urban spectacle, whose texts fed off and into the city. Even Ackroyd's narrative presentation took the form of a myriad of connections, continuities and recurrent themes, like the city itself. All of these elements – as is born out in Part 2 of the book – are to be found in Benjamin's formulation of urban experience as well as in Dickens's imaginative engagement with the city. Again, this is merely an acknowledged resemblance – Ackroyd never makes any mention of Benjamin. But the fact that Ackroyd highlights qualities in Dickens's imagination that feature prominently in a project that compares Dickens with Benjamin, is of interest. As this study will bear out in Part 2, Dickens's fictional treatment of the city, and Benjamin's formulation of that urban experience, has a legacy in city representations: a legacy that stretches from Surrealism to Situationism, from W.G. Sebald and Iain Sinclair to Peter Ackroyd.

# PART 1
# Exquisite Agony: Elements of Messianism and the Baroque in Dickens and Benjamin

# Part 1 Introduction

In October 1930 in Berlin, Walter Benjamin read Dickens's 1840–1841 novel *The Old Curiosity Shop* in German translation.[1] He and his colleague Theodor Wiesengrund Adorno were fascinated by the novel, Adorno producing an essay on it in 1931[2] and Benjamin quoting the essay next to an excerpt from *OCS* in his magnum opus, *The Arcades Project*.[3] Benjamin would later note that 'The Curiosity Shop as Interior' ought to be considered for a motif in the *Arcades*; and he included as one of his *Arcades* entries Chesterton's notion that the novel is the key to the whole of Dickens's creative output.[4]

But the point of connection being pursued in Part 1 of this book goes deeper than the intertextuality resulting from Benjamin's fascination with *OCS*. What is suggested, through a lengthy analysis, is that Benjamin and Dickens, in *OCS*, shared a vision of the religious and semantic crisis at the heart of modern life. German Romanticism and the German Baroque are the source of these ideas, and it must be acknowledged at once that Dickens is not usually discussed in relation to these eras. But he may have had a 'conduit' to these artistic movements – this can only be a speculative suggestion – through the influence of Thomas Carlyle (1795–1881). German Romanticism and Baroque culture does come together in

---

1 The only other evidence that Benjamin read Dickens's fiction is in a letter to Theodor Adorno, written in 1936, in which he claims he read *Great Expectations* in French: 'a very substantial book by Dickens, the first thing of his I have seen since The Old Curiosity Shop'. It impressed him with its 'significant constellations and rather wonderful figures,' but, like Forster, he disliked its 'inadequate' ending (Theodor Adorno and Walter Benjamin, *The Complete Correspondence 1928–1940* [Polity Press, 1999], p. 164).

2 Adorno's 'Rede über den Raritätenladen von Charles Dickens' appeared in the liberal newspaper *Frankfurter Zeitung*. It is in Adorno's *Gesammelte Schriften*, ed. Gretel Adorno and Rolf Tiedemann, vol. 11, pp. 515–22. English translation by Michael Hollington, *Dickens Quarterly* 6.3 (September 1989): pp. 95–101. The translated version will be referred to as 'Adorno's essay'.

3 *The Arcades Project*, H2a,4 and H2a,5, p. 208. [Benjamin divided the Arcades Project into 36 convolutes or files, collecting material under headings with capitalized letters from A – Z; followed by headings with uncapitalized letters from convolute 27 onwards. Further sub-divisions include numbers and uncapitalized letters. The cited references refer to Convolute H 'The Collector' in the English translation of the text.] 'Das Passagen-Werk', in *GS*, V, 1 and 2; trans. by Howard Eiland and Kevin McLaughlin as *The Arcades Project* (Cambridge, MA; London: Belknap Press of Harvard University Press, 1999). The English translation version is hereafter referred to as 'Arcades'.

4 *Arcades*, A 11,3, p. 57. Michael Hollington, 'Adorno, Benjamin and *The Old Curiosity Shop*', *Dickens Quarterly* 6.3 (September 1989): pp. 87–95 (p. 91), hereafter referred to as 'Hollington'.

Carlyle's thinking.[5] Benjamin 'rediscovered' his own Jewish religion through the metaphysics of the German Romantics, themselves deeply interested in the Jewish Kabbalah.[6] He then developed his theory of allegory in an essay on Baroque drama.[7] In a discussion of three essays by Benjamin, this book brings out a vision of a fallen modern world, a world so cruel, unjust and grotesque, there are only tiny sparks of meaning and redemption available in a life. When one considers Nell's trajectory, this appears to be an outlook that is relevant to a reading of *OCS*.[8]

The argument is this: *OCS* is a powerful delineation of passionate suffering and desolation, both Nell's and the world's. The peculiar energy of this mournful depiction of pain and decline is puzzling and has yet to be satisfactorily explored by criticism. Some Dickens criticism tends to steer clear of any metaphysical or religious interpretation of the novelist.[9] Malcolm Andrews throws doubt upon approaching the novel from the notion of the pilgrimage, with its religious connotations, since 'this approach is not sustained at any level comparable to Bunyan's allegory'.[10] The contention here is that a more sensitive reading of the deeply melancholic tone and incredibly mournful Nell passages is available when the novel's allegorical form is seen as operational throughout; when Dickens's delineation of the decay of the physical world, of its harshness and cruelty and violence is seen as a religiously inflected, allegorical vision. A philosophical reading, through Benjamin, of Dickens's allegorical turn of mind may seem counterintuitive, but it is worth bearing with. The melancholy passages of the novel are genuinely moving, and this approach allows an appreciation of them while avoiding, importantly, reading 'the death of Nell' as sentimental or vulgar.[11] Certain tendencies and elements in the novel – its masochistic hawking upon suffering and death, its lamentation

5 He was steeped in the Calvinist and emblematic religious traditions. And he used aspects of German Romantic metaphysics to bolster his view that God's divine nature is traceable in all things – but that humans had lost the capacity to apprehend this truth.

6 Benjamin was interested in, among others, the Jena Circle: Friedrich Schlegel (1772–1829), August Wilhelm Schlegel (1767–1845), Dorothea Schlegel (1763–1839) and Novalis (1772–1801) who set up the journal *The Athenaeum* to deal with aesthetic, metaphysical and political issues (1798–1800).

7 *Ursprung des deutschen Trauerspiels* revidierte ausgabe besorg von Rolf Tiedemann (Frankfurt a.M: Suhrkamp, 1963) – also in *GS*, I, 1, pp. 205–430; trans. by John Osborne as *The Origin of German Tragic Drama* (London: Verso 1977). The English translation version will be referred to as 'the *Trauerspiel* essay' or abbreviated as *OGTD*.

8 A tracing of Benjamin's and Dickens's religious/metaphysical concerns back to the German Romantics and the German Baroque will be conducted in detail in the conclusion to Part 1.

9 This is an understandable view. But some critics are convinced that Dickens treats religious issues in his novels: 'It is evident that Dickens's concerns with the nature of the human soul and the existence and nature of evil are present throughout his works', Loralee MacPike, *Dostoevsky's Dickens* (London: Prior, 1981), p. 31.

10 Professor Andrews's introduction to *OCS*, (Penguin, 1972), p. 16.

11 Aldous Huxley, *Vulgarity in Literature* (London: Chatto & Windus, 1930), p. 57.

and handwringing phrases and passages, Nell's peculiar status as both sinful and angelic, the meaning of objects in the novel, the position of comedy and the Lord of Misrule, Quilp – are brought into play in this reading in ways that throw an intriguing light on the work. Critics have given a lot of weight to the question of comedy in *OCS*, even arguing that the humor: 'controls the form of the novel and makes effective its pathos'.[12] While the comedy does indeed provide, formally, a brilliant contrast with the sadness of Nell's decline, this reading resists the idea that it is the most important structuring feature. And there is little focus upon comedy and how it works in the novel here.[13] This could be seen as the drawback of this reading. However, there are advantages, and rather than schematizing comedy in opposition to the dark side of the novel, as a number of critics do, this Benjaminian reading emphasizes how both lightness and, more forcefully, darkness are two aspects of the declining physical world, a cruel world where Nell will suffer and die, and no amount of vibrant comedy will save her from her fate.

Chapter 1 argues that *OCS* exhibits distinct notes of messianism within the contours of the text, a central component of a theological worldview Benjamin formulated in the early part of his career. The discussion examines two of Benjamin's early essays: the 1916 essay, 'On Language as Such and On the Language of Man' (Über die Sprache überhaupt und über die Sprache des Menschen), and the 'Theological-Political Fragment' (Theologisch-Politisches Fragment), which was probably written in 1920–1921, although Adorno dates this piece later, at 1937.

What will become clear in the précis of these essays is that Benjamin's concern at this point was to explore what role theological truth, or religious experience, played in everyday experience. How could one live an ethical, meaningful life when the uncertainties thrown up by war and the progress of science appeared to augur the death of God? What was it about modern existence that seemed to allow truth and meaning to fall away? The historical moment of writing was a poignant one – one of the essays was written during the First World War, the second, just afterwards, in 1920–1921. Not only hellish world events but philosophy itself had contributed to what Benjamin viewed as a loss of 'fullness' in experience. Kant, for instance (in 1781), had removed the absolute – totality and immediacy – from the realms of the theoretically knowable.[14] Benjamin came up with a fairly clear response to the problem: the absolute did indeed play a role within the experience of everyday life. The immanent absolute, reality as theological truth, made its

---

12 James Kincaid, *Dickens and the Rhetoric of Laughter* (Oxford: Oxford University Press, 1971), p. 89.

13 For critics who do focus upon comedy, see, for e.g., Mark Hennelly, 'Carnivalesque "Unlawful Games" in *The Old Curiosity Shop*', *Dickens Studies Annual* (1993): pp. 67–120; and Rachel Bennett, 'Punch vs Christian in *The Old Curiosity Shop*', *RES* 22 (1971): pp. 423–34.

14 In his philosophical project, the *Critique of Pure Reason*. An account of Benjamin's understanding of and engagement with Kant in his 1918 essay 'On the Programme of the Coming Philosophy' (Über das Programme der kommenden Philosophie) can be found in Appendix 1.

appearance in distorted, partial, veiled forms. The revelation of these 'redemptive moments' in experience involve the notion of a dialectical relationship between the historical world and its redemptive 'other' – a messianic realm.

There is a revolutionary political dimension to this. 'The Theological-Political Fragment' stages Benjamin's messianism as an understanding of the historical (capitalist) world as a realm in constant dialectical tension with a redeemed or utopian paradise.[15] The 'profane' historical world is mired in a context of utter devastation and corruption; but it burns with present hope for a different future. According to Talmudic texts, the messiah, the redeemer famed to bring about the end of history, comes only in an era of total corruption and guilt. And the historical world of Benjamin's apocalyptic vision is the site of such injustice, cruelty and devastation for the oppressed that its destructive end and redemption cannot, one imagines, be far off. Material conditions are so hellish for the poor, the messiah must surely be on his way soon. A positive yearning for the world's explosive, violent and abrupt cutting off permeates this worldview, then – this is the revolutionary aspect of it. The politics of the real world generates a desire for a better, completely different world, in Benjamin's 'Fragment'. Its view of time involves an energetic yearning for an end to suffering at each and every moment; an understanding of the future – as an instant possibility in the present – which culminates not only in a better world but a totally different one.

These areas of complexity will be opened up in an extended discussion of Dickens's novel. This line of enquiry argues that there are aspects of the fictional world of *OCS* that bear a resemblance to the messianic vision of the fallen world of modern capitalism articulated by Benjamin. *OCS* is caught up in the politics of the real world, Nell and grandfather are losers in the economy of profit and exchange. Dickens's fictional delineation of the nature of money and property avarice (Quilp and grandfather), of tainted relationships (Nell and grandfather, among others) and his focus upon Nell's suffering and the destitution of other poor people, comes close to Benjamin's messianic notion of the historical world as a constantly declining, lamentable place. Like Benjamin's vision of the historical world, Nell's is cruel, wanton and corrupt. Dickens's insistence upon this conversely brings its 'other' into play – Nell's world is simultaneously in mourning for redemption and reparation and is in constant tension with it. Through Dickens's continual use of the imagery of death, there is an omnipresent yearning for the world to be cut off, for it all to end. But it is when Nell's suffering is at its most grotesque, when she is at her lowest, that Dickens conversely represents how theological truths or 'redemptive moments' appear in the otherwise bleak and apparently 'godless' urban life. While Nell is

[15] Critics such as Michael Löwy in *Redemption and Utopia: Jewish Libertarian Thought in Central Europe*, trans. Hope Heaney (London: The Athlone Press, 1992); and James Mcbride, in 'Marooned in the Realm of the Profane: Walter Benjamin's Synthesis of Kabbalah and Communism', *Journal of the American Academy of Religion* 57, part II (Summer 1989): pp. 241–66, have argued for the obvious affinities between Jewish messianism and revolutionary Marxism or socialism.

essentially dying, Dickens interposes that trajectory with messianic moments; these take the form of revelatory, even paradoxically climactic experiences in Nell's life.

Echoing Benjamin's mournful vision, Dickens places the blame for the world's piteous state squarely at the door of industrialization, capitalism and the struggle for and obsession with money, property and possessions.

Of course, Dickens is influenced by the Christian biblical and emblematic tradition, by Carlyle and Calvinism. Benjamin is rooted in German Romantic/Judaic metaphysics. This will be discussed at the end of Part 1. As unlikely as it seems, there are aspects of the novel that can be productively read in terms of these Benjaminian ideas. It could even be suggested that Dickens's vision of Nell, her humorous grotesques, the novel's comic antics and unrelenting sorrow has more of an affinity with the Judaic comprehension of the material/political world as an imperfect reality to be violently overcome, than to, say, Carlyle's insistence that only the immaterial world has any status as 'real'.

Chapter 2 turns to the significance of allegorical form in *OCS*. This argument is conducted in relation to Benjamin's theory of allegory set forth in his study of seventeenth-century Baroque drama in *OGTD*. This concern with allegory in the novel, inspired by Adorno's reading, is not a departure from Chapter 1. As will become clear, Benjamin's theory of allegory is deeply steeped in his early metaphysics and is a natural continuation of it.[16] Allegory is the linguistic device that, rather than instantly naming essences (as symbol does), represents absences. The fall of language and the 'loss' of the absolute mean that allegory, for Benjamin, is the linguistic figure par excellence to evince the truth about the fallen nature of the historical world. Resembling the model of the messianic worldview, allegory's attempt to embody and redeem meaning is a gesture whose fulfillment is ponderously deferred. Dickens shares with the writers of the seventeenth-century *Trauerspiel* an attachment to allegorical form and to the melancholy religious meanings and resonances that use of this literary figure represents. And, beyond the theory of allegory, like the Baroque *Trauerspiele* playwrights, Dickens depicts grotesque violence as a natural part of a doomed world, which is replete with villains apparently succeeding in bringing characters to ruin. He mixes a deep melancholic tone with farcical comedy to conjure the image of the chaotic space of the material world, a world where the good will suffer along with the rest.[17]

Searching out and discussing elements of messianism and the Baroque, then, will form the backbone of Part 1's investigation into Benjamin's essays and *OCS*. So, to begin with Chapter 1: an investigation into the ideas that constitute Benjamin's early theological period.

---

[16] In fact, the heavily Judaic tendencies in Benjamin's reading of the Lutheran world of seventeenth-century German *Trauerspiele* can be seen as a weakness.

[17] It has been noticed among scholars, including R.H. Horne, that *The Old Curiosity Shop* 'had a sort of German look' (*A New Spirit of the Age*, vol. 1 [London: Smith Elder & Co, 1844], p. 49). See also, Dennis Walder, *Dickens and Religion* (London: Allen & Unwin, 1981), p. 88.

# Chapter 1
# Benjamin, Dickens and Messianism

## Benjamin's Language Theory: The Language of Objects

Benjamin can be placed within the parameters of the Modernist movement, if one understands Modernist writers and poets – say, Eliot and Pound – as being profoundly interested in formulating a theory and language of the object. Benjamin's essay of 1916, 'On Language as Such and on the Language of Man', does just that. He sets out a language theory that is a co-option of Jewish metaphysics; specifically, a delineation of the mystical writings and speculations of the Jewish tradition of Kabbalah. In this difficult essay 'On Language', itself an enactment of how baldly stated sentences can somehow fail to live up to the task of encompassing the metaphysical, Benjamin argues that the seemingly inadequate ability of language to get a grip on reality; the, on the face of it, peculiar attempt to grasp the nonconceptual (the object) through the conceptual, is due to the fallen nature of human language itself.

This notion of human language as 'fallen' is one worked through a reading of Kabbalistic speculations on Genesis.[1] In the beginning, according to the Kabbalists, the world was brought into existence in the very expression of language. If the Torah was a divine notepad upon which God scribbled out his Creation, in the expression of that divine plan in divine language, life, the very substance of being, was breathed into existence. This original and divine language, an *Ursprache*, saw no split, then, between the word and the thing, signifier and signified – there was no distinction between the thing and its expression, in Paradise. The Word was expressed and there was. The existence of a thing was inextricably linked to its acoustic linguistic expression. God's divine language expressed God's intellectual substance, it was the combination of God's thinking and being.

While God's divine language is the archetypal model of language, human language shares in this set up to the extent that thinking is of a linguistic nature; man's intellect and being is expressed in language too. More than that: Adam was allotted the gift of naming the objects of the world – nature and animals – with

[1] Michael Löwy argues in *Redemption* that the timing of Benjamin's encounter with Kabbalistic writings means he could not have been directly influenced by the Kabbalists during the composition of 'On Language as Such and On the Language of Man'. Following Menninghaus, Löwy asserts that Benjamin's 1916 essay was influenced by his reading of the German Romantics: Novalis, Schlegel, Hamman and Herder, who themselves borrowed extensively from the Kabbalah. Wohlfarth remarks (in Andrew Benjamin [ed.], *The Problems of Modernity*, 1989, p. 159) that, for Benjamin, early German Romanticism seems to converge with mystical Kabbalah – in Schlegelian metaphysics, there are no objects, only subjects, which unfold their being in infinite reflection.

their proper names. This was not to open up a split between the object and Adamic language. Adam studied the animals closely and they expressed their substance to Adam, who merely acoustically uttered the expression of their being. For the Kabbalists, nature cannot help but express its inner core of language. In nature's expression of this inner core of language, there was an uninterrupted relationship between being, knowing and naming in Paradise:

> Man is the namer; by this we recognize that through him pure language speaks. All nature, insofar as it communicates itself, communicates itself in language and so finally in man. Hence, he is the lord of nature and can give names to things. Only through the linguistic being of things can he get beyond himself and attain knowledge of them – in the name. God's creation is completed when things receive their names from man, from whom in name language alone speaks. (Benjamin, 'On Language as Such and On the Language of Man')[2]

If Adam uttered the name unique to the thing, there was one substance that was ineffable. The Divine Name, the Inexpressible, was not pronounceable and, hidden in all of nature, it was at the core of all naming.

It is the suggestion of what happens to human language after the fall that is of real interest for our present purposes. On the expulsion from paradise, Adam's magical language loses the immediate and divine nature of naming. Human language no longer calls perfection by its name, simply by an expression. Having eaten of the tree of knowledge, so the story goes, the profane distinction between good and evil is opened up, and name and substance come apart. Language must now be understood in terms of translation and mediacy. Human language is a mere mode of communication through which the arbitrary linguistic relation between word and thing is articulated. The profane is the realm of word and thing, subject and object; where, with the damaged immediacy of name and named, many words can be used to denote the same object. It is here that Benjamin's attachment to allegory comes in, since allegory is the literary figure whose meaning is conventional and can proliferate and change and is not, therefore, an immediate embodiment of the transcendent. Its structure foregrounds the position of fallen language as Benjamin sees it.

The fallenness of the world means a differentiation opens up between the thing's being (its intellectual substance) and the linguistic substance which articulates the thing's being. It can no longer express itself immediately, as nature had to Adam. And there is a graduated scale of 'profanity' in things in nature and human life; the further they are from the 'sacred' realm, the less of themselves they are able to voice: the less immediate apprehension of them becomes. In other words: 'Through the reduction of the difference between the *geistigen Wesen* (intellectual substance) and *sprachlichen Wesen* (linguistic substance) of a thing, we are permitted to bear

---

2 Michael W. Jennings and others (eds), *Walter Benjamin, Selected Writings*, 4 vols (Cambridge, MA and London: Belknap Press of Harvard University Press, 1996–2003), I, p. 65. *Selected Writings* will hereafter be abbreviated as *SW*.

likeness to the divine.'[3] The world of things, nature, in this profane world, cannot communicate their substance completely. They no longer possess a linguistic substance through which their being is communicated. Benjamin, then, is left to contemplate the idea of an existence beyond the possibility of expression. In other words, a world where meaning has fallen away.

The 'fallen' object's appearance now voices this veiled expression of the thing's substance in the profane world. This is not to suggest a 'deeper truth' behind the veil; what is most proper to the thing is its veiled nature.[4]

Hence, Benjamin's preoccupation with identifying the precious few singular and unique images of 'redemption' available in the otherwise bleakly profane historical world. In the essay 'On Language as Such', he claims that there remains a divine 'residue' lodged in profane language itself, a God-given presence which is, as it were, unpronounceable: 'all language houses its own incommensurable uniquely constituted infinity' (*SW*, I, p. 64). There exists an immanent absolute within language. The further suggestion is that there are moments in experience when the reflection of this 'residue' becomes apparent: 'the notion of the *magic* of language refers to something else at the same time: its infiniteness' (*SW*, I, p. 64).

While Benjamin posits the 'fallenness' of language in the profane realm and thinks its effect upon the 'knowledge' of a thing in terms of a 'loss', in terms of the problem of the 'inexpressible' – yet 'magically' there is a substance of the thing which expresses itself without intention. Without a means of expression – it has no linguistic substance – it expresses itself nonetheless.

This is an elaboration of a 'language of objects'. The object's appearance gives voice to the veiled expression of the thing's substance – and this 'magically', and occasionally, shows itself.

This notion that the absolute can be understood to show itself within objects at particular moments, this play upon the language of objects, could be opened up with respect to *The Old Curiosity Shop* and Benjamin's analysis of nineteenth-century material culture, *The Arcades Project*. Physical objects, old commodities, rubbish take up a lot of available space within the fictional world of Dickens generally and in *The Old Curiosity Shop* in particular, and they are the lifeblood of the *Arcades*. In Dickens, bric-a-brac, stuff, even dilapidated buildings are often used by the novelist to create a particular scenic effect; occasionally an

[3] Eric Jacobson, *Metaphysics of the Profane* (New York, Chichester: Columbia University Press, 2003), p. 98, hereafter abbreviated as 'Jacobson'.

[4] This notion of truth is comparable with that of Benjamin's contemporary, Heidegger. Drawing on Aristotle, Heidegger rejects truth as correspondence between subject and object. The character of truth is *aletheia* (unconcealment), a phenomenon whereby the thing itself is allowed to show itself as itself, is allowed to be uncovering something of its truth. But this uncovering is a manifestation in a way that conceals as much as it reveals. This covering up belongs to the nature of Being, for Heidegger. The conception involves a founding propriety which has always already been there and which manifests itself in a more fundamental way than things that are manifested through the logos – through a subject/object relationship.

object may even harbor its own 'character'.[5] And Dickens's tendency to play the physiognomist, to attempt to '[read] the immaterial in the material, the soul in the face, or, by metonymy, the clothes, gestures and environment of the human individual', is matched by Benjamin's physiognomy in the *Arcades*, as he tries to read the meaning of the nineteenth century in his material fragments.[6] Both writers' physiognomic tendencies echo Benjamin's characterization of the allegorist, who gazes at the mournful human condition which is 'not to be named, only to be read, to be read uncertainly by the allegorist'.[7] The significance of this aspect of both Dickens and Benjamin will deepen as the argument goes on.

But for now, the second essay of importance in an understanding of Benjamin's theology, the 'Theological-Political Fragment,' must briefly come under discussion.

## Messianism and Redemption as Understood in the 'Theological-Political Fragment'

Messianism, from the Hebrew noun *mashiah* (the anointed one), denotes a set of beliefs, expectations, an attitude toward time that developed within the Jewish faith. This political theology evolved out of the idea that a divinely sanctioned Israelite monarch would lead the Jews out of foreign bondage and back to a restored Golden Age of peace and prosperity. Some scholars suggest that the notion that a divine order intervenes in the affairs of Jewish history may have been influenced by ancient myth.[8] The Israelite version of the myth involves a promise that God, who had triumphed over chaos and evil in a cosmic battle in the Beginning, would defeat the historical forces of evil and death at the end, too, and restore Edenic harmony.

Messianic ideas were crystallized through the experience of disillusionment with the careers of kings who failed to compare well to the past, to the idealized tales of the reigns of David and Solomon, and who failed to fulfill the 'prophecy' of ending suffering and bringing about a new (the old, golden) world order. Significantly, the ideas were influenced by material conditions, then, and operated upon a political as well as a theological level. Adorno's entitling Benjamin's fragment the 'Theological-Political Fragment' underscores this.[9] Jewish metaphysics is not an

---

[5] For a development of this position, see Taylor Stoehr, *Dickens: The Dreamer's Stance* (Ithaca, NY: Cornell University Press, 1965).

[6] 'Hollington', p. 93.

[7] *OGTD*, p. 225.

[8] See R.J. Zwi Weblovsky, 'Messianism in Jewish History', in *Jewish Society through the Ages*, ed. by H.H. Ben-Sasson and S. Ettinger (London: Valentine, Mitchell, 1968), pp. 30–45.

[9] Benjamin had read it out to Adorno and his wife the last time they met, in 1938. Adorno gave the piece its title and believed it dated from the year before, 1937; Benjamin's other great friend, Gershom Scholem, believed that the piece dated much earlier, 1920–1921. See Scholem's *Walter Benjamin: The Story of a Friendship, New York Review of Books*, 2001, p. 112. This text will hereafter be abbreviated as 'Friendship'.

intellectual turning away from the material, modern world. It concerns the people, political events and social conditions of the present historical world, and includes a conception of revolution, a complete disruption of historical time.[10] Such an idea of a complete break with everything that went before has an analogous model in political revolution. Benjamin writes of the French Revolution as a kind of model of the messianic kingdom.[11]

### *Suffering/Redemption in the Messianic Worldview*

The greater the contrast between the present and the anticipated utopian, better world, the more energetically the redeemer was hoped for and the more omnipresent the 'restorative' future seemed. The evil present was pregnant, traced through with utopian possibilities. As the present became more catastrophic, contrasting more and more with its redemptive other, the idea became potent that only when the realms were at their most contrasting, would the redeemer arrive.

And Talmudic texts suggest that the messiah will come only in an era of total corruption and guilt. The messianic event is, then, a massive uprooting and total destruction of the existing order:

> this catastrophic element remained an essential feature of the dialectic of messianic utopia: ultimate salvation was accompanied, or preceded by destruction and by the terrors of the "birth pangs" of the messianic age.[12]

Such an anticipation of extreme suffering followed by utter devastation resulted in many Jews in different eras interpreting persecution or horrendous cruelty as a heralding of the messianic era.[13]

Paradoxically, the more suffering there was, the closer redemption was understood to be. It is in this concept of suffering, a suffering that brings the sufferer closer to redemption – and in suffering taking place within, and being attributable to, material/social conditions/causes – that it is claimed *The Old Curiosity Shop* has an affinity to Jewish messianism.

---

10 As suggested, Michael Löwy sets out his convincing account of the intellectual proximity of revolutionary socialism, libertarianism and messianism in *Redemption and Utopia*; see especially, ch. 2 (pp. 14–46) and ch. 6 (pp. 95–126). Gershom Scholem argues that there is an *anarchic* element in the very nature of messianic utopianism. See his *The Messianic Idea in Judaism and Other Essays on Jewish Spirituality* (New York: Schocken Books, 1974).

11 Number XIV of his 'Theses on the Philosophy of History', in *Illuminations*, p. 253. This text will hereafter be abbreviated as 'Theses'. Dickens, of course, fictionalizes the French Revolution in *TTC*. It is suggested in Appendix 2 that he also expresses a messianic yearning in his representation of historical time in that novel. See 'Dickens, Benjamin and Revolution', p. 234 of this book.

12 H.H. Ben-Sasson, p. 33.

13 Ibid.

### *The Role of Ultimate Redemption in Messianism*

Ultimate redemption, involves the notion that a messiah erupts onto the world stage – like a revolutionary explosion – and rights all the injustices committed during historical time:

> Only the Messiah himself completes all history, in the sense that he alone redeems, completes, creates its relations to the messianic.[14]

The *tikkun*, accomplished when the messiah arrives, is the reestablishment of the harmony disturbed by the Fall. All historical things come to an abrupt end and there is a return to the beginning, as the broken are returned to their original completeness. The messiah's arrival is the redemption, the return of all things to their original contact with God. The injustices that took place within history and befell 'the oppressed' – primarily the poor whose 'history of oppression' will have been overwritten by the victorious – will be righted. The messiah's settlement of affairs is, unlike Christian redemption (a case of individual or personal salvation), collective, public:

> In Christianity, the Redeemer lives and the repentant, individual soul is saved. In Judaism, the Messiah is promised and life is lived in view of this deferment; redemption, when it comes, will be universal – it is promised to the whole world, not just to the Jews.[15]

This collective political strain of messianism – which pays attention to the weak, the powerless and the poor – will become more of a point of emphasis in Benjamin's later work.[16] In this chapter, the suggestion will be that Dickens's attention to the poor in *OCS*, and his redemptive tying up of loose ends at the close of the novel, bears a similar political messianic strain.

### *Redemptive Moments*

The two realms, the divine (messianic) realm and the profane (historical) realm, are as intimate as any oppositional model can be. If one thinks of their relationship on the model of identity/difference, the profane order is defined by everything that it is not – the divine identity having, in that sense, always already been inherent within the profane before the world fell away into 'difference'.

---

[14] 'Theological-Political Fragment' in *SW*, III, p. 305.

[15] Gillian Rose, *Judaism and Modernity: Philosophical Essays* (Oxford: Blackwell, 1993), p. 183.

[16] Most obviously in the above-mentioned 'Theses'; for example, he insists upon the *ur*-history of the oppressed, which it is the duty of future generations to messianically 'remember' and reauthenticate. This point is made in his famous statement: 'There is no document of civilization which is not at the same time a document of barbarism' ('Theses', VII, *Illuminations*, pp. 245–55, [p. 248]).

Moreover, this dialectical model is crucial because of the context it provides for what this book argues is Benjamin's main interest: in how the realms, as it were, intersect in moments of dialectical insight; in how evanescent moments of truth are revealed. These moments of immanent transcendence are achieved when the divine makes its fleeting appearance within the everyday.

Benjamin's constant return to the problem of how one enables the absolute, or truth, to appear in fragmented, precious moments of revelation within the present is a leitmotif of this book. In one of Benjamin's earliest essays, he was claiming: 'the historical task is to expose this immanent state of perfection and make it absolute, to make it visible and dominant in the present'.[17] And there are tiny moments of redemption in the profane world for Benjamin, moments textured with shards of the messianic – which one must look out for. The task is to witness the immanent, temporal index of redemption in every moment of the present under the strain of the catastrophe enveloping it. However, these redemptive moments are not to be confused with the final messianic redemption, when history is brought abruptly to an end and all wrongs are righted.

This is a vision of the historical world as hell with tiny sparks of redemption – one that, it will be argued, Dickens shares in *OCS*. And this prophetic image of the world as a catastrophic landscape is further explored in Benjamin's reading of the Baroque *Trauerspiel* (the essay discussed in Chapter 2 of this first part).[18] Hence, the profane, historical world's fallen status allows a manifestation of the absolute within the profane, historical realm that would express itself only in a limited form: 'in complex, tortuous and even violent forms'.[19]

Moreover, such occurrences would be rare and critics, historians and artists must be vigilant in seeking them out. The task of the critic is to redeem such moments from their hiding places within works of art – making them the focus of present hope.[20] As for the historian, she too must locate immanent moments of transcendence in the past. And we are all, in this sense, historians. As Benjamin will state in the 'Theses' (1940):

---

[17] Quotation from Benjamin's 1914 essay, 'The Life of Students' ('Das Leben der Studenten') in *SW*, I, p. 37.

[18] The image of history viewed as a causal chain of disaster, a catastrophic pile of detritus, haunted Benjamin until the end of his life. It prompted, among other things, a thinking of temporality as a blasting of the past out of the continuum of history, in an attempt to break the progressive unfolding of historical ruin particularly developed in his 'Theses'.

[19] Phrase taken from Howard Caygill, *The Colour of Experience* (London and New York: Routledge, 1998), p. 2.

[20] This position is worked out in detail with respect to literary criticism in Benjamin's 'The Concept of Criticism in German Romanticism' (Der Begriff der Kunstkritick in der deutschen Romantik) of 1919, but it takes on an increasingly political flavor. See especially the speech Benjamin gave to the Institute for the Study of Fascism in Paris on April 27, 1934, 'The Author as Producer' ('Der Autor als Produzent') in *SW*, II, pp. 768–82.

> The past carries with it a temporal index by which it is referred to redemption. There is a secret agreement between past generations and the present one. Our coming was expected on earth. Like every generation that preceded us, we have been endowed with a weak Messianic power.[21]

## Dickens's *The Old Curiosity Shop*

This project has developed an introduction to Benjamin's early metaphysics. A key aspect of this all-too-brief delineation, is the notion that, for Benjamin, while the world is a fallen, bleak place, the absolute, totality does play a role in experience – it appears in flashes of insight or revelation and often in the most unlikely, in even the most destitute, of places in our lives. I have called these precious experiences, 'moments of redemption'; they are interventions of the messianic within ordinary life. But these moments may not, according to the early Benjamin, prevent the fallen world from declining toward the ultimate redemptive event, the arrival of the messiah.

Dickens, it will be argued, fictionalizes messianic or redemptive moments. He portrays pockets of immanent transcendence in the bleak world of *OCS*. While his well-known Christian background means he did not share Benjamin's focus upon Jewish metaphysics, I believe there are interesting and productive areas of convergence in their outlook on the world.[22] There is evidence that Dickens may have read and known something about the Talmud: 'He thinks [...] that the four Gospels are all derived from some anterior written scriptures – made up, perhaps, with additions and interpolations from the Talmud, in which he expressed great interest and admiration.'[23] Both men, Dickens and Benjamin, seem intent upon redeeming precious moments of transcendence that occur all too briefly and evanescently in the modern, profane urban life.

Secondly, Benjamin's messianism involves an important relationship between suffering and redemption; one that can be productively applied to a reading of Dickens's depiction of suffering in *OCS*. Again, it must be emphasized that they are coming from different religious traditions, but there is a point of convergence in their understanding of how suffering and redemption work which will be developed and argued for in this chapter.

Thirdly, this chapter involves a discussion of Dickens's treatment of objects. The narrative describes Nell and the omnipresence of objects in the shop as

---

21 *Illuminations*, p. 245.

22 As John Forster (Dickens's biographer) puts it, Dickens 'never had sympathy so strong as with the leading doctrines of the Church of England' (bk. 4, ch. 1, p. 298), while in the same biography Dickens says, 'the form of religion does not so greatly matter, if you try to do good' (bk. 4, ch. 5, p. 349), both in *The Life of Charles Dickens, 1812–1870*, ed. J.W.T. Ley (London: Cecil Palmer, 1928), hereafter abbreviated as 'Life'.

23 Annie Fields, *Memories of a Hostess: A Chronicle of Eminent Friendships, drawn chiefly from the diaries of Mrs. James T. Fields*, ed. M.A. DeWolfe Howe (Boston: Atlantic Monthly Press, 1922), pp. 167–8.

'a kind of allegory'.[24] And Dickens's insistence upon the quiddity and palpability of the objects does conjure up a fallen, capitalist world, awash with remaindered commodities and hollowed out ruins. There are two instances, though, where there is a kind of language, a magical quality attached to the objects, and this will be discussed. This reading of Dickens's objects takes place in view of Benjamin's essay on language.

Finally, it is suggested that there is something of the *tikkun*, a reestablishment of harmony or a messianic righting of wrongs, about the way Dickens ties up the novel's loose ends.

To begin, then: an exploration of the second highlighted point of affinity between the two writers – the material reality of suffering and its relationship to the divine realm.

## Introductory Remarks: The Allegorical Habit of Mind and the Context of Nell's Progress

The trajectory of Nell's existence in this novel is, quite simply, one of decline. She starts out as a lost, depressed, suffering orphan; but her suffering is set to get worse as she loses her home, becomes a tramp and embarks on a poverty-inducing pilgrimage leading to her collapse, death and resurrection.[25]

The novel's universe is, then, an undeniably dualistic, religious one. In terms of the interpretative process, the reader is presented with simultaneous levels of meaning: the material and the immaterial, the worldly and the spiritual, within which the fictional events and activities can be placed.[26]

Her progress is entirely rooted in fairly historically accurate, capitalist economics. This is a story about material, social conditions, about the gain and loss of money and property. Her neglect, abuse, harsh treatment and destitute social conditions all follow from the unsuccessful effort by Grandfather Trent to manipulate the ruthless economics of industrial capitalism – by gambling.[27] The repossession of the curiosity shop – and the intensification of Nell's suffering as she becomes homeless – is a direct result of her guardian's failed attempt to gain

---

[24] *OCS*, ch. 1, p. 19.

[25] Eileen Cleere argues that Nell's abiding status as 'child' makes a mockery of her exposure to the cruel vicissitudes of human nature; '"Implicit Faith in the Deception": Misanthropy, Natural History and *The Old Curiosity Shop*', *Dickens Studies Annual* 35 (2005): pp. 51–2.

[26] As pointed out in the introduction, this approach contrasts to those critics who read the novel's structure as divided into the dichotomous 'forces' of the sorrowful Nell camp and the comedic, energetic Quilp camp – with the Swiveller/Marchioness camp occupying the center ground. See Loralee MacPike, *Dostoevsky's Dickens* (London: Prior, 1981), p. 27; and James Kincaid, *The Rhetoric of Laughter*, pp. 76–104.

[27] A number of critics refer to grandfather as 'Trent' or 'old Trent' – although it is worth bearing in mind that he is her maternal grandfather and may well have a different surname to Nell.

a fortune. Borrowing cash and gambling is, significantly, the economic model of industrial capitalism. For Dickens as well as for Benjamin, 'the stock market is the bourgeois equivalent of the gaming table'.[28] In gambling, then, Grandfather Trent loses. Nell's 'pilgrimage' – which can be understood as an allegorical representation of a life – is not caused by a religious crisis, then, as in the case of Christian in Bunyan's book. When Nell utters Christian's phrase: 'What shall I do! Oh! What shall I do!'[29] it is in response to a concrete, material situation – her grandfather's mental decline, their financial destitution – rather than in apprehension of an abstract, metaphysical crisis.

However at the same time, and this is what is so compelling, the social conditions and their ample measure of unhappiness are inextricably caught up with a religious level of meaning, not least because of the novel's obvious and self-conscious allegorical form and biblical language and emblematical resonances.[30] Dickens's allegorical habit of mind here is interesting in view of the fact that in the messianic worldview, worldly suffering comes in the form of social conditions; the material world has an intimate relationship to a divine realm.

Even the most banal or degrading of the world's mundanities, gamblers luck, is presented in terms of God's justice:

> every piece I staked, I whispered to myself that orphan's name and called on Heaven to bless the venture, which it never did. Whom did it prosper? Who were those with whom I played? Men who lived by plunder, profligacy, and riot. (Grandfather, *OCS*, ch. 9, p. 84)

Here, if we follow this reasoning, the messianic injustice of the profane world is represented in Grandfather's view; but there is ample evidence (in addition to the allegorical form) that the novelist depicts events as working within the context of divine justice. For instance, while the odds of winning a fortune are pretty low, the novel appears to suggest that Grandfather could never win. The pitiable degradation of Grandfather's gambling losses and the decline and death his actions cause to Nell force the reader toward recognizing gambling in terms of a divine realm, as 'detrimental', 'immoral' or even, unusually for Dickens, 'sinful'. Grandfather's addiction to gambling, its capacity to cause him to betray Nell, steal and possibly murder (one of Nell's fears), follows the patterns of thinking in conventional religious discourse where one 'sin' committed is thought to lead to another. In messianic parlance, a sin, committed in the hope of bringing 'happiness' (wealth), instead causes suffering to the sinner. In the messianic worldview, the notion of human happiness – worldliness – is thought, within the framework of its ability, to bring on the event of the messianic: its ability to work to the rhythm of the eternal decline of the world.

This tendency is especially clear, one could argue, in the main didactic point of *OCS*. Dickens's novel is suggesting that the processes and forces of capitalism

[28] 'Hollington', p. 88.

[29] *The Old Curiosity Shop*, ed. Angus Calder (Oxford: Clarendon Press, 1997), ch. 6, p. 58. Abbreviated as *OCS*.

[30] The significance of Dickens's allegorical form is analyzed in Chapter 2.

cause the profane world to hurtle onwards toward decline. Gambling, money-making, capitalism – especially when the stakes are high and there is much to lose – can *never* produce a winning situation, the novel seems to suggest. The coveting of money *always* leads to suffering. Despite this, the profane world continues its obsession with mammon. And, even the less 'sinful', the Nells of this fictional world, will be subject to humanity's suffering fate.

Nell, at first, sees flight from financial ruin simply as a way of escaping 'unhappiness' – an unhappiness she can only make sense of if she conflates it with Grandfather's need for money and property. It is a concrete problem and a human response – to escape unhappiness, let's flee. But the biblical language, the Romantic connotations (of escaping the corrupt city into pastoral bliss) and the allegorical form Dickens uses, underscore the religious significance of her escape from the financial disaster. As Nell puts it,

> Let us be beggars, and be happy, [...]
> I have no fear but we shall have enough, I am sure we shall. Let us walk through country places, and sleep in fields and under trees, and never think of money again, or anything that can make you sad. (*OCS*, ch. 9, p. 81)

Nell will later revise her view (and the novelist, Nell's language) and the full extent of the religious significance of the flight from the 'temptation', 'greed' and the 'sinfulness' of city life will emerge.

If Nell initially associates turning away from the temptation of money and possessions as a way of being 'happy', she is to be disappointed. Her flight into the country only accelerates her destitution and furthers her suffering, ending in her death.

The consequences of the economics of her situation are, according to Dickens's fiction, then, an aesthetics of suffering, the intensity of which increases and insists at every moment. But such suffering would merely be that – an elongated depiction of suffering – if it did not point to a religious level of meaning, if it did not adumbrate the possibility of redemption. An interesting way to make sense of the novel's emphasis upon degradation, corruption and suffering ahead of death and redemption is in terms of its affinity with Benjamin's messianic theology. Nell's attempt to be happy becomes a way of accelerating her fallen state, her suffering – a state of affairs that, in Jewish messianic thinking, is one of the harsh realities of living in the fallen world. And the suffering takes a material form, it is psychological, physical. It is experienced in poverty, hunger, anxiety, pain. It comes about as a result of the economic realities of the profane world; it is perpetuated by the cruelty of others or sometimes, by bad luck.[31] Just to be clear, this is not to claim Dickens set out to express messianism in his work, but to

[31] See Gershom Scholem, *The Messianic Idea in Judaism and Other Essays on Jewish Spirituality* (New York: Schocken Books, 1974) for the role of bad luck and melancholy in Jewish thought. The ideas he discusses have a bearing upon how one interprets Benjamin and his particular strain of melancholy. See also Hannah Arendt's introduction to *Illuminations*, pp. 7–55.

point to some interesting affinities between messianism and certain contours and tendencies in his outlook in this novel.

Taking this further: at some junctures of the novel, the suffering depicted takes on a sort of heightened, even a strangely beautiful quality; it is a representation of exquisite agony. Dickens orchestrates a huge tension in the way he presents the variations of Nell's suffering in contrast to brief moments of joy or relief, or in relation to her ultimate 'redemption', her fictionalized resurrection. This, it could be argued, might also be viewed in terms of the messianic outlook. The, at times, grandiloquent, sentimentalized depictions of heart-wrenching suffering can be understood to simultaneously work to adumbrate the imminent possibility of relief or (in messianic terms) redemption at every moment. The novel, in these instances, is exhibiting a messianic view of life which can involve a wallowing in suffering – with a heightened, sentimentalized use of language and elicited emotion – because it augurs hope of redemption's imminence.

### *Nell's Suffering*

To put flesh upon these introductory remarks, we must look more closely at the nature of the suffering Nell endures.

#### ***(a) Neglect***

Those who are meant to protect and love Nell are unreliable (Grandfather, Mrs Quilp). As an orphan – *the* Victorian character of novels and evangelical publications – living with her elderly relative, she has to accept a large amount of responsibility from an early age. Her state of mind is often one of anxiety because her guardian is unreliable and weak.

Moreover, even while they have a roof over their heads, Grandfather exposes Nell to danger and indignity. The novel opens with Nell 'lost' in the London streets – surely one of the most potent metaphors of the modern world available to imagination, with obvious biblical/emblematical resonances.[32] She has to rely upon the narrator, a stranger, for direction. And she has to explain herself to him, when he asks her who has put her in this vulnerable position in the dead of night: 'Somebody very kind, sir', is her defensive reply. Such an answer – which could have been 'my guardian' – is aware of the accusation in the question. This is where shame comes into play, the shame felt at her own neglect. Moreover, she cannot even account for her nighttime wandering – she is inadvertently borrowing money from the villain moneylender, Quilp.

In a state of anxiety, then, caused by witnessing her grandfather's mental suffering and being vaguely aware that he may be judged harshly by others, her efforts go into alleviating (obeying) him and furthering his projects.

[32] The city is viewed primarily as a site of corruption and worldliness in Quarles's *Emblemes* (1643) – as it is in Bunyan's *The Pilgrim's Progress (1678–1684)*. Being lost in the city's physical labyrinth is an allegory of moral/spiritual atrophy.

Her acquiescence is motivated by the fear that, disobeyed, his behavior might worsen and result in his being thrown into an asylum. This is a determined loyalty born out of love and pity. It is also a loyalty based on fear – of being left to cope alone. It is a love that suspends judgment, but aids wrongdoing. And aids it at first, with a vague suspicion, but later, in full knowledge of, the 'temptation' she has become complicit in. Again, Grandfather's gambling is not only financial misjudgment or the desperation of an elderly man, but sinfulness, Dickens seems to insist. Even if one puts to one side the evangelical view of gambling, Dickens's elaborate descriptions of Grandfather's grotesque decline, his temptation/resistance, addictive relationship to the pastime, push the point home. Nell's vulnerability, her anxiety and humiliation, also persuades that Grandfather's actions are in the area of not only wrongdoing but sinfulness.

This is a world, then, where Nell's loving someone and needing to survive results in her own corruption and the furtherance of sin. More than that, refusing to become complicit in sin – her grandfather's gambling – might cause further harm. In other words (and this equally applies to both Grandfather and Nell) with the best intentions, one ends up committing sin. In terms of Benjamin's theology, one could argue that Nell's profane world has a rhythm of inevitable decline that comes close to his Jewish worldview.[33]

To keep her guardian 'happy'/sane, Nell must aid sin. To prevent the eventuality of being left alone, she must do the same.

Nell's neglect is clear in the issue of her safety, too. Unusually in Dickens, the narrator, Master Humphrey, upbraids Grandfather for neglect of it. In effect, what her position does is make the narrator so anxious for her safety, he dreams about her and returns to the shop to satisfy himself that she is surviving:

> Yet I lingered about, and could not tear myself away, thinking of all possible harm that might happen to the child – of fires and robberies and even murder. (Narrator, *OCS*, ch. 1, p. 17)

Here the narrator highlights a world in which the most vulnerable are not protected from harm, even in the home. And then there are the possibilities of harm from an unexpected source upon the road. One passing character comments:

> 'A pair of queer travelers to be walking all night', observed the man who had first accosted them. 'One of you is a trifle too old for that sort of work, the other a trifle too young […] I thought somebody had been robbing and ill-using you […] That's all. Good day.' (*OCS*, ch. 43, p. 333)

And the stranger in the city anticipates the fear of both Nell and the reader, when he says, 'Don't be afraid. There's nobody here will harm you' (*OCS*, ch. 44, p. 341) as she is led into an industrial hovel to warm herself by a furnace.

---

[33] See 'Jacobson', p. 21.

Dickens repeatedly draws attention, then, to the physical danger from outside/others in this dark world. The vulnerability of Nell, her youth, her tiny physique, her sexual innocence renders this danger all the more dramatic. And the neglect that exposes her to it is therefore all the more sinful.

Dickens spends much time, too, depicting Nell as emotionally neglected, as depressed and lonely. One of many fine passages evokes her solitude and introversion at the curiosity shop by describing her as staring out of the window for hours, attaching herself to the curiosities for company, watching neighbors switch lights on and off – all while her grandfather is away gambling. One of the most poignant episodes depicting her loneliness is her following of two reunited sisters and secretly sharing in their pleasure:

> Why were the eyes of Little Nell wet, that night, with tears like those of the two sisters? [...] thank God that the innocent joys of others can strongly move us, and that we, even in our fallen nature, have one source of pure emotion which must be prized in Heaven! (*OCS*, ch. 32, p. 251)

Notice how the events of the world are automatically viewed within a religious context.

Nell is reduced, then, to clinging to a relative who neglects her, exposes her to danger and humiliation and, later, betrays her. She attaches herself emotionally to objects[34] – the curiosities – and attains happiness only vicariously. As will become clear, Nell's ambivalent status as both subject to her material conditions and as remote from them, will ensure that her treatment by Grandfather is read as 'sinful' or 'evil'.

### *(b) Exploitation*

> 'It always grieves me', I observed, roused by what I took to be his selfishness, 'it always grieves me to contemplate the initiation of children into the ways of life, when they are scarcely more than infants. It checks their confidence and simplicity – two of the best qualities that Heaven gives them – and demands that they share our sorrows before they are capable of entering into our enjoyments'. (*OCS*, ch. 1, p. 11)

Here, Master Humphrey expresses a fear that Nell is being exploited by Grandfather Trent, that she is denied childhood and made to work before she is old enough to consent to such responsibility. Grandfather, though, insists Nell's actions are voluntary acts of love:

> She gives it cheerfully as you see, and it would break her heart if she knew that I suffered anybody else to do for me what her little hands could undertake. (*OCS*, ch. 1, p. 12)

[34] In Adorno's Benjaminian-inspired essay on *OCS*, he suggests Nell's special relationship to objects could be read as a pre-lapsarian ability to read/name their essential substance. The postlapsarian relationship to them, for Adorno, would be to treat them as hollowed-out commodities. See Adorno's essay, especially p. 101.

Here, Nell's 'act of love' simultaneously 'benefits' Grandfather – foregrounding the uncomfortable idea that even the most intimate relationships are attended (or should one suggest *tainted*) by a practical arrangement, a capitalist material exchange. This emotional entanglement makes it difficult to categorize Grandfather's 'exploitation' of Nell as deliberate cruelty. And Dickens is intentionally ambiguous in indicating how the reader should read this situation. Yet the arrangement of his life and his treatment of Nell is an issue the reader must wrestle with. It is one that Master Humphrey brings up immediately, but it is hardly settled, even by Nell herself. When asked to attest to Grandfather's behavior, she is less than forthcoming and he has to positively lead her to the conclusion:

> 'Do I love thee, Nell?' said he. 'Say – do I love thee, Nell, or no?'
> The child only answered by her caresses, and laid her head upon his breast.
> 'Why dost thou sob', said the grandfather, pressing her closer to him and glancing towards me. 'Is it because thou know'st I love thee, and does not like that I should seem to doubt it by my question? Well, well – then let us say I love thee dearly.' (*OCS*, ch. 1, p. 13)

Nell's tears confirm in her a mixture of awareness of Grandfather's faults, forgiveness and emotional masochism – understandable and convincing psychological elements, considering her situation.[35] Yet, there is a less emotionally complex exploitation to come, when Grandfather steals money from Nell for gambling.

Moreover, it is not long before Fred Trent puts the worst-case interpretation on the domestic set-up, one that, perhaps, the reader has reluctantly begun to suspect:

> I want to see my sister, that you keep cooped up here, poisoning her mind with your sly secrets and pretending an affection for her that you may work her to death, and add a few scraped shillings every week to the money you can hardly count. (*OCS*, ch. 2, p. 21)

The difficulty with this perspective is that – apart from the notion that Grandfather is rich – it does contain truth. There are scenes depicting Nell's isolation and loneliness. As for 'poisoning her mind', even Master Humphrey raises this issue:

> this reply [...] caused me to look at the little creature with an involuntary expression of surprise; for I wondered what kind of errand it might be that occasioned her to be prepared for questioning. (*OCS*, ch. 1, p. 8)

In addition, the suspicion the reader feels toward Grandfather is deliberately stoked-up by Master Humphrey's narrative, as a mysterious quality is attached to him:

---

[35] Such psychological cogency is important in view of the fact that Dickens is often accused of producing unconvincing characters. Adorno, meanwhile, celebrates that the novel's characters are, as he sees it, not hamstrung by bourgeois realism or psychology.

> At the street-corner he [Grandfather] stopped, and regarding me with a troubled countenance said [...] he must take his leave [...] summoning up more alacrity than might have been expected in one of his appearance, he hurried away [...] thrice he looked back as if to ascertain if I were still watching him, or [...] following at a distance. The obscurity of the night favoured his disappearance. (*OCS*, ch. 1, p. 17)

So, the ambiguity of Nell's relationship with her grandfather – exploitative? intimate but painful? – is deliberately left unresolved.

The issue of exploitation, of using those dependent upon you as profit-making objects, is made explicit in the case of Jerry's performing dogs, and in the discussion among the traveling performers about the fate of giants and dwarfs once they become too old to perform (*OCS*, ch. 18, p. 148 onwards).

Jerry's dogs are led by a bandy-legged old mutt whose harsh existence justifies his constantly mournful expression. Because eking out an existence through performing is so difficult in a capitalist set-up, any lost revenue even vaguely attributable to inadequate performance is severely punished. The elderly dog, on this occasion, then, is blamed for the loss of a few pennies, his food is withheld, and he is condemned to grind out mournful music and to howl as he watches the other dogs being fed. In this context, his fate seems obvious – once too old to perform, he will be discarded as a valueless object and, like the elderly performing giants, abandoned to starvation. Bizarrely – as if to highlight the perverse arbitrariness of the capitalist market – the dwarfs become more valuable as commodified freaks when they age, since their elderliness increases their curiosity-value. The performers, like the curiosity objects, have a price as a commodity which is liable to rise and fall with the market. They resemble allegories in their arbitrary meanings. The performers' existence as commodities puts one in mind of Benjamin's quoting of Christoph Männling's *Theatre of Death or funeral orations*, in the *Trauerspiel* essay. Männling's allegory claims that the material world is a general store overseen by the merchant, death, who trades in man, the merchandise.[36]

The model of an intimate relationship, then, is, in Marxian vein, one of exchange, of the relationship based upon mutual profit. The vulnerable (Nell, the dogs, the performing freaks), instead of being protected and loved, are objectified, exploited, subject to cruelty – the severity of which is driven by the desperate need to make money. The topsy-turvy morality applied here is necessitated by the capitalist system. Yet these unfortunate social conditions are still inextricably linked to the divine world in Dickens's novel. The vulnerability, the powerlessness of the victims depicted heightens the suggestion that their treatment is 'sinful' – that the events and actions of the material world impinge upon, have an effect upon the divine realm.

[36] *OGTD*, p. 159.

### *(c) Betrayal*

An act of betrayal is an original trust, promise or bond reneged upon by a friend. Grandfather's neglect and possible exploitation of Nell can be viewed as a betrayal of a trust between guardian and child.

The material and the religious senses of betrayal work simultaneously. Grandfather's neglect, his exposure of Nell to danger and humiliation, is driven by his psychological need to gamble. He betrays Nell because his craving for the jouissance of gambling takes precedence over the welfare of a child. With the psychological dishonesty of the addict, he claims he will bequeath his winnings to her; yet it is not a win that is the true object of desire. The gambler's addiction concerns the repetition of thrill and risk.[37] This is the material side of Grandfather's betrayal; the extreme risk he takes and the extreme wealth he covets, forces a material destitution upon not only himself, but his charge.

But there is another side to Grandfather's betrayal – the religious resonances. Dickens suggests that the trust between parent/guardian and child is a sacred one. He does this by emphasizing the dependence, the vulnerability and the goodness of Nell; by stoking up the pathos of her helplessness, her powerlessness. Her passive acceptance and even forgiveness of her treatment conjures up the New Testament's betrayal of Christ by Judas, the passage, 'Suffer the little children to come unto Me', or even the idea of the sacrificial lamb.[38] Like the betrayal of Nell by Quilp, Codlin and Short and Fred, Grandfather has worldly motives which harm Nell. But the harm is done by those claiming to be an intimate. In fact, it is only the intimate who can be a betrayer: the closer the intimacy, the greater the betrayal. It is this intimate/betrayer model that Dickens's takes so seriously and stages so dramatically in Nell's betrayal by Mrs Quilp:

> 'Dear Quilp', faltered his wife, 'I *love* the child – if you could do without making me deceive her'. (my emphasis, *OCS*, ch. 6, p. 55)

Mrs Quilp betrays Nell; whether under duress or no, the outcome is that she betrays her.[39] It is this involvement of love which makes the betrayal so significant and dramatic in this case and in the case of Grandfather.

The ubiquity of betrayal in the novel has the effect of eroding the distinction between intimate and enemy. Since only intimates can be betrayers, betrayal corrupts/taints all relationships. A further upshot is confusion over who is friend and who is foe. Characters begin to misinterpret all behavior as betrayal, as Nell does of Kit. While Grandfather is obviously an intimate, his behavior smacks of

---

[37] As will be discussed in Chapter 3, the repetition and anxiety of the gambler becomes an important image in Benjamin's formulation of his theory of urban experience.

[38] Betrayed with a kiss: Mark 14:45. See also Matt. 26:47–56; Luke 22:47–53; John 18:1–12. A kiss was the customary greeting for a rabbi from a disciple (Luke 7:45). 'Suffer the little children': Mark 10:14.

[39] Like Nell, Mrs Quilp is forced by a cruel male into sinfulness – further underpinning the notion of the necessary decline/sinfulness of the profane world.

betrayal, though Nell refuses to recognize this. There is an ironical pronouncement by Grandfather: 'Nobody is true to me. No, not one. Not even Nell!' (Grandfather, *OCS*, ch. 24, p. 188). Here Grandfather betrays the most intimate love of all: he betrays himself.

***(d) Abuse***

As a female child, it is important to pick up on the constant sexual/paedophiliac threat Nell lives under.[40] She is threatened by her jealous sibling, Fred Trent, who would happily divest her of Grandfather's subsistence by farming her out in marriage – Dick Swiveller teams up with Fred and Quilp to 'marry' her. In the discussion with Fred, Dick concedes that Nell is 'very pretty', declaring his sexual admiration, despite simultaneously claiming her youth excludes her from being a potential spouse.

She escapes the unspecified danger posed by Short and Codlin, a pair of puppeteers who revel in Punch's physical violence and executions, yet perversely talk about 'friendship' with her. Here is one of the instances in Dickens where the dark area of abuse of the child, sexual or psychological, is subtly nuanced. There is also a hint of sadism in this relationship. Codlin, who is cold and misanthropic, suddenly declares that he is Nell's true friend, not the amiable Short. Both puppeteers – as the reader knows but Nell doesn't – intend to betray Nell and Grandfather to the authorities. Possible physical abuse is also the subtext of Nell's stay upon the barge, where a drunken bargeman demands that she sing to him.

Finally, of course, Nell is at danger from Punch's double, Quilp. Nell's space in the crowded shop, her nook of purity, where she enjoyed peace of mind, is invaded by Quilp during his audacious encampment. It is a metaphorical rape. Grandfather and granddaughter are literally squeezed out of their home by Quilp's moral pollution. Quilp is both grotesquely cruel, reveling in causing harm to the vulnerable; and he is a moneylender – this again points to an inextricable dialectic between the profane world of money-making and the religious level of meaning. He is driven by the material urge to make money and he is, at the same time, undoubtedly a sinner.

There is, too, a distinct element of sadism involved in Quilp's relationship to Nell. It is when she is at her most frightened and vulnerable that he is sexually suggestive to her. While the old man is lingering between life and death, and Nell is sick with worry, Quilp accosts Nell, is plainly suggestive, even deriving pleasure from watching her weep:

---

[40] A threat that is absent in the case of a male child, for example, Paul Dombey. Hollington argues that Dostoevsky takes the 'abuse' of Nell as a Dickensian given and develops it further in his own fiction: in his lecture 'Remaining Modern: Dickens and the 19th Century European Novel', delivered at University of Exeter, March 15, 2009. See also MacPike's *Dostoevsky's Dickens*, part 1, pp. 19–92, especially p. 36.

> there's such a scratching and bruising in store for you, my young friend. Aha! Nelly! How is he now, my duck of diamonds?
> 'He's very bad', replied the weeping child.
> 'What a pretty little Nell!' cried Quilp.
> 'Oh beautiful, sir, beautiful indeed', said Brass [...]
> 'Has she come to sit upon Quilp's knee', said the dwarf, in what he meant to be a soothing tone, 'or is she going to bed in her own little room inside here – which is poor Nelly going to do?' (*OCS*, ch. 11, p. 96)

Here is Quilp at his most repulsive, mocking the feelings of the vulnerable child with 'poor Nell' when it is he who initiated the crisis and intends to profit by it.

And Nell cannot even escape the horrible Quilp when she is on the road. He haunts her physically and mentally throughout her journey. His threat is an articulated sexual one: 'How should you like to be my number two, Nelly?' (*OCS*, ch. 6, p. 52). He also wants any money she might inherit.

### *Nell's Messianic Status*

It has been argued that much of Nell's suffering is caused by the actions of characters engaged in a struggle to earn enough money to live; her misfortune and suffering can be traced to the material, social conditions in which she and others are rooted. Nell is a character as steeped in the profane world as any other, then. She is not innocent and pure, but corrupted by, complicit in sin; she does not escape injustice, anxiety, poverty and pain, but endures suffering just as much, if not more than, many others.

Nevertheless, there is textual evidence that, paradoxically, Nell still somehow transcends social conditions; that she has a spiritual quality, an otherworldliness that suggests she remains untouched by, while still being drawn into, the material reality of conditions around her.[41]

How does one explain, for instance, Nell's startling capacity for self-abnegation, forgiveness and loyalty? These are the opposite qualities to those fostered by many of the profit-based intimacies depicted in the novel.

One answer is that she is a child. Dickens is drawing on the Romantic tradition in suggesting that children have an inexperience, naivité or lack of cynicism that sets them apart from the adult world (this opposes the evangelical view that children are originally sinful). The Romantic child has an absence of self-interest and a purity of heart that adults lose through experience. Nell is the Romantic child in that she has a natural goodness, a child's simple frankness in a troubled, morally ambiguous material world. At the same time, though, she is still involved in sinfulness:

---

41 The possibility of Nell being 'redeemed', even while trapped in the profane world, will also be explored in an analysis of the allegorical image of Nell surrounded by curiosities in Chapter 2.

> She took from her pocket a little purse. He seized it with the same rapid impatience which had characterized his speech, and hastily made his way to the other side of the screen. It was impossible to restrain him. (*OCS*, ch. 29, p. 230)

She is also forced into self-consciousness. Her natural openness is checked by bitter experience:

> now and then she stole a curious look at my face as if to make quite sure that I was not deceiving her. (*OCS*, ch. 1, p. 8)

It is exceptional for a character to be afraid of a narrator in Dickens. Here, Nell is not only vulnerable, she knows she is.

Hence Nell has this ambivalent status. She is, as is the case in a profane world, a sinner. She is one who suffers. Yet she can relate to others on the basis of affection and pity, not profit. She displays selfless motivations and actions wholly at variance to the rigorous individualism and self-centeredness of the social context. This duality bears the anatomy of messianism. In messianism, while one is mired in sin and/or suffering, one can at the same time experience oneself as, or appear to others to be, 'redeemed'. The experience of suffering, as it were, alters the perceived structure of time, such that the present hope of future redemption becomes more intense, redemption itself appears to be closer, even present in the midst of suffering.

The paradox of Nell extends to the fact that, while she is a child, her selfless attitudes make her more mature, more adult than many of the adults around her.[42] Indeed, not only must she play adult to Grandfather's childlike whims: 'What are we to do, Nell? … Say what we're to do' (Grandfather, OCS, ch. 25, p. 194), but her concern and pity for others lends her an aura of quiet strength and authority which attracts attention. Master Humphrey is taken with her immediately; and her special quality of otherness is also spotted by Mrs Jarley, who wants to sell it to the public. Nell becomes more of a crowd-puller than the waxworks she displays. Her aura of gentle wisdom and selflessness is undoubtedly rather freakish in a world where profit and pragmatism are central components within the emotional economy.

But Nell also bears an air of spiritual authority/moral wisdom. There are dozens of episodes depicting her acts of kindness as verging upon holiness:

> She would have the old man refresh himself in this way too, and making him sit down upon the grass, cast the water on him with her hands, and dried it with her simple dress. (*OCS*, ch. 15, p. 126)[43]

[42] The uncanny notion of a wise child is one that often crops up in Dickens. Two obvious instances are Paul Dombey and Jenny Wren in *Our Mutual Friend*. Then there are the adults, particularly women, who appear to remain within the body of the child: Amy Dorrit is an instance of this.

[43] A gesture towards Mary Magdelene. Edwin M. Eigner claims Nell is a 'Madonna figure', *The Metaphysical Novel in England and America* (Berkeley; London: University of California Press, 1978), pp. 146–8.

And it is in this sense that the neglect, exploitation, abuse and betrayal of Nell has such an appearance of sinfulness in the novel. In the early stages of the text, even a wrongdoing as apparently trivial – albeit harmful – as Mrs Quilp's interrogation of Nell takes on a rather more serious quality because of the child's extraordinary quality of 'goodness'. Dickens stokes up this representation of Nell as vulnerable and trusting, too (*OCS*, ch. 6, pp. 55–9), such that Mrs Quilp's betrayal of her appears all the more unforgivable, a 'sin' against a blessed, even a strangely holy child. Unaware that she is betrayed, Nell is grateful to Mrs Quilp, her betrayer: a response to evil that, as has been mentioned, bears comparison to that other great holy figure who was betrayed with a kiss.

So while there are hints throughout the early part of the novel that Nell has a special quality of goodness, it is in the later phases of the novel (from chapter 42 onwards) that her role as spiritual leader or holy guide becomes explicit. But the notion of her as an exceptional person was plainly there from the very beginning. This development in the depiction of Nell comes about partly because, in terms of the character's psychology, the more suffering she endures, the more becoming conscious of her quest as a spiritual one is necessary to keep her going.

But the more explicitly spiritual Nell, as presented in these latter stages, is much more than a question of a character's convincing psychology. It is a question, it can be argued, of depicting the pilgrimage toward redemption; of delineating the trajectory of the homeless exile journeying inexorably toward home. In messianic terms, as a homeless person, as one expelled from paradise, Nell is exposed to suffering and sinfulness in the profane world. And the more suffering she undergoes, from the messianic point of view, the closer to redemption she approaches. Remember, the greater the contrast between the present evil state of affairs and the anticipated utopian, better world, in messianism, the more energetically that redemption was hoped for and the more omni*present* the 'restorative' future seemed.

Dickens fictionally depicts Nell's movement toward redemption by dovetailing the increasing intensity of Nell's physical and mental suffering with a gradually more explicit emergence of Nell as a holy figure. As her suffering causes her to start to leave the material/physical world behind – as she succumbs to illness and moves toward dying – her spiritual life becomes more intense; it is a capacity that allows her to redeem not only Grandfather but herself, too.

Dickens effects this *gradual* emergence of Nell as holy by his representation of time and space. For the pilgrims, traveling through space is a case of the sequential emergence and the fading away of people, things, buildings, landmarks and landscapes. Time's chronology, simultaneously, is mimed within the text through this sequential emerging and dwindling of phenomena and events – an episodic movement echoed, of course, by the reading process. As the reader gets further in the novel, and the pilgrims move further along their road spatially and temporally, it becomes clear that two lines of progress are being traced. The latter stages of the novel put a heavy emphasis both upon the world's downward decline, its worsening sinfulness and the increased suffering this causes Nell; whereas, in a contrapuntal movement, the increasing intensity of Nell's spiritual life is delineated, as her status emerges as that of a combination of the sacrificial lamb and spiritual figure.

Nell becomes a fully blown moral savior, for instance, when she overhears the gamblers persuading Grandfather to steal Mrs Jarley's money. Horrified by Grandfather's acquiescence, she flees:

> homewards as quickly as she could, torn and bleeding from the wounds of thorns and briars, but more lacerated in mind. (*OCS*, ch. 43, p. 330)

Here Dickens incorporates connotations of the scapegoat[44] or the holy hermit into the description of Nell's effort to summon up emotional courage to tackle this problem. Here, the immolation of Nell's flesh by the natural/material world is an iconographic indication of the access to spiritual strength and wisdom she has. Holy men fast in the wilderness, lash themselves or don hair shirts to express their scorn for the material; Nell's flesh is torn by thorns and briars. Scapegoats, wounded and sent out into the wilderness, take the sins of the community upon their heads. Like saints or holy men, then, she is strangely untouched by fleshly injuries; pain even serves to heighten the sense of moral crisis, to strengthen her capacity to make a decision and take action. Fleshly agony is in this sense *exquisite* since it is a rite of passage into a spiritual realm of experience. This is one journey which Nell is not afraid to make.

As a spiritual savior under extreme duress, Nell is now in possession of a lurid imagination which views the Manichean world in extreme and grotesque terms:

> she was distracted with a horrible fear that he might be committing it at that moment; with a horrible dread of hearing shrieks and cries piercing the silence of the night; with fearful thoughts of what he might be tempted and led on to do, if he were detected in the act, and had but a woman to struggle with. It was impossible to bear such torture. (*OCS*, ch. 43, p. 330)

And she wards off Grandfather's temptation with a spiritual fervor reminiscent of the holy figure in deadly combat with the devil. She has a frightening energy that cows Grandfather into action:

> 'What's this!' he cried, starting up in bed, and fixing his eyes upon her spectral face. 'I have had a dreadful dream', said the child, with an energy that nothing but such terrors could have inspired. 'A dreadful, horrible dream […] It is a dream of grey-haired men like you, in darkened rooms by night, robbing the sleepers of their gold. Up, up! […]. I cannot sleep, I cannot stay here, I cannot leave you alone under the roof where such dreams come. Up! We must fly.' (*OCS*, ch. 43, p. 330)

Again, here is Nell as the rhapsodic seer prophesying the future in dreams. Grandfather, enchanted by the child's strange aura and her apparent ability to anticipate his plans, follows her like a disciple.

---

[44] Lev. 16:8 and 21; Isa. 53:6.

Nell's selflessness now takes on the form of an explicit physical and psychological suffering (a suffering that was less obvious, but present, from the beginning), again resembling the traditional penance of the holy man or scapegoat:

> the child felt cold, being but poorly clad, her anxious thoughts were far removed from her own suffering or uneasiness, and busily engaged in endeavouring to devise some scheme for their joint subsistence. The same spirit which had supported her on the previous night, upheld and sustained her now. Her grandfather lay sleeping safely at her side, and the crime to which his madness urged him, was not committed. That was her comfort. (*OCS*, ch. 43, pp. 335–6)

Again, the messianic structure of Nell's situation is clear in this passage: the suffering involved in minimizing or avoiding sin is what sustains 'the same spirit' – the spirit that achieves the redemption of Grandfather.

Indeed, Nell keeps herself going by recounting this messianic set-up to herself; she braces herself to endure all possible suffering in the knowledge that she is redeeming Grandfather from an action that is sinful:

> 'I have saved him', she thought. 'In all dangers and distresses, I will remember that.' (*OCS*, ch. 43, p. 332)

Like the conventional holy figure, then, Nell's determination is only sharpened by obstacles and difficulties. This paradoxical spiritual willfulness is traditionally a focus of awe, incomprehension and even fear. And, likewise, those around the holy figure of Nell are, in traditional style, puzzled by her willingness to endure pain and suffering:

> 'Rough people – paths never made for little feet like yours – a dismal, blighted way – is there no turning back, my child?'
> 'There is none', cried Nell. (*OCS*, ch. 44, p. 345)

*Exquisite Agony*

The argument so far has made the central claim that aspects of the novel show recognizable elements of messianism. It is now time to elaborate this suggestion more fully.

The first aspect to consider is Nell's and Grandfather's homelessness. They are divested of all property and possessions and wander around without any clear destination – sometimes traveling in circles. Like the Jews, then, they are destitute exiles. But rather than viewing their ruin with fear and trepidation, Nell's response is

> 'Yes, let us go', said the child earnestly. 'Let us be gone from this place, and never turn back or think of it again. Let us wander barefoot through the world, rather than linger here [...] We will be happy [...] We never can be here.' (*OCS*, ch. 12, p. 103)

This rhapsodic attachment to a life in exile, and the certainty with which she declares it, has the ingredients both of childlike naivité and a mature sense that while suffering is possible, its endurance will yield something better. It is, then, an acceptance of possible suffering – including enduring an existential homelessness – for which enthusiasm makes sense if one considers Nell's meaning as echoing a messianic possibility of redemption, of a coming home at last.

But it is when physical suffering takes place that the depiction of Nell is really interesting:

> The child walked with more difficulty than she had led her companion to expect, for the pains that racked her joints were of no common severity, and every exertion increased them. But they wrung from her no complaint, or look of suffering. (*OCS*, ch. 45, p. 347)

Here, Nell endures pain – with the poetic echoes of the tortured saint in the language used: 'racked', 'joints', 'wrung' – but wills herself to internalize it. Acceptance of pain and suffering in a wholly private capacity can be a case of dysfunctional psychology, a familiarity with suffering. But it can also involve an inner conviction about the meaning of suffering and what is beyond it. For Nell, something good will come of it. Not only is suffering the logical punishment for sin, then – sin into which by necessity she has been plunged – but it indicates a kind of endgame, as if bringing on intense unhappiness will lead to a quicker resolution, to an arrival of redemption all the sooner. The emotional structure of the messianic existence, then, necessitates fortitude and asceticism. Nell exhibits this aplenty. But further, she actually intensifies, revels in, her suffering by remaining silent when she could be screaming. Profane suffering involves an intensification of the present through pain – which is survived by the idea that one is touching redemption in the heat of the moment. One can almost embrace agony during such an intense experience. Agony is, it is suggested, Nell's in silent embrace.[45]

During some parts of the journey, though, Nell wants Grandfather to be aware of the suffering she endures:

> 'We shall be very slow today, dear', she said as they toiled painfully through the streets, 'my feet are sore, and I have pains in all my limbs from the wet of yesterday'. (*OCS*, ch. 45, p. 347)

This is, of course, merely information for Grandfather: but it is also an interesting dwelling upon and declaration of pain. It is less a complaint against it than a pathetic acceptance or avowal of it: a reminder to herself and Grandfather of what suffering is required to attain redemption. It also suggests a belief that the acceptance of suffering somehow renders one more deserving of redemption.

[45] MacPike reads Nell's journey psychologically: as a masochistic expiation of the guilt she feels for unconsciously wishing for the death of her grandfather. See *Dostoevsky's Dickens*, p. 83.

It announces the conventionally rather masochistic willingness to trust in God – as did Abraham – that the paradox of life will ultimately make sense.

And it is not just Nell who talks of suffering with acceptance and pathos. The narrative itself can be seen to use pathos just as much, dramatizing the trajectory of Nell's deterioration with a repetition of passages like

> Much weaker, diminished powers even of sight and hearing, and yet the child made no complaint. (*OCS*, ch. 45, p. 350)

and

> She felt a hopelessness of their ever being extricated together from that forlorn place, a dull conviction that she was very ill, perhaps dying. (*OCS*, ch. 45, p. 350)

Notice how the matter of fact tone – 'perhaps' – contrasts with the mournful content. This passage of free indirect speech emphasizes the idea that Nell has a messianic notion of suffering as a familiar part of existence, something to be endured in the anticipation of happiness.

An explicit account of how suffering can become not only a familiar part of life, but a complex site of pain, love and beauty occurs when Nell meets a woman mourning a loved one by a grave. Nell mistakes the elderly mourner for the dead youth's mother and is shocked to hear that the mourner was, in fact, his wife; the youth died 50 years before:

> She told her how she had wept and moaned and prayed to die herself [...] But that time passed by, and although she continued to be sad when she came there, still she could bear to come, and so went on until it was pain no longer, but a solemn pleasure, and a duty she had learnt to like. (*OCS*, ch. 17, p. 138)

The woman's pain has become a site of pleasure because it is a reminder of the happiness and redemption she will have when she meets her husband 'in another world', as Dickens puts it. Further, redemption and happiness are, in a sense, already with the mourner since she claims that her former suffering self 'seems to have died with him'. In traveling through and beyond suffering and achieving 'death' and reminding herself of her own suffering/death by revisiting the same place mentally and physically, the agony of loss transforms into exquisite pleasure and becomes a source of redemption.

Another form of wallowing in suffering traceable in the narrative is in the way it presents the element of chance. Nell and Trent's existence on the road means that life will become governed by the exigencies of luck. They have a little good luck, but mostly bad luck; and the bad luck is heightened to a pitch where it becomes melodramatic. For instance, having found stable employment and somewhere to stay, Nell and Grandfather accidentally come across a gambling den which will lure Grandfather back to his ruin. What is more, the travelers do not see the gambling tavern because of a rainstorm and are about to walk past without stopping. But, as luck would have it, the landlord hails them in from the rain – an event that is their undoing. Like the fact that Grandfather never wins at cards, this is a kind of reveling in the injustice of the profane world by the novelist which comes close to a messianic viewpoint. Here Dickens indulges in a fascinating aesthetics of suffering, a heightened dramatization of bad luck and sadness which is set against the novel's anticipation and witnessing of Nell's redemption.

Yet another tendency toward a 'wallowing in sorrow', and a yearning for an end to suffering, lies in the narrative's repetitive hints of Nell's imminent death (*OCS*, chs. 52–5, pp. 400–426). These comprise a strange anticipation of the novel's denouement, an aesthetic and somewhat masochistic dwelling upon, and relishing in, her demise. For example, in entering what will be her final security from destitution, her final home, she shivers. The schoolmaster says,

> 'A peaceful place to live in, don't you think so?' [...]
> 'Oh yes', rejoined the child, clasping her hands earnestly. 'A quiet, happy place – a place to live and learn to die in!' (*OCS*, ch. 52, p. 401)

This is an extraordinary utterance for a child – although, as discussed, Nell is no 'ordinary' child. Implied in the instance of her shivering is the cold she feels having entered her 'tomb'. This is her last resting place. Her surroundings, decrepit and ancient, are physically tomblike, too. For the first time reader, this is a play upon death, tickling the reader's suspicions so that drawing toward the end of the novel becomes a question of the raising and/or the gazumping of one's expectations. For those who have already read the novel, this is a repetitive reminder, a variation of the crescendo of death to come. But why the obsession with, the relishing of, death? Again, Nell's passive acceptance, even her desire for death – 'I will learn to die' – makes sense within the framework of messianic sentiment argued for; moreover, Dickens's persistence with these anticipatory gestures toward Nell's fate throughout this latter section point to a narrative echoing of Nell's messianic fervor for an end and a new beginning – for redemption.

The physical and psychological suffering of the travelers persists through a number of encounters; but there are two episodes when it could be argued that the narrative aesthetics of suffering really reaches a crescendo. For instance, take the following:

> Towards the afternoon, her grandfather complained bitterly of hunger. She approached one of the wretched hovels by the way side and knocked with her hand upon the door.
> 'What would you have here?' said a gaunt miserable man, opening it.
> 'Charity. A morsel of bread.'
> 'Do you see that?' returned the man hoarsely, pointing to a kind of bundle on the ground.
> 'That's a dead child. I and five hundred other men were thrown out of work three months ago. That is my third dead child, and last. Do you think I have charity to bestow, or a morsel of bread to spare?'
> The child recoiled from the door, and it closed upon her. (*OCS*, ch. 45, pp. 350–51)

Here we have an evocation of life that comes close to the state of perpetual and relentless suffering evinced in Jewish theology. When the travelers are desperate and in need of help, those they call upon are in a similar state of desperate and piteous poverty. Notice the inclusion of the economic/political reasons for the poor man's state of affairs. Suffering comes about through the material conditions of the profane world. The interest of this intervention of historical realism is not only that it is an attack upon the conditions of the poor by Dickens, but that it comes close to the Jewish messianic notion that the politics and social conditions of the profane world are the root of suffering, itself having meaning in relationship to a divine realm.

The other passage worth considering in this light is the one depicting the city (of Wolverhampton) as a cruel, mechanistic hell:

> The child and her grandfather [...] stood amid its din and tumult, and in the pouring rain, as strange, bewildered, and confused, as if they had lived a thousand years before [...] They withdrew into a low archway for shelter from the rain, and watched the faces of those who passed, to find in one among them a ray of encouragement or hope. (*OCS*, ch. 43, p. 337)

The quintessence of the profane, historical world – the city – is a harrowing, mournful site that exacerbates the travelers' woes. The vertiginous routine of the streets ensures they are physically stranded among strangers who, while jostling them, do not see/know them. Only in the crowd can one be visibly present yet invisible. They are lost – but not only in space, physically. They are lost in moral/human terms too; their suffering is not witnessed. No befrienders guide them away from the confusion and pace that obfuscates their destitution. This city morality, where other people represent not potential friends but obstacles that must be bypassed in the crowd, is a result of the physical constitution of the space. Beggars, the directionless, those without a clear sight and sense of their own physical and moral route, feel the hard end if this. They are the ignored and the jostled. They are abandoned to their fate. The revolutionary critique of laissez-faire city sensibility is echoed in Friedrich Engels:

> No one even bothers to spare a glance for the others. The greater the number of people packed in a tiny space, the more repulsive and offensive becomes the brutal indifference.[46]

This is the nadir of Nell's and Grandfather's suffering because the suggestion is their suffering could be endless in the city: not only do they fail to attract anyone's attention to their plight, but attempts to orient themselves ends in a fruitless circuitous route. This is the city as purgatory. Like everyone around them, they are mesmerized by, and powerless before, the city's frenetic relentlessness:

---

[46] Benjamin quoting Engels's *The Condition of the Working Class in England* in 'Motifs', *Illuminations*, p. 163.

> the child continued to gaze upon the passing crowd with a wondering interest, amounting almost to a temporary forgetfulness of her own condition. But cold, wet, want of rest [...] soon brought her thoughts back. (*OCS*, ch. 44, pp. 338–9)

Here Nell rehearses the familiar notion that city experience involves a vertiginous loss of subjectivity.[47] But this is a disaster for the poor; they are not only without help but are unable to exact much control over their helplessness. Moreover, the crowd reduces the specificity of the beggar's plight to being that of all other beggars, whose presence on the street becomes a familiar sign. The intention to argue one's case as deserving attention becomes disrupted in the context of the destitution of masses. As Dickens phrases it, Nell and Grandfather are a mere 'atom [...] in a mountain heap of misery' (*OCS*, ch. 44, p. 339). This is the cruel city at its loneliest and most dispassionate. It is the loneliness of the crowd consisting of miles and miles of strangers, with all that that means to the individual in need. The city resembles an inhuman, monstrous machine that, as the train does to Carker, devours its inhabitants.[48]

Dickens's more explicit delineation of the city as hell follows immediately from this passage. Nell and Grandfather, afraid and desperate and failing to solicit any help, retreat into a doorway, where they are accosted by a shadow who leads them to his furnace bed through sanitary pollution and excrement:

> In a large and lofty building, supported by pillars of iron with great black apertures in the upper walls, open to the external air; echoing to the roof with the beating of hammers and roar of furnaces, mingled with the hissing of red-hot metal plunged in water, and a hundred strange unearthly noises never heard elsewhere, in this gloomy place, moving like demons among the flame and smoke, dimly and fitfully seen, flushed and tormented by the burning fires, and wielding great weapons, a faulty blow from any one of which must have crushed some workman's skull, a number of men laboured like giants. (*OCS*, ch. 44, p. 342)[49]

---

[47] One textual source of this notion is Benjamin's reading of Baudelaire's 'A Painter of Modern Life', itself involving a reading of Poe's 'The Man of the Crowd' (1845) – which, briefly, delineates a man's experience of the frenetic electricity of the city crowd and a dissolution of his subjectivity into it. Benjamin reads Baudelaire reading Poe in his essay 'The Paris of the Second Empire in Baudelaire', ch. X, 'The Flâneur', in *SW*, IV, pp. 3–94. An analysis of the metropolis and mental life, including the effect of the crowd upon the individual psyche, will be pursued in Part 2 of this book.

[48] Statistically, the number of infants that died in the city as opposed to those in rural environments during the first half of the nineteenth century meant that the city was literally (as well as fictionally/mythically) a devouring monster. See esp. F.S. Schwarzbach, *Dickens and the City* (London: The Athlone Press, 1979), intro., pp. 7–10.

[49] It is difficult not to speculate that the 'industrial sound world' created towards the end of act I, scene 3, of Wagner's *Das Rheingold* (the first part of his tetralogy *Der Ring des Nibelungen*) composed in 1853–1854 (performed on its own in Munich in 1869 and as part of the Ring cycle at Bayreuth in 1876), was influenced by Dickens's delineation of a hellish industrial scene in *OCS*. Wagner was interested in English Literature, having adapted

Here is the manmade profane physical world resembling nothing less than hell. As is the case in the messianic worldview, it is only when the world is at its most catastrophic that redemption 'draws nearer'. It is clear, then, that Nell had to reach this nadir to be redeemed. Once she has been, as it were, 'purified' by excrement, pollution and fire, the route toward redemption and death is opened up. It is amid the tormenting fires of hell that Nell and Grandfather find a kindly word and a charitable gesture from a grotesque stranger. It is at the most catastrophic moment that the world can be interpreted as on the verge of a cataclysmic inversion.

> as a force is capable, through its direction, of promoting another in the opposite direction, so too is the profane order of the profane in the coming of the messianic kingdom. The profane, therefore, is not a category of the kingdom but a category [...] of its most quiet nearing.[50]

## *Moments of Revelation*

It was suggested at the start of this chapter that Benjamin was fascinated by the idea that everyday existence involved encounters with or glimpses of religious experience or immanent transcendence. And it was maintained that Dickens's fiction appears to share this idea, with his characters sometimes experiencing the world or moments that could be understood within the framework of such a theory of experience. It is now time to discuss this line of argument in detail.

There are a number of episodes in the travails of Nell that can be considered here. Firstly, we shall examine a passage which depicts Nell and Grandfather's experience of leaving the city of London. The passage begins with the experience of traveling itself: a representation involving the chronological emergence and dwindling away of buildings, landmarks or landscapes. Then, the depiction of spatial distance is evoked with the idea that the traveler's glance back over his route ties together the separate spatio-temporal episodes through which he has traveled, and a whole journey emerges:

> Then came a turnpike; then fields again with trees and haystacks; then a hill; and on top of that the traveller might stop, and – looking back at old Saint Paul's looming through the smoke, its cross peeping above the cloud (if the day were clear) and glittering in the sun; and casting his eyes upon the Babel out of which it grew until he traced it down to the furthest outposts of the invading army of bricks and mortar whose station lay for the present nearly at his feet – might feel as last that he was clear of London. (*OCS*, ch. 15, p. 125)

Dickens's friend Bulwer Lytton's novel, *Rienzi, Last of the Tribunes* into his third opera in 1840. See also Katherine Inglis's thinking upon the presence of the automaton in Dickens's fiction, which includes an interpretation of this passage in 'Becoming Automatous: Automata in *The Old Curiosity Shop* and *Our Mutual Friend*', *19*: *Interdisciplinary Studies in the Long Nineteenth Century* 6 (2008), <http://www.19.bbk.ac.uk>.

[50] Benjamin, 'Theological-Political Fragment', trans. by Jacobson in 'Jacobson', p. 21. See Appendix 1 for an outline of variations on the translation of this fragment.

This passage begins to open up an experience that includes a totality of apprehension not available in the moment by moment hustle and bustle of movement. Spatially, the perspective over and above London allows for a piecing together, a mastering, of the evanescent encounters and fragmentary viewpoints one collects on a journey through the city space. Here, it is suggested, is an example in Dickens's fiction of Benjamin's fuller experience, a redemptive moment, the idea that totality (of time and space) or the absolute can break in upon everyday experience. This is especially the case when the narrative continues as follows:

> The freshness of the day, the singing of the birds, the beauty of the waving grass, the deep green leaves, the wild flowers and the thousand exquisite scents and sounds that floated in the air – deep joys to most of us, but most of all to those whose life is in a crowd or who live solitarily in great cities as in the bucket of a human well, – sunk into their breasts and made them very glad. The child had repeated her artless prayers once that morning, more earnestly perhaps than she had ever done in all her life, but as she felt all this, they rose to her lips again. (*OCS*, ch. 15, p. 125)

Here is the idea that the physical and mental exertion of traveling and achieving a vantage point from which to review one's progress, can become an experience of the absolute. Having got beyond the city confines where the senses were bombarded with a shock-inducing and mechanistic rhythm, the travelers relax in the natural landscape, within its less frenetic sensual context. The feeling of well-being this entails, as well as the feeling of mastering the journey as a whole, opens up a space for an apprehension of God. Nell expresses thankfulness in prayer that progress has been made and that rest has arrived. She understands the progress and reward of their journey as God's dispensations; looked at in hindsight, the journey is, for Nell, a mini-allegory of the Christian life. And she goes on to compare, at that point, *The Pilgrim's Progress* with their own 'pilgrimage'. Her experience of the absolute is, in this sense, an opening up of meaning not only within her own fictional world, but simultaneously, at the meta-fictional level as well.

Another representation of a moment of the absolute flooding into Nell's world, is toward the end of the novel, when Nell is sitting pensively in a chapel surrounded by sarcophagi, tombs and reliefs of the dead (*OCS* ch. 53, pp. 412–13). The passage begins with a fascinating depiction of the power of objects to make present the past:

> Broken and dilapidated as they were, they yet retained their ancient form, and something of their ancient aspect. Thus violent deeds live after men upon the earth, and traces of war and bloodshed will survive in mournful shapes, long after those who worked the desolation are but atoms of earth themselves. (*OCS*, ch. 53, p. 412)

Here is an evocation of the language of objects: old objects that indicate their whole story dialectically in their very fragmentariness. To this evanescent glimpse of the past – a past made present, a totality erupting and contracting within the present – is added the following:

> The child sat down in this old, silent place, among the stark figures on the tombs – they made it more quiet there, than elsewhere, to her fancy – and gazing round with a feeling of awe, tempered with a calm delight, felt that now she was happy, and at rest. She took a Bible from the shelf, and read; then laying it down, thought of the summer days and the bright spring-time that would come – of the rays of sun that would fall in aslant upon the sleeping forms – of the leaves that would flutter at the window, and play in glistening shadows on the pavement – of the songs of birds, and growth of buds and blossoms out of doors – of the sweet air, that would steal in and gently wave the tattered banners overhead. What if the spot awakened thoughts of death! Die who would, it would still remain the same [...] It would be no pain to sleep amidst them. (*OCS*, ch. 53, pp. 412–13)

This, it is suggested, is a complex representation of a moment of redemption. Sitting among effigies of the dead, Nell anticipates her own death and beyond, and feels no fear – only contentment. In imagining the changing of the seasons, the beautiful flux of the world, Nell contrasts it with the safe, unchanging silence of the tomb where she will (in Victorian euphemism) go to sleep; but the tomb is not untouched by the world of the living. There is still life after death. After the battle of life, while Nell looks forward to a quiet resting place, she also envisages her tomb as penetrated by rays of sunlight and wafts of air.[51] Death, then, is inextricably caught up with the material world. The onslaught of time, nuanced in the changing seasons, will decay not only the stone effigies but the body too. But this is part of the natural pattern of things. And the tomb's silence will remain, like the soul, unchanged, eternal. Nell's feeling is that death is a kind of safe haven from the world, that death means redemption, because its endorsement of finitude is merely the obverse side of eternity. Death as redemption is reinforced by her Bible reading. The future as eternal redemption is made present for Nell within the context of religious belief, then, a fictional representation of a glimpse of an immanent absolute. It is an experience brought about by Nell's sitting in a chapel and opening herself up to the objects and ruins around her.

But the passage goes on. Nell physically enacts the metaphysical notion of redemption, in fact, of resurrection. She climbs out of the tomb, like Lazarus:

> She left the chapel – very slowly and often turning back to gaze again – and coming to a low door, which plainly led into the tower, opened it, and climbed the winding stair in darkness; save where she looked down through narrow loopholes on the place she had left, or caught a glimmering vision of the dusty bells. At length she gained the end of the ascent and stood upon the turret top.
>
> Oh! The glory of the sudden burst of light; the freshness of the fields and woods, stretching away on every side and meeting the bright blue sky; the cattle grazing in the pasturage; the smoke, that, coming from among the trees, seemed

[51] 'The Battle of Life', the title of Dickens's 1846 Christmas book.

> to rise upward from the green earth; the children yet at their gambols down below – all, everything, so beautiful and happy. It was like passing from death to life; it was drawing nearer Heaven. (*OCS*, ch. 53, pp. 413–14)

This is not only a moment of redemption for Nell, but a meta-fictional moment for the reader, a presentiment of Nell's fate. It is a redemptive moment whose content is the religious moment of redemption itself. For Nell, the physical effort of climbing opens up a sudden vision of heaven and eternity. There appears a sudden apprehension of theological truth. For the reader, it is a dramatized preview of Nell's death, complete with the eschatological notion of her rising to heaven. She is, as we suspected all along, to be redeemed, yet this enactment, together with the illustration of Nell in the arms of angels on the last page of the novel, amount to a strangely clunky literary attempt to evoke the Christian litany. Dickens's apparent anxiety to get this image across is, perhaps, why critics such as Wilde thought the death of Nell laughable.[52] It is not so much a sentimentality that grates at the end of the novel, but an overkill, an excess of the pointing up of Nell's redemption which is clearly not required if the novel's presentation of Nell is read closely.[53]

Another appearance of the evanescent absolute within everyday life is also represented in the kind actions of strangers:

> But the woman had observed, from the young wanderer's gait, that one of her little feet was blistered and sore, and being a woman and a mother too, she would not suffer her to go until she had washed the place and applied some simple remedy, which she did so carefully and with such a gentle hand – rough-grained and hard though it was, with work – that the child's heart was too full to admit of her saying more than a fervent 'God bless you!' nor could she look back nor trust herself to speak, until they had left the cottage some distance behind. When she turned her head, she saw that the whole family, even the old grandfather, were standing in the road watching them as they went, and so, with many waves of the hand, and cheering nods, and on one side at least not without tears, they parted company. (*OCS*, ch. 15, p. 130)

Here, the narrative opens up the idea of transcendence with the biblical resonances of the loving act of the washing of the feet, added to the only phrase which can rise to the occasion for Nell, 'God bless you!' The contrast asserted between the gentleness of the treatment effected by the woman and the work-calloused hands with which she washes Nell's foot is an interesting example of Dickens's

---

[52] Oscar Wilde sought refuge at the home of the literary socialite Ada Leverson between his trials. According to Leverson's daughter, Wilde 'Never liked even the grotesque part of Dickens. To those who praised Dickens, he said, "One must have a heart of stone to read the death of Little Nell without laughing"', Violet Wyndham, *The Sphinx and Her Circle: A Biographical Sketch of Ada Leverson, 1862–1933* (London: André Deutsch, 1963), p. 119.

[53] See Nicola Bown's convincing defense of sentimentality in Dickens and its importance to Victorian culture in 'Introduction: Crying Over Little Nell', *19: Interdisciplinary Studies in the Long Nineteenth Century* 4 (2007), <http://www.19.bbk.ac.uk>.

literalizing of the transcendent – a form of dramatic oxymoron or dialectic the novelist sets up between the physical and the spiritual/moral, to suggest the immanent transcendence or moral importance of an action within ordinary or common life.[54] The significance of the woman's action is clear in its contrast to the actions of other characters: her palliative act is instinctive and motherly, unrequested and unconditional, unplanned and spontaneous. It is in stark contrast, then, to the self-interested, considered, conspiratorial actions of villainous characters, such as Quilp or the Brasses. And, at one level, we see here the traces of melodrama: villainous characters are wealthy/moneylenders and conspirators; the poor are simple, pure and good. But even at the level of realism, Dickens wants to suggest that the family's simplicity, its lowly poverty gives it greater access to the harshnesses of life and therefore, to redemption. With their firsthand experience of hardship, the poor have a greater awareness of the possible suffering of others – and take uncomplicated and direct action to help.

The messianic worldview that emphases degradation, corruption and suffering ahead of redemption is pregnant with contradiction. As the world declines and things and events become more depraved and deprived of meaning, it is there, in the most destitute areas of life and experience, that one will locate redemptive moments. Dickens appears to express this. The poor, the oppressed will suffer most intensely and therefore come to 'know' the possible redemptive qualities about it, sensing it in others who suffer. There is, then, something special about the poor, they exchange a unique experience, from Dickens's point of view as well as from the messianic one. Only they have the eyes to see, and bear witness to, the suffering of others. Only they have the generosity of spirit to meet suffering head on, to help and be glad, in what Wohlfarth terms 'a Messianic will to fulfilment which ecstatically affirms the world'.[55] That the woman's actions 'aid' Nell's decline, allowing her to continue walking to her death – yet making both Nell and the woman tearfully 'happy' – is a contradiction that is only as it should be:

> To the spiritual [...] corresponds a worldliness that ushers in the eternity of the decline and the rhythm of this eternal passing away, passing away in its totality [...] the rhythm of messianic nature is happiness.[56]

---

[54] While Dickens can be understood to suggest in his own work that there is a glimpse of transcendence traceable within the kindnesses of common folk, he rejects the idea that the holy family might be depicted as ordinary people in art. The Pre-Raphaelite artist John Everett Millais painted *Christ in the House of His Parents* in 1850, and, literalizing the transcendent, he depicts the holy family as realistic working people. Dickens hated the painting, and appears to believe Millais blasphemed. See *Household Words*, June 15, 1850, in *Dickens' Journalism*, ed. Michael Slater, 4 vols. (London: J.M. Dent, 1994–2000), II, pp. 242–8. Millais's painting is online at: <http://www.victorianweb.org/religion/type/ch4b.html>.

[55] Irving Wohlfarth, 'On Some Jewish Motifs in Benjamin', in *The Problems of Modernity*, ed. Andrew Benjamin (Routledge, 1989), p. 166. This essay will hereafter be abbreviated as 'Jewish Motifs'.

[56] 'Theological-Political Fragment', trans. Jacobson in 'Jacobson', p. 21.

The family's genuine sympathy and concern for Nell and Grandfather is underlined in their moving farewell, their reluctance to let the pilgrims out of sight. The family wave – a gesture that indicates to the receiver that the waver still has them in view across space and through time. This confirmation that the pilgrims are watched, that their plight is known, is significant since the increasing rapidity of travel and the greater frequency of travelers arbitrates against noticing travelers at all. The family's watching, then, is in stark contrast to the people of the city crowds who, despite Nell and Grandfather's desperate plight, do not appear to see them at all.[57]

## Conclusion: *The Old Curiosity Shop* and Messianism

Nell and Grandfather shared short-lived bouts of happiness and finally found a restful place to die, but their existence was dominated by aimless wandering, suffering and poverty, and the narrative's trajectory does not suggest their pain served any conceivable purpose or effected any real change in the profane world. The poor, meanwhile, continue to endure suffering, the novel asserts, and other Nells will suffer and die and be forgotten along with our heroine.

From a messianic point of view, it is right that Nell should die and that no real progress should be made. Benjamin's messianic understanding of history, outlined most powerfully in his last work, the 'Theses', dismisses the notion of history as progress. The increasingly catastrophic events of historical time are, on the contrary, a mounting pile of debris, the junk-heap of history – a melancholy image echoed by the objects of Grandfather's curiosity shop as well as by the heaps of decaying stone ruins in which the pilgrims end their days. The world, then, is a charnel house whose destitution will only be ended by the catastrophic revolutionary event of the messiah's arrival, not by any evolutionary move toward decency. Nell's life and death appear to ratify the position that a huge event would be needed to change the world's melancholy and fallen state.

The fall from paradise does not, of course, feature among the objective facts of history. For Benjamin, the present not only features a fall away from paradise, then, but a forgetfulness of that very fall itself. The fall is a self-perpetuating act of forgetting. A forgetfulness of theological truths characterizes modern sensibility.[58] For Benjamin, there is an urgent need for remembrance, for recognition of redemptive moments and religious meaning, then. Even Dickens recognizes the melancholy reality of forgetfulness in modern sensibility – which he inscribes upon the very fabric of the city. Kit remembers Nell but:

> He sometimes took (his children) to the street where she had lived; [...] new improvements had altered it so much, it was not like the same. The old house had been long ago pulled down, and a fine broad road was in its place. At first he

[57] *OCS*, ch. 44, p. 338.

[58] 'obliviousness to the Fall may prove to be one of its most baleful historical consequences' (Wohlfarth, 'Jewish Motifs', p. 162).

> would draw with his stick a square upon the ground to show them where it used to stand. But he soon became uncertain of the spot, and could only say it was thereabouts, he thought, and that these alterations were confusing.
> Such are the changes which a few years bring about, and so do things pass away, like a tale that is told! (*OCS*, ch. 73, pp. 574–5)

Here, then, is the melancholy Dickensian strain denying any purpose and progress with respect to Nell and her suffering life. Much was made in the novel (schoolmaster's speech, *OCS*, ch. 54, p. 421) of the notion that redemption in death consists in that the deceased live on in the memory of others. But at the close of the novel, Dickens slams that door shut. For Benjamin, the lives of the oppressed are forgotten and covered over, and urgently need to be remembered and redeemed. His intellectual life was aimed at finding ways in which this redemption could be carried out.

Yet despite this melancholy strain, there is another tendency in *OCS*, a yearning for, as it were, a messianic solution. Even if one discounts the repeated image of Nell's redemptive flight to heaven – and it is difficult to do so since Dickens is so insistent upon it! – Dickens rights all wrongs at the close of the narrative, a novelistic sleight of hand which echoes a revolutionary Jewish *tikkun*. Having dealt with all characters, rewarding some while doling out a violent death to Quilp, imprisoning and impoverishing the villainous Brasses, exiling and killing off Fred Trent in a drunken fight, the novelist continues:

> Those who had been kind to them, did not escape his search. The sisters at the school – they who were her friends, because themselves so friendless – Mrs Jarley of the wax-work, Codlin, Short – he found them all; and trust me that the man who fed the furnace fire was not forgotten. (*OCS*, ch. 73, p. 573)

Dickens knows that one of the most disturbing depictions of poverty evoked in the novel was the pauper living in the city factory. Here, Dickens reassures the reader that the anonymous pauper, too, is to be remembered, in Benjaminian vein. Without pushing the point too far, then, here is Dickens playing a kind of novelistic messiah. Viewing the narrative from the point of utopian perfection, with hindsight, he dramatically interrupts the 'history' and goes about righting all wrongs, resolving the unresolved, returning the broken to themselves, completed. While the narrative comes to an abrupt end, there is also a beginning, an attempt to reestablish the harmony disturbed by the profane world's/narrative's exigencies.

# Chapter 2
# *The Old Curiosity Shop*, Allegory and *Trauerspiele*

> Whosoever would grace this frail cottage, in which poverty adorns every corner [...] would be making no inapt statement nor overstepping the mark of well-founded truth if he called the world a general store [...] in which man is the merchandise, death the wondrous merchant, God the most conscientious book-keeper.[1]

The form and content of *OCS* is allegorical and emblematical, influenced as it is by John Bunyan's *The Pilgrim's Progress*. In Bunyan's text of 1678, the character of Christian, burdened and 'lost', is guided by Evangelist toward 'the promised land' where his burden will be eased. Christian is, of course, an 'everyman' – he responds to specific circumstances, but his life journey is meant to represent ours at a more general level. The text is designed to be read didactically. Similarly, Little Nell makes a journey with her grandfather away from the evil city into the countryside in search of salvation (echoing another of Quarles's emblems).[2] Rather than being guided, she is the moral and spatial guide. Her efforts will culminate in her death and redemption. This is, then, a straightforward allegorical/emblematic representation of an innocent trapped in a material, corrupt and cruel world, which, at a certain level appears to have been abandoned by God. The only route to transcendence appears to be relentless suffering followed by death. Indeed, that is what the novel appears to imply.

## The *Trauerspiel* Study, Baroque Playwrights and Benjamin's Metaphysics

The novel's allegorical structure is extremely important in view of the discussion of Benjamin's early metaphysics. It is also crucial to another discussion: that of *OCS* in relation to Benjamin's theory of allegory – and the novel's resemblance to German *Trauerspiele*.

1 Benjamin quoting Christoph Männling's *Theatre of Death or funeral orations*, the opening allegorical motif of the final chapter in *The Origin of German Tragic Drama* (*Ursprung des deutschen Trauerspiels*) trans. John Osborne (London & New York: Verso, 1998), p. 159. This text will be abbreviated as *OGTD*.

2 Embleme VII in bk. 4 features an illustration of two travelers surveying picturesque countryside accompanied by Canticle 7.11, 'Come my beloved, let us go forth into the fields, and let us remain in the villages' (Francis Quarles, *Emblemes* [Cambridge, printed by RD for Francis Eglefeild: St Paul's Churchyard, 1643], pp. 212–15).

The two areas of Benjamin's oeuvre – his early theological essays already adduced, and his *Trauerspiel* Study – intellectually converge. Benjamin's early essay '*Trauerspiel* and Tragödie' was written in the same year, 1916, as 'On Language as Such and On the Language of Man', and was working within the Jewish language theory formulated in the 'On Language' essay.[3] Indeed, Benjamin told Gershom Scholem that his epistemological framework for *OGTD*, his famously difficult 'Epistemo-Critical Prologue', would only be understood by those versed in the mysteries of the Kabbalah.[4] Hence, biographically, the *Trauerspiel* study can be viewed as part of Benjamin's earlier, Romantic-theological phase.

The points of convergence between the Baroque *Trauerspiele* and Benjamin's Jewish theological interests include a 'hallowing of the word'; the Lutheran and Counter-Reformation drama's preference for allegory echoing Benjamin's language theory.[5] For Baroque artists and Benjamin, language is the site of the loss and possible redemption of the absolute. Benjamin claimed that the loss of Adamic naming after the Fall resulted in the 'over-naming' of the thing, which was dramatized in the verbosity and melancholy of *Trauerspiele*:

> one notices an extravagant tone of plaintive lamentation, which acquires the character of a fixed mannerism; an incessant hand-wringing mode of expression. (*OGTD*, 64)[6]

The bombastic language characteristic of the *Trauerspiel* is an indication, for Benjamin, that the dramatists understood the desolation of humankind. The world portrayed by the *Trauerspiele* playwrights was God-forsaken, a space where anxious verbosity testified to the inability to embody meaning. Like the messianic worldview, *Trauerspiel*'s allegorical form was eschatological (as opposed to the theophanic expression of symbol). It expressed salvific anticipation. The power of its expression of the world's passion simultaneously gestured toward something beyond itself. That 'something' (the absolute) was there and not there at the same time.

In writing the *Trauerspiel* study, Benjamin buried himself not only in the wholly neglected Baroque plays of Lohenstein, Gryphius, Opitz[7] and others but

---

3 Benjamin claims on the title page of the thesis *The Origin of German Tragic Drama* that it was conceived in 1916, but written in 1925. It was published in 1928.

4 *Friendship*, p. 152.

5 See George Steiner, introduction to English translation of *OGTD*, pp. 7–24.

6 'Benjamin differentiates the silences of tragedy from the torrential prolixity of the *Trauerspiel*' (Steiner, intro., *OGTD*, p. 17).

7 Daniel Casper von Lowenstein (1635–1683): he wrote, among others, *Cleopatra* (1661) and *Sophonisbe* (1680). Andreas Gryphius (1616–1664), among whose works are *Catharina von Georgien* and *Carolus Stuardus*; Martin Opitz (1597–1639), whose *German Poetics* (Buch von der deutschen Poeterey) is considered the theoretical groundwork of German Baroque literature.

also in Baroque emblem books and theological tracts – in the broader baroque worldview.[8] He found that

> *Trauerspiele* expressed time and history. The dramatists were masters of celebrating desolation and melancholy – a reflection of the historical state of affairs during and after the 30 years war.[9]

In viewing *OCS* in terms of the ideas from the early essays as well as from the *Trauerspiel* study, one is in effect plowing the same field of theological ideas. Indeed, Benjamin has been accused of conflating Judaic and Lutheran metaphysical notions with respect to his reading of seventeenth-century drama. This need not worry us too much. Of relevance to our exploration of *OCS* is firstly, Benjamin's reading of allegory; and then, secondly, a discussion which teases out elements of a Baroque aesthetic in Dickens's novel.

## The Theory of Allegory in *The Origin of German Tragic Drama* (or Mourning Plays)

Allegory is the main poetic and stylistic element of the plays of the seventeenth century and Benjamin theorizes this in his 1925 essay. And, as mentioned, it is the perfect linguistic figure to capture the sorrowful struggle for absolute meaning in that fallen world.

As opposed to the aesthetic figure of symbol, which attempts an immediate unity with that which it intends, overlapping with the universal and thus carrying the moment of transcendence within itself – or at least representing that set up to the imagination – allegory, argues Benjamin in *OGTD*, presents the world in fragmentation and imperfection. It does this because it is a figure of speech in which an object or element comes to signify or stand for something else, and while its meaning is conventional, it is also, in that sense, contingent and arbitrary. The meaning of allegorical images are not self-evident, they are part of a worldview which claims that all meaning has ceased to be self-evident. Allegory, then, always needs completion from an outside source, from the allegorist: it lacks immanent meaning. It is subject to proliferation; referents can multiply so much, they can even negate former meanings. In contrast to

---

[8] It has already been mentioned that Dickens was influenced by Quarles's emblem books. According to Benjamin's friend, Gershom Scholem, Benjamin was fascinated by 'Dürer's Melencolia I and the emblem books of the sixteenth and seventeenth centuries' (*Friendship*, p. 82).

[9] Bertold Brecht (1898–1956) – with whom Benjamin took up a close intellectual relationship in later life, writing a number of essays on the German playwright published in Germany in 1966 as 'Understanding Brecht' – wrote *Mother Courage*, set during the Thirty Years War. Moreover, the original score of *The Threepenny Opera*, which premiered to acclaim in Berlin in 1928, is intriguingly understood by many Brecht/Weill scholars to have distinct strains of Lutheran morality, rather than just being a work of Marxist polemic.

symbol, then, which condenses and concentrates meaning intensively in a single image in a momentary totality, allegory consists of an excessive ornamentation of strained associations, working through a 'displacement' of meaning along a horizontal chain of signifiers.

Allegory, following Benjamin's language theory, is, then, the perfect literary figure of the profane world. Allegorical figure has (aesthetically speaking) no immediate or necessary connection to the absolute. It is, as it were, an empty shell without any immanent meaning. It fails to name that which it intends. Its 'knowledge' does not yield the absolute, just as profane language fails to do so, after the Fall. In Jewish theology, the Torah of the Exile (which replaces the divine Torah after the Fall) is figured in allegorical language. Kabbalists speculated, interpreted and read this sacred text in a bid to gain insight into sacred truths and possible utopian futures. Such truths were expressed immediately in the Torah of Redemption (the sacred text of the Messianic era). Here, then, Benjamin's reading of allegory in seventeenth-century *Trauerspiel* is rooted in radical Jewish metaphysics.

For Benjamin, the Baroque world and hence the world of the *Trauerspiel* is a 'fallen' one. Plots were little more than a mechanical procession of catastrophic events, rooted in the representation of existence as terrifying and bleak, an emptiness of unfulfilled time. A sovereign ruler, the summit of all creation, might erupt into madness like a volcano, destroying himself and his entire court. His divinely invested position as monarch is weighed against his depravity and impotence. An audience gains little satisfaction (or catharsis) from such a representation of his downfall: there is just a sense of disgust.

The dominant tone of such an artistic production, then, is melancholic and mournful. Hence '*Trauerspiel*' sometimes being translated as 'mourning play'; George Steiner uses the term 'horror-drama'.[10] Yet Baroque dramatists were writing about life itself, they contained the Baroque age:

> 'Historical life, as it was conceived at that time, was its content.'[11]

A central theme for all Baroque artists – not only playwrights – was how the material and spiritual worlds could be shown to interrelate during a period of history when the world seemed to have lost all contact with the absolute. All art, so Benjamin insists, is concerned with the representation of man's relation to the absolute.[12] For Benjamin, the ostentatious expressions of lamentation were

[10] *OGTD*, intro., p. 15.

[11] Opitz's description of *Trauerspiel*, *OGTD*, p. 62. *Ursprung des deutschen Trauerspiels*, revidierte ausgabe besorgt von Rolf Tiedemann (Frankfurt a. M: Surkamp Verlag, 1963), p. 51. Hereafter abbreviated as '*Trauerspiels*'.

[12] In Benjamin's essay 'The Concept of Criticism in German Romanticism', he claims that the absolute appears in the work of art – but only in a veiled, fragmentary way. The critic's job is to make something in the work appear. See *SW*, I, p. 359.

the logical result of the historical situation of the Baroque age.[13] The playwrights felt existence was such a torment that the answer as to what exactly the relationship of the world of the *Trauerspiel* is to transcendence, to God or redemption, was that there was no relationship at all.

> The *Trauerspiel* 'is confined to a context of strict immanence without any access to the beyond'.[14]

In the world of the *Trauerspiel*, for Benjamin, one is thrown back onto the material world – there is nothing else. And material objects, with their undeniable quiddity as well as their tendency to decay, attest to the finite nature of everything, of the tendency toward change and decline. The emphasis upon decay in the *Trauerspiel* has echoes in *OCS*. Flux, change, decay and death are the modus operandi of the profane world.

Yet, totally in line with the messianic underpinnings of 'On Language as Such' and the 'Theological-Political Fragment', there is what Benjamin terms 'the antinomy of allegory'. For Benjamin, allegorical structure is dialectical. *Trauerspiel*'s allegorical content amounts to an inverted picture of the divine world: it functions as a kind of negative theology. The work's content becomes transformed into its opposite – based upon the theological conception of the diametrically opposite relation between the profane life and that of the divine.[15]

Nothing is as it appears, in the *Trauerspiel*, then. Things are of little interest or value in and of themselves – their significance lies utterly in the determination of their allegorical meaning, in relation to the theological concept of redemption. In fact, all claims to knowledge, all representations in the profane world of the *Trauerspiel* are totally undermined, since neither can yield the absolute. Even the grotesque and lively representation of evil is comfortingly 'unreal' in the final estimation of the play. The corrupt and ruined world of the *Trauerspiel* becomes like a puppet-play or the shadows in Plato's cave – or like a tale told by a novelist – its negative semiology rendering the relationship of appearance and essence as one of inversion.

---

[13] Seventeeth-century Germany was dominated by the so-called Thirty Years War, which was, briefly, the struggle of a number of German princes backed by foreign powers such as France, Sweden, Denmark and England, against the unity of the Holy Roman Empire and the house of Hapsburg which ruled vast territories in Europe. It was a bloody and terrible situation. Beginning in 1618, by 1648 Germany was in ruins, depopulated and starving. The idea is that *Trauerspiel* playwrights expressed that appalling state of affairs (*OGTD*, p. 81).

[14] *OGTD*, p. 80.

[15] See Richard Wolin, *Walter Benjamin: An Aesthetic of Redemption* (Berkeley, Los Angeles, London: University of California Press, 1994), p. 72.

## The Allegorical Tableau of *The Old Curiosity Shop*

It is becoming clearer why *OCS* can be situated within this framework. The novel is an allegory. And, as was the case in the world of the *Trauerspiel*, an almost obsessive need to read the allegory – to make sense of its representations, to attribute meaning to its events and its material objects, the curiosities, plays a huge role in *OCS*. Take the following passage:

> the heaps of fantastic things I had seen huddled together in the curiosity-dealer's warehouse. These, crowding upon my mind, in connection with the child, and gathering round her, as it were, brought her condition palpably before me. I had her image, without any effort of imagination, surrounded and beset by everything that was foreign to its nature, and furthest removed from the sympathies of her sex and age. If these helps to my fancy had all been wanting, and I had been forced to imagine her in a common chamber, with nothing unusual or uncouth in its appearance, it is very probable that I should have been less impressed with her strange and solitary state. As it was, she seemed to exist in a kind of allegory; and having these shapes about her, claimed my interest so strongly, that [...] I could not dismiss her from my recollection, do what I would. (Narrator, *OCS*, ch. 1, p. 19)

Here, it is suggested, is one of the central tableaux of the novel. It represents Nell and the curiosities as an allegory within the novel's allegorical form – but the passage was only added later, a deferral of meaning that echoes allegory's structure.[16] And the source of this textual allegorical representation is the Williams illustration.

Referring to the textual excerpt first, here we have an allegory being presented by the allegorist (the narrator, Master Humphrey). As has been mentioned, the allegory, for Benjamin and for the Kabbalists, is *the* literary figure. Through that critical process something of the original 'truth' of the work is redeemed. In visiting Nell and the curiosity shop, Master Humphrey recalls that experience in one image, in which he surrounds Nell with the strange, haunting objects, the 'curiosities'; he then claims this image has disclosed her situation truthfully to him. Bringing the objects together with Nell shows him clearly that she is living in 'a kind of allegory'. Pushing Master Humphrey's interpretation of Nell as living in an allegory further, it can be suggested that the image claims that she lives in a fallen, capitalist world that is in mourning for meaning. It is only right that Master Humphrey should see Nell and the remaindered commodities and come up with an allegorical image, since 'Allegories are in the realm of thoughts what ruins are in the realm of things' (*OGTD*, p. 178).

---

[16] This passage is part of material Dickens added to the first separate volume edition in 1841, following the review of the story by Thomas Hood halfway through its serialization in *Master Humphrey's Clock*. In the *Athenaeum 7* in November 1840, Hood claimed that Williams's picture of Nell sleeping amid the objects was 'a kind of allegory'. Dickens liked this idea and inserted four paragraphs toward the end of chapter 1 elaborating the notion of Nell and the objects as allegory.

Fig. 2.1 'The Child Asleep in her Bed', wood engraving by Samuel Williams (1788–1853). This image appeared with the first chapter instalment in No. 4 of *Master Humphrey's Clock* on 25 April 1840. Reproduced by courtesy of the Charles Dickens Museum, London.

And what are curiosities? They are the detritus of society, commodities no longer wanted, without use-value. For these objects, their completion was in the past. Now they have lost their meaning; they are as 'fallen' as their price; they are objects for which to mourn. They have gone the way of all worldly objects, they have become ruins and remainders, physical embodiments of a world subject to the onslaught of time and the market, the world as decaying, fragmented and ostensibly without redemption.

The objects' ruination, their fragmentariness is what gives them their Gothic texture and ambiguity. On the one hand they are shadowy, dusty ghosts of their former selves; on the other hand they are unquestionably 'there', their remains palpably insist upon their quiddity. This Gothic quality might resurrect their exchange value for a while. They occupy the dialectic space between past and present: as objects of the past, objects of memory, they insist upon haunting the present, and in this sense, they seduce the window-shopper and the passerby. But even this meaning must be allotted to them by the allegorist; this act of remembrance, this redemption, can only be done by the curiosity seeker. In and of themselves, they are devoid of meaning, empty shells. They are forgotten objects.

And what is Nell in this allegorical tableau? She is entombed among inanimate objects and is, metaphorically, a corpse: she too is the quintessential emblem of the ruin. The corpse is material testament to the body's immanence and decay. Nell, on this reading, is a piece of rubbish. She has no exchange-value, she is 'homeless', no one takes care of her, no one wants her; she has no source of salvation or transcendence. She is just another of the out-of-date commodities, a ruin.

> That which lies here in ruins, the highly significant fragment, the remnant, is, in fact, the finest material in baroque creation. (*OGTD*, 178)[17]

Yet, rather like the moment of magic within language when the 'inexpressible' appears – and, as Benjamin indicates, being a highly significant fragment – Nell is simultaneously redeemed within this tableau. She is diminutive in comparison to the piles of junk. And as Master Humphrey's passage suggests, she is crowded out by them. There is a play upon the otherness of the objects in relation to Nell: the idea that their ruinousness, their decay and quiddity is somehow 'contrary' or contrasted to the pure and ethereal Nell. As Master Humphrey puts it: 'everything that was foreign to its nature, and furthest removed from the sympathies of her sex and age' (*OCS*, ch. 1, p. 19).

Dickens emphasizes Nell's smallness, her tiny stature and body, her youth and beauty, the perfect, incorruptible being that Nell represents.[18] His depiction of Nell's size is presumably influenced by the Judeo-Christian notion of the body or matter as 'abject', as the substance that decays and corrupts in contrast to the untouchable spirit. Hence her 'un-fleshy', tiny body. His is a desire, then, to represent Nell as pure and therefore, as waiflike.[19]

Her tiny stature is significant. For Benjamin, tiny things contain in concentrated form, everything else; the more they are compacted by dialectical insight, the more monadic they become. He concentrates upon the overlooked, the transitory: 'to detect the crystal of the total event in the analysis of the small, discrete object'.[20]

Nell discloses, in monadic form, the fallenness and simultaneously, the salvation, of the historical world in this allegorical image. So even before Nell's pilgrimage gets underway, right at the start of the novel, Nell's fate and its meaning

---

[17] *Trauerspiels*, p. 198.

[18] Dickens probably read Carlyle's 1824 translation of Goethe's *Wilhelm Meister's Wanderings*, and it is possible that Nell's stature was modeled on Goethe's tiny princess. Paul Schlicke claims Dickens had a copy of the novel in 1844 (*Oxford Reader's Companion to Dickens* [Oxford: Oxford University Press, 1999], p. 40), but it is here suggested that Nell's resemblance to Goethe's heroine points to an earlier acquaintance with the book. Benjamin mentions Goethe's 'Neue Melusine', the princess in the little casket in 'Conversation above the Corso' (1935) in *SW*, III, p. 29. Carlyle's influence on Dickens is discussed in the conclusion to Part 1.

[19] As Hollington points out, Adorno's reading of *OCS* relates the youthful Nell to the topos of 'Death and the Maiden'. See 'Hollington', p. 88.

[20] *Arcades*, N2, 6.

is nuanced in Master Humphrey's allegorical image within the allegorical form of the novel. This can be read off from the allegorical image of Nell and the curiosities around her. The reader becomes the allegorist.

But the image of Nell sleeping among curiosities is itself a montage,[21] an assemblage of fragments of the narrator's memory of his visit to the curiosity shop. In this sense, the allegory itself could be understood to be foregrounding its own arbitrariness. Moreover, since the objects are fragments of memory, the allegory is an image of objects in the process of redemption. The narrator himself calls his allegorical image a 'recollection', an act of remembrance:

> We are so much in the habit of allowing impressions to be made upon us by external objects, which should be produced by reflection alone, but which, without such visible aids often escape us; that I am not sure I should have been so thoroughly possessed by this one subject, but for the heaps of fantastic things I had seen huddled together in the curiosity-dealer's warehouse. These, crowding upon my mind, in connection with the child, and gathering around her, as it were, brought her condition palpably before me. (Narrator, *OCS*, ch. 1, p. 19)

The fragments of memory 'crowding' the narrator's mind are, he acknowledges, the result of the astounding and indelible impression material objects have upon the viewer. The insistence of material objects, the weight of their presence and juxtaposition, their 'connection' with Nell and with each other, demands of the narrator reflection and interpretation. They demand remembrance and 'redemption'.[22] As has been suggested, messianism reads remembrance and redemption as approximating to similar activities.

Master Humphrey's image of Nell surrounded by curiosities is significant, too, in view of Benjamin's interest in the imaginative world of associations.[23] Benjamin even takes this notion as far as claiming 'Ideas are to objects what constellations are to stars' (*OGTD*, p. 34). It is in respect of the juxtaposition of objects/fragments, from an unmediated juxtaposition of material elements, that ideas or truth emerge. What could be suggested is that Dickens's panoply of objects, here, rehearses such a notion. Dickens here has a fascination for objects: for juxtaposing objects and

---

21 Montage is a significant form for Benjamin. His later work, especially *The Arcades Project*, was structured in 'literary montage'. Montage also points to the influence of the Surrealists on Benjamin. For an in-depth study of Benjamin and the Surrealists, see Margaret Cohen, *Profane Illumination* (Berkeley, Los Angeles, London: University of California, 1993).

22 Benjamin's fascination with Proust involves understanding Proust's theory of 'memoire involuntaire' (involuntary memory) as a possible route to the absolute in an unredeemed modern world – a full discussion is conducted in Chapter 3.

23 Gershom Scholem says of Benjamin, 'In Paris, he led me, offering highly appreciative remarks along the way, to such places as The Cabinet des Illusions and also to Madame Tussaud's waxworks, whose unexpected juxtapositions of figures equally evoked his aesthetic-associative delight' (*Friendship*, p. 82).

creating new and incredible associations and meanings; for closely focusing upon them and gleaning their meaning or redeeming their truth.

There is further reason to ratify Master Humphrey's claim that the allegory discloses Nell's state of affairs: 'These, crowding upon my mind, in connection with the child, and gathering around her, as it were, brought her condition palpably before me' (*OCS*, ch. 1, p. 19).[24] While Nell is haunted by the ruins of the past, the image of her surrounded by curiosities foreshadows her future, too. It is a presentiment of the 'fantastic' people and objects she will encounter on her journey toward death; an anticipation of the fallenness of the corrupt, broken characters she will encounter, the gothic ruins and spaces she will inhabit. Her lying as if dead among the ruins is, too, an anticipation of her future. Her future, then, will also be haunted by ruins. This is only as it should be, for Benjamin. The ruin is the figure for the demise of the creaturely as natural history:

> In the ruin history has physically merged into the setting. And in this guise history does not assume the form of the process of eternal life so much as that of irresistible decay. (*OGTD*, pp. 177–8)[25]

The allegorical image of Nell and the objects opens up not only the present, then, but the past and the future as well. Little Nell is an unwanted object among the detritus of the profane historical world. Yet, as discussed, there is also a hint of the redemption of this profane state of affairs; the redemption that, as it were, always already lives in the profane 'now'. For Benjamin, in the profane world, there is a constant tension within time itself – a case of redemption appearing alternately 'close at hand or out of reach'.[26] This applies to Nell in her position within the allegorical image – and in her ambiguous status in the rest of the novel's text: she will be fallen, homeless trash, yet redeemed and otherworldly.

The textual account of Nell and the curiosities is complemented, as was suggested, by the famous illustration by Williams (reproduced above).[27] The narrator's vision in illustration compounds the indelible quality of the image that he specifies. (Dickens used woodblock engraving which could be 'dropped into' the text rather than steel etchings on separate pages – allowing illustration and text to be more closely identified).[28] In Blakean tradition, then, Dickens provides a composite artwork. The narrative detail 'I cannot get this image out of my mind',

---

[24] Benjamin cites a passage from *OCS* which includes this quotation in Convolute H 'The Collector' of *The Arcades Project*, H2a, 4. The quotation Benjamin uses is part of the allegory 'addition' Dickens made to the 1841 separate volume edition.

[25] *Trauerspiels*, p. 197.

[26] Quote from Wohlfarth, 'Jewish Motifs', p. 161.

[27] *OCS*, ch. 1, p. 18.

[28] On first receiving the sketch in March 1840, Dickens asked Williams to add 'a few grim, ugly articles' to the depiction of the curiosity shop and to make Nell look 'more childish'.

with the implied intention, 'I try to redeem these objects' or 'I try to give this allegory meaning' is compounded by a pictorial representation.

The textual boundaries between the literary narrative and the pictorial narrative are insecure. The position of the illustration in relation to the text renders it difficult if not impossible to establish the 'source' of specific aspects of the mental image conjured up in the mind of the reader. Rather than a question of addition in respect of the two images (textual and illustrative), then, the production of meaning is more an issue of multiplication – the conjuring up of new or original meanings. Moreover, Dickens foregrounds in the mind of the reader this complex relationship between meanings and their source. He does this by suggesting a dialectical relationship between the material objects (the objects in the curiosity shop) and their effect upon the mental life of the narrator (the objects are a montage of memory). While the narrator's mind arranges the objects around Nell, condensing the curiosity shop into a compact image – the 'actual' objects in the 'actual' curiosity warehouse are themselves only fictional images in the mind of the reader. And this circuitous chasing for sources of meaning echoes allegory's inability to encompass the absolute.

Like the textual allegorical image, the illustration denotes futural events. Nell is in a deep exhausted sleep. Care and anxiety are etched upon her face. While she is unaware of it, an intricate and scheming world is going on around her, some of it dark and threatening to her. This is nuanced by faces or masks worked into the grain of wooden furniture, into the grain of the composition, available to the eye only if one traces the lines of the illustration carefully. There is a hidden arrangement in the objects around her, then, once one moves one's focus away from the sleeping Nell to study the concatenation of objects that surround Nell's bed. The faces, spotted and foregrounded by the eye, 'disappear' into the scene again once the eye settles back to resting on Nell. The hidden connections of even the most remote things in time and space are an important Dickensian trait, reproduced here in illustration. The juxtaposition of objects/ruins is also, as has been pointed out, an important epistemological moment in the *Trauerspiel* study. For Benjamin, ideas or patterns of meaning emerge from the combination of fragments or things themselves.

## The Waxworks[29]

Along with Master Humphrey's allegorical image and its illustration, Dickens also foregrounds allegory in the text through his portrayal of the waxworks. Take the following passage:

> divers sprightly effigies of celebrated characters, singly and in groups, clad in glittering dresses of various climes and times, and standing more or less unsteadily upon their legs, with their eyes very wide open, and their nostrils very

[29] 'In *The Old Curiosity Shop*, Dickens speaks of the "unchanging air of coldness and gentility" about the waxwork Dream House' (*Arcades*, Q2a2).

> much inflated, and the muscles of their legs and arms very strongly developed, and all their countenances expressing great surprise. All the gentlemen were very pigeon-breasted and very blue about the beards; and all the ladies were miraculous figures; and all the ladies and all the gentlemen were looking intensely nowhere, and staring with extraordinary earnestness at nothing. (*OCS*, ch. 28, p. 221)

Here we have a powerful image that literalizes the metaphysical state of affairs in Benjamin's understanding of allegory, his understanding of the fallen world of the *Trauerspiel*, as well as representing the metaphysics of the melancholy human condition of Benjamin's early theology. Significantly, the novel depicts the life of performers: Nell, the performing dogs, the freaks, the puppets: they are sold to the public – they are commodities. As the novel's title implies, they are curiosities in a great curiosity shop.[30] Moreover, as if taking his cue from Marx, Dickens depicts the relationships of those struggling to survive the exigencies of the capitalist economy as 'tainted' – characters relate to each other on the basis of an exchange of benefit or profit. Subjects then, become objects – while commodities or objects are fetishized and are treated like subjects. The waxworks and the curiosities in the curiosity shop have a 'home', while Nell and grandfather have none. In a profane world of fallen language and objects, in the world where meaning has fallen away, the human sphere in *OCS* starts to appear like a crowd of empty waxwork shells.[31] Dickens's inclusion and treatment of the waxworks is a brilliant allusion to that state of affairs.

The waxworks' uncanniness is an echo of the uncanniness of the everyday. While they are made of wax, they stare 'intensely' and 'earnestly', facial expressions familiar to us. Seeing them is an echo of an everyday occurrence of looking at the Other looking. This is the unseeing, staring face that one might be jostled by in a crowd – and is one of the empty faces that Nell tried to read for signs of pity in Wolverhampton. The strange moment of recognition in seeing a waxwork is further augmented by the way they are strangely halted in mid-action, their 'muscles' flexed as if at the ready, as if trying to figure forth the energy of life: instead of representing its absence. But the lack of animation is a shock for us – the shock of confronting the corpse, the ultimate Otherness.

While there is an obvious Otherness about the figures, sameness plays an important role in any understanding of their structure, too. This manifests itself in a weird resemblance to each other: 'All the gentlemen were very pigeon-breasted'; as well as in their resemblance to one's everyday experience of the Other – as a lot of similar 'others' in the crowd or on the street. Sameness has an importance in the anatomy of decay. It underlines the fact that decay, the ravages of time, reduces all individuality to sameness in the end – the sameness of the corpse.

---

30 See cited allegory by Christopher Männling, Theatre of Death or funeral orations, above, p. 32.

31 See also Katherine Inglis, 'Becoming Autonomous: Automata in *The Old Curiosity Shop* and *Our Mutual Friend*', 19.6 (April 2008), <http://www.19.bbk.ac.uk/issue6/papers/inglisautomata.pdf7>.

There is a further element of horror or uncanniness about waxworks. The models are not only corpses, ruins, but attempt to represent people of another time and space. So while there is a 'sameness' and an 'otherness' about them – while they are corpse-like empty shells – they also remind the onlooker of the fact that humans have some sort of resemblance to them. Further, their owners are selling that resemblance to the public. More profoundly, the waxworks allegorically represent human beings in the fallen capitalist world: like the performers and puppets, humans are reduced to little more than empty ruins. This is surely where the Dickensian lamentation (comic and uncanny though it is) over, and critique of, capitalist economics and its dire social consequences is at its most powerful.

The materiality of the waxworks' allegorical representation of the human condition is, significantly, played up by instances of misrecognition recounted in the novel, when the instability of the waxwork identities, and the proliferation of possible referents, becomes apparent.

This is manifest, firstly, in the habit of spectators mistaking humans for waxworks:

> Nell dismounted amidst an admiring group of children, who evidently supposed her to be an important item of the curiosities, and were fully impressed with the belief that her grandfather was a cunning device in wax. (*OCS*, ch. 28, p. 218)

This is a set-up whereby a spectator's ability to recognize is thrown into disorientation by the waxworks; she starts to believe that anything is possible, even a moving waxwork. The interesting irony is that the spectator substitutes the allegorical referent (the human) for the allegorical figure itself (the waxwork).

Another manifestation of this tendency to play on the materiality of allegory, is when the narrative comically colludes with the waxwork illusion:

> a highly ornamented table placed at the upper end for Mrs Jarley herself, at which she was to preside and take the money, in company with his Majesty King George the Third, Mr Grimaldi as clown, Mary Queen of Scots, an anonymous gentleman of the Quaker persuasion and Mr Pitt holding in his hand a correct model of the bill for the imposition of the window duty. (*OCS*, ch. 28, pp. 222–3)[32]

Here, the narrative deliberately declines to state 'the waxwork figure of …', although it is comically implied by its very absence. Yet this absence/presence play using the signifiers (not using but implying the presence of the phrase 'the waxwork figure of') results in an absence/presence play on the level of the signified (are they the 'real' characters or are they waxwork?).

[32] Dickens edited the *Memoirs of Grimaldi* – the clown Joey Grimaldi (1778–1837) – in two volumes for Bentley's *Miscellany*. He had seen Grimaldi, the greatest of pantomime clowns, perform as a child. See Forster's '*Life*', bk. 2, ch. 2, p. 104: Dickens did not particularly rate this piece of work.

A third example of this tendency, is through the notion that the wax models can change from one identity to another, with the minimum of adjustment and attention to detail:

> Mr Pitt in a nightcap and bedgown, and without his boots, represented the poet Cowper with perfect exactness; and Mary Queen of Scots in a dark wig, white shirt-collar, and male attire, was such a complete image of Lord Byron, that the young ladies quite screamed when they saw it. (*OCS*, ch. 29, p. 225)

Working like the allegorical linguistic device, the waxworks' referents are unstable and contingent, not essential. Here again is the strange allusion to the quality of 'sameness' inherent in the waxworks, the uncanny sameness of the mass produced commodity. As in the example of the corpse, all individuality in the waxwork is eroded by time.

The final example of a tendency for Dickens to play up the materiality of allegory is in the constant textual play in the narrative that suggests the substitution of humans with waxworks:

> He was very patient and willing, happy to execute any little task, and glad to be of use; but he was in the same listless state, with no prospect of improvement – a mere child – a poor, thoughtless, vacant creature – a harmless fond old man, susceptible to tender love and regard for her, and of pleasant and painful impressions, but alive to nothing more. (*OCS*, ch. 29, p. 227)

This is a view of Grandfather seen through Nell's eyes. He sounds uncannily dummy-like.

A similar example is the snobbish derogation of the child by the school mistress, an event which identifies the otherness of the lower classes with the otherness of the waxwork:

> 'You're the wax-work child, are you not?' said Miss Monflathers.
> 'Yes, ma'am', replied Nell, colouring deeply, for the young ladies had collected about her. (*OCS*, ch. 31, p. 244)

Nell's status as a human being here withers under the predatory gaze of the authoritative seeker of curiosities. Nell is herself objectified into a curiosity, allegorizing both her own class position and the human condition at the same time.

If there are a series of 'misrecognitions' of humans for waxworks or vice versa in the novel, there is one substitution of the one for the other that is perhaps most convincing of all:

> Quilp indeed was a perpetual nightmare to the child, who was constantly haunted by a vision of his ugly face and stunted figure. She slept, for their better security, in the room where the wax-work figures were, and she never retired to this place at night but she tortured herself – she could not help it – with imagining a resemblance, in some one or other of their death-like faces, to the dwarf, and this

> fancy would sometimes so gain upon her that she would almost believe he had removed the figure and stood within the clothes. (*OCS*, ch. 29, p. 226)

This passage suggests that, for both Nell and the reader, there is something more horrifying, empty and shell-like about Quilp than any other character. Indeed, Quilp is presented as intentionally attempting to become waxwork-like, getting in among the waxworks' clothes. And for Nell, he is the figure of terror who initiated her downfall. The disgust she feels for the otherness of the waxworks resembles the disgust she feels for the otherness of Quilp. For the reader, in view of what has been argued, Quilp's status as moneylender, wheeler-dealer, villainous manipulator of others, user of others for profit, surely makes him the figure who most clearly represents the fallenness of the human state. His grotesque, earthy physique is an index of that state of affairs, an index of pure materiality, supported by his grotesque sexual appetites and violent tendencies. As a walking waxwork, he is pure immanence, the figure most representative of the absence of transcendence and the moral decay into which human nature has fallen.

In his essay on *OCS*, Adorno suggests that Nell's death is inevitable in the fallen, capitalist world of the novel, because of the special status she has. This is indexed, he suggests, in her, as it were, pre-lapsarian (pre-capitalist) appreciation of objects. In his Marxist-dialectical terms, Nell does not relate to objects as commodities with use and exchange value that, with the exigencies of the market, wax and wane and get thrown aside as ruined and valueless. (Commodities, as suggested, in this sense resemble allegories, whose meanings are contingent, changeable and conventional, not essential.) Nell has insight into the essential meaning of objects, for Adorno, since their value to her is not influenced by convention (the market). This is evidenced, he insists, in the passage where she is leaving the curiosity shop:

> There were some trifles there – poor useless things – that she would have liked to take way; but that was impossible. (*OCS*, ch. 12, p. 104)[33]

Adorno's interesting view of Nell can be pushed further, using evidence of her relationship to the waxworks. Mrs Jarley shows Nell each waxwork, and Nell has to name them:

> All this Nell repeated twice or thrice […] and then passed on to the next. (*OCS*, ch. 28, p. 222)

This passage is supported by an illustration (p. 221) of Nell pointing authoritatively to the waxworks with a wand, as if, like the animals in front of Adam, they had lined up to be endowed with a name for the first time. A little later, Nell's relationship with the waxworks is brought up again:

---

33 Adorno's essay, p. 101.

> they looked so like living creatures, and yet so unlike in the grim stillness and silence, that she had a kind of terror of them for their own sakes, and would often lie watching their dusky figures until she was obliged to rise and light a candle. (*OCS*, ch. 29, p. 226)

While she does experience the waxworks as anyone would, fearfully sensing their Gothic otherness and sameness, and their immanent mutability of meaning; there is certainly a heightened ability on Nell's part to make something appear within these allegorical waxworks, bringing them to life like the Gothic revival of a corpse. And this ability to read the fleeting transcendence in the object is uppermost in her, to the extent that she cannot sleep because the works' meanings are keeping her awake. Adorno is right, then, to claim Nell has a unique relationship with objects: it is an ability to redeem glimpses of the absolute in everyday objects. The contradictory structure of Nell's experience of the waxworks – she experiences them as an ordinary person would, and she sees something in them – reflects the contradictory status of Nell, as already argued for. On the one hand, she is sinful, fallen, a ruin like any of the curiosities; on the other, she is redeemed and even takes on an increasingly holy aura as the novel proceeds.

## Affinities between *The Old Curiosity Shop* and the Baroque *Trauerspiel*

> The novels of Dickens contain some vestige of that afterlife of the baroque that haunts the nineteenth century. (Theodor Adorno, 'An address on Charles Dickens's *The Old Curiosity Shop*')[34]

As well as reading Dickens's allegorical image of Nell, the objects, and the waxworks in terms of Benjamin's theory of allegory, there are other aspects of the novel which exhibit distinct elements of the Baroque *Trauerpiel* aesthetic.[35]

The plot of *OCS* does not involve a ruler wreaking destruction upon all around him in an orgy of violence and madness, but Grandfather does resemble the *Trauerspiel* tyrant in some respects. He is indecisive, can be cruel and his moral will is 'increasingly undermined by his sensibility: and he ends in madness'.[36] He destroys those closest to him, gets into debt, ends up weak-minded, destitute and unable to help himself, a total collapse. His motivations and actions, which lead to his grand-daughter's death, remain largely unaccounted for.

Meanwhile, Quilp resembles the villains of the *Trauerspiel*. He is a ruthless intriguer, a creature of his own devices who, like Iago or Aaron, needs no 'reason' or incentive for his villainy, just an enjoyment of it. He breeds plots to lead others

---

[34] *Dickens Quarterly* 6.3 (September 1989): p. 96.

[35] It is interesting that, on viewing work by Baroque sculptor Pietro Bernini (1562–1629) in Italy, Dickens opined its lack of naturalism, its distortion and ugliness. These are 'drawbacks' often levelled at Dickens's own work.

[36] *OGTD*, p. 99.

to disaster – yet he does so through farcical comedy and violence. This too has an affinity with *Trauerspiel*, a form of drama – 'spiel': play – in which play, theatricality and grotesque violence foreground the hollowness of allegory and the immanence of life. *Trauerspiele* feature scenes of horrendous torture and physical violence before death, but such scenes can only be borne by an audience when they take on a grotesque comedic quality. Even without such scenes, *OCS*'s dwelling on Quilp's violence against his wife and his young helper, and Quilp's similarities to Punch has its parallel in the *Trauerspiele*. Benjamin mentions the 'highly important medium of the puppet-theatre to the grotesque' and insists that 'Such play need not be thought of as accidental, it might just as easily be planned and calculated and might therefore be seen as a puppet play, with ambition and desire holding the strings'.[37] This is a most fitting description of Quilp's motivations and actions.

The Baroque worldview of the *theatrum mundi*, the image of the world as a stage, also feeds into this take on Quilp. The *theatrum mundi* privileges fakery and theatricality, an important currency which paradoxically discloses a form of truth, the immanence of existence. (The novel's form, too, emphasizes its own fakery. It is framed within the narrative of Master Humphrey, who withdraws after a few chapters like some puppet master; and the novel closes with the 'self-negating' phrase: 'so do things pass away, like a tale that is told!') Part of the game is the fact that one is being watched: the image created is privileged as an important signifier of meaninglessness, not in itself meaningless, false or unreal. A character like Quilp, the consummate faker, the manipulator and the lord of misrule who does things for effect, fits into such a worldview. His schemes, such as setting out to destroy Nell and her grandfather, or fitting up Kit, are like petty games; the joy he gets out of them and the apparent absence of reason for his mischief-making, merely underline his fiendish otherness (see *OCS*, ch. 21, pp. 172–3). But while Quilp's ruses, conspiracies and manipulations within the world of the novel coalesce with the ludic nature of the *theatrum mundi*, this character's unclear status at the meta-fictional level also projects the whole novel away from realism into the realms of storytelling, fakery and theatricality.[38] Moreover, if life is a game, an ever-changing, restless form of activity, with man as an eternal player, Nell and Grandfather's travels and travails come into the picture. Their unstable and ever-changing fortunes mean they can be seen as the vain plaything, even the puppets, of time and chance, an expression of the *theatrum mundi* too.

Nell, too, has a place within this comparison with *Trauerspiele*. The 'hero' of the 'martyr drama' (*trauerspiele* were either in the form of tyrant-dramas or martyr-dramas) must be 'the perfect embodiment of all virtues, and must be afflicted by the faithlessness of friends and enemies'.[39]

Nell had a somewhat ambiguous status with respect to sin, but it is certainly conceivable that her physical suffering and stoicism, her goodness and betrayal are

37 Both ibid., p. 83.

38 For instance, what exactly is Quilp meant to be? See Appendix 1 for a discussion.

39 *OGTD*, p. 72.

ingredients that put her in the area of martyrdom. Her chastity, too, is significant: 'The hallmark of domestic devotion is replaced by physical asceticism. Thus it is in the martyr-drama the chaste princess takes pride of place.'[40] And the pointlessness and inevitability of her suffering also figures: 'it is not the moral transgression but the very estate of man as creature which provides the reason for the catastrophe'.[41] It is here that Dickens's affinity with the German playwrights runs very deep. Nell's complicity in sin is, as has been suggested, down to her being a human being, a human being 'forced' in a sense to commit sin to survive in a profane world; the world of capitalist economics.

### *Melancholy*

Another point of connection between *OCS* and the *Trauerspiel* is the quality of melancholy – the '*trauer*' (sorrow/lamentation) of the *Trauerspiele* – which dominates both:

> A play which now one man enters and another leaves, with tears it begins and with weeping it ends.[42]

*OCS* begins with Master Humphrey's contemplation of shadows and 'air built castles' in the night where the destitute and hungry 'pause with heavier loads [...] remembering to have heard or read in some old time that drowning was not a hard death but of all means of suicide the easiest' (*OCS*, ch. 1, p. 6). The dénouement of the novel is Nell's death. So, echoing the *Trauerspiel*, there is something of the 'Dance of Death', the grievous pageant about *OCS*.[43] Death, of course, is a constant theme; as is decay.

The ruin is a ubiquitous presence, not only in the form of the old man, Nell herself and the defunct objects, as mentioned, but in terms of the dark decaying stone crypts, vaults and gravestones among which many scenes are played out.

While the ruin is the quintessence of the ravages of historical time and earthly, physical immanence, it is also, paradoxically, an index of the Baroque obsession with infinity. The ruin is both and neither part nor whole, it invokes and annuls, invokes by annulling, the idea of the whole in a constant dialectic of reflection. It contains within itself, then, like the monad, its own absolute, its own completion. A ruin is an allegorical representation of the infinite.

The Baroque age was obsessed with the idea of infinity. *OCS* has the notion of infinity at its heart. Its allegorical form can be seen itself is a case of fallen

---

40 Ibid., p. 74.

41 Ibid., p. 89.

42 Benjamin citing Lohenstein's *Sophonisbe*, ibid., pp. 82–3.

43 See Michael Hollington, 'The Dance of Death in Charles Dickens's Dombey and Son' where he assesses the importance of Holbein's 'Dance of Death' to the representation of Paul's death, in *Schriften zur Literaturwissenschaft*, Band 8, 'Tanz und Tod in Kunst und Literatur, herausgegeben von Frank Link' (Berlin: Duncker & Humblot, 1993).

language always attempting to exceed itself in the direction of the infinite (and never being coextensive with it). And, as already mentioned, Dickens places yet another allegory within the allegorical novel; the image of Nell surrounded by the curiosities, staged at the beginning of the novel and supported by an illustration. Both textual and illustrative allegories are 'fragments' whose meanings are inexhaustible.

In terms of the world of the novel (as well as in terms of the profane language of allegory), what is present is incomplete and apparently trivial; what is complete is absent, unrepresentable except through the trivial. The finite world of the pilgrims is always pointing beyond itself toward infinitude, even or perhaps especially when it is at its most horrifyingly immanent.

Infinitude is even evoked in the way Dickens delineates space. Baroque painters often shaped space in a way that unites the painting and the viewer in a single coextensive space. Further, painters even projected space beyond the work, by representing objects which simultaneously breached the space of the onlooker. For instance, in Murillo's oil 'The Immaculate Conception' (1678), the Virgin raises her eyes to heaven in a direction above and beyond the painting's frame. Other figures below her lean out of the frame, as it were, fixing their gaze 'below' and beyond the painting's edge. Murillo implies an infinite expansion of space above, below and beyond the composition of the painting: an expansion that starts within the work's confines, and expands and projects out into the world of the onlooker.[44]

Dickens uses this Baroque technique of 'breaching' the frame of a scene; he does it to help stoke up Quilp's palpably fiendish qualities:

> 'Ah!' said the dwarf, who with his hand stretched out above his eyes had been surveying the young man attentively, 'that should be your grandson, neighbour!'
> 'Say rather that he should not be', replied the old man. 'But he is.'
> 'And that?' said the dwarf, pointing to Dick Swiveller.
> 'Some friend of his, as welcome here as he', said the old man.
> 'And that?' inquired the dwarf, wheeling round and pointing straight at me. (*OCS*, ch. 3, p. 27)

Quilp, apparently catching the narrator, Master Humphrey, off guard, projects himself out of the scene by pointing unexpectedly at him. Moreover, the speed with which the dwarf performs this dramatic action ('wheeling round') augments the menace and surprise of it. The reader, silently standing beside, and listening to, the narrator simultaneously feels herself singled out by Quilp: the frame Quilp breaches is the reader's imaginative one. Hence the space between the reader and Quilp's presence is suddenly an extended, united one.

Dickens achieves the quality of melancholy in the novel in the way he uses light and darkness. Baroque aesthetics – in sculpture, architecture and theatrical productions – involved the use of chiaroscuro: artificial light/shadow was

---

[44] Bartolemé Esteban Murillo (1617–1682), 'The Immaculate Conception', oil on canvas in the New York Metropolitan Museum of Art.

contrived for dramatic effect. Baroque architects, of course, were trained in how light could be shaped within space. The church interior or crypt, for example, could become the locus for spectacle and vision in the religious or the dramatic sphere. This interest in the dramatic significance of light and darkness within a space is traceable in *OCS*, not least in the number of scenes involving backdrops of ruins, graveyards or shadowy curiosities – and interiors such as the curiosity shop and the chapel. Chiaroscuro accentuates the illusion of depth, meaning the fictional objects have greater mass and weight in the imagination. Their three-dimensionality could almost jump out of the fictional frame that contains them, because of the light/shade of the dramatic setting they inhabit.

Such settings also have metaphysical significance, of course. Darkness and shadows dramatize the presence of an invisible sphere, lending the spiritual and the unseen significance. Dickens here dramatizes, as it were, Benjamin's messianic worldview, or his antinomy of allegory. Dickens's fictional images become fascinatingly anamorphic, suggesting that there is a hidden element or concealed meaning that requires interpretation.[45]

In some uses of Baroque chiaroscuro, the lighting effect evinces tension, a juxtaposition between, on the one hand, an intense spirituality and on the other, sexuality and ravishment. Such a dual quality is present in a number of scenes in *OCS*, an obvious one is when Nell crosses paths coincidentally with Quilp:

> the old gateway of the town, leaving the low archway very black and dark; and with a mingled sensation of curiosity and fear, she slowly approached the gate, and stood still to look up at it, wondering to see how dark, and grim, and old, and cold, it looked [...] The instant he appeared, she recognized him – Who could have failed to recognize, in that instant, the ugly mis-shapen Quilp! [...] he seemed to have risen out of the earth. But there he was. (*OCS*, ch. 27, pp. 214–15)

While darkness/shadows are often comforting to Nell, evocative spaces of spiritual goodness and contemplation, here darkness is a harbinger of fearful surprises, substance and sexual threat. Such a juxtaposition of contraries is central to what the technique of chiaroscuro – surface/depth, visible/invisible, shadow/substance, seen/heard – is all about.

'*Trauer*' denotes lamentation and the ceremonies of sorrow and grief. As Benjamin makes clear, the mourning play is ostentatiously, even hyperbolically plaintive. *OCS* even seems to express this aspect of *Trauerspiele*. At certain moments, for instance, the narrative adopts the pessimistic mindset of the relentless sufferer; it suggests, for example, that destitution and poverty attracts bad luck:

[45] Benjamin's fascination with the Baroque's onus upon the anamorphic quality of the image underpinned his aesthetics. As a critic in search of the truth or the absolute within a work of art, he concludes in 'The Concept of Criticism in German Romanticism' (1919) and in 'Goethe's Elective Affinities' (1922) that truth never discloses itself completely. Both essays are published in English in *SW*, I, pp. 116–200 and 297–360.

> At noon it poured down more hopelessly and heavily than ever, without the faintest promise of abatement. (*OCS*, ch. 43, p. 337)

Like the idea that Grandfather could never win a fortune at cards, this is the narrative in melancholy mood.

And if Benjamin claims *Trauerspiel* exhibits 'an incessant handwringing mode of expression',[46] the narrative can oblige here too:

> Why had they ever come to this noisy town, when there were peaceful country places, in which, at least, they might have hungered and thirsted, with less suffering than in its squalid strife! (*OCS*, ch. 44, p. 339)

This histrionic expression of lamentation, so resonant of the *Trauerspiel*, comes most often through Grandfather:

> how poor we are, and what a life it is! The cause is a young child's, guiltless of all harm or wrong, but nothing goes well with it! Hope and patience, hope and patience! (*OCS*, ch. 2, p. 26)

and

> 'Ah! Poor, houseless, wandering, motherless child!' cried the old man, clasping his hands and gazing as if for the first time upon her anxious face, her travel-stained dress, and bruised and swollen feet: 'has all my agony of care brought her to this at last!' (*OCS*, ch. 44, p. 340)

Here is the novel's display of *tristesse* expressing not only a shattered characters's state of mind but extending *acedia* to the entire novelistic universe itself. This can be traced to the seventeenth-century physiology of humors: an overactive spleen and too much bile has its irrational astrological complement in Saturn and planetary maleficence.[47]

*Otherness, Change and Instability*

Another part of the Baroque aesthetic is an interest, among painters and sculptors, in evoking change, movement or metamorphosis. Dickens even appears to include this element of the Baroque in *OCS*. He achieves this through his depiction of Quilp as having an unstable identity. The dwarf pops up in innumerable guises in the text: he emerges from the shadows, a gargoyle come to life (*OCS* ch. 27, pp. 214–15), he appears as a crowd (p. 216), a gas (p. 216); he goes from himself

---

[46] Benjamin quoting Erdmannsdőrffer on the sources of *Trauerspiele*, *OGTD*, p. 64.

[47] *Hamlet* comes close to this notion of a world dominated by Saturnine melancholy, and the prince himself as being a character dominated by an overactive spleen. Benjamin argues that Shakespeare's 1601 play should be read as a *Trauerspiel* rather than as a 'Tragedy'. See *OGTD*, pp. 135–8.

to a waxwork and back again (p. 217); he becomes a waxwork, Mrs Jarley and a barrel organ all at once (p. 217), and, even appears as a fictional evocation of pure otherness: 'and yet not exactly any of them either' (p. 217).

This incapacity to attribute positive and stable predicates to Quilp, this apparent impossibility for Quilp to be identical with himself, anticipates Stevenson's character Mr Hyde (1886), whose physical appearance also defied definition. Stoker's character Count Dracula (1897), who has an apparently infinite capacity to transform into animals, also bears comparison.

Quilp's breaching of the reader's space is consistent with a carnivalesque exuberance which needs to subvert authority. It also dramatizes in no uncertain terms his invidious tendency to defy spatial and temporal limits. He turns up at the most inopportune and crucial moments in the plot, horrifying onlookers (and the reader) with his apparently magical or demonic ability to be anywhere at anytime needful.

# Part 1 Conclusion

Reading *OCS* as an expression of Dickens's allegorical, melancholy turn of mind allows the critic to do a number of things. She can pay close critical attention to, and perhaps bring out the significance of, the deeply melancholy mode in which this work operates. What can one make of an artwork the subject of which is suffering, anxiety, pain and death? Though punctuated by moments of relief and joy, and by a fictional resurrection, this is a desolate vision.[1] It is an emotional, moving piece about wasted youth and the loss of childhood, and, for Dickens the great entertainer, it is an unusually anxious work.[2] What is being argued is not so much that Dickens is a religious writer, but that an allegorical reading does justice to certain elements, perhaps not consciously crafted, that have a 'metaphysical' resonance. The sheer power of Dickens's expression of Nell's passion, the way the novel relishes suffering, the sentimental passages, the at times bombastic handwringing language, together gesture toward a meaning beyond the confines of the novel's world. Dickens can be understood to be in mourning for a fallen world, and this approach allows us to take a representation of misery and sadness seriously and to view it sincerely.

The novel is, of course, firmly fixed within the temporal setting. *OCS* concerns itself with the physical experience of social disadvantage, hunger and pain, with the mechanisms of exchange, of money and capitalist economics, the realities of debt, of alienation, betrayal and homelessness. And in this sense, it is a political critique about the plight of the poor. In its lively treatment of objects, violence and the themes of decay, it revels in, as Dickens often does, the sheer physicality of the world itself. No doubt, the material world of suffering, decay and death can be seen as a portrait of just that and nothing else. But at the same time, it is in the midst of all this materiality and immanence that the messianic worldview comes into view. And what is being suggested is that in the lurid depiction of Nell mired in the physical degradations of suffering, in the deep sadness of his depiction, Dickens seems to open up, dialectically and ironically, the possibility of another restorative level of meaning to the reader, and to keep it in play throughout the novel. The urgency of the depiction of Nell's suffering augurs the possibility that it could all be so different; and this is an issue that Dickens, like Benjamin, asks the reader to consider as much upon a revolutionary political level, perhaps, as upon a metaphysical one.

---

[1] As Dickens admits to Forster by letter, he could not believe in a doctrine of progress, that people learned from suffering and death. 'Old wounds bleed afresh when I only think of the way of doing it [representing Nell's death] […] I can't preach to myself the schoolmaster's consolation, though I try', *The Letters of Charles Dickens*, ed. Madeline House and Graham Storey, vol. 2, 1840–1841 (Oxford: Clarendon Press, 1969), p. 181.

[2] We know the biographical and productive background to this work: the death of Mary Hogarth, and the teething problems of *Master Humphrey's Clock*.

This interpretation attributes a unity to a novel that at times seems fragmented and improvisational, positioning Nell's trajectory at the center[3] and viewing the comedic, grotesque, unruly elements as part of this picture of a declining world. It also allows the critic to account for the simultaneously unreal, apparently trivial quality of many of the actions, characters and antics depicted. Like the qualities Benjamin found in the *Trauerspiele* and the Baroque, Nell's world is, on the one hand, harrowing and real, and yet seems staged, fake or ultimately unimportant, 'a tale that is told'.[4] As is the case with *Trauerspiele*, the novel's scenes of suffering seem at some level unimportant because they simultaneous signal the 'quiet nearing' of a place where all injuries and injustices will no longer matter.[5]

Like all readings, this approach cannot encompass everything, and there are two issues it does not deal with adequately. The first is the role of sentimentality. The construction of a sentimental scene and the emotion it evokes in a reader cannot be satisfactorily accounted for by a theory of fallen language or an allegorical worldview where communication fails and is dominated by verbosity and lamentation. Affect or emotion are integral to the experience of this novel, since the representation of a child's suffering, a character's failure to find any meaningful way to exist or to communicate in the world is what is at stake. And yet, the allusion to the *Trauerspiel* and its representations of meaninglessness and sorrow does at least start to open up the area of how audiences respond to artworks depicting suffering and injustice. Perhaps sentimentality could be seen within this framework of a failure of language or meaning – as a failure to represent convincingly or to respond adequately to suffering and sorrow.

Secondly, the role humour plays in this novel. Very little has been said here about the subversive, the irreverent and the carnivalesque aspects of this novel's comedy and laughter and its importance as a point of contrast to the melancholy passages. And of course the comic couple, Swiveller and the Marchioness, appear to gesture toward a possible happy existence in the physical world, escaping this reading altogether. These are issues that are in excess of this reading. However, the focus here has been upon seeing something in the melancholy mode of this novel, and hopefully, making it appear.[6]

---

[3] See Malcolm Andrews's comment, *OCS* introduction (Harmondsworth: Penguin, 1972), p. 16.

[4] The final phrase of the novel, excluding the exclamation mark.

[5] The phrase 'quiet nearing' lifted from Benjamin's 'Theological-Political Fragment', 'Theologisch-politisches Fragment', in *GS*, II, 1, pp. 203–4; trans. Edmund Jephcott as 'Theological-Political Fragment', in *SW*, III, pp. 305–6. See Chapter 1, note 9 (p. 20) above, on the dating of this fragment.

[6] The idea that the critic must not explain away the enigma of the artwork, but gently make something appear through an elaboration of how the ontology of the artwork works, is part of Benjamin's thinking in 'The Concept of Criticism in German Romanticism', *SW*, ibid., see especially p. 351.

## Postscript: The German Influence in Benjamin and Dickens

Discussing one of Dickens's novels (*OCS*) in relation to Benjamin's German/Jewish metaphysical context is not to make an entirely arbitrary connection. One possible reason why *OCS* – as has been argued – appears to come so close to the early Benjamin, could be due to a connection Dickens has to the German Romantics and seventeenth-century theology through Carlyle.[7]

One can speculate that Dickens's uncanny affinity with the melancholy world of the seventeenth-century German *Trauerspiel* in *OCS* can be viewed in terms of the influence of the seventeenth-century Protestant movement, coming both through Carlyle and the emblematic tradition. This is a difficult suggestion to back up without extensive discussion. But the aesthetic and theological ideas, the flavor of the seventeenth century did appear to have some effect, as the discussion of *OCS* bears out. Something of Carlyle's influence in this area has been discussed elsewhere and will not be taken any further, here.[8]

As for the German Romantics and Dickens – this is a more intricate argument. If Benjamin's reading of Schlegel, Fichte and other German Romantics helped shape his theory of language – the Germans themselves being deeply interested in the Jewish Kabbalah – Dickens's mentor, Carlyle, was also an avid reader of the Jena Circle.[9]

Carlyle, steeped in the Calvinist religious tradition, of course, was to use aspects of Schlegel's and Fichte's metaphysics to bolster his view that God's divine nature is traceable in all things – but that humans had lost the capacity to apprehend this truth. At a simple level, what both Carlyle and Benjamin had in common with German Romanticism was a critical view and suspicion of modern industrial growth, technology and science, the Enlightenment project's challenge to religion and metaphysical thinking.[10]

They were both, if a convenient term might be used, Romantic anti-capitalists. Carlyle and Benjamin were convinced that industrialization and its accompanying effects and ideologies resulted in a loss of absolute/religious experience. They mourned the apparent loss of fuller experience and attempted to find ways of combating its loss. The Part 1 discussion suggests that Dickens, too, expresses something of this position in *OCS*.

Benjamin was part of a tendency among Jewish intellectuals who, from about the 1880s onwards in Central Europe, were questioning industrialization, their

[7] See William Oddie, *Dickens and Carlyle: The Question of Influence* (London: Centenary Press, 1972) and Michael Goldberg, *Carlyle and Dickens* (Athens: University of Georgia Press, 1972).

[8] Oddie, Goldberg and C.F. Harrold, *Carlyle and German Thought 1819–1834* (New Haven: Yale University Press, 1934).

[9] August Wilhelm Schlegel (1767–1845) and Johann Gottlieb Fichte (1762–1814).

[10] This statement must be qualified with respect to Benjamin, who appears to 'celebrate' the changes technology has wrought upon human experience in some essays – for example, in 'The Work of Art in the Age of Mechanical Reproduction'. Chapter 3 examines the essays in which Benjamin shows concern about this process.

bourgeois upbringing, modern society and commodity culture. But coming from an assimilated Jewish background meant the university-educated Benjamin was steeped in German Romantic writers. His rediscovery of his own Jewish religion, then, took place through the lens of the Romantics. As Michael Löwy puts it:

> charged with German romantic spirituality [...] through German neo-romanticism, these young Jewish intellectuals rediscovered their own religion: their path to the prophet Isaiah went by way of Novalis, Hölderlin or Schelling.[11]

In Benjamin's 1919 doctoral dissertation, 'The Concept of Criticism in German Romanticism', Benjamin outlines a notion of time which he claims is a 'romantic messianism'. The concept involves the idea of an extraordinary fullness issuing from each and every moment as opposed to the unrelenting unfolding of an empty end-determined time. For Benjamin, messianism was a crucial component of German Romanticism. In a letter to Schoen (April 7, 1919), he claimed he wanted to place messianism at the center of his thesis on German Romanticism.[12] For Benjamin, the messianic dimension was present in the writings of Schlegel and Novalis,[13] and among his quotations concerning Schlegel, was this one:

> the revolutionary desire to realize the Kingdom of God [...] is [...] the inception of modern history. (*SW*, I, p. 185, note 3)

Carlyle modified terms and concepts habitual to German Romanticism to re-elaborate his view of a universe in which clear knowledge is wedded to religion in the life and business of man, but in which 'clear knowledge' was becoming less and less of a factor in modern life. Taking elements from Goethe and Fichte, Carlyle insisted that there is a constant immanence of God in common things – a position close to Benjamin's notion of an immanent absolute in language/things.[14]

In common with Benjamin and the German Romantics, the problem for Carlyle was that language had become 'de-sacrilized'. Carlyle's answer was to compose his writings in biblical language and language that reflected the emblematic tradition. Using language in this way helped re-engender the religious context of life in Carlyle's reader. The only language available that was charged with metaphysical reality was that of the 'extinct Hebrew', for Carlyle. Indeed, in a view of language intriguingly close to Benjamin's in 1916, Teufeldrockh's conversion in *Sartor Resartus* is a matter of 'speaking' his vision. Carlyle's character acoustically utters his natural connection to the godlike, which he sees:

---

[11] *Redemption and Utopia* (London: The Athlone Press, 1992), p. 35. (Novalis [1772–1801]; Friedrich Hölderlin [1770–1843]; Friedrich Wilhelm Joseph von Schelling [1775–1854]).

[12] *The Correspondence of Walter Benjamin*, ed. and ann. by Gershom Scholem and Theodor W. Adorno (Chicago: Chicago University Press, 1994), p. 139.

[13] Benjamin uses the term 'Romantic messianism' in 'The Concept of Criticism', in *SW*, I, p. 168, and in notes to the essay, note 3, p. 185.

[14] Johann Wolfgang von Goethe (1749–1832).

> Could I unfold the influence of Names, which are the most important of all clothings, I were a second greater *Trismegistus*. Not only all common Speech, but Science, Poetry itself is no other, if thou consider it, than a right Naming. Adam's first task was giving names to natural Appearances: what is ours still but a continuation of the same [...]?[15]

Of course, Dickens's works in relation to the emblematic tradition and his use of biblical language in his novels has attracted much scholarly attention.[16] But Dickens's apparent absorption of the messianic outlook with all that that means in terms of the fallenness of the world and its need for redemption – in relation to the German Romantic/Judaic traditions – has attracted less attention.

Carlyle, like Benjamin, would reinterpret Kant's delineation of the function of the Understanding and Reason in the Subject, ignoring the strict distinction Kant set up between them.[17] Carlyle misreads Kant's conclusion in the *Critique of Pure Reason* that space and time are subjective forms with no existence independent of the perception of objects, using it to claim that the material world is therefore an 'illusion' or 'unreal'.[18] As the discussion in Part 1 has demonstrated, Carlyle's apparent relegation of the material world to the status of 'unreal' or 'illusory' is one pathway along which Dickens will not tread. Dickens here comes closer to Benjamin: the material world is 'real,' it expresses the human relationship to the absolute and is an essential part of human experience and meaning. Indeed, for Benjamin, 'truth'/ the absolute inheres within objects themselves, if one pays close attention to them. Dickens too, as has been argued, has a fascination with objects in his novels pointing to the idea that there is something of a Dickensian language of objects at work within his fictions. Dickens has a tendency toward physiognomy in his fiction, he attempts to 'read' the universe, to focus almost obsessively upon, to pay close attention to, objects and the environment, in order to glimpse meaning from it.

Where Carlyle, Dickens and Benjamin can be understood to share a Romantic outlook is in the notion that the mechanistic/materialist view of the world does not adequately describe the world as it really is. The attempt to charge the fallen world with a religious quality, to nurture a relationship to the absolute in a world devoid of meaning, was for all three men in their different ways, an important project. Carlyle and Dickens gained inspiration from German Romanticism and their Christian biblical and emblematic traditions. Benjamin was rooted in German Romanticism and Judaism. It has been argued that Dickens comes closer – in a number of ways – to Benjamin in his attempt to fictionalize a world 'charged with the grandeur of God'.[19]

---

15 *Sartor Resartus* (Edinburgh: Canongate Classics, 2002), p. 100.

16 See especially Barry V. Qualls, *The Secular Pilgrims of Victorian Fiction* (Cambridge University Press, 1981), ch. 3.

17 See Harrold, pp. 127–46. Immanuel Kant (1724–1804).

18 Harrold points out that this is a misreading of Kant. Indeed, Kant expressly argues against this idealist position in the 1st Critique [The Critique of Pure Reason].

19 Part of the opening line of Gerard Manley Hopkins's sonnet 'God's Grandeur' in *Gerard Manley Hopkins: Poems and Prose*, ed. W.H. Gardner (Harmondsworth: Penguin,1983), p. 27.

# PART 2
# Dickens, Benjamin and the City

# Part 2 Introduction

Chapters 3 and 4 are a continuation of the project to identify and explore areas of mutual interest and concern in the writings of Dickens and Benjamin. The point of focus here, though, is the topic perhaps most associated with both writers: the metropolis.

Benjamin's formulation of modern experience places city existence at its core. Not only *The Arcades Project* but also a number of his other works take the city (or the experience of it) as central to an understanding of Benjamin's own present at the philosophical, as well as at the political and aesthetic levels.[1]

As critical studies attest, Dickens is one of the greatest London novelists.[2] The city and its vertiginous variety or strange points of connection are at the heart of his creative imagination. Most novels, if not set in London, at least visit there; and though the novelist's travels abroad yielded depictions of other towns and cities – he is particularly taken with Paris and set *TTC* in both London and Paris – it is London that remains his constant point of reference and inspiration. In fact, Dickens's depiction of the city of London has left an indelible inscription upon its surfaces, upon how one now sees or reads that city. As G.K. Chesterton put it, 'Dickens Dickensized London'.[3] And George Gissing, if one of the earliest to say so in print, was certainly not one of the last to see London through the lens of Dickens's fictions:

> I had but to lean, at night, over one of the City bridges, and the broad flood spoke to me in the very tones of the master [...] The very atmosphere declared him; if I gasped in a fog, was it not Mr Guppy's 'London particular?'[4]

Forster claimed that with *Nicholas Nickleby*, Dickens's acuity and sharpness of vision helped open his eyes afresh to London: 'we hardly knew anything of the places we supposed that we knew best'.[5]

---

1 'Das Passagen-Werk', in *GS*, V, 1 and 2; trans. Howard Eiland and Kevin McLaughlin as *The Arcades Project* (Cambridge, MA; London: Belknap Press of Harvard University Press, 1999).

2 This is what studies like Peter Ackroyd's *Dickens* (London: Sinclair-Stevenson Ltd., 1990) and F.S. Schwarzbach's *Dickens and the City* (London. The Athlone Press, University of London, 1979) amount to. But these are two among innumerable studies which bear this out. John Forster himself implies as much in *The Life of Charles Dickens*, ed. and annotated with an introduction by J.W.T. Ley (London: Cecil Palmer 1928) bk. 2, ch. 4, p. 123. Hereafter referred to as '*Life*'.

3 *Charles Dickens*, 11th ed. (London: Methuen & Co. Ltd., 1917), p. 42. See Appendix 1.

4 *The Immortal Dickens* (London: Cecil Palmer, 1925), pp. 9–10.

5 Forster, *Life*, bk. 2, ch. 4, p. 123.

For Benjamin, getting to know a city naturally involves Gissing's and Forster's experiences. One cannot avoid approaching a city via a concatenation of speculative textual cities. Dickens himself experienced London through his childhood reading. Impressed by the description of Covent Garden in George Colman's *Broad Grins*, Dickens

> stole down to the market by himself to compare it with the book [...] He remembered [...] snuffing up the flavour of the faded cabbage-leaves as if it were the very breath of comic fiction.[6]

Cities (real or imagined), then, throw light upon one another reflexively, as a matter of course: 'More quickly than Moscow itself, one gets to know Berlin through Moscow.'[7] This holds despite, or even because of, their differences. Counterfactuals in one city lead to an uncovering of shards of information in the other city that might otherwise have remained hidden or overlooked. Dickens saw Genoa through the lens of London. Commenting on Italian streets, he tells Forster they are 'narrower than Albany-street and [...] less wide than Drury-lane or Wych-street'. He does the same in his description of Naples.[8] This pertains to memory as well as to imagination. As Benjamin's essay 'A Berlin Childhood around 1900' illustrates, the memories of a childhood city frame the adult's experience of that city and of subsequent cities.[9] Hence Dickens's 'Gone Astray' is an imaginative recapitulation of an experience which would have affected not only Dickens's subsequent urban experiences and his production – including a representation of just that specific experience – but would affect the reader's urban experiences as well.[10] But these and other matters will be opened up in the discussion to come.

For now we must press on with Part 2, which, like Part 1, is divided into two chapters. Chapter 3 is a focus upon urban experience: which for Benjamin centers on the notion of the 'shock'. Benjamin uses a Franco-German coinage to denote this new conception, *Chockerlebnis* (shock experience). His concern with developing a theory of expanded or fuller experience, his fascination with the idea of an immanent absolute within the structure of experience, it will become clear, continues into his later thinking of the poetics of the urban and of the everyday as

[6] *Life*, bk.1, ch. 1, p. 12. The humorous poet George Colman (1762–1836) wrote the coarse and comic *My Gown and Slippers* (1797), reprinted as *Broad Grins* in 1802.

[7] Opening line of Benjamin's 'Moskau', published in 1927, *GS*, IV, pp. 316–48; trans. Edmund Jephcott as 'Moscow', in *SW*, II, pp. 22–46.

[8] *Life*, bk. 4, ch. 4, p. 336 and bk. 4, ch. 7, p. 370, respectively.

[9] 'Berliner Kindheit um 1900' (two versions): 1934 version in *GS*, IV, 1, pp. 235–304; 1938 version in *GS*, VII, 1, pp. 385–433; trans. Howard Eiland as 'A Berlin Childhood around 1900' in *SW*, III, pp. 344–413.

[10] 'Gone Astray' appeared in *Household Words* on August 13, 1853. It is reproduced in *Dickens's Journalism*, 4 vols, ed. Michael Slater (London: J.M. Dent, 1994–2000), vol. III, pp. 155–65. References to *Dickens' Journalism* will hereafter take the form of 'Slater', followed by volume and page details.

he enlists the help of memory to 'redeem' moments of truth in what he sees as an increasingly hollow and depthless modern experience.

It will be suggested that Dickens himself recognized and experienced this new urban '*Chockerlebnis*'; that he recorded as much in an article for *Household Words*. And, it will be maintained, he expressed this urban experience in the form and content of his novels.[11] In an exploration of Dickens's delineation of Bradley Headstone, Jonas Chuzzlewit and Grandfather Trent, the question is raised as to whether Dickens depicts characters as experiencing the urban in a way that anticipates Benjamin's 'theory'.

Furthermore, memory's role in experience will be explored in Dickens. The relationship of the city to one's memories and therefore to one's experience of the self is the theme in a close study of Dickens's autobiographical depiction of the autobiographical process, *DC*. Dickens's novel provides another angle on how urban existence involves an encounter between the self and the mnemonic city; on how a continual process of reciprocity between oneself, memory, time and space amounts to the city becoming the site of a kind of psycho-geo-auto-biography, a continual process of revision and renewal of one's sense of self which Dickens delineates in *DC*. The discussion of *DC* aims to deepen the understanding of Benjamin's theory of experience; it attempts to demonstrate how it might work.

Chapter 4 turns to and discusses two important motifs within *The Arcades Project* – 'the flâneur' and 'the crowd' – and explores them in relation not only to Dickens's novels but also to his journalism. And the gothic mode comes under discussion in relation to modern urban experience and the elliptical appearance of truth. But for now it is time to get the discussion underway with Chapter 3, 'Experience and Memory'.

---

[11] F.S. Schwarzbach argues that one way Dickens comes to terms with the shocking impact of city life is through an investment in the myth of the town-country opposition (p. 23 of this book). This book argues that he does indeed do this – but that he also goes further. He finds a way of expressing and making conscious through literature, in form and content, urban experience.

# Chapter 3
# Experience and Memory

## Three Essays on Experience

This chapter examines three essays in the attempt to outline a Benjaminian theory of experience: 'The Image of Proust' published in 1929; his 1936 piece on Nikolai Leskov, 'The Storyteller'; and, from Benjamin's penultimate year, 'On Some Motifs in Baudelaire' (1939).[1]

'The Storyteller' and 'Motifs' (among other things) trace the notion that modern urban existence involves a sealing off, or a reduction of, experience. This position, very simply, is inspired by a Marxist analysis of relations of production and alienation; and is also informed by sociological thinkers of the urban, such as German philosopher Georg Simmel (1858–1918), who viewed urban space as a correlative of consciousness, a materialist formulation suggesting that the experience of the city's physical geography has an effect upon how one experiences and represents the world.[2]

The essay on Proust presents the possible redemption of this state of affairs by a turning to the past. Benjamin suggests that memory – understood as something analogous to Proust's notion of the *mémoire involontaire* (*eingedenken* in German) elaborated in his novel *À la recherche du temps perdu* (1913–1927) – is a possible locus for the salvaging of atrophying experience in modern existence. The idea that memory could be the site of a gathering together of fragments of already lived experience is not an astoundingly original one, if one considers the importance memory played in the Romantic theorization of the 'problem' of perception and representation.[3] But the astonishing importance in terms of redemption that

---

[1] 'Zum Bilde Prousts' in *GS*, II, 1, pp. 310–24, trans. Harry Zohn as 'The Image of Proust', in *Illuminations*, pp. 197–210; 'Der Erzähler' in *GS*, II, 2, pp. 438–65, trans. Zohn as 'The Storyteller' in *Illuminations*, pp. 83–107; 'Über einige Motive bei Baudelaire' in *GS*, I, 2, pp. 605–53, trans. Zohn as 'On Some Motifs in Baudelaire', in *Illuminations*, pp. 152–96. This latter essay will be abbreviated as 'Motifs'.

[2] 'The Metropolis and Mental Life' (1902–1903), in *The Sociology of Georg Simmel*, ed. K.H. Wolff (New York: New York Free Press, 1950), pp. 409–24. This essay will be referred to as 'Metropolis'. Benjamin attended Simmel's lectures at the Friedrich Wilhelm University in Berlin in 1912–1913.

[3] Paul de Man in his essay 'The Intentional Structure of the Romantic Image' discusses Wordsworth's 'Tintern Abbey' in terms of the Romantic attempt to represent the nature of the object without losing the privilege of the immediacy of perception. See *Romanticism and Consciousness*, ed. Harold Bloom (New York: W.W. Norton, 1970).

Benjamin wants to claim for memory, and the emphasis he places upon the present as a locus of 'loss', is perhaps the area of uniqueness.[4]

These essays concerning experience come at the point in Benjamin's career when he starts to engage with Marxist concepts and ideas. But some critics have proposed that Benjamin's theory of experience can be understood to be a mnemonic messianic theology: one bound to the idea that the historian must read the world theologically through the mediation of remembrance.[5] To ask just how religiously inflected this ostensibly more materialist theory of expanded/redemptive experience is, then, is to return again to the constant conundrum within Benjamin's thought – how does his materialist/Marxist analysis of experience coalesce with his theological/metaphysical side? How is one to understand this apparent conflict?

One way is biographically. It was from about 1924 onwards that Benjamin came into contact with Marxist theory. He read Lukács's *History and Class Consciousness,* which was published in Berlin in German as *Geschichte und Klassenbewußtsein: Studien Über marxistische Dialektik* in 1923.[6] He was profoundly moved by it. He became firm friends with the Marxist thinker Ernst Bloch who introduced him to Lukács's work; and, while visiting the island of Capri for six months in that year, 1924, he met and fell in love with a colleague of playwright Bertold Brecht, Asja Lacis. She was a socialist actress, director and agitator who encouraged Benjamin toward a serious engagement with Marxist theory and communist political practice. She had a lasting influence upon him; he wrote an important essay 'Naples' ('*Neapel*') with her in the year they met, and dedicated *One-Way Street* ('*Einbahnstraße*') to her in 1926.[7] Hence, Benjamin elaborates, in the essays cited for this chapter, and from 1924 onwards generally, a markedly more Marxist-inflected/materialist account of experience and truth.

Yet there remains the preoccupation with the possibility of an immanent absolute within experience – a preoccupation that can be traced directly back to

---

[4] Both the importance of remembrance as a form of redemption and the notion of the present as a site of loss are more explicitly present in Benjamin's last essay, 'Theses on the Philosophy of History', written in 1940. It is suggested here that they are also implicit in the three essays under analysis, although there will not be space to argue for this assumption. The apparent unity of Benjamin's project – the way he addresses the same concerns from his early writings to his last essays is a topic that will be discussed in the conclusion to this book.

[5] James McBride, 'Marooned in the Realm of the Profane: Walter Benjamin's Synthesis of Kabbalah and Communism', *Journal of the American Academy of Religion* 57.2 (Summer, 1989): pp. 241–66 (p. 249).

[6] György Lukács (1885–1971) had escaped from Hungary to Vienna in October 1919, where he continued both his intellectual and political activities – often under threat of arrest.

[7] The translation of the dedication reads: 'This street is named/ Asja Lacis Street/ after her who/ as an engineer/ cut it through the author' (*One-Way Street*, trans. Marcus Bullock and Michael W. Jennings, in *Walter Benjamin*: *Selected Writings*, 4 vols (Cambridge, MA; London: Belknap Press of Harvard University Press, 1996–2003), I, p. 444. *Walter Benjamin: Selected Writings* is hereafter abbreviated as *SW*.

the earlier theological concerns with the nature of the present (Modernity) as a site of loss and fallenness – discussed in Part 1. Moreover, Benjamin's conclusion (elaborated fully below) that modern experience is 'stuck' at a depthless level of immediacy converges with the Marxist analysis of Lukács in *History and Class Consciousness*, and Benjamin himself recognizes the convergence (letter to Scholem, 1924).[8] Lukács arrives at a position close to Benjamin's, however, by quite a different route: via an engagement with Hegel and a study of reification (the notion that bourgeois consciousness is transfixed at the level of capitalist social relations).

How one understands Benjamin's preoccupation with auratic experience and the roots it has in both theology and Marxism gets to the heart of the difficulty of reading Benjamin.[9]

## The Modernism of Benjamin's Methodology

But there is another difficulty, too, to be found in Benjamin's style. The striking factor about his writings in his later phase – not only 'The Storyteller', 'The Image of Proust' and 'On Some Motifs in Baudelaire', but other essays including *One-Way Street*, his city portraits, his two versions of 'Paris, the Capital of the 19th century' and *The Arcades Project* itself – is that they are written in the form of unmediated 'literary montage'.[10] Fragmentary descriptions, citations or linguistic snapshots of nineteenth-century Parisian life are juxtaposed with longer insights about writers or personal impressions and quotations from newspapers and other texts.

This method is integral to Benjamin's overall project. For him, the present was a moment of crisis. He was engaged in rethinking historical time, memory and the task of the historiographer in relation to the present. He was forging a new structural form, a new way of thinking about history that turned on the notion that there is no presentation that represents the totality of what there is. This is a form of thinking temporality as interruption, a way of understanding history such that the 'moment' picks out the totality, in temporal terms. Hence, in his writings, he articulated the breaking up of totalized visions – such visions being impossible in the 'fallen' world. He presented a series of visions, juxtapositions, fleeting

[8] See *The Correspondence of Walter Benjamin 1910–1940*, ed. and annotated by Theodor W. Adorno and Gerhard Scholem, trans. Manfred R. Jacobson and Evelyn M. Jacobson (Chicago; London: University of Chicago Press, 1994), p. 248.

[9] The adjectival use of the term 'aura' is deliberately used here – it alludes to a concept Benjamin discusses in his famous essay 'The Work of Art in the Age of Mechanical Reproduction' of 1935. See Appendix 1.

[10] Material gathered in volume 5 of Benjamin's *Gesammelte Schriften* and entitled *Das Passengen-Werk*, was published in Germany in 1982, edited by Rolf Tiedemann. It is published in English under the title of *The Arcades Project*, translated by Howard Eiland and Kevin McLaughlin (Cambridge, MA; London: Belknap Press of Harvard University Press, 1999). Hereafter abbreviated as 'Arcades'.

moments or images which he tore out of their context (in the past) and revivified in conjunction with the present.

His use of the fragment is central to this procedure. Retrieving the overlooked detail required a scrutiny that was close up to prevent the loss of valuable material – material that might be the magic route to opening up a crucial historical truth.

The constellation of ideas that surface in Benjamin's rapid, quick-fire methodology are not developed in any traditional or systematic way, then. It makes manifest what Modernists understood to be the thought processes of Modern urban existence. That is to say, it is fragmentary, but also, at times, illuminating.

## The Loss of Relaxation and the Community of Listeners

The 19 short 'reflections' which make up the 1936 essay 'The Storyteller' (Der Erzähler)[11] are observations taking the Russian writer Nikolai Leskov (the storyteller) as the starting point for a discussion of how an evolving capitalist economy alters the shape of communities, the reception of tradition within culture and in consequence, experience itself.[12]

In the very first section, Benjamin informs the reader that the age of storytelling is coming to an end, putting this phenomenon down to the loss of 'the ability to exchange experiences'.[13] This, he goes on to assert, can be understood as a consequence of the loss of the conditions for the proper reception and retention of stories and their retelling, in modern culture.

Inchoate mercantile communities were ripe to hear the stories and absorb the wisdom of those seamen whose tales were shaped by the 'lore' of distance, and craftsmen at home whose narratives inhered the 'lore' of local ideas and tradition. What is more, the stories were about wisdom: they contained a moral, practical advice or a maxim:

> But if today 'having counsel' is beginning to have an old fashioned ring, this is because the communicability of experience is decreasing. In consequence we have no counsel either for ourselves or for others.[14]

For the story to have a claim upon the memory (*Gedächtnis*) of the listener, for someone to integrate the story into his own experience and retell it to others – and therefore for the story's ongoing survival – there needs to be a particular context

---

[11] 'The Storyteller' in '*Illuminations*', pp. 83–107.

[12] John Bowen discusses a number of phrases from 'The Storyteller', showing how Dickens's Sam Weller is 'a storyteller' in the vein of Benjamin's understanding of that concept, *Other Dickens: Pickwick to Chuzzlewit* (Oxford; New York: Oxford University Press, 2000), pp. 69–70.

[13] *Illuminations*, p. 83.

[14] Ibid., p. 86.

for assimilation, suggests Benjamin. Listeners need to be relaxed or self-forgetful. While traditional patterns of working, cottage crafts for example, allowed one to work and listen at the same time, the more industrial-based modes of work cut off that source of social intercourse. The right context for the retention of a story in memory, then, has become rare in modern existence, Benjamin continues. Relaxation or the activities associated with boredom 'are already extinct in the cities and are declining in the country as well'.[15]

Storytelling is about an exchange of experience: the storyteller takes what he tells from experience – either his own or that learnt from others – and he makes it the experience of others who are listening. This sets up a reciprocity between the activity of storytelling and the community. It is an oral and collective experience in contrast to, for Benjamin, the novel. Moreover, the fascinating aspect of stories is that, although repeated, each repetition will be a unique event, weaving a yarn with the traces of both a collective and of an individual thread: 'Thus traces of the storyteller cling to the story the way the handprints of the potter cling to the clay vessel.'[16]

And, unlike the self-contained, delimited novel, the story defies death. The story is like a flawless pearl, 'the product of a long chain of causes'. But, Benjamin adds, the pace and heightened concentration required moment by moment by modern working patterns means the patience for a narrative is fading: 'Modern man no longer works at what cannot be abbreviated'.[17]

## Two Types of Experience: Erfahrung, Erlebnis and 'the Shock' (*Chockerlebnis*)

In the 1939 essay 'On Some Motifs in Baudelaire' (über einige Motive bei Baudelaire), Benjamin focuses not upon the demise of storytelling but upon Baudelaire's poetry and Proust's prose.[18] He begins by considering why Baudelaire's lyric poetry seemed (to Baudelaire himself) to be unsuited to mid nineteenth-century audiences: 'This may be due to a change in the structure of their experience', Benjamin asserts.[19]

What Benjamin means by this statement is that modern urban experience is characterized by 'the shock' (*Chockerlebnis*). Because of overstimulation by the urban landscape, with its machinelike rhythms, new signs and designs and the Subject's jostling by the crowd, the job of consciousness becomes a case of shielding the Subject as much as possible from constant bombardment by

---

15 Ibid., p. 90.

16 Ibid., p. 91.

17 Both quotations, Benjamin quoting Paul Valéry, ibid., p. 92.

18 In ibid., pp. 152–96.

19 Ibid., p. 153.

urban stimuli.[20] Following Freud's formulation that consciousness, in a heightened state of awareness, registers stimuli in a bid to prevent them from penetrating the unconscious and exacting a really destructive shock, Benjamin develops the idea that, by necessity, modern existence reduces what could be a deeper, more reflective and meaningful experience, *Erfahrung*.[21] *Erlebnis*, rather, reduces the ability to assimilate or retain the data of the world around us – thanks mostly to the vigilance of consciousness in warding off the urban shock. Modern existence as *Erlebnis* becomes a case of living the immediate and trivialized passing moment and in an anxious, hyperconscious state. This, claims Benjamin, is hardly any kind of experience at all. And, as Eagleton puts it, such a short-lived and shallow event hardly leaves any trace or impression that lasts: 'that which is lived cannot be traced'.[22] This description of modern existence is in dramatic contrast to those who lived in the communities whose relaxing patterns of work and play allowed them to assimilate the story and hence retell it in 'The Storyteller'. 'Perhaps the special achievement of shock defence may be seen in its function of assigning to an incident a precise point in time in consciousness at the cost of the integrity of its contents.'[23]

*Erlebnis* involves the experience of time as chopped up, isolated and without depth, in contrast to the 'integration' of time implied by the narrative. Benjamin gives three analogies or models through which to view this notion of the temporality of *Erlebnis*. The principles of journalism – freshness of news, brevity, immediate comprehensibility, lack of connection between news items – all militate against a reader assimilating the information it supplies, says Benjamin. Newspapers 'isolate what happens from the realm in which it could affect the experience of the reader'.[24] Moreover news, by definition, is of the moment – its focus quickly moves on to the next new event or idea, in turn dropping that in favor of yet another new item ad infinitum.

Press information, for Benjamin, feeds the experience of time as discrete, unconnected repetition. And such a temporality also exists in the two other

---

20 Ibid., p. 159. The importance of the concept of 'the shock' to the wider debate about the nature of experience conducted during the late teens and early twenties of the twentieth century – and involving such thinkers as the already mentioned Georg Simmel, Sigmund Freud (1856–1939), Henri-Louis Bergson (1859–1941) and Martin Heidegger (1889–1976) as well as Benjamin – cannot be emphasized enough. The surrealist André Breton (1896–1966) was also part of the debate. See *Nadja* (1928) where he claims that subjectivity and objectivity commit a series of assaults on each over a lifetime, with subjectivity coming off worst.

21 See Sigmund Freud, *The Standard Edition of the Complete Psychological Works* (London: Hogarth Press and The Institute of Pychoanalysis, 1955), trans. under the general editorship of James Strachey in collaboration with Anna Freud, vol. 18, 1920–1922, 'On the Pleasure Principle', pp. 7–64, especially section 2, pp. 12–13. Freud's favorite Dickens novel was *David Copperfield*, the focus of this chapter.

22 Terry Eagleton, *Walter Benjamin: Or, Towards a Revolutionary Criticism* (London: Verso, 1981), p. 35.

23 *Illuminations*, p. 159.

24 Ibid., p. 155.

analogies Benjamin provides: the experience of the modern factory worker at his machine and that of the gambler.

In line with a Marxist analysis of the factory worker being alienated from the means of production, Benjamin suggests that the experience of the worker on the assembly line exemplifies the quintessential temporality of modern existence as *Erlebnis*. Conjuring up the image which had been used to such comic effect by Charles Chaplin in the film *Modern Times* (1936), Benjamin suggests that the worker at the machine performs a task which has no connection with the preceding operation; he is, rather, involved in an exact repetition of previous events which is a discrete and complete renewal of them.[25] Each movement is totally new, it is isolated, relating to nothing before and to nothing after it. Significantly, in contrast to his apparent celebration of the possible further changes in experience wrought by new technologies (photography and film) in his essay 'The Work of Art in the Age of Mechanical Reproduction' (of which there are three versions, the first being written in 1935), Benjamin in 'Motifs' shows no sign of welcoming the change that modern existence wreaks upon the fabric of experience. The present is, rather, a site of loss; experience has atrophied: 'The unskilled worker is the one most deeply degraded by the drill of the machines. His work has been sealed off from experience; practice counts for nothing there.'[26]

Benjamin's dark, almost dystopian vision of modern experience extends beyond the workplace and feeds into all areas of modern life: including perhaps that quintessence of urban living, the experience of the crowd. He alludes to Edgar Allen Poe's depiction of the masses in his short story, 'The Man of the Crowd':

> Poe's [...] pedestrians act as if they had adapted themselves to the machines and could express themselves only automatically. Their behaviour is a reaction to shocks. 'If jostled, they bowed profusely to the jostlers.'[27]

In contrast to those living in pre-capitalist communities, when one assimilated one's own past experience and the experience of others (it was an age when communities had a relationship to tradition), modern individuals inhabit a world governed by a complete break from tradition.[28] One of the most common elements

[25] Benjamin wrote two fragments on Chaplin: 'Chaplin', which was not published in the author's lifetime, and 'Chaplin in Retrospect', published in *Die literarische Welt* in February 1929. Both are published in English in *SW*, II, pp. 199–200 and pp. 222–4, respectively. Chaplin was a devoted fan of Dickens (David Robinson, *Chaplin: His Life and Art* [London: William Collins & Sons, 1985], p. 30).

[26] *Illuminations*, p. 172.

[27] Benjamin and Benjamin quoting Poe, ibid. 'The Crowd' as a motif in both Benjamin and Dickens is discussed in Chapter 4.

[28] Benjamin's concern here with the erosion of tradition's continuity can be compared with the position of Matthew Arnold (1822–1888). As F.R. Leavis puts it, Arnold saw that 'the massive and rapid growth of material civilization, the changes in human habit and the human condition brought about by technological advance, will entail a lapse of that creatively human response [...] which a cultural tradition is', Leavis, *English Literature in*

given in the definition of Modernity is (viewed in terms of history) the idea that it involves a complete break between the past and present.

Benjamin sets up another tantalizing image which equally evinces the chopped up temporality, as well as the decadence of, modern existence: the image of the gambler. At first, it seems paradoxical and comic to align the factory worker in any way with the gambler; one is at work, the other at play: but Benjamin does so. Factory work, says Benjamin,

> lacks any touch of adventure, of the mirage that lures the gambler. But it certainly does not lack the futility, the emptiness, the inability to complete something which is inherent in the activity of the wage slave in a factory.[29]

Hence, it is the experience of time that connects the worker at the machine with the gambler, for Benjamin:

> each operation at the machine is just as screened off from the preceding operation as a *coup* in a game of chance is from the one that preceded it, the drudgery of the labourer is, in its own way, a counterpart to the drudgery of the gambler.[30]

Benjamin picks up the image of the gambler from Baudelaire, the writer he views, with Proust, as expressing modern experience. Arguably, Baudelaire's innovation and radicalism lie in his risky subject matter; the poet depicts the psychological turmoil of the man in the crowd; or the decrepit degradation of the whore and the gambler. He even introduces the image of the fencer in the city – a weird personification of the efforts consciousness makes to ward off the multitude of urban shocks in the city.[31]

As will be argued in more detail later in this chapter, there is evidence that Dickens, as early as August 1857, appreciated that some change in experience was resulting from factory work, from working with the tempo of machines: 'they want more amusement, and particularly […] something in motion […] [looking at paintings] is too still after their lives of machinery'.[32]

---

*Our Time and the University* (Cambridge: Cambridge University Press, 1979), p. 43. This is a rich and complex area of research and cannot be gone into here.

[29] *Illuminations*, p. 173.

[30] Ibid.

[31] Baudelaire's exploration of the psychological turmoil of the man in the crowd can be found in his essay 'The Painter of Modern Life', trans. Johnathan Mayne, in Calhoone, L. (ed.), *From Modernism to Postmodernism* (Blackwell, 1996), ch. 9, pp. 136–44. Two poems addressing the whore are 'La Muse Vénale' (The Venal Muse) and 'Hymne à la Beauté' (Hymn to Beauty); the gambler features in, among other poems, 'Le Vampire' (The Vampire). These and others can be found in *Charles Baudelaire*: *Selected Poems,* trans. Carol Clark (Penguin, 2004) p. 11, pp. 18–19, and pp. 31–2, respectively.

[32] Graham Storey and others (eds), *The Letters of Charles Dickens*, The Pilgrim/British Academy Series, 12 vols (Oxford: Clarendon Press, 1965–2002), vol. 8, p. 399.

Benjamin could also have taken Dickens's exploration of Grandfather Trent's gambling addiction, the opium addiction of John Jasper or the psychological turmoil of a Jonas Chuzzlewit or a Bradley Headstone – not to mention Dickens's numerous depictions of down-and-outs and prostitutes – as perhaps equally useful for his search for the essence of modern experience. There is, however, an important difference in tone in the way Dickens and Baudelaire treat their subject matter. Dickens is usually understood to be more engaged, didactic, empathetic than Baudelaire, whose ironic and detached tone was the inspiration for *l'art pour l'art*.[33] Much of this project, though, is concerned with highlighting the modernity of Dickens, in suggesting that he anticipates aesthetic concerns in form and content that feed into *l'art pour l'art*, symbolism, surrealism and modernism.

There are two aspects to Benjamin's theory of modern experience: 'Contact as failed or contact as [...] violent'. Failed contact is *Erlebnis*, sterilized for memory, while violent contact is the experience of the shock [*Chockerlebnis*].[34] Benjamin, of course, does not argue for this; but the formulation (or constellation of ideas in which he presents his essays) adds up to such a claim. Modern existence is the place where the shock is the norm, and a relentless rhythm of emptied-out, discreet renewal results in an atrophying of experience.

## Proust and the Redemptive Quality of Memory

Benjamin outlines how philosophy has attempted to find a model of 'true' experience in a world where, for him, the masses enjoy only a 'standardized, denatured' one (*Erlebnis*). And evidently, the only way one can redeem or take possession of some remnants of the substance of our experience is retrospectively, since

> none of us has time to live the true dramas of the life that we are destined for. This is what ages us – this and nothing else. The wrinkles and creases on our faces are the registration of the great passions, vices, insights that called on us; but we, the masters, were not home.[35]

Proust – whose novel Benjamin translated into German with Franz Hessel between 1925–1929 – appears to come up with a convincing answer to the 'problem' of atrophying modern experience in his theory of the *mémoire involontaire* (involuntary memory). Proust's novel, *À la Recherché du temps perdu* (*In Search*

[33] Art for art's sake was the term given to a set of aesthetic ideas reacting against the perceived moral, didactic and political purposes to which art was put by Victorians such as Dickens – although this is an oversimplification, since the reaction was also a case of technique and style. The oppositional model is exemplified in the dispute between John Ruskin and James McNeill Whistler, which escalated into a libel trial after Ruskin accused Whistler of 'flinging a pot of paint in the public's face' in 1877.

[34] This point is made by Margaret Cohen, *Profane Illumination* (Berkeley; Los Angeles: University of California Press, 1993), p. 181.

[35] Benjamin, 'The Image of Proust', *Illuminations*, p. 20

*of Lost Time*) 'may be regarded as an attempt to produce experience synthetically [...] under today's conditions, for there is less and less hope that it will come into being naturally'.[36]

Proust distinguishes between *mémoire volontaire* (voluntary memory) and *mémoire involontaire* (involuntary memory).[37] Voluntary memory, the deliberate intellectual attempt to retrieve past experiences, results in only poor recollections. As Proust himself puts it:

> I must own that I could have assured any questioner that Combray did include other scenes and did exist at other hours than these. But since the facts which I should then have recalled would have been prompted only by voluntary memory, the memory of the intellect, [...] the pictures which that kind of memory shows us preserve nothing of the past itself.[38]

Proust's insistence that conscious or 'intellectual' effort fails to really gain a purchase upon the past, implies that there is another means to access it. His novel depicts scenes where an auratic and lucid opening onto the past occurs following an event governed by the senses: memory is triggered by sensations such as taste or smell, or via the hearing of a piece of music. The prompted 'memory' or rather, its contents, which unfold in an epiphanic rush, and, as it were, involuntarily (without conscious effort or guidance), consists of material that has been assimilated unconsciously. This is clear in the example of the character of Swann in *À la Recherche*. He hears a piece of music, which initiates the most intense recreation of a past moment, an experience which he recognizes involves the remembrance of details and sensations he had not noticed at the time. Both Benjamin and Dickens describe their own experiences of Proustian 'involuntary memory' – pointing to the idea that rather than 'inventing' this experience, Proust discovered it. In an account of his two-month trip to Soviet Russia in 1926–1927, Benjamin shops for Russian toys:

> I myself felt a memory from the very distant past stir within me as I caught sight of these rather ugly playthings. My father must have bought something of this sort during some summer vacation [...] when I was young.[39]

---

[36] Benjamin, 'Motifs', *Illuminations*, p. 154.

[37] Proust was by no means the first to make such a distinction. For instance, Dugald Stewart in his *Elements of the Philosophy of the Human Mind* (1792) does as much. See Jenny Bourne Taylor and Sally Shuttleworth (eds.), *Embodied Selves* (Oxford: Clarendon Press, 1998), p. 141; hereafter abbreviated as 'Selves'. The library catalog for Gad's Hill (Dickens's permanent home from 1860) shows he had a copy of Stewart's work.

[38] Proust, *A la Recherche du temps perdu* [In Search of Lost Time], 6 vols, trans. C.K. Moncrieff and T. Kilmartin (London: Vintage, 1996), I, 'Swann's Way', p. 50.

[39] *Moscow Diary*, ed. Gary Smith, trans. Richard Sieburth (Cambridge, MA; London: Harvard University Press, 1986), p. 119.

Dickens, too, describes such an epiphanic opening up of memory. While inspecting the suitability of a chariot for a friend, Dickens takes the reader on a journey to Paris, Strasbourg and Switzerland – at the end disclosing the fact that the trip was an imaginary one which took only half a minute. Dickens's own travel to those sites fueled his vivid depiction of traveling.[40]

Not noticing much at the time, being transfixed in the immediate level of hyper-awareness, as consciousness concentrates upon registering stimuli at an increasing pace, is a natural consequence of modern experience as *Erlebnis*. In contrast, the flowering of the past opened up in involuntary memory is the very opposite of this limited version of experience: 'For an experienced event is finite – at any rate, confined to one sphere of experience; a remembered event is infinite, because it is only a key to everything that happened before it and after it.'[41]

In 'The Image of Proust', the dual structure of memory as unconscious/conscious, involuntary/voluntary – is further developed. In fact, the involuntary/voluntary memory dichotomy is posited in terms of a nighttime weaving and a daytime unraveling of Penelope's tapestry. Modern life is nothing less than a struggle to make something of the fragments of experience retrospectively: an interaction between the warp of forgetting and the weft of attempting to remember.

At night, in one's dreams, one weaves an ornate text consisting of the content of experience that seeped into the unconscious – in spite of efforts to consciously register and parry shocking stimuli. This nocturnal activity with precious, textured traces and threads of experience is the material that constitutes involuntary memory. Involuntary memory, in flooding the mind with lucid past experience, maintains a relationship to truth, then. Paradoxically, Benjamin characterizes the weaving of dreams as closer to a 'forgetting' than to remembering. The contents of such a web of experience can only survive in the dreamlike state of self-forgetful retention; memory is only prevented from fading like invisible ink by the relaxation that goes with sleep.[42]

In our waking hours, the converse process dominates. During the light of day, the ornate nighttime fabric is 'unraveled'. Like the empty repetition of the factory worker at the machine, daytime mental processes, goal-oriented and conscious as they are, begin *all over again* the process of gathering up the fragments of experience. But conscious attempts to 'remember' or to pay attention to past experience merely undermine and unravel the truthful lucidity and depth of the nighttime revelations already woven in dreams.[43]

---

[40] *The Uncommercial Traveller*, 'Travelling Abroad', originally published in *All the Year Round*, April 7, 1860 – in 'Slater', IV, pp. 83–96.

[41] *Illuminations*, p. 198.

[42] Ibid.

[43] It is worth raising again the point of connection between Benjamin's reading of Proust and the Surrealist André Breton. Benjamin's Proust and Breton are concerned with the quality of experience in modern life and both put an onus on the unconscious, on the importance of the dream. See *Les Vases Communicants* of 1932 (*Communicating*

Hence, the warp and weft of life's memory work in this way to move toward a general trend of forgetting. It is in this sense that Benjamin claims experience is slipping away like water through fingers. Yet the discovery Proust makes of the riches opened up by the dream world, and by the unconscious traces of involuntary memory, represents a powerful intervention in that trend toward general amnesia in human life.

Proust's illness allows him to eschew daylight, to, as it were, shut out the conscious world, and to remain in the world of phantasms and dreams in his bedroom. This in turn means the material of involuntary memory and the traces of nighttime dreams linger on – and he can record them in his novel. It is in this sense that Proust (re)produces experience 'synthetically', as Benjamin phrases it. Proust redeems his fading, limited experience artificially. He recreates *Erfahrung* retrospectively, spinning *Erlebnis* into *Erfahrung* through the articulation of fuller experience in his writing.[44]

*Memory/City*

There is a further application of Benjamin's development of Proust's theory of memory where the city dweller chances upon some 'trace' that opens up the past within the present – this will prove important for a reading of urban Dickens. The traces of the 'truth' (or the absolute) inherent within objects pertains at the level of the physical experience of the city; the encounter with past time comes about through the encounter with urban space. One can pick up this line of thinking particularly from a reading of Benjamin's city portraits, *One-Way Street* and Convolute K of the *Arcade*s, 'Dream City and Dream House' – as well as from other essays.[45] For Benjamin, city spaces and surfaces are a powerful source of memory and of fuller experience: and this insight has been taken up by scholars and artists, especially novelists, in many different disciplines.[46] One scholar, Ivan Vladislavić, goes as far as claiming that the city can be understood as

*Vessels*, trans. Mary Ann Caws and Geoffrey T. Harris [Lincoln; London: University of Nebraska, 1990], p. 5). Benjamin's writings on urban experience were hugely influenced by Surrealism; in 1929 he wrote 'Der Sürrealismus': in *GS*(2), II, 1, pp. 295–310, trans. Edmund Jephcott as 'Surrealism' in *SW*, II, pp. 207–21.

44 At least two critics speculate on the influence Dickens had upon Proust. Proust read Dickens in translation according to George D. Painter, *Marcel Proust* (London: Penguin, 1990), p. 121. His favorite novel was *Bleak House*. Edmund Wilson argues: 'It seems plain that Proust had read Dickens and [...] learned from him' (Wilson, 'Marcel Proust', in *Axel's Castle* [London: Fontana, 1979], p. 114).

45 Such as 'A Berlin Childhood around 1900' and 'Central Park'. Benjamin's city portraits include 'Moscow', 'Marseilles', 'Hashish in Marseilles' and 'Naples'. Also see p. 155 of this book for an outline of the relationship of *The Arcades Project* to a number of supplementary essays.

46 One could cite W.G. Sebald as particularly representative of this position – but there are many others, too numerous to mention.

'no more than a mnemonic'.[47] And one could trace this evocative notion through to Situationism, established in 1957.

The encounter with the city is a crucial moment for Benjamin, producing what he terms a 'dialectical image'. The dialectical image is not an experience of the past 'as it was' but offers the past in a new relation, one that relates it to the present moment. The 'dialectical image' could be understood, then, as a temporal version of Benjamin's preoccupation with the absolute. History, even prehistory, as traced upon the intricate folds of the cityscape itself – and a 'remembrance' of lost time – does seem to take on a redemptive role in Benjamin's thought. Modern, urban life for Benjamin, then, is Janus-faced. While involving an attenuation of experience for the Subject, the city's physical presence offers traces of redemption: traces which the city dweller may just chance upon.

## Dickens, Experience and Memory

### *Storytelling and Serialization*

In 'The Storyteller', Benjamin pits oral wisdom against the rise of the novel, a form which, as he narrowly defines it, neither comes from the oral tradition nor feeds back into it. He also claims that the delimited nature of a novel cannot, like the story, defeat 'death'. While the story is ongoing, the novel closes at the final page.

But one could contend against Benjamin that Dickens's novels were part of a kind of oral tradition. Dickens's serialized form meant the novel was not a stable or delimited text at all but an open, fluid one, one that was often dramatized on stage before serialization had even ended. The public, then, was reading Dickens's material through the lens of, or in conjunction with, popular performance.

In terms of content, Dickens has an interesting relationship to the 'wisdom' of oral tradition. Storytellers gave voice to 'localized' conflicts and problems; Dickens treated the concerns of the new urban population. He depicted the social conditions of the disenfranchised and the poor, class conflicts, and explored common fears, beliefs and aspirations. He discussed and satirized political and religious issues of the day with the perspective of the wise common man.[48] He was a storyteller of a mass audience.[49] In terms of style and imagery, Dickens is not without his Romantic and German fairy tale influences – again expressing a fantastical and grotesque nuance that positions him in relation

---

[47] 'Street Addresses, Johannesburg', in H. Judin, and I. Vladislavić (eds.), *Architecture, Apartheid and After* (Rotterdam, Nai; New York: D.A.P., 1998), p. 309.

[48] See Humphry House, *The Dickens World* (Oxford: Oxford University Press, 2nd ed., 1942), pp. 41–2.

[49] Julian Wolfreys explores the serialized form with relation to *The Pickwick Papers* in *Dickens to Hardy 1837–1884* (Basingstoke; New York: Palgrave, 2007), pp. 18–19.

to traditional storytelling.[50] His interpolated tales in *The Pickwick Papers* undoubtedly gestures back to the Gothic medievalism of Mrs Radcliffe and Walpole, a tradition that thrives on the materiality and drama of storytelling and tales within tales.

The dramatic expression of language was what Dickens's oeuvre was about. His work could indeed be read by the lone reader, but it was also designed to be read as a dramatic playtext by more than one reader. As Philip Collins puts it: 'Dickens's public readings developed [...] from the way in which his novels were often in fact read aloud in private households.'[51] The aural quality of the words on the page, Dickens's attention to marginal as well as mainstream voices, his use of slang, patter and accent in dialogue as well as his theatrical narrative style and melodramatic tone – implied more of a collective, dramatic audience than an isolated bourgeois reader.[52] During the writing process, members of his household heard Dickens talking aloud in the voices of characters – he was 'listening' to the dramatic fluency of his dialogue. Daniel Maclise (1806–1870) sketched him in typical pose reading his stories out loud to friends to gauge their opinion.[53] And, of course, he took his dramatized excerpts on reading tours to huge acclaim in England and abroad. The effects he achieved were known to stir audiences to near hysteria, the kind of experience associated more with live theater and storytelling than sedate novel-reading.[54]

Without attacking the integrity too much of Benjamin's attempt to define storytelling as the exchange of experiences within a community, it could be argued

---

[50] The fairy tale form was immensely important to Dickens as a reader – and undoubtedly had an influence on his production. He wrote the fairy tale 'The Magic Fishbone' (1968) and his Christmas books often consciously took on the form, with *The Chimes* being 'A Goblin Story' and *The Cricket on the Hearth* being subtitled 'A Fairy Tale of Home'. Critics who discuss this issue include Harry Stone, *Dickens and the Invisible World* (Bloomington and London: Indiana University Press, 1979); Michael C. Kotzin, *Dickens and the Fairy Tale* (Bowling Green, OH: Bowling Green University Press, 1972); and Elaine Ostry, *Social Dreaming: Dickens and the Fairy Tale* (New York; London: Routledge, 2002). As for Dickens and his relationship to Romanticism, much critical discussion exists. See Robert Higbie, *Dickens and the Imagination* (Gainesville: University Press of Florida, 1998); D. Hartog, *Dickens and Romantic Psychology* (Basingstoke: Macmillan, 1987); Robert Newsom, *Dickens on the Romantic Side of Familiar Things* (New York; Guildford: Columbia University Press, 1977); Donald Fanger, *Dostoevsky and Romantic Realism* (Cambridge, MA: Harvard University Press, 1965); and Taylor Stoehr, *Dickens: The Dreamer's Stance,* (Ithaca, NY: Cornell University Press, 1965).

[51] *Reading Aloud: A Victorian Métier* (Lincoln: Tennyson Society, 1972), p. 11.

[52] See Deborah Vlock, *Dickens, Novel Reading and the Victorian Popular Theatre* (Cambridge: Cambridge University Press, 1998), p. 12.

[53] Dickens reading his 1844 Christmas book *The Chimes* to Carlyle, Forster et al.: reproduction in *The Life of Charles Dickens*, 2 vols (London: Chapman and Hall), vol.1, bk. 4, ch. 6, p. 242.

[54] See Appendix 1 of this book on the dramatic quality of Dickens's reading tours.

that Dickens is a storyteller in the age of mechanical reproduction.[55] While telling stories in print according to the mechanical rhythms of deadlines, Dickens's texts evolved over time and had an oral and aural quality that resembled the vitality of storytelling. He also tackled the topics and entertained the fancies that mattered to a community of readers, appealing to a collective experience.

Dickens's serialization came out of technological developments in publishing, distribution and illustration. Hence, it is no surprise that the parts or numbers, as installments, enact the rhythmical repetition of *Erlebnis*.[56] But they do not represent stable, short-lived or isolated moments of text. Comprising between two and five chapters, the installments are fluid entities, reaching out across time to the continuation of the narrative. Dickens not only published but wrote serially, too. He enacts the change in the structure of experience in his very production. He also 'plays with' *Erlebnis*, often closing on a cliffhanger which evinces pleasure in the interruption, and desire for the connectedness, of narrative. The installments were also influenced by huge numbers of alternative and simultaneous adaptations with which Dickens had, at times, to compete. Unlike instantly verifiable news or information, whose value does not last beyond the moment, Dickens's installments made an impression that lasted across time. Excited audiences awaiting each weekly or monthly number were buoyed up by a desire to continue the narrative, a desire fed by interim speculation and gossip, editorial teasers and even dramatizations that created an ending.[57]

The popularity of Dickens's work, even if one grants Benjamin that new working patterns resulted in a loss of the conditions for the proper reception and retention of conventional storytelling, implies that the appetite for the new 'mechanized form of storytelling' was intense. Dickens's 'storytelling' can be understood as a hybrid oral and written textual form that had evolved with the new working patterns and technological developments: a kind of storytelling that Benjamin does not allow for in his essay.

[55] This phrase is a deliberate echoing, of course, of the title of Benjamin's seminal essay about the fate of art in technological times, 'The Work of Art in the Age of Mechanical Reproduction' (first published in French in abbreviated form in 1935). *Kunstwerk im Zeitalter seiner technischen Reproduzierbarkeit* is translated by some scholars as 'The Work of Art in the Age of Its Technological Reproducibility'. Benjamin produced three versions of the essay, one in 1935, one in 1936 and one in 1939. I will stick with Harry Zohn's translation of the title in *Illuminations*.

[56] Compare John Bowen and Robert L. Patten (eds.), *Palgrave Advances in Charles Dickens Studies* (Basingsoke, Hampshire: Palgrave Macmillan, 2006), p. 33, 'serial publication's rhythms [...] accommodated to the industrial world which reformed human bodies and psyches under the regimes of temporal control and repetitive labour'.

[57] See Appendix 1 on the 'exploitation' of Dickens's material and his response.

*Dreaming Dickens*

The notion that novel-writing redeems experience via an artistic engagement with the unconscious – as Benjamin claims of Proust – could be thought in terms of Dickens's techniques of production. Like Proust, Dickens often spent nights occupied with the memories and phantasms of the city as he walked the streets.[58] This was crucial to a fluent productivity. If Dickens was not able to perform the act of walking, reading and dreaming the city, his productivity suffered. Benjamin himself recorded this phenomenon:

> Dickens could not remain in Lausanne because, in order to write his novels, he needed the immense labyrinth of London Streets where he could prowl about continuously. (*Le Temps*, May 22, 1936)[59]

Again, like Proust, the nighttime weaving of dreams and unconscious fantasies – accessed via Dickens's nightly wandering – formed a crucial part of his novelistic and journalistic production. And there is other evidence of Dickens's relationship to his creative dreams. Dickens's son, Charles Dickens Jr., visited his father at the offices of *All the Year Round* in May 1870, where the ailing novelist was working on the sixth installment of *The Mystery of Edwin Drood*:

> He found his father 'writing very earnestly', and said a few words to him. Dickens looked up, but showed no awareness of his presence. His son spoke out again, and Dickens looked at him. But he did not see him. He was so enveloped in the world of Cloisterham and Jasper that he saw nothing around him. 'He was in dreamland with Edwin Drood', Charles Jr. wrote later, 'and I left him – for the last time'.[60]

Dickens had the ability to immerse himself in dreams and fantasies, to interact with the gothic city that contained them, out of which his fictional world evolved.[61] Strolling in the city, the novelist accessed memories and dreams whose combination was to prove so important for literature.

## Dickens and Benjamin's Theory of Experience

Dickens, always the consummate observer of urban life, records the effect a speedy, crowded urban existence has upon the Londoner's sensibility from early in his career. In 'The Last Cab-driver and the First Omnibus Cad', one of his 'scenes' of urban life (1833–1836), he describes the urban dwellers' adaptation to something

---

58 Dickens and flânerie will be discussed in detail in Chapter 4.

59 *Arcades*, M9a,5.

60 Peter Ackroyd, 'The Eternal Mystery of Edwin Drood', *Guardian*, December 4, 2004, Review section, pp. 42–3.

61 A detailed discussion of 'the gothic city' can be found in Chapter 4.

akin to 'the shock', an adaptation which evolves into an enjoyment of, or even an addiction to, such stimulation 'in these days of the derangement of the nervous system [...] people are content to pay handsomely for excitement'.[62] Here Dickens not only describes the assault upon the senses of urban stimuli, but the populace's growing familiarity and even enjoyment of it, as well as the leisure industry's commodification of it. The passage satirizes traveling by cab in overcrowded, traffic-laden London, a city where, he comically asserts, cabs crash at least every three miles traveled. Where, he asks the reader, can excitement (the urban dweller's craving for 'the shock') 'be procured at a cheaper rate?' Furthermore, part of the implication of pieces like 'The Amusements of the People' is that while the urban populace may be becoming inured to the daily shocks, noise and stimulation of city life, this comes at a cost to the individual's capacity to experience fully:

> There is a range of imagination in most of us, which no amount of steam engines will satisfy; and which The-great-exhibition-of-the-works-of-industry-of-all-nations, itself, will probably leave unappeased.[63]

Here Dickens occupies a position that steals a march on Benjamin. Benjamin worried that the masses enjoyed only a 'standardised, denatured' experience. Dickens similarly identifies a state of affairs where modern experience of the noise, confusion and excitement of urban life ultimately leaves the Subject unfulfilled.

Dickens registers the tendency of the city dweller to ward off the shocks by adopting a protective mental state, an autopilot against stimuli. Observing commuters in 'Shops and their tenants', Dickens declares, 'we meet them everyday [...] Nothing seems to make an impression on their minds; nothing short of being knocked down by a porter or run over by a cab' (*SB*, Scenes: ch. 3, p. 80). Again, this comes close to Benjamin's Freudian formulation of *Erlebnis* in which consciousness forms a protective barrier against shocks entering the unconscious.

Later, Dickens's 1851 article on railway travel, 'A Flight', was published in *Household Words*.[64] This, it is suggested, is a revolutionary piece in the context of nineteenth-century writing and the expression of modern urban experience. In the way Georg Simmel viewed urban space as a correlative of consciousness in 1902, Dickens 'makes the connection between a physical process of railway travel and the mental state that it engenders' in 1851.[65] Rail travel, of course, with its 'rapid crowding of changing images, the sharp discontinuity in the grasp of a single glance, and the unexpectedness of onrushing impressions',[66] is modern

[62] *Sketches by Boz*, ed. Dennis Walder (London: Penguin, 1995), Scenes: ch. 17, p. 172.

[63] 'The Amusements of the People, I', Slater, II, p. 181. The first part of 'Amusements' appeared in *Household Words* on March 30, 1850, the second part, on April 13, 1850.

[64] It was published on August 30, 1851. Reproduction in Slater, III, pp. 26–35.

[65] Grahame Smith, *Dickens and the Dream of Cinema* (Manchester; New York: Manchester University Press, 2003), p. 93. Hereafter referred to as 'Smith'.

[66] Georg Simmel, 'The Metropolis and Mental Life', p. 410.

urban experience crystallized.[67] Dickens hints at this in the writing of 'A Flight'. The primary source of vertiginous thoughts and sensations during rail travel derive from the optical experience at the window. Dickens declares: 'Here we are – no, I mean there we were, for it has darted far into the rear -'[68]

The actuality of the sheer speed of the train, confounds expectation 'no, I mean', it delivers a shock, and represents a disruption, moment by moment, of time and space and one's position in relation to both. Now a ruffled, disoriented Dickens, must anxiously attempt to play catch up with reality: 'no, I mean there we were'. (Shock and temporal disorientation are simultaneously mirrored at the level of the sentence. The interjection 'no, I mean' disrupts the narrative flow; it is an interruption and shock to the reader. The immediacy and excitement of speed, evoked through use of the present tense, is interrupted and revised into the past tense.) This self-interruption and modified repetition has the structure of Erlebnis. Dickens's thought pattern, mirroring the rhythm of the stimulus – and echoed at the level of the sentence – is a tiring cycle of discontinuity and discreet repetition, the rhythm of Erlebnis. The experience is a bombardment by visual stimuli, hard work to perceive and process at such a pace. In fact, the train's speed disrupts the perceptual faculties: Dickens depicts how the passenger experiences the optical illusion of his being fixed in relation to a moving landscape – a moving panorama – which 'darts far into the rear' (with the word 'dart' depicting a jerk in the train's movement).[69] The power and excitement of 'the shock of the new' is that it produces sensations in a body to which it is entirely unfamiliar. Unfamiliarity turns into uncanniness as these immediate effects are interpreted in a way that is at variance with what technologically one knows to be happening: 'I wonder why it is that when I shut my eyes in a tunnel I begin to feel as if I were going at an Express pace the other way?'[70] Here Dickens indulges in the pleasurable, disorientating sensations of technology which he claimed could not completely satisfy a human being. Yet he takes pleasure in them all the same.

Dickens suggests more: if, moment by moment, one's spatio-temporal orientation is so repeatedly attacked, and one is dizzily uncertain of one's ability to cope with these assaults; this anxiety is dwarfed, hours later, by the complete shattering of spatio-temporal level headedness: 'I wonder where England is, and when I was there last – about two years ago, I should think.'[71] It was, of course, only a matter of hours ago. Yet Dickens's acknowledgment of this disorientation, his

[67] For a wide-ranging discussion of this assertion, see Ian Carter, *Railways and Culture in Britain: The Epitome of Modernity* (Manchester & New York: Manchester University Press, 2001).

[68] 'A Flight' in 'Slater', III, p. 28.

[69] Film scholars have identified the perceptual experience of the rail passenger with that of the watcher of a film. Both observe an ongoing rush of visual impressions. Smith, pp. 90–91.

[70] Slater, III, p. 29.

[71] Ibid., p. 32.

self-consciousness in the midst of it, is evidence, again, of the pleasure principle involved in the city's vertiginous 'derangement of the nervous system'. This terror and disorientation coupled with a self-conscious awareness of these effects, and a belief that one will ultimately be safe, is akin to the complex structure of painful or 'negative' pleasure within Kant's Sublime: this is Dickens's urban sublime.[72]

In another passage of 'A Flight', Dickens's poetic use of language works more explicitly on two levels: semantically it evokes the repetitive rhythm, of sound and image, confronting the passenger at the window: at the same time, the structure and order of the words on the page graphically take on the shape of the traveling experience itself (a strategy Benjamin uses in *One-Way Street*):

> The distant shipping in the Thames is gone. Whirr! The little streets of the new brick and red tile, with here and there a flagstaff [...] have been fired off in a volley. Whizz! Dustheaps, market-gardens and waste grounds. Rattle! New Cross Station. Shock! There we were in Croydon. Burrr! The tunnel.[73]

This is an evocation of a pattern of experience consisting of glimpses punctuated by interruption, the fractured form of *Erlebnis* governed, as Dickens puts it significantly, by 'Shock!' Dickens includes onomatopoeic neologisms (a shock for the reader), together with exclamation marks for explosive emphasis, which imitate the sound and are placed at that point in the sentence that suggests the syncopated rhythm of the train's machinations: 'Whirr!', 'Burrr!' – as well as one word which evokes the sound of speed 'Whizz!' (Benjamin's 'shocking' invention of the portmanteau part-French, part-German coinage, *chockerlebnis*, also performs its own semantic meaning in its utterance). Short sentences between interruptions get shorter, evoking growing speed, and greater haste and anxiety as the perceptual faculties begin to breakdown under the pressure. As the passenger struggles to get a purchase upon the bombardment of images, upon experience, the sentence structure reflects this vein process: sentences diminish in length, eventually collapsing into a series of montages, a fractured naming of whatever is before one: 'market-gardens and waste grounds', 'New Cross', 'Croydon', 'The Tunnel'. The train's speed only allows one to announce the present, to encompass it, as a spatio-temporal fragment.

This snapshot articulation at the verbal level is buoyed up by the evocation of its visual counterpart: 'The streaks grow stronger – become continuous – become the ghost of the day.'[74]

As the train speed increases and the perceptual shocks become too many and too quick to manage, impressions merge into one another, the landscape resembles an 'impressionistic' painting, becoming evocatively insubstantial, like a ghost. Dickens has little choice but to relinquish the effort to assimilate the data, to allow the content of experience to become ghostly. As Benjamin describes in his essays,

---

72 Immanuel Kant, *Kritik der Urteilskraft*, trans. J.H. Bernard as *Critique of Judgement* (London: Collier Macmillan Publishers; New York: Hafner Press, 1951), pp. 82–188 (p. 83).

73 Slater, III, pp. 28–9.

74 Ibid., p. 29.

not noticing much at the time, being 'transfixed in the immediate level of hyper-awareness' is the consequence of experience as *Erlebnis*. The fluctuation and impermanence, the speed of the city with its discontinuity and fractured nature was what the Impressionists struggled to find new form to articulate.

Dickens describes at least two ways the traveler responds to all this. There is the 'Demented traveller', tormented by terror and anxiety, whose disorientated belief is that the journey's speed requires him to hurry. His lurid experience is constantly interrupted by staff telling him not to do so: to which Dickens's sympathetic repost is 'No hurry! And a flight to Paris in eleven hours!'[75] Then there is one of Dickens's responses: 'I have but to sit here, thinking idly as I please and be whisked away.'[76]

This draws attention to the utter contrast between the awesome machine that exacts total control over the fragile body, whisking it away to France at high speed, while the human body remains idle and vulnerable. While he also suggests a certain relaxation or even reverie is possible, Dickens's own reverie on the differences between rail and carriage travel is, predictably perhaps, interrupted. Another passage puts one in mind of Benjamin's notion that *Erlebnis* involves the warding off of shocks by consciousness:

> There might be neither a Reigate nor a London for me, as I fly away among the Kentish hops and harvest. What do I care![77]

Here Dickens takes an attitude toward the difficulty of processing the concatenation of visual images flashing by him – he gives up the effort to process them altogether, hence distancing himself from the content of his experience. Benjamin's claim that modern experience involves a reduction in the ability to assimilate one's experience, a direct result of the need, by consciousness, to ward off the urban shock, could be a fair approximation of what is Dickens is getting at, here. Bombarded by visual stimulation, Dickens resorts to giving himself up to the experience, as if allowing experience to wash over him. He no longer challenges his optical and spatio-temporal illusions: 'what do I care?' *Erlebnis*, for Benjamin, involves a case of living the immediate and trivialized passing moment, with the integrity of the content of experience being sacrificed to a general trend toward amnesia. Dickens seems to register this situation. The quality of his assimilation of the experience is not going to be as full as, for example, the engagement with the landscape he recalls experiencing during the slower-paced carriage travel.

In 'A Flight', Dickens, like Benjamin's Proust, is turning to memory and writing about it. Yet, significantly, rather than offering an epiphanic opening up of the contents of Dickens's experience which he did not notice at the time – redeeming, say, the missed details, sights, sounds and smells of Dickens's journey

75 Ibid., p. 28.

76 Ibid.

77 Ibid., p. 29.

in a revelatory rush – his piece is, rather, an epiphanic celebration of the strange sensations that result from the experiential limitations the city dweller appears to be lumbered with in the face of modern technology.[78]

There are further aspects that could be discussed in terms of the Benjaminian formulation of modern experience as '*Erlebnis*' and '*Chockerlebnis*'. There is evidence, for example, of Dickens's 'miming' the experience of *Erlebnis* and *Chockerlebnis* in the form of his fiction; and of characters experiencing their world in a chopped-up, fast-paced or anxiety-laden way.

A good example to adduce is Dickens's depiction of Carker's death in *Dombey and Son*. *Dombey* (written and serialized in 1846–1848) has been read by a number of critics as Dickens's great railway novel.[79] As Dickens's own railway piece suggests, the early years of railway travel involved a vertiginous anxiety as to speed and disruption of space and time, a significant factor in how railway travel was perceived and experienced generally. Hence, Dickens's scene depicting the violent crushing of Carker under a train should be viewed as part of a general anxiety in the public mind over the safety of this new form of travel:

> He heard a shout – another – saw the face change from its vindictive passion to a faint sickness and terror – felt the earth tremble – knew in a moment that the rush was come – uttered a shriek – looked round – saw the red eyes, bleared and dim, in the daylight, close upon him.[80]

The passage evokes, through dislocating rhythm and a sparing use of words, the depthlessness and pace of sensations and thoughts flooding Carker in the moment before death. Dickens piles up fleeting sense perceptions (he heard, he saw) – sense perceptions whose syncopation and content amount to a series of shocks. Carker must adjust himself to information rapidly assaulting his body's senses; before the final assault that will tear his body apart. He has time to think one thought – that the train will run him down: 'knew in a moment the rush was come'. Notice Dickens's inclusion of sensation and thought. 'The shock' as described by Benjamin is both a mental and physical phenomenon. One scholar views it as a neurological category:

> From the factory to the battlefield the experience of shock, physical and psychic, constitutes the norm […] adaptation was […] widely demanded. The city itself is a cauldron of shock-effects. These shocks daily assault the dismantled individual.[81]

---

[78] Philip Davis concurs with this analysis, referring to 'Dickens's vertiginous turn of mind', *The Oxford English Literary History*, 13 vols, vol. 8 (1830–1880) 'The Victorians' (London: Oxford University Press, 2002), p. 235.

[79] See Ian Carter, *Railways and Culture in Britain: The Epitomy of Modernity*, (Manchester and New York: Manchester University Press, 2001), pp. 71–99.

[80] *Dombey and Son*, ed. Alan Horsman (Oxford: Clarendon, 1974), chapter LV, p. 743.

[81] Esther Leslie, *Walter Benjamin: Overpowering Conformism* (London; Sterling, VA: Pluto Press, 2000), p. 182.

While Carker's is an extreme situation, an encounter with death, this does not make the depiction any less of a depiction of *Chockerlebnis* as understood by Benjamin. Indeed, Benjamin speculates upon the ultimate version of urban shock – which for him would be death through military service:

> 'the concept of 'total experience' that is fatal from the outset. War is its unsurpassed prefiguration.[82]

Significantly, Dickens's use of language with respect to his train journey in 'A Flight' is an imaginative conflation of the technologies of speed with that of weaponry or warfare:

> Bang! We have let another Station off […] Bang, bang! […] we stop![83]

In the Dombey passage, not only can Dickens be understood to be representing the ultimate dark fantasy of public consciousness; he is presenting the ultimate modern experience, the ultimate example of *Chockerlebnis*: death. If the scene makes manifest a Victorian anxiety about railway travel, Benjamin's preoccupation with how technology develops takes a similarly dark turn in some essays, as in his 1933 essay, 'Experience and Poverty', for instance:

> A generation that had gone to school in horse-drawn streetcars now stood in the open air, amid a landscape in which nothing was the same except the clouds and, at its centre, in a force field of destructive torrents and explosions, the tiny, fragile human body.[84]

While Benjamin's apocalyptic image is primarily a poetic threnody to the shell-shocked soldiers of the First World War, the fear that both Benjamin and Dickens express of the human body's vulnerability before the onslaught of technological advancement, is clear. It is worth noting here that while Benjamin gave a radio talk on 'The Railway Disaster at the Firth of Tay' on Berliner Rundfunk in February 1932, Dickens was to live out the ultimate fear of railway travel: he was involved in the Staplehurst rail disaster in 1865.[85]

---

[82] *Arcades*, Convolute M – 'Idleness', M1a,4, p. 801. The 'history' of the phenomenon of 'the shock' is inextricably caught up with warfare. Schivelbusch suggests 'the shock' begins to be recognized as an experience at the moment mechanized warfare is developed, concomitant with the mechanized production of commodities: see Wolfgang Schivelbusch, *The Railway Journey: Trains and Travel in the 19th Century* (Oxford: Basil Blackwell, 1980), p. 149.

[83] Slater, III, p. 29.

[84] '*Erfahrung und Armut*', in GS(2), II, pp. 213–19. Translated by Rodney Livingstone as 'Experience and Poverty' in *SW*, II, p. 732.

[85] 'Die Eisenbahnkatastrophe vom Firth of Tay', in *GS*, VII, 1, pp. 232–7; trans. Rodney Livingstone as 'The Railway Disaster at the Firth of Tay', in *SW*, II, pp. 563–8.

Returning to the quoted excerpt, Dickens generalizes the train's relentless machinations, making it contiguous with industrialized life – which, as industrial accidents attested to, tears up everything, human and natural, in its path: 'was beaten down, caught up, and whirled away upon a jagged mill, that spun him round and round, and struck him limb from limb'.[86] A more specific fantasy, an equivalent of which can perhaps be seen in the 'runaway train' sequences of early cinema,[87] was the early Victorian terror that trains were little more than speeding projectiles or bombs hurtling through time and space.[88] Dickens himself describes the feeling that the train he rides on 'exploded, blew into space somehow'.[89] The immense speed and weight of a locomotive meant a stationary observer on the platform experienced a train's force as a roaring 'rush', in the wake of which the human body was a mere rag doll: 'cast his mutilated fragments in the air'. Dickens's inclusion of the image of the mindless monster, the fiery dragon, which devours and licks up the life of Carker is a natural extension of this fear of the unfathomable, sublime 'otherness' of the machine that relentlessly feeds on coal to generate huge amounts of energy.

Each of Carker's shocks must take, in 'real time', a tiny fraction of a second at most. This is implied by Dickens's short sentence structure, his use of the dash, the instant movement from the delineation of one perception to the next: 'He heard a shout – another – he saw the face – he felt the earth shake', and so on. Yet while the depiction of Carker's sensations intends to imply this speedy succession, the time it takes the reader's eye to traverse Dickens's words slows the process of Carker's experience down. Hence, unlike the visual depiction of this event in, say, film – which could undoubtedly achieve the required 'real time' rapidity through fast-cutting and editing techniques – Dickens's delineation of Carker's last moments takes on an eerily slow-motion quality. But the slower pace of the literary depiction enhances the drama and realism of Carker's experience: it is as if he is suffering a personalized, heightened and dislocated sense of time, a terrifyingly slowed-down temporality, so accurate to the truth about extreme moments of crisis.

---

86 As Raymond Williams points out, there was something of a conflation, what he calls a 'confusion', between the idea of the city and the idea of industry in Dickens's time. *The Country and the City* (New York: Oxford University Press, 1973), ch. 15, p. 153.

87 Émile Zola's *La Bête Humaine*, part of *Les Rougon-Macquart* cycle (1871–1893), features the depiction of a runaway train – and Jean Renoir's 1938 adaptation of it includes one of the first cinematic runaway train sequences.

88 Schivelbusch argues that while in the early years of railway travel compartments were designed to minimize the effect of mechanical jerks and rhythms, passengers – as Dickens himself attests to – felt they were flying and were disturbed by the experience. See *The Railway Journey*, ch. 8, 'The Accident', pp. 131–51. See also Jill Matus, 'Trauma, Memory, and Railway Disaster: The Dickensian Connection', *Victorian Studies* 43.3 (Spring 2001): pp. 413–36, where Matus argues that there was little in 1860s trauma discourse for Dickens to draw upon to help him respond to his traumatic experience in the Staplehurst disaster. 'The Signalman', she claims, was the result.

89 'A Flight', in Slater, III, p. 29.

The 'filmic' quality of Dickens's fiction has not gone unremarked among major filmmakers. Sergei Eisenstein argued at length that Dickens influenced early filmmaking. Of real interest for Eisenstein was Dickens's 'montage' technique (the narrative's interruption by a shift to parallel action):

> the works of Dickens, considered not only against a background of English literature, but against a background of world literature of that epoch, were produced as the works of a city artist. He was the first to bring factories, machines, and railways into literature. But indication of the 'urbanism' in Dickens may be found not only in his thematic material, but also in that head-spinning tempo of changing impressions with which Dickens sketches the city in the form of a dynamic (montage) picture.[90]

As persuasive and passionate as Eisenstein is, it is of course the invention of film (well after Dickens's death) that allows him to retrospectively ascribe such proto-filmic qualities to Dickens's prose. But this is hardly a sin: Dickens's extraordinary tendency to think in images and strange angles, to evoke sounds and movements of all kinds, both at a micro and macrological level, is surely crying out for a cinematic reading.[91] Rather than 'influencing' cinema, though, Dickens prefigured it. However far one wants to follow Eisenstein down this particular route, of importance here is the fact that the filmmaker spotted that Dickens engages in a breaking up of totalized visions or smooth narratives, that he evoked experience in shot and montage form, which can be seen as not only an anticipation of filmic montage but, more significantly for this project, as an anticipation of the *chockerlebnis* quality of modern experience as described by Benjamin.

That is not to downplay the apparently mimetic relationship between early filmic techniques and modern urban sensibility – which is an important area of scholarship. As Benjamin scholar Esther Leslie puts it: 'film records the complexity and fluctuating impermanence of city life, its speed, fracture, the incessant movement. Experience in the city is montaged and discontinuous'.[92] And Benjamin himself is not adverse to thinking about film on these terms. In his 'Work of Art' essay, he explicitly describes film in terms of the theory of *chockerlebnis*:

---

[90] 'Dickens, Griffiths and Film Today', in *Film Form*, trans. Jay Leyda (London; San Diego; New York: Harvest, Harcourt Inc., 1949 repr. 1977), pp. 215–16. See also pp. 206 and 213 where Eisenstein discusses Dickens's 'optical quality', 'frame composition', 'close-ups' and 'dissolves'. See Appendix 1.

[91] Undertaken by Grahame Smith, whose *Dickens and the Dream of Cinema* (Manchester; New York: Manchester University Press, 2003) – already cited – is a lively and comprehensive exploration of Dickens's relationship specifically to film. See also, 'Dickens and the City of Light', Smith's 1998 conference paper, <http://www.victorianweb.org/authors/dickens/turkey/turlit10.html>.

[92] *Overpowering Conformism*, p. 67.

> The spectator's process of association in view of these images is indeed interrupted by their constant, sudden change. This constitutes the shock effect of the film, which, like all shocks, should be cushioned by heightened presence of mind.[93]

The 'Work of Art' essay famously goes on to discuss how the medium of film has a reciprocal mimetic/creative relationship with experience, both reflecting and even modifying modern experience – especially with respect to evolutions in the field of perception. Incidentally, in an evocative fragment on Chaplin, Benjamin makes a connection with Dickens, pointing to an area of comparison between Chaplin and Dickens in terms of their flânerie and creative engagement with London. Frustratingly, he does not pursue this line of thinking himself.[94] Chaplin, meanwhile, was an obsessive reader of *Oliver Twist*.[95]

But rather than being a claim about the filmic qualities of Dickens, or a discussion of how Dickens contributed to the cultural crucible that nurtured film's evolution – as interesting and convincing as these areas are – this is a claim about Dickens's delineation of modern urban experience.[96] Dickens's work prefigures cinema as a parallel response to the shock of modernity. What is being claimed is that not only does Dickens 'play with' the temporality of *Erlebnis*, with the mechanistic interruption and repetition of the form in which he publishes his texts – that is to say, in his installments. More than that: Dickens actually underwent *chockerlebnis*, he experienced the city on these terms, and wrote about it in 'A Flight' as an important, new form of experience that readers were probably having and might be interested in bringing, as it were, into full view. And what the cited Dombey passage (written in 1848) and 'A Flight' (written later, in 1851) have in common is that in both pieces, Dickens built in the rhythms, syncopations, sudden disruptions and shocks of urban experience into their narrative form. His use of vocabulary, punctuation and imagery enable a hyper-aware, fast-paced, dislocated and anxious vision of the world to be experienced by the reader through an engagement with the narrative. In this sense, Dickens, at least in these passages, is more intent upon delineating how urban life is experienced, than in delineating urban life itself. Dickens does all this while simultaneously suggesting, in the Dombey passage, that the character at the center of the scene, Carker, experiences his death in these terms.

---

[93] 'Kunstwerk im Zeitalter seiner technischen Reproduzierbarkeit', trans. Harry Zohn as 'The Work of Art in the Age of Mechanical Reproduction', in *Illuminations*, pp. 211–44 (pp. 231–2). See especially sections XIII and XIV, but basically the whole essay.

[94] 'Rückblick auf Chaplin', in *GS*, III, pp. 157–9; trans. Rodney Livingstone as 'Chaplin in Retrospect', in *SW*, II, pp. 222–4 (p. 223). This book, alas, cannot pursue this line either, here. But Dickens and flânerie will be discussed in Chapter 4.

[95] David Robinson, *Chaplin: His Life and Art* (London: William Collins & Sons, 1985), p. 628.

[96] As was hinted at in the introduction, this is one of the crucial differences between my project and that of Professor Grahame Smith in his 2003 project, *Dickens and the Dream of Cinema*.

And there are other novels and characters to be seen in light of what has been argued. In *Hard Times*, Dickens, like Simmel and Benjamin, has no hesitation in making the causal link between the physical presence of technology and the structure of experience. He describes how machine tenders have difficulty concentrating after a day's toil in the factory:

> Many ears and eyes were busy with a vision of the matter of these placards, among turning spindles, rattling looms, and whirling wheels, for hours afterwards.

And evokes the pacey, repetitious rhythm of Stephen Blackpool's thought processes by claiming:

> the old sensation [came] upon him which the stoppage of the machinery always produced – the sensation of its having worked and stopped in his own head.[97]

While Benjamin uses the image of a factory worker to conjure up the depthlessness and pace of *Erlebnis*, Dickens's fictional version of the factory worker suggests the same conclusion about technology, the pace of modern life and experience.[98]

If Dickens describes city dwellers in his *Sketches* as so acclimatized to the urban shock that they desire heightened stimulation even in their leisure time, there is one character who could be understood to be suffering from a case of 'urban fatigue'. Bradley Headstone, the self-taught working-class teacher who has fought his way out of the gutter, is in such a state of heightened anxiety, London is probably the last place for him to be living. His mercurial constitution – what the narrator and other characters call his 'over-passionate nature' – is caused by the lethal cocktail of an exhausted effort of will, self-doubt and repressed class resentment, which is then exacerbated by thwarted sexuality. Dickens's convincing psychological delineation includes an account of how Headstone, through sheer effort of will, made himself into a schoolmaster. Dickens's sketch provides the clue to Headstone's relationship to the modern experience of *Erlebnis*:

> He had acquired mechanically a great store of teacher's knowledge. He could do mental arithmetic mechanically, sing at sight mechanically, blow various wind instruments mechanically, even play the great church organ mechanically. From his early childhood up, his mind had been a place of mechanical stowage [...] There was a kind of settled trouble in the face. It was the face belonging to a naturally slow or inattentive intellect that had toiled hard to get what it had won, and that had to hold it now that it was gotten.[99]

---

97 *HT*, Book 3, Ch. 4, p. 267 and Book 1, Ch. 10, p. 103, respectively. Both quotations from *HT* cited by Herbert L. Sussman in *Victorians and the Machine* (Cambridge, MA: Harvard University Press, 1968), p. 67.

98 The notion that a worker would mentally pick up a rhythm in his labor is hardly a new or radical claim. The long, documented existence of shanties (work songs) attests to this.

99 Description of Bradley Headstone, *Our Mutual Friend* (London: Penguin, 1981), bk. 2, ch. 1, pp. 266–7.

Dickens here shows his scorn for what Sussman terms the 'mechanization of the spirit in education'.[100] Headstone's effortful learning process takes on a similarity to the factory worker's mechanistic repetition at the machine. If the worker's movements lack integration and are unrelated to that which went before and that which comes afterwards, the data Headstone attempts to master appears to be registered in similarly discreet gobbets, and his assimilation of it has a depthlessness that resembles the workers' alienation from the work. The anxiety surrounding Headstone's retention and recalling of his material suggests as much:

> He always seemed to be uneasy lest anything should be missing from his mental warehouse and taking stock to assure himself. (*OMF*, bk. 2, ch. 1, p. 267)

This is a similar scrambling to retain the data of experience that Benjamin describes in his theory of *Erlebnis*. Headstone's consciousness seems too overworked, too vigilant to allow him a reflective, deep assimilation of his material. Even if this is pushing the point too far, Headstone is certainly a personality transfixed in the immediate level of hyper-awareness. The 'settled trouble in his face' smacks of his concentration not only upon registering 'the shock' of urban stimuli but also on attempting to retain information that could be useful for his personal archive. Moreover, it shows his lack of confidence: he scrutinizes the behavior of others, parrying 'the shocks' of their opinion of him. Such an anxious state, with the Subject trying to get an integrated grasp upon fragmented experience, is the natural consequence of modern experience as *Erlebnis*.

Another character worth discussing in this light is Jonas Chuzzlewit. Unlike Headstone, Jonas's extreme anxiety is related to a specific event; it takes hold just before and after he murders Tigg Montague (ch. 42 onwards).[101] Furthermore, his is the hyper-awareness of the villain attempting to escape moral and legal justice. For a villain, he has a highly developed sense of the moral universe.[102] As soon as he decides to murder Montague, even ahead of actually doing it, he wallows in self-loathing and becomes paranoid about being detected. It is as if the truth of what he really is, is too massive a blow for his psyche. If *Erlebnis* involves a heightened state of awareness which prevents 'a shock' from penetrating into the unconscious and causing damage, here Jonas is unable to parry 'the shock' of his own intention, and later, the reality of his own foul deed:

[100] See Sussman, pp. 41–75 (p. 65). See also Dinah Birch's analysis of how Headstone and Miss Peecher are institutionalized products of 'mechanical processes' (pp. 36–7), in *Our Victorian Education* (Oxford: Blackwell, 2008).

[101] At the start of *Martin Chuzzlewit*, as a poor swindler, this character is called Montague Tigg. He reappears (ch. 27, p. 427 onwards) having undergone an inversion of fortune matched by an inversion of name.

[102] In this sense, Dickens's Jonas anticipates Dostoevsky's 'villains'. See N.M. Lary, *Dostoevski and Dickens: A Study of Literary Influence* (London: Routledge, 1973).

> This made him, in a gloomy, murderous, mad way, not only fearful *for* himself but *of* himself.[103]

Psychologically dismantled by 'the shock' that he is a murderer, he seems no longer able to cope with urban existence; he can no longer adequately cope with or ward off the normal 'shocks' of urban living. Urban stimuli, rather, become an intolerable source of horror. Macbeth-like he is appalled by church bells and knocking:

> They had not sat very long, when there was a knocking within.
> 'What's that?' cried Jonas.
> 'Can't say, I'm sure,' replied the man.
> He made no further enquiry, for the last question had escaped him, in spite of himself. (*MC*, ch. 47, p. 723)

His extreme anxiety and watchfulness is not only a question of psychological damage and moral terror though; it is about fear of being discovered. His crime and attempts to avoid detection mean he takes on the consciousness of the urban detective. Survival, moment by moment, becomes about protecting his secret in the city. He knows the urban space, the crowd, the labyrinthine streets afford him a certain amount of cover. The crowd as passersby, as bystanders, are useful for his alibi; he can disclose himself in one place, but not another, in disguise or in his own garb. This only serves to increase his anxiety and paranoia to grotesque proportions, though. Every aspect of urban stimulus is integral to, speaks to, his shameful secret. The flaring up or extinguishing of lights afford spaces of exposure or corners in which to hide; the texture or shape of buildings either conceal or disclose; the sounds of footsteps or voices indicate obliviousness to, or suspicion of, his crime. Every event is a signifier concerning his fate as a criminal:

> Footsteps in the court! Two men. He fell back from the door on tiptoe, as if they could have seen him through its wooden panels.
> They passed on, talking (he could make out) about a skeleton which had been dug up yesterday, in some work of excavation near at hand, and was supposed to be that of a murdered man. 'So murder is not always found out, you see,' they said to one another as they turned the corner. (*MC*, ch. 46, p. 717)

To bury his secret he needs to master urban space – but instead, he becomes a slave of it. The city's complexities, its constant 'assaults' on consciousness and its plethora of chance events and surprises means he is always improvising,

---

[103] *Martin Chuzzlewit* (Oxford: Clarendon Press, 1982), ch. 47, p. 724. John Carey in *The Violent Effigy* (London: Faber & Faber, 1973), pp. 18–19, reads the heightened, lurid delineation of Jonas's murder of Tigg Montague and its aftermath as an imaginative fascination with the psychology of murderers. I argue here, in contrast, that Dickens expresses the experience of his character Jonas as an extreme form of anxiety-ridden city sensibility or *Erlebnis*.

evading, lurking. The urban shocks have become just too shocking, too heartfelt. The city space becomes oppressive, claustrophobic. Space, from which one cannot escape, itself becomes fearful:

> Dread and fear were upon him. To an extent he had never counted on, and could not manage in the least degree. He was so horribly afraid of that infernal room at home. (*MC*, ch. 47, p. 724)

As well as being fearful of space, he is even afraid of time. Before the murder, it dragged on wearily, but afterwards, like the temporality of *Erlebnis*, it is experienced as chopped-up, speeding up, even predatory:

> Setting off from this point, and measuring time by the rapid hurry of his guilty thoughts, and what had gone before the bloodshed, and the troops of incoherent and disordered images, of which he was the constant prey. (*MC*, ch. 47, p. 724)

And, of course, time does catch up with him. Jonas's guilty speculations that something – possibly 'the night' – sees his evil deeds, proves accurate, but at a less metaphysical level: Mr Nagett, a 'private eye', has been watching Jonas's every move and unveils him. Dickens's treatment of Jonas through the delineation of the character's psychological suffering and through the narrative's judgmental, free, indirect speech, virtually guarantees that such an unveiling will come. Such Dickensian didacticism and moralism is what, as has been suggested, *l'art pour l'art* and later artistic movements 'reacted against'. But the modernity of the representation of the character's experiences is something such artists would surely have approved of.

The most obvious character to be viewed in terms of Benjamin's *Erlebnis*, perhaps, is Grandfather Trent, the gambler. If, for Benjamin, modern existence as *Erlebnis* involves an anxious, hyperconscious state triggered by the shock, then when Grandfather comes across gamesters playing cards by serendipity (no less), his is that state:

> The child saw with astonishment and alarm that this whole appearance had undergone a complete change. His face was flushed and eager, his eyes were strained, his teeth set, his breath came short and thick and the hand he laid upon her arm trembled so violently. (*OCS*, ch. 29, p. 230)

Benjamin adduces the gambler's coup to evoke the temporality of *Erlebnis*, the pattern of pure repetitive presentness, the depthless immediacy in this structure of experience. Such experience comes about, remember, because consciousness, alert as a screen against shocks, allows few impressions to enter experience (*Erfahrung*) – and Benjamin sees this as a reduction of an experience that could be so much more expansive. The result is that one lives the immediate, discreet and trivialized passing moment accompanied by the shock, the 'drudgery' and depthlessness of which Benjamin compares with the 'drudgery' of the gambler's repetitive throw of the dice.

Dickens, too, does not flinch from depicting the gambler's experience as a series of emptied-out, discreet moments. But in delineating the gambler, he explores an area which Benjamin does not cover in his cited essays: the area of what happens when a Subject becomes so acclimatized to 'the shock', he becomes addicted to it. As already mentioned, Benjamin was concerned that modern experience involved something 'standardized and de-natured'. Dickens implies, at least in the case of Grandfather, that such indulgence in a depthless present is dangerously irrational, unnatural and even immoral:

> Let me go, Nell. The means of happiness are on the cards and in the dice. (Grandfather, *OCS*, ch. 29, p. 232)

The opposite, of course, proves to be the case: it brings Grandfather and Nell ruin. But Dickens also shows that the opposite is the case even while Grandfather is playing:

> Exulting in some brief triumph, or cast down by a defeat, there he sat so wild and restless, so feverishly and intensely anxious, so terribly eager, so ravenous for the paltry stakes, that she [Nell] could have almost better borne to see him dead. (*OCS*, ch. 29, p. 233)

Grandfather, gripped by irrational lust for the repetitive, momentary shock of the coup, evokes Benjamin's connection between the worker and the gambler in 'Motifs'. Transfixed at the immediate level of hyper-awareness, and like the worker at the assembly line, Grandfather performs a task which has no connection with the preceding operation: an exact, discrete repetition, the drudgery of which Benjamin notes. Dickens's portrait of a pathetic figure is underpinned by an equally irrational attempt by Grandfather to justify his actions. It is an evocation of a gambler's tendency to have a kind of 'faith' which is ultimately self-delusion:

> We must rise from little winnings to great. (Grandfather, *OCS*, ch. 29, p. 232)

and

> Be of good heart, it's all for thee [...] I don't tell them, no, no, or else they wouldn't play, dreading the chance that such a cause must give me. Look at them. See what they are and what thou art. Who doubts that we must win! (Grandfather, *OCS*, ch. 29, p. 232)

Even after he has, Dickens suggests, been cheated out of his cash and the gamblers have left the table, Grandfather continues dealing the cards and checking the hands in a bid to grasp a rationale for why he has not won the game. Not playing for long enough, not having enough money to continue is what he comes up with. Again, this conjures up the hellish, eternal repetition that Benjamin hints at in the factory workers' activity. Grandfather, here, is like the wistful city dweller who has experienced many coincidences: he needs to envisage a system beneath apparent randomness. But this is, as Benjamin calls it, a mere 'mirage'. Grandfather, like all gamblers, is just offsetting criticism that, while he said he would win, he has not. But his self-delusion is clear again since he can have no real interest in systems which lower the stakes, and lower the intensity of the shock for him. And this subjective feeling of intensity and anxiety, moment by moment, is just that – a subjective feeling accompanying the relentless and emptied-out moments. The normally disinterested and childlike Grandfather only really comes alive in the midst of the repetitive, momentary jouissance of risk because he is an addict, lured by that 'touch of adventure' which is in reality only the futility and eternal drudgery of gambling:

> the inability to complete something which is inherent in the activity of the wage slave in a factory.[104]

It is a futility that dwells in the fact that the reader knows that even if Grandfather did have funds to continue the game, his gambling cohorts would have cheated him out of it. Grandfather himself may even suspect as much, yet still he craves the excitement of the moment, dismissing the thought of ends. Here, one can compare Grandfather's addiction to gambling's 'shock' with the people in 'The Last Cab-driver and the First Omnibus Cad' who 'are content to pay handsomely for excitement'.[105] Like all seekers of intense yet depthless experience, which has no purpose other than the momentary experience itself, Grandfather must pay for his pleasure.

The dangerously irrational aspect of Grandfather's addiction lies in his willingness to subject himself to intensities of feeling which his frail frame can hardly withstand, and further, to endlessly ruin himself and Nell into the bargain.

The selfishness of his actions is sharply offset by Nell's much less selfish, non-gambler's view of the situation:

> The child sat by, and watched its progress with a troubled mind. Regardless of the run of luck, and mindful only of the desperate passion which had its hold upon her grandfather, losses and gains were to her alike. (*OCS*, ch. 29, p. 233)

In contrast to this concern for her guardian, Grandfather's explicit cruelty to Nell when she pleads with him not to gamble, suggests an unnatural, dysfunctional and even an immoral aspect to his addiction:

> 'Give it to me, I say', returned the old man fiercely. 'Hush, hush, don't cry Nell. If I spoke sharply, dear, I didn't mean it. It's for thy good.' (Grandfather, *OCS*, ch. 29, p. 230)

[104] All quotations, *Illuminations*, p. 173.

[105] *Sketches by Boz*, ed. Dennis Walder (London: Penguin, 1995), Scenes: ch. 17, p. 172.

As if stuck at the depthless level of immediacy of *Erlebnis*, Grandfather is totally unable to respond to her distress. Instead,

> He seized [the purse] with the same rapid impatience which had characterized his speech, and hastily made his way to the other side of the screen. (*OCS*, ch. 29, p. 230)

Part of the 'loss' Benjamin identifies in the onset of *Erlebnis* is an inability to fully experience and therefore to respond to 'the great passions, vices, insights that called on us; but we, the masters, were not home'.[106] A diagnosis of the city dweller that comes close to what Grandfather might be suffering here is given by Georg Simmel:

> A life in boundless pursuit of pleasure makes one blasé because it agitates the nerves to their strongest reactivity for such a long time that they finally cease to react at all.[107]

Dickens's Grandfather Trent displays how incapable he is of recognizing the importance of the exchange with Nell and the need to rise to it.

It is difficult not to read Jonas Chuzzlewit, Grandfather Trent and perhaps even Bradley Headstone, whose lives 'burn [themselves] out in a pure repetitive present': 'as suffering from a kind of lack of Proustian remembrance'.[108] In other words, in Benjaminian terms, they are suffering from an inability to assimilate and integrate the content of experience and are without any means by which to redeem experience, to make it fuller and more meaningful. If the three characters analyzed can be understood to be experiencing the world in this reductive way, it is not a happy portrait. And Benjamin's (and Dickens's) suggestion that this state of affairs involves a 'loss' makes sense.

Yet there is also the problem, seen in Grandfather Trent, that becoming accommodated to *Chockerlebnis* could even involve a form of pleasure which, Dickens notes wryly, everyone is prepared to pay for – and even Dickens himself enjoyed ('A Flight'). One could take this thought further and suggest that – if one accepts that early film has a mimetic relationship to the structure of experience as *Chockerlebnis* – this might be a clue to film's aesthetic pleasure and popularity. Conversely, then, in this light, it might seem a churlish, pedantic and somewhat conservative position for Benjamin and Dickens to hold that modern experience as *Erlebnis* involves a loss and is something lamentable. But it is one that they both seem to maintain. And both of them, as was argued in Chapter 1 and continues to be argued here, rely upon the eruption of epiphanic experience within the everyday as a means of redeeming the situation.

---

[106] 'The Image of Proust', *Illuminations*, p. 207.

[107] 'The Metropolis', p. 414.

[108] Eagleton, *Walter Benjamin*, p. 28.

## Memory and Morality

In his essay 'The Storyteller', Benjamin suggests that the ability to retain data and exchange experiences is reduced, due to a hyper-awareness that parries the shocks of urban life. He does not touch upon, in any explicit way in the essays mentioned, the role memory plays in forming identity; or how identity might be affected by the suggested reduced ability to retain the data of everyday life. For Benjamin the focus is that the modern phenomenon of *Erlebnis* represents a reduction of experience, a 'maimed experience'[109] that needs to be redeemed at every and any opportunity.

In the Christmas book of 1848, *The Haunted Man*, Dickens does explicitly explore the issue of memory and identity. The eponymous antihero, Redlaw, is a character whose identity is entirely defined temporally: he views his life through the lens of the past, while Dickens's tale suggests his essential humanity disappears with the removal of his memories.

Redlaw is hounded to distraction by a painful past. Hence, in contrast to Benjamin's fear that the modern condition is one governed by the inability to retain data and a general drift toward amnesia, Redlaw's problem is not only that he cannot forget but that the past constantly overwhelms the present. Returning to and repeating a past experience involves a strange split in the self: while one re-experiences the past event, one is simultaneously aware that one is doing so. The doubleness involved in the process of memory is dramatized by Dickens in the form of the specter, Redlaw's double. Yet the ghostly presence is not one that lasts for the duration of a revivification of the past experience and then fades – it lurks in the background, a constant at the corner of Redlaw's eye. Redlaw's uncanny visitor symbolizes the way in which one does not always have to be reliving the 'narrative' of memory for it to effect the present. Like an unwanted guest or a silent entity – it remains and haunts one at an intimate level.

In line with psychologists of the time, the Dickens of *The Haunted Man* appears to take inspiration for his account of memory and identity from John Locke (1632–1704). Identity is 'produced by' memory, for Locke. What is crucial to the notion of 'person' is a continuity of the rational being. This is ensured by maintaining a consciousness of one's own ideas, by perceptions of one's own perceptions. Therefore, memory plays a crucial part in this set up. Memory of past conscious states ensures continuity and a singularity of the self. Simply put, self-conscious awareness (the present) plus memory (the past) equals 'the person'.

Viewing the character of Redlaw from within this framework, one starts to understand the strange state within which he is trapped when he decides to take up the offer of forgetting his tragic past.

---

[109] Tomoko Masuzawa, 'Tracing the Figure of Redemption: Walter Benjamin's Physiognomy of Modernity', *Modern Language Notes* 100.3 (April 1985): pp. 514–36 (p. 519).

> He looked confusedly upon his hands and limbs, as if to be assured of his identity, and then shouted in reply, loudly and wildly; for there was a strangeness and terror upon him, as if he too were lost.[110]

And, in a sense, he is 'lost': Redlaw's identity, the continuity of which memory provides, has been eliminated. Redlaw exists, then, in the moment, with each moment being totally discreet and unconnected with any other that precedes or succeeds it. In a sense, the essence of his new, forgetful life is improvisation. This alienation of the self from the self, this instant form of existence comes close to the alienation, repetition and renewal involved in Benjamin's understanding of *Erlebnis*.

*The Haunted Man* implies that one's memories 'maketh' the man. Dickens invests as much importance in the past, in this sense, as does Benjamin. And like Benjamin, there seems to be a blurring of categories in understanding memory not only as fundamental to subjectivity and experience – but also as having a moral function. For Benjamin remembering the past involves, especially in his later thinking, taking up a moral duty to redeem the history of the oppressed: remembrance is central to redemption.[111] With Dickens's delineation of Redlaw, memory lends a moral dimension to human psychology – it is the foundation of the ability to empathize with the human condition. It is indeed what makes us able to be human at all. Without it, we are merely robotic agents, reacting to the moment. Hence, when a wild and destitute boy crosses his path, what would be Redlaw's natural reaction appears to be stunted, blocked by a malfunction of the psyche:

> The time had been, and not many minutes since, when such a sight as this would have wrung the Chemist's heart. He looked upon it now, coldly; but, with a heavy effort to remember something – he did not know what. (*HM*, ch. 1, pp. 397–8)

Redlaw's feeling of repugnance and coldness toward the boy stems from his inability to grasp the possible causes of the boy's miserable situation or to imagine the boy's feelings – something that past trials and tragedies, even long forgotten traumas, allow one to get an insight into. Indeed, it is often the sight of others' misery which triggers – in Proustian vein – the flood of long-buried past experience in one's self. This is the moment when memory's involvement in response and action becomes an ethical input. Loss of access to our own (past) experience results in a catastrophic loss of human empathy or humanity, then, for both Benjamin and Dickens.

Memory also features prominently in the more famous Christmas book, *A Christmas Carol* (1843). Memory here is crucial to the power of self-discovery and self-making.

At the start of the story, Scrooge has shut out a painful past and comforts himself with the present immediacy of money-making. Disappointment and

---

[110] *The Haunted Man*, in *Charles Dickens's Christmas Books* (Oxford & New York: Oxford University Press, 1998), ch. 1, p. 396.

[111] See especially, Thesis II, 'Theses', in *Illuminations*, p. 245.

bitterness have shaped him into an ogre of insularity and insecurity; he needs no perspective upon himself to survive, and does not have one. Scrooge the miser merely functions in the present.

It is not that Scrooge is determined by or is the result of his past choices that is of importance. What Dickens is interested in is what happens when he is made conscious of this state of affairs. In a sense, the problem with the miserly Scrooge had been that he was too much of a determinist: vague determinism allowed him to exist for the 'now' and take no responsibility for outcomes. Miserly Scrooge has no interest in either the past or the future. The past and the future were merely the antecedent to, and the consequent of, the present activity of gaining profit. Like Baudelaire's gambler and Grandfather Trent, Scrooge is locked in a repetitive present: the *Erlebnis*-like repetitive present of capitalist money-making. His embrace of laissez-faire philosophy and Malthusianism is a crucial part of this. Both theories resign themselves to the inevitability of economic determinism; Malthus even claims the harshnesses and inequalities that result from it are beneficial to the greater good. Similarly, Scrooge can pour scorn on carol-singers and charitable organizations and, with Malthus, view Tiny Tim as surplus to the population – which is only consistent with an understanding that things inevitably unfold as they must, and that no moral responsibility need be taken for any of it.

Scrooge's psychological flaws are the natural result of life's griefs; he is not an essentially evil man. He is the result of the tragic choices of the past. It is by revivifying the feelings and attitudes of his childhood and young adulthood, by showing Scrooge the scenes of Christmases past, that the ghost begins to shake Scrooge from his rigid rootedness in the present. Whether the scenes are his memories or supernatural representations of them, Scrooge recognizes them as his old concerns and feelings – and he enters into them again. By piecing together scenes of his past through memory, Scrooge gets a sense of himself as part of an evolving pattern or narrative, a pattern that is playing itself out in the present and which will, without intervention, inexorably roll on into an unhappy future. But notice an affinity to Benjamin's understanding of how memory works: access to the past for Scrooge comes in auratic flashes and fragments, experiences over which Scrooge has no personal control. It is through the piecing together of these fragments that Scrooge attains some sense of continuity and identity.

Scrooge's change of heart results, the story implies, in generosity toward the Cratchits and the survival of Tiny Tim. His new self-awareness, gained through a crucial engagement with memory, prompts actions that have a moral outcome. This again is where Dickens places memory in relation to morality. In a move similar to that made in *The Haunted Man*, Dickens claims that it is one's sense of oneself as part of a narrative that enables one to engage with the world responsibly. Yet, significantly, the idea of oneself as a stable continuity can only be attained retrospectively and precariously through the discontinuous, fragmentary experience of memory (in this case specific memories chosen by Scrooge's spectral companions). It is here that one can view Dickens as coming close to Benjamin's suggestion that modern sensibility (a context of capitalist money-making so central to Scrooge) involves a repetitive onus upon the present and a falling away of the past – in other words, experience as *Erlebnis*. And in a Benjaminian world where exchanging and sustaining narratives becomes less and less possible, the implication is that acting responsibly and morally becomes less and less possible.

## The Operation of Memory in *David Copperfield*

> Reminiscences, even extensive ones, do not always amount to an autobiography ... For autobiography has to do with time, with sequence and what makes up the continuous flow of life. I am talking of a space, of moments and discontinuities. For even if months and years appear here, it is in the form they have at the moment of recollection.[112]

This section explores Dickens's semi-autobiographical novel, *David Copperfield* (*DC*, 1849) which involves not only the possible inclusion of a selection of Dickens's memories: but a fictional construction of the processes of memory itself.

There were two theories of memory current in the 1860s: that memory is something unreliable and fictional, and that it is something that clarifies and revivifies an experience in the present.[113] Both have a bearing upon how one could look at *DC*.

On the one hand, in writing *DC*, Dickens, for Cobbe, is producing a text with as much 'truth value' vis-à-vis his own past as simply having a memory of it (which is a fiction itself). Dickens began writing an autobiography at some point between 1845 and 1847, dealing with the first 13 years of his life. It was unfinished and he abandoned it, significantly, when he began writing *DC* in 1849. However, the material was published in fragmentary form in Forster's biography of Dickens in 1872. Scholars have speculated as to the meaning of several discrepancies in the accounts of, especially, his early life in Chatham, in London and his employment at Warren's Blacking Factory. Some critics believe that the traumatic content of his past meant Dickens had to, emotionally, edit and re-edit his past in his articulation of it. As F.S. Schwarzbach puts it, 'It is at least possible that these errors [the discrepancies in Dickens's accounts of his past] were the result of Dickens not correctly remembering the past, but rewriting it'.[114]

On the other hand, Carpenter cites Dickens as a case study of how the creative imagination can reproduce with the force of actual experiences.[115] And, as will be examined, the narrator, Copperfield, claims a number of times that his memories revivify experience in the present moment.

---

[112] Benjamin, 'Berliner Chronik' (1932), in *GS*, VI, pp. 465–519; trans. Edmund Jephcott as 'A Berlin Chronicle', in *SW*, II, pp. 595–637 (p. 612).

[113] See Frances Power Cobbe and Carpenter in *Selves*, pp. 151 and 156, respectively.

[114] *Dickens and the City* (London: The Athlone Press, University of London, 1979), p. 17.

[115] Selves, p. 156.

Both theories put Dickens's autobiographical and favorite novel in a particular light. The question as to how close the content of the novel comes to Dickens's 'actual life' becomes a redundant one. All autobiography, like all memory, is representation. The novel's content has the same problematic relationship to 'truth' or 'the real' as does all representation and memory to 'reality'.

### *Fragmented Narrative*

*David Copperfield* is presented in the form of autobiography. The writer/narrator of the biography (also the narrated protagonist, Copperfield) suggests the book will have the forward momentum one expects of autobiographical discourse. The narrative will begin with 'the beginning of my life – Chapter 1 – I am born' and it will continue relentlessly forward, eventually revealing 'Whether I shall turn out to be the hero of my own life'. Moreover, there is an extra dimension, here. Forster (Dickens's biographer) tells us that *DC* is an evocation of his own childhood and adult relationships in fictional guise.

So Dickens the writer, like Proust, raids his 'memories' and weaves them into fiction. Whether one describes Dickens as accessing his mnemonic material via the processes of Proust, dreaming and thinking through his nocturnal wanderings, there is certainly a similar urge to 'redeem' past time in the author. The reader of *DC*, meanwhile, is encouraged to expect narrative biography. The story will mirror our usual understanding of historical time, the inevitable unfolding of one event after another in a necessary flow.

But it immediately emerges that the narrative is anything but a smooth unfolding of events. Rather it fragments. It features an opening which interrupts itself, is punctuated by a number of beginnings and false starts and a retrospective which refuses the conventional linear understanding of the past, present, future continuum of time.

The opening of the novel is a beginning. It seems fair to begin at the beginning: 'To begin my life with the beginning of my life', as the narrator tells us in the chapter called 'I Am Born'.

Yet, one must remember that, for the narrator to begin, it must also be a 'beginning-again', a repetition for him. For him to write his history, for him to rewrite his history, the narrator must interrupt his history and begin (verb) at a new beginning (noun). This, then, is an interruption and a repetition: an interruption of the unfolding movement of the narrator's history with the conjuring up and writing down of memory; and a repetition, an access to earlier events. It is here that the narrator appears to undertake what for Proust would be the 'mistake' of intellectually 'willing' remembrance (voluntary memory) in a bid to write it down.

The novel's opening is also a renewal for the narrator. He begins at the beginning, at chapter 1. Chapter 1 is titled, 'I Am Born'. Notice the present tense, I *AM* born. This suggests, does it not, that on the back of the repetition, is a rebirth; a renewal of birth through the making of a new beginning. So this raises the opportunity of a 'renewal' of 'my history' as well as a repetition of it – an opportunity for a 'rewriting', for a reworking, or for an editing of history in the 'writing' of it. Such a repetition and a renewal, allows space for immediacy and difference, then.

To recapitulate: to begin, the narrator must 'interrupt' and begin again, in a moment of wresting the beginning from the past and repositioning it in the now. This is not a state of affairs where the narrator 'goes back' to the past in some way and recreates it 'as it was'. What is being staged comes close to the Benjaminian 'dialectical image'; it is a temporal montage of past and present; an event that leaves room for newness in the experience.

At the start of the novel, the narrator does not commence with 'I was born at such and such a time, at such and such a place' – as one might expect. He, as it were, interrupts the start with:

> Whether I shall turn out to be the hero of my own life, or whether that station will be held by anybody else, these pages must show. (*DC*, opening line, ch. 1, p. 1)

Here is another deferral of any beginning: with a questioning of the process of biography itself and the narrator's role within it. Rather than giving away information, the author, Copperfield, withholds it – he declines to state the case of whether he will be the hero or not. Is this an indication of modesty of temperament? Or is it an acceptance that only when the fragments of memory are gathered together, can such a decision be made? It stokes up the anticipation of the reader, as well as obfuscating the narrator's omniscience. It sloughs off authorial responsibility for judgment, throwing doubt upon his ability to control how the events of the past are recounted. Again, this allows space for not only repetition and renewal but for difference.

What it also does, importantly, is allow the instances of revisiting the past in the text to be experienced unencumbered by any preconceived judgments or ideas. The narrator will describe and 'experience' his activities in the past in as immediate a way as it is possible to experience the past in the recounting of it. His narration mimes the actual experience of experiencing the past, as understood by Benjamin and Proust. It implies that there is space for the discovery of traces that suddenly initiate a lucid opening onto an area of the past that was perhaps not expected. Seen in this light, experiencing the past in Dickens's novel is a risky event and one over which little control can be exerted. So while Copperfield's narrative is an attempt to will the recovery of the past – the Proustian act of 'voluntary memory' – it contains an acknowledgment of the inability to master such material and appears to allow space for 'involuntary' revelations.

There are yet other interruptions. The narrative gets waylaid yet again with the discussion of the selling of David's caul to an elderly woman. After a lengthy diversion into what happens to the caul, the narrator declares, 'Not to meander myself, at present, I will go back to my birth' (*DC*, ch. 1, p. 2).[116]

[116] The obvious precursor to the notion of autobiography posing an acute difficulty in terms of just getting underway is Laurence Sterne's *The Life and Opinions of Tristram Shandy* (1760). This is a comic exploration of the incoherences involved in attempting

There is another beginning in chapter 11, which is entitled 'I begin Life on my Own Account, and don't like it'. This is the episode David spends as a drudge in the factory cleaning and packaging wine bottles.

And in chapter 15, he is called upon to 'make another beginning'. This is his attempt to forge a bond with his aunt, Betsey Trotwood – who rejected him at his birth. As well as being a beginning it is a repetition – a repetition of the meeting between the two. But the repetition opens up the possibility of difference – a difference of outcome. Which is exactly what happens – she takes to him against the wishes of the Murdstones.

Falling in love is often a repetitive process throughout a young life, and David is guilty of a number of false starts in this area. As a boy he wants to marry Emily; while later, in Canterbury, he claims he is in love with the dancing school student, Miss Shepherd, before falling for Miss Larkins – who marries a hop-grower. He fails to recognize the great love of his life, Agnes; marriage to her is still deferred as the novelist plumps to marry Dora. It is only her death that leads him to 'return' again to his life and Agnes after an extensive 'absence' to begin afresh.

David is not the only character with a penchant for new beginnings. Mr Dick can be doubled with Copperfield in needing to begin his memorial again and again and, perhaps, in his being unconcerned to finish it.

Micawber, too, can be compared with David in his constant wish for fresh starts: but his motivation is to break the continuum of bad luck in his personal history. His famous repetition of the phrase 'something will turn up', conjures up the picture of a longing for a chance interruption in his life that is so messianic, it completely resolves his situation.

With a multitude of beginnings, repetitions and false starts, then, Dickens and Copperfield interrogate the biographical form rather than expressing themselves straightforwardly through it. The question to ask is, why does the narrative follow a sequence of interruption, repetition, renewal and new beginnings, rather than a smoothly evolving narrative? The short answer is that Dickens/Copperfield highlight the impossibility of capturing the traces of past time, and of making any totalized narrative out of them. The narrative also apes, it is suggested, the structure of *Erlebnis*. Dickens delineates through David's 'narrative', an anxious, fragmentary and repetitive experience of modern life, which is then strung loosely together. The best the narrator can do is to gather material under such headings as 'I begin Life on my Own Account, and don't like it'.

Retrospectively gathering fragments under themes or headings, of course, is the approach Benjamin took in, among other projects, his written account of the Berlin of his own childhood in the posthumously published 'A Berlin Chronicle' (1932) and 'A Berlin Childhood around 1900' (1932–1934, revised in 1938).

---

to 'tell the complete truth' in novel form. To start at the beginning of the hero's life story involves a lengthy digression into endless genealogies and, even 200 pages later, Tristram Shandy is yet to be born. The paradox of the situation is evoked wonderfully in the narrator's comment: 'I shall never overtake myself!'

As was the case in Dickens's writing of 'A Flight', rather than bearing an emphasis upon the Proustian success of weaving *Erfahrung* (a fuller experience) out of the fragments of *Erlebnis*, *DC*, rather, evinces the attempt at 'autobiography' and the process of memory itself as falling most frequently toward a pattern of anxiety and repetition: aping Benjamin's structure of *Erlebnis*. The narrator's attempted remembrance/redemption of his experience positively confirms repetition rather than linear narrative as being the formal shape of autobiographical and memorial 'redemption'.

Dickens/the narrator gather up fragments and piece them together to imply continuity at another, later moment in the novel. The narrative is punctuated by a retrospect (ch. 18, 'A Retrospect', p. 226). This proves to be a strategy to 'fast-forward' to events later in the narrator's life. There is even a suggestion that there is a smooth temporal flow: 'As I look back on that flowing water.'

Yet one only has to take a cursory look at the chapter to recognize that in 'recovering' the past, the narrative can only snatch a couple of snapshots. Like Zeno's arrow, then, there is no depiction of smooth transition or movement (whatever a literary depiction of this might look like), only a sequence of unconnected moments.

Look at two examples of Dickens's delineation of the passage of time in this retrospective chapter. Firstly, on page 229 (ch. 18), David states: 'Time has stolen on unobserved for Adams is not the head boy.' Secondly, he asks, 'And the little girl I saw on that first day at Mr Wickfield's, where is she? Gone also. In her stead, the perfect likeness of the picture [...] moves about the house; Agnes – my sweet sister – is quite a woman'.

Both of these attempts to depict the passage of time work through a quick comparison of two images of the same space. In the first example, temporal flow is evoked by the successive image of school with Adams as head boy compared with another image of school with him absent. The other example works similarly: an image of the interior of Mr Wickfield's home with Agnes as a little girl is swiftly juxtaposed to an image of Wickfield's home with Agnes as a woman. Continuity lies in a recognition of 'perfect likeness' or similarity of the subject, and of identity of spatial context. It is the repetition of spatial context coupled with the difference between the two subjects which prompts the recognition of time's passage. Here, Dickens anticipates Eadweard Muybridge's proto-cinematic depiction of locomotion through the rapid succession of stills, whose slight degrees of difference create the illusion of movement. Hence, the flow of time passing is evoked through the sequence or juxtaposition of snapshots, stills or fragments. The narrative, again, is interrupted: indeed, it is using interruption to imply narrative flow. Dickens's use of interruption, once more, anticipates Benjamin's understanding of how memory works. As he puts it in 'A Berlin Chronicle': 'the mysterious work of remembrance – which is really the capacity for endless interpolations into what has been'.[117]

[117] *SW*, II, p. 603.

Yet Dickens seems reluctant to give up on the idea that time can be configured as a continuum. This is evident in his insistence upon depicting time's 'extension' in spatial terms – as a road. He says, 'That little fellow seems to be no part of me: I remember him as something I have left behind on the road – as something I have passed, rather than have actually been – and almost think of him as someone else' (*DC*, ch. 18, p. 229).

The disjunction the narrator sets up between himself in the 'now' and the boy of the past, as well as his use of 'road', implies distance. But in the very establishing of distance, in the attempt to situate 'the boy' as 'no part of me', David paradoxically sets up contiguity. Through disjunction he sets up conjunction: namely, the image of spatial continuum and consequentially, temporal continuum between himself and the boy. The transition from 'boy' to 'man', though, is implied by the absence of its depiction, by the difference between one image 'the boy' and another, 'I'. Hence the continuum of David's life is again represented through the juxtaposition of two fragments of it – the image of boy with the image of 'I'.

The idea that the self can be 'something I left behind on the road', a suit of clothes one can take off, emphasizes the objectivity of images of the past. The 'self' is merely an 'object', as if captured as an image in photography rather than the memory. Here, in *DC*, memory resembles photographic paper: interesting in view of the fact that Dickens believed and told others that his observation of urban life involved capturing images upon the photographic plate of his mind.[118] Dickens's language in the excerpt implies that he is dealing with a glimpse of himself – a literary image which, due to the brevity and speed with which it is mentioned and the moving position from which it is viewed, has an ephemeral, delicate, possibly photographic or snapshot quality to it. Coupled with the description of that boy as 'something' left behind, the image of the boy is a thing, a collectible, disposable object, a quality which photographs, as opposed to paintings, were soon to have.[119]

But in collecting such an 'object', in the remembrance and the redemption of it, a connection is made by the Subject doing the collecting.[120] In the field of photographic theory, for instance, Roland Barthes depicts in gothic terms that interim space inhabited by the 'self' when 'collecting' an object of memory.[121] Barthes's description of the uncanny experience of moving between subjectivity and objectivity in viewing an image of the self is echoed in Dickens's excerpt at the point when the 'familiar' image of the boy converts into a stranger, when Copperfield thinks 'of him as someone else'.

---

[118] See *Life*, bk. 3, ch. 5, p. 246.

[119] See Regina B. Oost, 'More Like than Life': Painting, Photography, and Dickens's Bleak House', *Dickens Studies Annual* 30 (2001): pp. 141–58 (p. 143).

[120] Again, the surrealist connection should be pointed out. The problem of experiencing 'identity' as evanescently to-ing and fro-ing between subjectivity and objectivity is a conundrum that the surrealist André Breton attempted to encompass in the first part of his 1928 prose trilogy, *Nadja*.

[121] See *Camera Lucida*, trans. Richard Howard (London: Vintage, 2000), pp. 13–14.

The notion that the image of the boy is a 'thing' to be left behind on the road, gives it a disposable quality that reduces its importance. Like all disposable, reproduced images, it lacks aura, again resembling the photograph.[122] Yet, conversely, David is still obsessed with it and, as a 'thing', it still discloses an important truth to him. As Benjamin argues in his essays on photography and on collecting, photographs, memorabilia and objects disclose traces of 'the absolute', traces of 'truth' about the past and, by necessity, about the 'self' (and importantly, history) that insist in the present.[123]

The narrator conceives of the 'self' as a point in space, too: 'something I have left behind on the road – as something I have passed' (*DC*, ch. 18, p. 229). The self is a moment, a point traversed; one that will be traversed again; a point whose space is reoccupied later by chance or planned revisitation, opening up memory and an awareness of difference, of distance traveled in space and time. This is evoked most clearly during David's trip to London from Dover: which he hopes will result in his becoming a Proctor at Doctors' Commons. During the journey, the reverse of his penniless tramp from London to Dover, David looks out for landmarks in recognition of which he can reconnect with and measure the vast distance between his former experience of the space and his current one:

> It was curious and interesting […] to be sitting […] behind four horses well-dressed, and with plenty of money in my pocket; and to look for the places where I had slept on my weary journey. I had abundant occupation for my thoughts, in every conspicuous landmark on the road. When I looked down at the trampers whom we passed, and saw that well-remembered style of face turned up, I felt as if the tinker's blackened hand were in the bosom of my shirt again […] I stretched my neck eagerly to look for the place where I had sat, in the sun and in the shade waiting for my money. (*DC*, Narrator, ch. 19, p. 243)

David is traveling back along a route he has already trodden. But bear in mind that the passage is more than just a description of a retracing of footsteps – although it is that too. It is also a spatial and allegorical representation of Copperfield's life. And it is clear that his life is more than just a straight road. The labyrinth is the shape most suitable to a description of his location in time, with respect to his false starts, errors, repetitions, and memories.

Copperfield's return to London along the Dover road, is an experience of repetition and renewal for David. The repetition is in the recognition and reinhabiting of a space once occupied. The renewal lies in the difference one registers between one's original experience of the site and the repeated one.

[122] As already mentioned, in 'The Work of Art' essay, Benjamin claims an original painting loses its 'aura' once it is reproduced. See Appendix 1.

[123] 'Little History of Photography' (1931), in *SW*, II, pp. 507–30; 'The Work of Art in the Age of Mechanical Reproduction' (1935), in *Illuminations*, pp. 211–44. 'Unpacking My Library' (1931), in *SW*, II, pp. 486–93. 'Eduard Fuchs, Collector and Historian (1937), in *SW*, III, pp. 260–302.

But while one glimpses the difference between the new and the old experience, the original one still haunts the present lucidly: 'I felt as if the tinker's blackened hand were in the bosom of my shirt again.' This co-presence of the past and the present is a kind of fictional 'dialectical image' which opens up the truth about temporality's effect upon David's self.

There is a Gothic element to David's relationship to his past. It is space that affords the repetition of memory, and David's is an encounter with the city space, the space traveled and with himself. But the people involved in the scene are less than substantial:

> The atmosphere of the city that is here evoked allots them only a brief, shadowy existence. They steal along its walls like beggars, appear wraithlike at windows, to vanish again.[124]

Moreover even the 'self' encountered is ghostly and evanescent. The narrated David registers the difference in his situation (in comparison to his last visitation) with some relief but also with a certain perverse sense of loss. Here is a 'self' that dreads its connection to the past and wants to distance itself from it, that looks on its former 'self' as a stranger; yet is driven to reinhabit old spaces and to 'eagerly [...] look for the place where I had sat'. This obsessive need to revivify the spectral experiences of the past, and conversely, the insistent haunting of the present by the past's ghostly materialization, has its meta-literary version in Dickens's relationship to his own childhood.[125]

The Gothic resonances of ghostly revisitations to a city space in memory as well as physically, is evoked explicitly in the novel; and it implies a spectral, a much less stable sense of 'self', marked by a modern sense of anxiety.

On page 272 (ch. 22), the narrator says:

> my occupation in my solitary pilgrimages is to recall every yard of the old road [...] and haunt the old spots. I haunted them as my memory has often done and lingered among them as my younger thoughts had lingered when I was far way.

Here the narrator is interested not so much in focusing upon the difference in experience between the 'then' and the 'now', but in a sameness, a sense of connection. His obsessive 'haunting' and 'lingering' in the space is driven by a need to gather together fragments of experience into a narrative, into a stable sense of self. His repetition of haunting a space has, as he admits, been repeated many times before, in memory. He now physically follows in the footsteps of those spectral memories, follows up his thought processes in a bid to gain a purchase upon this evanescent self – which has become a kind of ghostly byproduct of space. The city

---

124 'A Berlin Chronicle', pp. 612–13.

125 This was mentioned earlier in the chapter, with Dickens's conflictual/painful relationship to his time at the Blacking Factory manifesting itself (possibly) as discrepancies in Dickens's written and oral accounts of his period of toil.

space is a palimpsest, somehow haunted by the fading traces of an earlier, elusive 'self' – a trace that is constantly reworked and overwritten with each revisitation. Rather than the 'self' being 'something' he left behind on a straight road, it is, rather, a multitude of intangible phantoms, to be sought out in a labyrinth. Such repetition and re-arousal of 'self-hood' in memory or as a result of a physical visit, then, is hopeless and relentless. The very repetition points to anxiety, an obsessive and vein hope to achieve a grasp upon a totality of meaning. David's 'spatial self', with its obsessive, anxiety-driven attempt to gather a fragmenting self into a conceivable whole, echoes the formal structure of the autobiographical narrative with its new beginnings, repetitions and retrospectives. And, as has been suggested, it echoes, and is determined by, the form of the cityscape with its unfathomable impenetrability. His self becomes a labyrinth, too; and thus 'straying', 'wandering' become the practice of existence within the city.

Benjamin emphasizes the need for aimless wandering in the city and would celebrate Copperfield's obsessive return to the same space, as being an integral part of the process of recovering the elusive fragments of memory and the past:

> Fruitless searching is as much a part of this as succeeding, and consequently remembrance must not proceed in the manner of a narrative or still less that of a report, but must, in the strictest epic and rhapsodic manner, assay its spade in ever-new places, and in the old ones delve to ever-deeper layers.[126]

Again, the process of anxiously wandering the streets, of seeking out the encounter with the self and with memory, and what it means for 'autobiography' takes on a meta-resonance when we recall Dickens's 'need' to wander the streets of London if his production was to be fluent.[127]

Dickens's habit of wandering the city streets, and his depiction of Copperfield (and indeed, of Master Humphrey, Sidney Carton and other characters) as doing so is a crucial moment in the exploration of Dickens and Benjamin. The importance of it cannot be emphasized enough. Benjamin himself iterates this quality in Dickens several times in *The Arcades Project*.[128] Its importance centers on the fact that, for both men, the city space determines a comprehension of the self, of memory and of experience. Such searching may, moreover, yield momentary encounters with the absolute or truth:

---

[126] 'A Berlin Chronicle', p. 611.

[127] As was signaled in the introduction, there is a clear convergence here with Peter Ackroyd's work. Reviewing Ackroyd's *London: The Biography*, Iain Sinclair remarks that the book 'very rapidly announces itself as Peter Ackroyd: The Autobiography' ('Maybe it's because he's a Londoner?' Iain Sinclair on Peter Ackroyd's London: The Biography', *Guardian*, October 14, 2000, <http://books.guardian.co.uk/print/0,,4076226-99937,00.html>.

[128] There are six citations on Dickens and flânerie in Convolute M entitled 'The Flâneur' of *The Arcades Project*: M4a,4; M9a,5; M11,1; M11,2; M11,3; and M11a,1.

> the city – where people make the most ruthless demands upon one another [...] and the struggle for existence grant the individual not a single moment of contemplation – indemnifies itself in memory and [...] the veil it has covertly woven out of our lives shows images of people less often than those of the sites of our encounters with others and ourselves.[129]

Dickens's exploration of the spatial qualities of time in fiction allows the insight that Dickens's/Copperfield's life could be compared to the topographical structure of the city itself. Dickens anticipates Benjamin's theorization of the fact that the labyrinthine city prompts one's encounter with oneself and memory, governing and recovering experience itself. If one sketched out the temporal life of Copperfield spatially – it would take on the structure of a city map. Not only would routes delineate the forward directions, the false starts and retracings, the errors, wrong-turnings and repetitions of the young Copperfield; it would also depict the coincidences and chance meetings – a quintessential part of city living – that arise in Copperfield's life, and which, as he becomes aware with hindsight, temporally anticipate the future.

Benjamin himself takes up the idea of exploring his life topographically. While sitting in a café on the Saint-Germain-des-Prés in Paris, he records:

> and with compelling force, I was struck by the idea of drawing a diagram of my life, and knew at the same moment exactly how it was to be done. With a very simple question I interrogated my past life, and the answers were inscribed, as if of their own accord, on a sheet of paper that I had with me. A year or two later, when I lost this sheet, I was inconsolable. I have never since been able to restore it as it arose before me then, resembling a series of family trees. Now, however, reconstructing its outline in thought without directly reproducing it, I would instead speak of a labyrinth.[130]

Another passage in *David Copperfield* suggesting the city as both palimpsest and archive is found in the chapter titled 'Agnes':

> I came into the quiet streets, where every stone was a boy's book to me. (*DC*, Narrator, ch. 60, p. 717)

The city space here is a text: it is inscribed with former experience; and conversely, experience is shaped in and by stone.[131] The streets are indelibly colored by Copperfield's younger imagination. He cannot return to a space with 'fresh eyes', despite the distance of time from which the older David approaches the city.

[129] 'A Berlin Chronicle', p. 614.

[130] Ibid.

[131] Particularly in *One-Way Street* (1923–1926, published 1928) but also in other works, Benjamin evinces how the street is in fact a concatenation of textual fragments, a linguistic cosmos: streets and traffic signs, names of places and buildings, billboards and adverts are juxtaposed in strange montages, yielding insights. Conversely, the text *One-Way Street* was penned to perform the spatial and linguistic form of a city.

Here is the paradox of repetition: despite the temporal or spatial distance from which one renews an acquaintance with a space, the haunting traces are close at hand and discernible; traces of old narrative cannot be avoided. David cannot but follow an old line of thought connected to that part of the pavement or to that window. Every object and surface is legible: space triggers old thoughts, old narratives: memory. Yet still difference remains. Notice Copperfield states, 'every stone was a boy's book to me', not 'every stone was a book to me'. This slight degree of difference, like the subtle magic of Muybridge's photographs, opens up the truth about experience. One cannot repeat the past experience as it was. One cannot but repeat the experience, knowing the narratives/routes one follows as one scans the city surfaces are/were 'the boy's'; yet one cannot retrace them without registering one's distance from them in the process of repeating it.

Benjamin, in some moods, laments that one can never repeat the experience of encountering a city 'for the first time'.[132] Dickens, or the narrator Copperfield, appear to be quite aware of, and even reconciled to, the re-inscriptive nature of experiencing the past and its articulation in autobiography. City experience is 'there' to be read and overwritten again and again in a series of repetitions and renewals: repetitions in the shape of visiting the city or in writing about such a visit.

The fact that one can never repeat an experience as it was is offset by the fact that painful emotions can be revived. Some routes or spaces are painful to revisit, even after years of distance. 'To be sure, there are parts of the city in which it was destined to have [...] deep and harrowing experiences, but in none of them was the place itself so much a part of the event.'[133]

At one point, Copperfield hesitates about wandering along one particular thought process/street:

> A dread falls on me here [...] I cannot bear to think of what did come [...] of what must come again, if I go on. (*DC*, ch. 31, p. 382)

The sense of the self being split during the experience of memory, then, does not prevent an experience from being lucid. When the narrator, Copperfield, claims, 'are things, not of many years ago, in my mind, but of the present instant. They are all before me, just as they were in the evil hour' (*DC*, ch. 11, p. 132), or 'I see and hear, rather than remember, as I write about it' (*DC*, ch. 45, p. 561), he exalts in the insistence of the past upon the present, an insistence which almost overpowers the present. And can involve strong, sometimes distressing emotion. But the very comment, 'these are things not of many years ago, in my mind', or 'I see, I hear' situates the narrator in a self-conscious relation to past events described, so the lens of 'the present' by necessity always remains. A strangely double, simultaneous exposure to events, or Benjamin's 'dialectical image' (a temporal montage of past and present) is the inevitable result. Dickens's/Copperfield's delight at the past's

[132] *One-Way Street*, p. 468.

[133] 'A Berlin Chronicle', p. 603.

seeming so present points to the notion, contra Proust, that within the parameters of intellectually willed memory – if one can define autobiography in such a way, even apparently uncontrolled and freewheeling autobiography – lucid moments and images can open up and preserve 'something of the past itself' (Proust's requirement, cited above).

Another example of how Dickens/David experience memory as forming something akin to Benjamin's 'dialectical image' is the following passage:

> Can I say of her face – altered as I have reason to remember it, perished as I know it is – that it is gone, when here it comes before me at this instant as distinct as any face that I may choose to look on in a crowded street? (*DC*, Narrator, ch. 2, p. 21)

This passage is a montage of temporalities, a pulling together, or simultaneity or arrangement of delicate fragments.[134] There is the present: Copperfield the narrator, recalling his past – as well as the moment from which his mother's remembered face emerges. But almost simultaneously – or in the tiny length of time it takes the reader to scan Dickens's words – an image from an 'altered' (older?) mother, plus yet another from her deathbed or a funeral scene are triggered, ahead of returning to the lively face of a presumably young, carefree Mrs Copperfield, which the narrator claims is so lucid and epiphanic, it breaks through into the present. Copperfield's astonishment at memory's capacity to, as it were, resurrect the dead in the present moment is echoed by Benjamin: 'This image [of Benjamin's friend] is already now that of a dead man.'[135] Its revelatory character comes close to the past's flowering in the Proustian involuntary memory:

> For an experienced event is finite – at any rate confined to one sphere of experience; a remembered event is infinite, because it is only a key to everything that happened before it and after it.[136]

As Benjamin attributes to Proust, Copperfield's recounting of this memory, then, is a representation of a delicate appearance of truth – or the absolute – a truth that a careful attention to memory makes available in everyday life.

Copperfield's choice of analogy is the characteristically modernist face in the crowd.[137] The face in the crowd is fleeting, difficult to spot and usually indistinct.

---

[134] As stated in the introduction, simultaneity of arrangement of significant fragments has been a key component of this project. The synchronic approach toward elements of Benjamin and Dickens brought together in comparisons – the kind of analysis which would not be possible through a diachronic perspective – echoes the 'dialectical images' of Benjamin's historiography, as well as, here, Dickens fictional delineation of how memory works.

[135] 'A Berlin Chronicle', p. 604.

[136] 'The Image of Proust', *Illuminations*, p. 198.

[137] Imagist poet Ezra Pound's ideogrammatic poem 'In a Station of the Metro' focused upon the face in the crowd as the most concrete image of modern life (*Poetry Magazine* 2.1 [April 1913]).

Even if one strains to pick out a face in the crowd, that image of a face is in a state of flux, and the self is in motion in relation to it. It is unstable and soon fades, though its impact is great. A face, a snatched moment caught in the context of the bustling city is, for Copperfield in the excerpt, analogous to the way memories appear and disappear in life itself. The mind's 'form' is like a city in which memories – whose content is often of the city and triggered by an engagement with the city – appear before melting into the shadows. Memories appear as isolated snapshots; they are delicate and unstable entities, which illuminate dramatically and then fade. But their textured, layered temporalities – in which months or years flash up in a single moment – are monadic and 'truthful. The 'truth' emerges from a tiny fragment.

## *Déjà Vu*

The experience of déjà vu feeds into the analysis of memory as a 'double exposure' to events of the past. In déjà vu there is an indistinct recognition at some level that one has 'been here' and 'done this' or 'said that' before. It is a recognition that simultaneously estranges us from and reconnects us to our environment. It is a vague mental impression of repetition and the result is uncanny. Here is Dickens's inclusion of déjà vu in *DC*:

> We have all some experience of a feeling, that comes over us occasionally, of what we are saying and doing having been said and done before, in a remote time – of our having been surrounded, dim ages ago, by the same faces, objects and circumstances – of our knowing perfectly what will be said next, as if we suddenly remembered it! (*DC*, Narrator, ch. 39, p. 483)

It is tempting to argue that the vagueness and disorientation of déjà vu belongs purely to the urban context; especially when Benjamin's theory of *Erlebnis* implies that the city dweller's ability to retain data is irrevocably eroded by the shocks of modern life. One could even understand déjà vu as the malfunction of the Proustian 'involuntary memory'. Rather than a chance encounter – a smell, a taste – prompting a moment of lucid opening onto the past, such a prompting is followed instead by a failure of unconscious data to flow out – a consequence, presumably, of Proustian 'unraveling' or amnesia. Even without Benjaminian theory, the habit of the repetitive rhythms of city life, where one follows the route to and from work on 'autopilot', affords a trancelike mental state in the commuter which is ripe for interruption by an uncanny experience like déjà vu.

Dickens can be understood to intend an analogy between the experience of déjà vu – 'of our knowing perfectly what will be said next, as if we suddenly remembered it!' – and the process of writing autobiography. Writing autobiography involves marshaling the fragmentary data of the past, just as does the process of memory. The quality of memory, like the quality of writing, varies according to the lucidity of its contents. The experience of déjà vu represents the most difficult and, in terms of power and clarity, the least productive 'memory' to work with for the Subject. Writer's block, when the autobiographer struggles to clarify an image in language is déjà vu's equivalent. Hard mental work needs to be done to coax the buried image of the (past) moment to the surface – both in writing and in the experience of déjà vu.

*Rendezvous*

Recognition is not only a reacquaintance with the original space, or with an old friend, but with ourselves – as temporal and spatial beings. On returning to Yarmouth, the narrator claims, 'The streets looked small, of course. The streets that we have only seen as children always do, I believe, when we go back to them' (*DC*, ch. 21, p. 258). Here, David experiences himself as 'spatial'. The movement implied by his altered viewpoint on the environment, affords a recognition or sudden confrontation with the self as subject to time, which is also a subjection to movement and space.

The self-reference involved in recognition is dramatized beautifully when David decides to pretend not to recognize Emily:

> a curious feeling came over me that made me pretend not to know her and pass by as if I were looking at something a long way off … (*DC*, Narrator, ch. 10, p. 121)

Here David is playing out the drama of the spatial self. While this encounter does not take place in London but in Yarmouth, and not amid tightly packed buildings, it has the structure of urban experience about it. There is a theatricality in it one can only attribute to the city space: which provides the backdrop – the crowd, reflective surfaces, traffic, empty streets or squares – that allows one to be for the other, to be seen 'distracted' or distant 'looking at something a long way off' in the public space regularly frequented by oneself and others. Copperfield could not convincingly stage his act of 'not seeing' Emily, unless there was a backdrop where distraction was possible. The irony of this pantomime of appearing self-contained in the encounter with the other is that the 'self' is anything but 'self-contained' – it is scattered spatially. In this example, Copperfield's selfhood is, as it were, the conjunction of three points – the point at which he appears, the distant point at which he gazes, and the point (Emily's) from which he imagines himself watched. There is an element of flânerie about it: the flâneur's sovereignty in the city was to be seen seeing or to be seen distracted in the street.

This evasion-encounter between David and Emily also has another significance, though. It is a symbolic anticipation of the couple's later relationship – a case, if you like, of 'futurity in the past', or novelistic prolepsis. When Emily is later 'ruined' by Steerforth, David will again avert his eyes and refuse to 'recognize' her. Again this second instance of failure to recognize tells us more about David than it does about Emily.

Dickens's staging of the coincidence is an evocation of the powerful reverberations such apparently trivial moments have. The character David reacts to the surprise of seeing someone he did not expect (though hoped) to meet by pretending not to see Emily: Emily just laughs at this masquerade. Coincidences of this sort punctuate the smooth surface of reality. They force one into self-consciousness about one's own space and time, in a trick of the light that déjà vu also works. And self-consciousness is exactly what the narrator, Copperfield, exhibits in his recounting of the event: 'a curious feeling came over me to pretend not to see her'.

### *Crossroads*

Coincidences, dramatized within space, within the space of the city, and within the space of the text, take place at a crossroads, or even at a nexus of many available routes. Decisions are sometimes forced upon characters and the narrator by chance events, which become a case of not going down this road, but that one. But the need to make a choice is itself of the greatest significance. Dickens reminds us that the mind is never stilled of the anxiety of what might have been. As the narrator says later: 'I considered how the things that never happen are often as much realities to us, in their effects, as those that are accomplished' (*DC*, ch. 58, p. 701).

Dickens, here, articulates how autobiography and memory, understood topographically, involve not 'a straight road' (as the narrator, Copperfield, suggested earlier) but a huge network or web of them. In some moods, Copperfield can look at the past as a kind of theater, a space where the writer and characters enact what could have been, as well as what was, and rehearse the circumstances and desires upon which decisions were made. Disappointment in the outcomes of what did occur often prompts the desire to play out parallel, alternative scenes. Here Dickens expresses the melancholy, regretful side of autobiography, of remembering. In piecing together fragments of what would have happened (conditional perfect tense) if one had continued down a route, some sort of relationship to truth is achieved, he suggests. At least, its effect (perhaps sadness) is real enough.

What is, in effect, Copperfield's thought experiment in imagining an alternative past has its equivalence in being lost in the city – in view of the suggested identity of mind, memory and the city in the novel. One might be lost, yet one would allow oneself to see how things turn out. Both Benjamin and Dickens write of such experiences:

> Now I was feeling quite contented with this forced, nearly pointless trip through a part of the city with which I was completely unfamiliar.[138]

> Long before I reached Wapping, I gave myself up as having lost my way, and, abandoning myself to the narrow streets in a Turkish frame of mind, relied on predestination to bring me somehow or other to the place I wanted, if I were ever to get there. (Dickens, 'Wapping Workhouse', *UT*, p. 44)

[138] *Moskauer Tagebuck* (Frankfurt a.M: Suhrkamp Verlag, 1980) – also in *GS*, VI, pp. 292–409; trans. Richard Sieburth as *Moscow Diary*, ed. Gary Smith (Cambridge, MA; London: Harvard University Press, 1986), p. 112.

Being lost, for Benjamin, opens up the city as gothic, uncanny and phantasmagoric more than if one knows it: the city's ability to shock and the necessity that one abandon oneself to its stimulation is all the more unalloyed. It offers an experience which is 'incomparable and so irrecoverable' because 'habit has not yet done its work'.[139] Inevitably, the self-reflexivity of the city means that being lost involves occupying a space so outside of one's usual physical and mental boundaries, it can lead to the crossing of an important threshold. In *OT*, for example, Dickens depicts two Londons in one city: having been lost to the well-heeled Londoners, Oliver discovers that underground, terrifying and grimy London inhabited by Fagin, his thieving boys and other criminals. In his topographic crossing of boundaries, then, Oliver crosses the threshold of his own class with everything that that means to his understanding of existence.

### *Narrative Structure, Reading, Rereading and Memory*

The structure of the narrative, as labyrinthine, fragmented and dominated by repetition – as 'miming' the formal structure of memory and the city – enables the reader to experience the operation of memory in the reading of the novel. An example of this is when Steerforth visits Yarmouth with Copperfield, and proceeds to tell a story of a shipwreck to the Peggottys. The narrator, David, is describing an event in his past – Steerforth's visit with him to Yarmouth and the Peggottys. But the event proves to be interpretable in relation to the future of the narrative; it is a symbolic anticipation of the emotional storm that will blow through the lives of the Peggottys and the deaths that will result from it (an example of prolepsis). Steerforth, the storyteller, is the author of the storm that will cause such destruction. This presentiment, too, is shared by Emily: 'little Em'ly's eyes were fastened on him all the time, as if she saw it too' (*DC*, ch. 21, p. 269). Emily's gaze, here, is a sign of her possible prescience of her part in the drama to come. The real shipwreck, foretold by Steerforth, then, will be a repetition for all characters concerned as well as for the reader – Steerforth's story comes first, then the event itself.

The recognition that Steerforth and Emily share the premonition of their fate comes to the reader only in retrospect – only after the reader has got toward the end of the novel. This process mirrors the model of how the narrator 'recognizes' this premonition in retrospect. As the reader gets further in the novel, she moves closer to the narrator's position of knowledge – that is to say, to a position where recognizing patterns in (past) events is possible.

Benjamin highlights what he terms a futurity in the past – the future which he calls 'that stranger' in the past – which one can only make sense of as an adult:

> the images, severed from all earlier associations, that stand – like precious fragments or torsos in a collector's gallery – in the sober rooms of our later insights.[140]

---

[139] Both quotations from *One-Way Street*, p. 468.

[140] 'A Berlin Chronicle', p. 611.

The same process is being staged in the reading of Dickens's novel. Much of Benjamin's writing concerns attempts to locate prophetic moments in what is past – moments that anticipate the future or await redemption in the future. And the shipwreck tale and death of Steerforth and Ham in the storm is an example of just this pattern of futurity in the past in Dickens's novel.

The reading process also mimes the way trivial events or details in life change meaning in retrospect. In his earlier memory of Steerforth, for instance, Copperfield's narrative if anything, directs us to the straightforward untainted view of Steerforth as hero, a view which is that of the boy David:

> 'You haven't got a sister have you?' said Steerforth, yawning.
> 'No', I answered.
> 'That's a pity', said Steerforth. 'If you had had one, I should think she would have been a pretty, timid, little, bright-eyed sort of girl. I should have liked to know her. Goodnight, young Copperfield.'
> I thought of him very much after I went to bed, and raised myself, I recollect, to look at him where he lay in the moonlight, with his handsome face turned up, and his head reclining easily on his arm. He was a person of great power in my eyes. (*DC*, ch. 6, p. 76)

Once we have read the novel, we can view Steerforth's question about David's having a sister being one laden with irony considering how he 'ruined' Emily, who could be seen as Copperfield's 'sister'. But on first reading of Steerforth's question, we view it as a question without any extraneous connotations, mirroring the view David takes of it at that point, mirroring the original experience Copperfield would have had in life. Similarly, in the writing of the 'autobiography', Copperfield knows Steerforth is to become a 'cad'; hence in the writing of his autobiography, in the repetition of it, he will view such a question as loaded with irony.

The novel's retrospective (autobiographical) stance stages the way viewing events in memory, in retrospect, allows one the insight that the meaning of events are always changing, the way the meaning of photographs change once the subject has died. This uncannily Benjaminian way of gathering up experience retrospectively, acknowledges the complexity and density of fragments of experience and memory, allowing the reader to do likewise.

## Experience and Memory: Concluding Remarks

This chapter has been an engagement with Charles Dickens and Walter Benjamin, in terms of their articulation of experience and memory – with an accent upon points of affinity and interconnection. For Benjamin, *Erlebnis*, an attenuated form of experience necessitated by the shock, and characterized by repetition and depthlessness, is a transformation in the structure of experience, a formulation suggesting that interaction with the city's physical pace and rhythm has an effect upon how one experiences and represents the world. Dickens, it has been argued, experienced city life in this way, and such experience made its way into his fictions – in terms of both form and content. He depicted characters as experiencing life in these terms too – yet it is not being suggested that Dickens consciously went out to represent *Erlebnis* in his writings. Rather, his evocation of *Erlebnis* and *Chockerlebnis*, of urban experience, is a result of Dickens's powerful creative imagination.

What is being suggested, in other words, is that Benjamin's theory of experience has provided a notion of Dickensian form. The amorphousness and fragmentariness that are such features of Benjamin's modern experience are analogous to the disclosures of fragmentary significance depicted in Dickens's novels, and which therefore amount to a form of mimesis on Dickens's part. Dickens gets hold of something about the nature of modernity which Benjamin will later also get hold of – by other means.

It can be argued that Dickens, the great literary figure, does not need further evidence to prove what a quintessential urban artist he is. Yet here, his literary expression of a modern urban experience, *Erlebnis*, as described by Benjamin, is precisely that. He does not just set his novels in the city, and depict the exigencies and disruptions of city life, then; he also expresses, through his narrative form, how the city is experienced.

For Benjamin, the transition from *Erfahrung*, a fuller experience, to the more attenuated *Erlebnis* represents something of a loss: a loss that can to an extent be redeemed retrospectively. One can make time and space for memory – which floods into view at the most contingent and unexpected of moments. By nurturing the unconscious life, the dreams and phantasms that harbor the data one is unable to experience fully at the time, one can, Benjamin claims with respect to Proust, even (re)produce experience synthetically. While Dickens does not, like Proust, depict the process of the epiphanic appearance of 'involuntary memory', he does depict the difficult process of gathering up memories in *DC*. It turns out to be an equally delicate procedure; one which collapses into fragmentation, infinite regress and recapitulation. This mnemonic process is generated by and dependent upon flânerie. Copperfield – like Dickens himself (as argued in detail in Chapter 4) – incessantly visits and revisits the site of his former experiences in the city, a gothic, phantasmagoric space that reflects, reconstitutes and reconstructs his experience of his selfhood with each visitation. This repetitive encounter with the self in the city space is, as has been suggested, the Dickensian version of the Proustian 'epiphany'. The importance to Dickens of flânerie, dreaming and memory in the city is also, of course, where Dickens comes into relationship with one of Benjamin's main figures in his urban writings, Charles Baudelaire. The affinities between Baudelaire and Dickens, together with Benjamin's use of fragments concerning Dickens in *The Arcades Project*, will be opened up, again, in Chapter 4.

But a number of points arise from the argument so far. If Dickens's representations include an expression of *Erlebnis* and *Chockerlebnis*, then it is suggested that these areas should be taken in conjunction with his breaking up of smooth narratives or totalized visions of the world as identified in the *Copperfield* analysis. And this conjunction amounts to Dickens's response to modernity. Dickens is expressing an urban aesthetic. Dickens is an urban artist whose fragmented forms, 'filmic' angles or montaged sequences emerge as an aesthetic normally attributed to much later London novelists and artists, literary Modernists such as Virginia Woolf or urban Impressionists like Whistler or Monet. Moreover, if Dickens delineates the discontinuity, the constantly mutating, noisy, nerve-wracking stimulation of life in the streets, he does it in the optical mode which, Benjamin notes, Georg Simmel announces as the preponderant way one experiences big cities.[141] As noted earlier, Dickens's tendency to think and represent in images – even evoking the movement of time and space through the representation of a close succession of images – is a quality that has captured the attention of filmmakers and critics alike.

Further, it should be added – though, alas, there is not space to argue for this at length – that Dickens's expression of, his debt to, the melodramatic mode is a fact which underlines Dickens's place as the greatest of modern urban writers. If it is assumed that melodramatic Dickens was exactly the Dickens from which the artists of Realism, *l'art pour l'art* and Modernism tried to distance themselves, what is being claimed here is that it is precisely the melodramatic strain within Dickens's fictions that underlines the success of his urban mimesis.[142] Benjamin's theory of *Erlebnis* is important, here. What governs *Erlebnis*, after all, is 'the shock', interruption, repetition. The nervous stimulation that city living involves must determine a variety of emotional states; but they must center around the experiences of 'an anxious, hyper-conscious state' as Benjamin puts it. The melodramatic mode, with its emotional contrasts, its highs and lows (the stripes in a side of streaky bacon for Dickens), provides the emotional register flexible enough to capture such city experience.[143] As Dickens himself described the relationship between modern urban life and melodrama: 'The transitions in real life from well-spread boards to death-beds, and from mourning weeds to holiday garments, are not a whit less startling' than those that occur in melodrama. 'We are busy actors [...] blind to violent transitions and abrupt impulses of passion or feeling', which, he claims appear 'outrageous and preposterous' when viewed from the outside (all three quotations from *OT*, ch. 17, p. 106).

If Dickens's art shows signs of breaking up totalized visions and expressing chopped-up, hyper-real fragments of urban reality, then, the melodramatic mode seems the perfect complement to such an aesthetics of the urban. The vampiric relationship that existed between urban and popular theatrical culture during Dickens's years of production has been brilliantly and comprehensively surveyed by at least three recent critics and does not need to be rehearsed here.[144]

---

141 'Second Empire', pp. 19–20.

142 Grahame Smith includes a fascinating chapter on Dickens, melodrama and film in 'Smith', pp. 102–18.

143 *Oliver Twist*, ed. Kathleen Tillotson (Oxford: Clarendon Press, 1966), ch. 17, p. 105.

144 Paul Schlicke, *Dickens and Popular Entertainment* (London: Allen & Unwin, 1985); Deborah Vlock, *Dickens, Novel-Reading and the Victorian Popular Theatre* (Cambridge: Cambridge University Press, 1998); and Juliet John, *Dickens's Villains: Melodrama, Character and Popular Culture* (Oxford: Oxford University Press, 2001).

Furthermore, Dickens's evocation of the emotional extremes and shocking sensations of living in the city, his, as it were, miming of *Erlebnis* and *Chockerlebnis*, must be related to the genre of the sensation novel. The Dombey passage and 'A Flight' discussed in this chapter are instructive here. As argued with respect to them, not only does Dickens's content depict city experience, not only do his characters experience the rhythms, syncopations, sudden disruptions and shocks of urban experience – but the narrative form is also designed to enable the reader to experience the fictional world on these terms. It cannot be argued at length here but, in this light, the sensation novel, the medium whose raison d'être was to bombard the reader with shocks and provide a hyper-aware, fast-paced, dislocated and thrilling vision of the urban world, is an important form in the development of Dickens's work. As will be argued further in the following chapter, the sensation novel is, possibly, the site where the notion of the urban 'shock', of epistemological uncertainty in the crowd, the gothic city and the detective's peripatetic attempt to master it all, come together in one genre.[145]

One last point needs to be made. Dickens's handling of fragments of memory, his nurturing of his own dreamworld and imagination in his flânerie (and in Copperfield's and many other of his fictional characters) and, as has been argued, his tendency to depict the appearance of revelatory ruptures or moments – in Benjaminian terms, the breaking through of an immanent absolute – brings him into a relationship with Surrealism. As André Breton puts it: 'The street [is] the only valid field of experience'; and, as has been suggested, Dickens devotes himself to delineating that experience.[146] This, it might be contended, is hardly surprising since, as has been intimated all along, Benjamin's interest in thinking a fuller experience, his concern with the rupture of the extraordinary within the everyday, his fascination with the Surrealist notion of 'Profane Illumination', guarantees that the comparison of Benjamin with Dickens presented here would imply as much. But it is an important point to pause upon. It points the way to understanding Dickens as an artist whose representation of experience involves an implicit and mature awareness of the variety of heightened moods, affective states, dreamlike perspectives necessitated by the urban environment; and an intention that any representation of experience of the world must encompass all or any of them. For Dickens, the material world is no more real than the imaginary one: in fact, Dickensian experience implies that the two are indistinguishable. His representation of experience reflects the fact that the everyday is an extraordinary place; his sometimes hallucinatory eye upon a scene, his 'imaginative empathy'[147] with violence in scenes of conflagration and riot, indeed, his delineation of the murderers Jonas Chuzzlewit or Bill Sikes, exhibits the eye of a proto-surrealist

[145] An essay by Benjamin, 'Detective Novels, on Journeys', claims the detective novel is essential reading for railway journeys because its thrills and spills eclipse the traveler's anxieties about traveling. *GS*, IV, 1, pp. 381–2.

[146] Breton quoted in Benjamin's essay 'Marseilles', in *SW*, II, p. 232.

[147] Carey, *The Violent Effigy*, p. 19.

who senses the world is experienced in more than flat, 'realist' terms. Benjamin's interest in the Surrealists opened him up to the disruptive, strange side of reality, as he searched for a materialist formulation of experience that allowed for the appearance of the absolute. Dickens's ability to build in the emotional or affective aspects of experience, back in the mid nineteenth century, involves a delineation of *Erlebnis* and *Chockerlebnis*, an incorporation of melodrama and sensation; and an uncanny anticipation of the fragmentary, revelatory nature of reality, which would explode into the Surrealist project.

# Chapter 4
# The Gothic City of the Flâneur and the Crowd

Chapter 4, the second part of this section on 'Dickens, Benjamin and the City', is a further opening up of urban themes in the novels of Dickens; this time, with respect to the more well-known material on modern urban experience identifiable in Benjamin's writings on the French poet, Baudelaire. The discussion will be organized around three main themes: the motifs of 'the flâneur' and 'the crowd' and the gothic city which they inhabit. Within this framework, an attempt will be made to bring out how Benjamin uses the concepts and what meaning(s) and nuances they appear to have, given that such assessments have to be pieced together from the inexhaustible fragments which make up Benjamin's kaleidoscopic presentation. The aim is to throw light upon what kind of urban subjectivity and existence Benjamin's engagement with Baudelaire can be understood to imply. And how does it relate to the quintessential urban novelist, Charles Dickens? Identifying how flânerie and the crowd work within Dickens's imagination, the other main thrust of the discussion, helps clarify and broaden the investigation of the themes, as well as providing an interesting reading of Dickens as an artist in his own right. An obvious corollary to this approach is the issue of how closely Benjamin's and Dickens's vision of the city and modern urban experience can be seen to relate; and what this state of affairs implies about their visions of the city, their imaginations and the intellectual and historical contexts which produced both writers.

Before the main discussion gets underway, it is important to outline the philosophical aims behind the main body of writings from which Benjamin's urban themes emanate. Those writings are *The Arcades Project*, a collection of materials Benjamin worked upon from 1927 until his death in 1940. Briefly, a relationship to Benjamin's earlier theological works – those works discussed in the first chapter of this book – will be established. Also, an affinity of Benjamin's project to Dickens's interest in objects, clues and fragments will be suggested. *The Arcades Project* is undoubtedly central to Benjamin's oeuvre and a little background to it will position the reader in terms of Benjamin's considerable output, as well as in terms of what is being attempted in this project.

### *The Arcades Project*

For 13 years Benjamin devoted himself to researching a project on material history, what was later entitled *The Arcades Project* (in English) – in German, *Das Passagen-Werk* or as Benjamin called it, *Das Passagenarbeit* or *Passagen*. This vast, unfinished collection of 36 files (convolutes) comprising citations, sketches, reflections and literary fragments – the manuscript of which was hidden by the philosopher Georges Bataille in Paris's Bibliothèque Nationale de France during the war – was an attempt by Benjamin to anatomize nineteenth-century material history and thereby to draw out an understanding of his historical present in the twentieth century.[1] Benjamin's Marxist-inspired, materialist methodology took commodities and other fragments of mass culture of the nineteenth century as objects of study. Benjamin, *contra* Marx, understood culture to be an 'expression' of the outcomes of relations of production of the economic base, not merely something determined by it:

> Marx lays bare the causal connection between economy and culture. For us, what matters is the thread of expression. It is not the economic origins of culture that will be presented, but the expression of the economy in its culture.[2]

Commodities, advertisements, material culture and so on, then, were not only the concrete manifestation of processes of production. They crystallized consciousness: they were symbols of, they expressed the pervading consciousness of nineteenth-century capitalism. And, since capitalist economy and the culture which 'symbolizes' it continues, these past traces were a source of politically empowering knowledge of both the collective past and concomitantly, of the present.

Benjamin's historiography honored the concrete material history of nineteenth-century Paris because Paris was the European capital which most represented the 'era of high capitalism'.[3] The inception of a mass consumer culture in Paris and its development opened up questions and issues that were crucial to an understanding of modernity and to formulating a Marxist critique of it.[4] The Parisian shopping arcades (popular between c.1820–1840) themselves became the central motif of the project because they symbolized, through their status as faded relics of the consumer economy, the relentless waxing and waning of the capitalist market; and the dashed dreams and hopes this literally implied.

Predictably, Benjamin's project did not only involve the seeking out and presentation of historical materials; it generated a philosophical investigation into the nature of historiography itself. *The Arcades Project* would not be a narrative

---

1 The *Passagen* material was secreted away by Bataille on Benjamin's request as he made his escape from the Nazis. For a fuller account of Benjamin's fatal journey, see Appendix 1 of this book. The *Passagen* material was retrieved from Paris and taken to New York in 1947. It was published as *Das Passagen-Werk*, volume 5 of Benjamin's *Gesammelte Schriften* (Complete Works) in German in 1982. It was published in English in 1999.

2 *Arcades*, N1a,6.

3 The English title for a collection of translated essays on Baudelaire was called *Charles Baudelaire: A Lyric Poet in the Era of High Capitalism*, trans. Harry Zohn and Quintin Hoare (London: N.L.B., 1973).

4 One or two theorists have questioned Benjamin's choice of Paris over London. This chapter implies a similar questioning.

overview of the nineteenth-century epoch.[5] The present was not determined by the past, nor was history an ongoing story of progress. What 'the past' and 'the present' actually are was undecided for Benjamin, amid the material and ideological struggles of our culture. The victor of such struggles announces his worldview and everything that supports it as the (official) past, consigning everything else to the dustbin of history.[6]

History, then, is always a site of struggle and Benjamin was trying to redeem the history of the oppressed, to recover and hear the voices who had never spoken.[7] The only way to listen to such neglected whispers was to gather the ruins and fragments, the ordinary experiences that history had always regarded as rubbish: and there one would discover an historical truth: 'the eternal [...] is far more the ruffle on a dress than some idea'.[8]

Finding the most banal, worthless objects and events, the most quotidian spaces and experiences, the smallest passed-over details was crucial, here. He sought the sort of material the grand narratives of official history excluded. Such zealous preoccupation with the redemption and remembrance of buried histories was, as the language suggests, not only inspired by Marxist concerns with historical injustices, but (as has been the case all along) was concomitantly driven by Jewish theological concepts, including Messianism.[9] Benjamin uses the concept with respect to its rôle in historiography several times in his 'Theses on the Philosophy of History',[10] claiming that historical materialism can always win the cultural struggles over history as long as its operations are guided by theology.[11]

Benjamin's findings were presented as concretely and discontinuously as possible. His paratactic form would scatter history 'through space like stars'.[12] He sought out his momentary, accidental, neglected fragments and 'allowed them

---

5 Here, one could argue, Benjamin comes close to Jean-François Lyotard's position that our era is one that has witnessed the collapse of the grand narrative: see Lyotard's *The Postmodern Condition: A Report on Knowledge*, trans. Geoff Bennington and Brian Massumi (Minneapolis: University of Minnesota Press, 1983). Benjamin's relationship to Postmodernism is a complex area which cannot be gone into here.

6 See Thesis VII, 'Theses on the Philosophy of History', in *Illuminations*, p. 248. Hereafter referred to as 'Theses'.

7 Thesis VII, 'Theses', p. 248.

8 *Arcades*, N3,2.

9 This point is developed in Rolf Tiedemann's 'Historical Materialism or Political Messianism?' in *Benjamin: Philosophy, Aesthetics, History*, ed. Gary Smith (London, Chicago: University of Chicago Press, 1989), pp. 175–209. Smith's book will hereafter be referred to as 'Smith, *Benjamin*'.

10 See Thesis II, 'Theses', pp. 245–6.

11 See Thesis I, the famous image of a puppet in Turkish dress (representing historical materialism) whose strings are being worked by a hidden 'hunchback' (representing theology), 'Theses', p. 245.

12 His use of parataxis even functions at the level of the sentence in some instances. It is literal as well as being an epistemological position.

to speak', rendering them in all their concreteness. This was achieved by omitting formulations, theory or abstraction. Paring down language to the bare necessities, excluding theory as much as possible, was crucial: historical truth is objectively present in the objects/material details themselves and the historian's job is to allow that truth to disclose itself. The subjective presence of the historian needed to be kept to a minimum. As Benjamin puts it: 'I needn't say anything. Merely Show. I shall purloin no valuables, appropriate no ingenious formulations. But the rags, the refuse – these I will not inventory but allow, in the only way possible, to come into their own.'[13] The resonances this position has with Benjamin's language theory, the language of objects discussed in Chapter 1, is clear.

Moreover, the significance of 'the rags, the refuse' was something Dickens explored in his writings. For the novelist, there was a serious moral error at the heart of a society that worshiped the profit motive, but advocated a laissez-faire approach toward the suffering of the poor. The omnipresence of objects and the trade in remaindered goods, antiques, rags and bric-a-brac in his fiction can be viewed as having a similar effect to the *Arcades*: it points to an unending and meaningless cycle of exchange, a state of affairs where human lives appear spectral and valueless in comparison to all important, palpable commodities. Marx's theory of commodity fetishism, a central component of the *Arcades*, can be found in Dickens's presentation of the economy in some novels.[14] For instance, Dickens satirizes society's obsession with status and wealth by presenting the Harmon legacy in *OMF* as built upon mounds of excrement, which works as literal and metaphorical. Evidence of a character's commodity fetishism from the same novel comes in the shape of Nicodemus Boffin's love of window shopping and his fetishistic attitude toward the purchase of books on misers. Similarly, Grandfather Trent's plans to make a fortune are equally based upon dust (gambling). His curiosities, which after all are just heaps of old commodities, have a home, while Nell and grandfather are expelled from the shop and are homeless. Meanwhile, there are a plethora of grotesque dealers in secondhand or stolen goods or rags clawing a living: Krook (*BH*); Fagin (*OT*); Sol Gills (*DS*). And the abject marginality of underground trade can take the form of characters literally feeding off corpses: Gaffer Hexam, Wegg and Venus (*OMF*); Smallweed (*BH*); Jerry Cruncher, body snatcher (*TTC*); Joe and Mrs Dilber, the cronies who pawn the dead Scrooge's cloths and bedlinen (*C*). By portraying money-making as a concern with 'dust' or 'corpses', Dickens suggests not only the metaphysical insubstantiality of the profit motive, but seems to be going further in claiming it is unnatural and cannibalistic.[15] While the cannibalistic Hexams and Dilbers

---

[13] *Arcades*, N1a,8.

[14] 'This fetish character of the commodity world has its origin in the peculiar social character of the labour that produces commodities', Benjamin quoting Marx, *Arcades*, G5,1.

[15] The image of capitalism as cannibalistic is in the *Arcades*, where Benjamin suggests that the temporality of fashion, its obsession with newness, has a link with death; desire and prostitution with the corpse: see *The Arcades Project*, B1,4.

are presented as revolting enough, what is really under attack, surely, are the lengths to which people must go to survive within the amoral world of capitalist economics.

Even the sexual economy's castoffs, prostitutes, while firmly positioned as 'immoral' and dealt with accordingly by Dickens (Martha Endell is exiled in *DC*, Nancy is killed off in *OT*), are simultaneously presented as victims of a system of exchange greater than themselves. Objects are omnipresent in Dickens's writings then and, like Benjamin, truths, meanings emerge from an attention to society's detritus and 'rubbish'.[16] Perhaps the most Benjaminian appreciation of the power of objects to offer up rich interpretations are two of Dickens's *Sketches by Boz*. 'Meditations on Monmouth-street' (*SB*, scenes: ch. 6, pp. 96–104), features an elongated improvisation upon a couple of suits of clothes spotted during a window-shopping session, which develops into the story of a man's life and ruin.[17] And 'Brokers' and Marine-store Shops' (*SB*, scenes: ch. 21, pp. 209–13): scrutinizing minor articles in a marine store, Dickens celebrates the fact that they disclose the quality and historical period of the neighborhood from which they come. Some of the goods have a theatrical flair to them, pointing to a fad for amateur dramatics that took hold at a certain time in certain sections of the London population (*SB*, scenes: ch. 21, p. 212).

In building imaginatively and creatively upon useless fragments/objects in this way, Dickens displays an uncannily Benjaminian tendency.[18] As was mentioned in Chapter 1, Dickens's physiognomic tendencies, his interest in reading the hieroglyphic language of the object, his producing a novel like *OCS*, is fascinating in view of Benjamin's language theory and his theory of allegory. Dickens's physiognomy of objects in the scenes mentioned from *Sketches* echoes Benjamin's allegorist collector, who, as both obsessive commodity fetishist and seeker after the truth of objects, Benjamin claims is both a rescuer and a physiognomist of 'the world of objects'.[19]

---

[16] A point made in Carey, *The Violent Effigy*, p. 49.

[17] This appreciation of the story objects, especially ragged or secondhand clothes, can tell is an important literary legacy that many writers, including Samuel Beckett, inherited. Estragon's boots and Vladimir's hat in *Waiting for Godot* (1955), for example, are a major source of meaning in that play.

[18] This is a rich area of study and, alas, there is not room to do justice to a discussion of Dickens, Benjamin and what could be entitled 'the poetics of the disposable' in this book. This would include a discussion of Benjamin's theory of the language of objects, his essays on collecting and Dickens's treatment of objects and collecting in his novels. Kevin McLaughlin in *Writing in Parts: Imitation and Exchange in Nineteenth-Century Literature* (Stanford, CA: Stanford University Press, 1995) does to some extent take up this topic, reading *SB* and *PP* in terms of Benjamin's collector. A brief discussion of Dickens's relationship to another important theme in *The Arcades Project*, the capitalist myth of progress, can be found in Appendix 1. See also Grace Moore, 'Turkish robbers, lumps of delight, and the detritus of empire: the east revisited in Dickens's late novels', *Critical Survey* 21.1 (January 2009): pp. 75–88, where Moore reads Dickens in relation to the empire through his treatment of objects.

[19] 'Unpacking My Library', *Illuminations*, p. 62.

To return to the methodology of *The Arcades Project*, Benjamin arranges his historical materials according to the principles of montage, constructions which were then the source of epiphanic images. The past's material trace, in a temporal montage with the present moment, enables the opening up of historical truth in a graphic flash. This intense, explosive moment Benjamin termed the 'dialectical image'. But there is no definitive theoretical account of what the 'dialectical image' is or under what conditions it can or cannot occur. In a fascinating exchange of letters, Adorno questions Benjamin's use of the 'dialectical image', throwing doubt on its efficacy as a valid methodological tool.[20] Yet it seems there is no question that the notion of the 'dialectical image' offers a radical alternative to how temporal relations are normally understood, of what 'the past' and 'the present' are in terms of each other. It was suggested in the introduction that the synchronic approach adopted for this study, the significant fragments of Dickens and Benjamin presented together, mirrors Benjamin's theory of how truth appears in this respect.

As David Ferris puts it, for Benjamin neither 'the past' nor 'the present' should be approached from the premise that they are fixed moments, as if they stood outside of time like an absolute.[21] Historical meaning lives beyond the moment it originally occurred and explodes into significance in the hands of later historical observers. But this historical experience is only legible at that specific moment; and Benjamin wants to cultivate a culture that is somehow more open to the precious occurrence of historical happenings. His immersion in the material history of nineteenth-century Paris yields essential information about the crucial issues of his day: 'The materialist presentation of history leads the past to bring the present into a critical state.'[22]

The project's material traces were monadological fragments, collectibles that, interpreted in a particular light – in the present – would provide an encyclopedia of their age and ours. If apprehended suddenly – through the 'dialectical image' – these precious hieroglyphs or clues opened the secrets of philosophical and historical truth. Like the ruins of the *Trauerspiele* (the Baroque mourning plays discussed in Chapter 1), they contain totality within themselves. And, brought together with the other fragments in *The Arcades Project*, like a curiosity shop window or the exhibits at a nineteenth-century exposition, they formed a curious mosaic.

---

[20] See the exchange of letters between Benjamin and Adorno in *Aesthetics and Politics*, trans. and ed. Ronald Taylor (London; New York: Verso 1977), pp. 100–134. Margaret Cohen points out that (mostly in response to the criticisms of Adorno) Benjamin refrains from using the term 'dialectical image' in his later synopsis of *The Arcades Project*, the exposé of 1939. But he had used it up until that point. See Cohen, 'Benjamin's Phantasmagoria: *The Arcades Project*', in David Ferris (ed.), *The Cambridge Companion to Walter Benjamin* (Cambridge; New York: Cambridge University Press, 2004), pp. 207–8. Hereafter referred to as 'Companion'.

[21] 'Introduction: Reading Benjamin', in *Companion*, p. 14.

[22] *Arcades*, N7a,5.

Fig. 4.1 'Dickens's Dream.' This famous watercolour, begun by Robert W. Buss (1804–1875) after Dickens's death in June 1870, is, in a sense, a montage. The source of the painting lies in a number of images brought together in one presentation. Its setting was taken from Luke Fildes's engraving 'The Empty Chair'. The figure of Dickens was painted from John and Charles Watkins's 1861 photograph of the novelist. The universe of characters of which Dickens 'dreams' were created by, among others, George Cruikshank. Buss died before completing the work. Reproduced by courtesy of the Charles Dickens Museum, London.

Benjamin honored his fragments' fragmentariness.[23] His aim was 'to detect the crystal of the total event in the analysis of the small, discrete object'.[24] The individual fragments had a relation to the whole, but it was a relation which ensured they were not merely sober details given their position within a master narrative.

[23] This theoretical turn of thinking fragmentariness was addressed by, among many others, French philosopher, Maurice Blanchot (1907–2003) – but Benjamin was also part of this body of scholarship. See Blanchot's 'The Athenaeum' and 'The Fragment Word' in *The Infinite Conversation* (Minneapolis: University of Minnesota Press, 1993).

[24] *Arcades*, N2,6.

The form of *The Arcades Project* ensured that historical meaning would, rather, be disclosed from 'the bottom' (the fragments) upwards.[25]

Verbal, pictorial or photographic/cinematic montage was the mode of representation Benjamin believed most capable of capturing the fluidity and dynamism of urban modernity, and, by implication, of one's experience of it.

Indeed, montage, parataxis, resembled the discontinuous and shockingly dissonant quality of one's experience of urban space with its rapid assault upon the senses.[26] The montage aspect of the 'dialectical image' was influenced by French Surrealism,[27] its shock 'awakening' the Subject from the enchanted sleep of capitalism, a political dimension to montage shared by many artists of interest to Benjamin.[28]

*The Arcades Project* can be viewed as part of a more general epistemological project, which included essays such as 'On Language as Such and On the Language of Man' (1916), 'The Concept of Criticism in German Romanticism' (1919) and *The Origin of German Tragic Drama* (1925).[29] His challenge in those works had been to assess the extent to which language could redeem meaning in a situation where 'the Absolute' could no longer express itself. His conclusion was that a certain style of writing – allegorical, aphoristic, esoteric – could express 'the Inexpressible', at least in part. Similarly for the Benjamin of the *Arcades*, the present, modernity, was a site of crisis, a place where a new way of disclosing philosophical and political truths needed to be thought. The time of writing, during the rise of fascism, generated this philosophical task – as much a political one as a need to think modernity. For Benjamin, the present was a site of loss, no longer capable of the kind of philosophical, historical and political truths that there had once been.[30] If one couches it in terms of his earlier theological concerns, modernity was a site of fallenness and part of the present's modernity would be expressed in the way it now comported itself toward an understanding of the past. Hence, exactly how knowledge and historical truth could be given to us within

[25] It is worth noting that *The Arcades Project* itself is an 'unfinished', literary fragment. See Appendix 1 for a brief rehearsal of the significance of this status.

[26] As has been suggested, a number of theorists view the techniques of early cinema as 'aping' the discontinuity and fragmentariness of modern experience.

[27] Esther Leslie argues that, for Benjamin, the Surrealist project was an engagement with the debate over 'experience', their forging of a new constructive aesthetic form being an attempt to expand experience – Leslie, p. 20.

[28] Benjamin was a great advocate of Eisenstein's cinematic techniques which included, famously, montage. He wrote on Russian cinema, including the essay 'On the Present Situation of Russian Film' published in *Die Literarische Welt* in March 1927 (in *SW*, II, pp. 12–15). Benjamin was also interested in the photomontage work of Weimar artist John Heartfield (1891–1968), whom he met in Paris in 1935.

[29] 'On Language', in *SW*, I, pp. 62–74; 'The Concept of Criticism', in *SW*, I, pp. 116–200.

[30] The philosopher Andrew Benjamin develops Walter Benjamin's construal of the present as a 'site of loss'. See his *Present Hope: Philosophy, Architecture, Judaism* (London; New York: Routledge, 1997).

the time of the now, at the time of crisis, was always the issue. And Benjamin always already foregrounds this issue/problem in the mind of the reader by his formulation of a style of writing (aphorisms, esoteric writing, digression) that was not so much a medium for his thought, as being a use of language that generates thought through its very form.[31]

The experience of historical truth as 'the dialectical image' is expressed in terms of a visual model – the image – resembling the Surrealist 'profane illumination'.[32] One recovers the past when it presents itself in terms of an image at the moment of interruption in a dialectical interchange between the past and present:

> To thinking belongs the movement as well as the arrest of thoughts. Where thinking comes to a standstill in a constellation saturated with tensions – there the dialectical image appears. It is the caesura in the movement of thought.[33]

Historical experience happens in images (rather than concepts). 'Dialectical images' had an immediacy which interrupted the flow of time and thought, disrupting conventional ways of thinking and perceiving while disclosing a precious truth. Again, this idea of 'awakening' the complaisant Subject from an enchanting dream of capitalist progress is important here; as Richard Sieburth puts it, for Benjamin 'History is a nightmare from which it is imperative to awake'.[34] The significance of 'interruption' in this process has attracted much scholarly attention.[35] But, the melancholy side of this is that such a monadic explosion though brilliant, soon fades. Historical truth, then, is fleeting and finite and is something that cannot be sustained. Yet nothing could deny that that evanescent, precious truth had occurred, and it is our messianic duty to redeem and learn from as many such truths as we can. In a similar tendency to that found in his theory of experience, outlined in Chapter 3, Benjamin turns to the past to redeem truth. He aims at a critical historiography of remembrance that somehow salvages the 'fallen' present.

## *The Arcades Project* and Dickens

While *The Arcades Project* ostensibly focuses upon nineteenth-century (as well as twentieth-century) Parisian material, its intellectual resonances reverberate far beyond the confines of that city. For Benjamin, Paris was the 'capital' of, the city

---

[31] See 'Reading Benjamin', *Companion*, p. 8.

[32] As mentioned in Chapter 3, Surrealism's 'profane illumination' of the world of things stems from a similar interest in an expanded concept of experience to Benjamin's, one which recognized and attempted to capture the mysterious, the absolute, within the contours of the everyday – bringing the theological into 'the profane'. One way of capturing it for the Surrealists was through the presentation of shocking juxtaposition, in montage.

[33] *Arcades*, N10a,3.

[34] Sieburth, 'Benjamin the Scrivener', in Smith, '*Benjamin*', p. 18.

[35] See especially Andrew Benjamin, 'Benjamin's Modernity', in *Companion*, pp. 97–114.

which most exemplified, the structure of urban modernity itself, and it was this phenomenon – urban modernity – which he was interested in opening up in the past and in his present. If the *Arcades* was to be an ur-history (*Ur-Geschichte*) of twentieth-century capitalism (if it was to open up truths concerning Benjamin's present), the insights it offers on anything from city experience, and the patterns of industrial capitalism and consumption, to commodity fetishism, utopian dreaming and phantasmagoric display could surely provide worthy paradigms for understanding urban modernity in cities other than Paris.[36] Even the shopping arcades themselves, the central motif of the project, were an international phenomenon and were a part of Dickens's London experience.[37] In his unpublished autobiographical narrative, cited by Forster, Dickens mentions frequenting the Lowther Arcade, a covered passage near the Strand.[38] Among Benjamin's *Arcades* fragments are citations from French and German as well as British writers and journalists, with no less than 15 citations concerning Dickens.[39] One of these fragments is an excerpt from *The Old Curiosity Shop* itself.[40] The consequences of industrial capitalism, a phenomenon Britain led the world in developing, was at the heart of Benjamin's investigation. The expansion of economies internationally began around 1870; but industrialization had got underway early in Britain, in the late eighteenth century, meaning urban populations were growing rapidly, attracting greater migrating populations, and were suffering any effects by the 1830s and 1840s (Dickens's manhood). Peter Gurney (University of Essex) locates the origin of consumer culture in

---

36 This is the view critic Scott McCracken takes, quoted in 'Random Patterns, Flashes of Insight: Walter Benjamin's *Arcades Project*', *Journal of Victorian Culture* 7 (Autumn 2002): p. 277. Special roundtable discussion on *The Arcades Project*, *Journal of Victorian Culture* 7 (Autumn 2002): pp. 263–96.

37 The Burlington Arcade (still in existence today) was the earliest London arcade, built by Cork and Burlington Estates in 1819. Other extant arcades in London include the Piccadilly Arcade and the Princes Arcade, both in Piccadilly, and the Royal Arcade in New Bond Street. But fine arcades exist all over Europe. A particularly celebrated grand arcade is the Galleries St Hubert in Brussels (1847); the grand GUM complex in Moscow (1890), Galleria Umberto I in Naples (1887), and the Galleria Vittorio Emanuele II in Milan (1865) are all still standing. Berlin and Vienna also boast beautiful arcades.

38 *Life*, bk. 1, ch. 2, p. 28.

39 For more material on flânerie in Dickens's life and as reported in *Household Words*, see Catherine Waters, *Commodity Culture in Dickens's Household Words: The Social Life of Goods* (Aldershot: Ashgate, 2008), chaps. 4 and 8. And Michael Hollington, 'Dickens, Household Words and the Paris Boulevards', part 1, *Dickens Quarterly* 14.3 (September 1997): pp. 154–64; and part 2, *DQ* 14.4 (December 1997): pp. 199–212. Among other things, Hollington discusses Dickens's and Collins's flânerie in Paris in 1855.

40 *The Arcades Project*, H2a,4. The quotation is the allegorical image of Nell surrounded by curiosities, *The Old Curiosity Shop*, end of ch. 1, p. 18, as mentioned, the passage Dickens added to the first separate volume edition in 1841 after Thomas Hood's review.

mid-Victorian Britain.[41] As Margaret Cohen puts it, 'London might seem to have a better claim to the designation, capital of emergent modernity'.[42] And world expositions, one of the most famous of which took place in London in May 1851, form an important section of material crucial in the *Arcades* for an understanding of commodity fetishism and the phantasmagoric nature of urban life.

Despite the, as it were, cosmopolitan reach of Benjamin's research, one must not overlook the specificity of much of the detail he scrutinizes. There is no direct London equivalent for the Haussmannization of Paris, its revolutionary causes and its consequences; Benjamin's preoccupation with the dialectical relationship between technology and the market as it pertains to newspapers or feuilletons and particular French writers yields specific insights into those specific forms.[43]

On the other hand, some parallels, if handled carefully, can be usefully drawn. For instance, the delineation of newspaper innovation and some of its consequences, including novel serialization, could be loosely applied to London newspaper history and to Dickens's publishing conditions.[44] Moreover, when Benjamin depicts the market pressures under which Baudelaire suffered, one is put in mind of some of the anxieties Dickens labored under to keep up his readership and earning power: '[Baudelaire] knew the true situation of the man of letters: he goes to the marketplace as a flâneur, supposedly to take a look at it but in reality to find a buyer.'[45]

In a constellation of fragments in convolute C about the city's physical transience, Benjamin includes a fragment on the artist Charles Meyron, whose ink sketches of Paris capture the essentially fleeting nature of modern history:

> His work as an engraver represents one of the profoundest poems ever written about a city, and what is truly original in all these striking pictures is that they seem to be the image, despite being drawn directly from life, of things that are finished, that are dead or about to die.[46]

---

41 Paper entitled 'The Sublime of the Bazaar' given at a conference, 'The Victorians and the Twentieth Century', at Leeds Centre for Victorian Studies, July 13, 2005.

42 *Companion*, p. 200. The critic Lynda Nead obviously concurs with this sentiment, having situated Victorian London within a Benjaminian urban framework (*Victorian Babylon* [New Haven; London: Yale University Press, 2000]).

43 From 1853 until 1869, during the Second Empire in France under the rule of Napoleon III, the Préfet de la Seine, Georges Eugène Haussmann, widened boulevards, built sidewalks and opened public parks – thus performing the 'Haussmannization' of Paris. Public space was enlarged and extended, providing the context for the *grand magasins*, or department stores. That was in effect the death knell of the arcades. Dickens lived in Paris for a while, writing *Little Dorrit* (1855–1857) there. He praised the 'great line of Boulevards in Paris' and 'the gallant beauty of the Place de la Concorde' ('The Uncommercial Traveller', Slater, IV, p. 279), which he contrasted with the 'meanness' of London streets.

44 'Second Empire', p. 13.

45 Ibid., p. 17.

46 *Arcades*, C7a,1.

Whistler's ink etchings of London are an exact parallel to this phenomenon. In the late 1850s and early 1860s, Whistler aimed, like Meyron, to capture portraits of city sites that were undergoing rapid physical change.[47]

Dickens, too, produced work that could be viewed in a similar light to the sketches of Meyron in Paris and Whistler in London. His *Sketches by Boz* were short, sharp, impressionistic observations penned to provide the reader with a punchy glimpse of a London milieu in a constant state of flux and activity.[48] The glimpse, as argued in Chapter 3, is the quintessential way of experiencing, as *Erlebnis*.[49] The style and tone of the narrative implied that the passerby or flâneur scribbled down notes on the moment and on-site. One of his 'Scenes', 'Gin-Shops', asserts that some of the physical change the city undergoes, driven as it is by relentless commercial pressure, is pointless:

> Six or eight years ago, the epidemic began to display itself among the linen drapers and haberdashers. The primary symptoms, were an inordinate love of plate-glass, and a passion for gas-lights and gilding. The disease gradually progressed, and at last attained a fearful height. Quiet dusty old shops in different parts of town were pulled down; spacious premises with stuccoed fronts and gold letters, were erected instead; floors were covered with Turkey carpets; roofs supported by massive pillars; doors knocked into windows, a dozen squares of glass into one; one shopman into a dozen; and there is no knowing what would have been done. (*SB*, Scenes: ch. 22, pp. 214–16)[50]

[47] James Abbott McNeill Whistler (1834–1903). Here is cited not so much Whistler's famous *Nocturnes* – although *Old Battersea Bridge* (1872–1875) from this series of oils does record a bridge that was soon torn down. Rather Whistler's earlier etchings are adduced: *Old Westminster Bridge* (1859) is a study of Westminster without a clock face, which was being hoisted into position at the time of drawing; and the 1861 *Westminster Bridge in Progress* shows the building process at an early phase. The earliest extant picture by Whistler is a study from a watercolor inspired by Dickens: *Sam Weller's Landlord in the Fleet*. See *The Art of James McNeill Whistler*, ed. T.R. Way and G.R. Dennis (London: George Bell & Sons, 1903), p. 95.

[48] Between December 1833 and October 1836, Dickens wrote a number of essays and short stories on the theme of London's urban life for various magazines and newspapers. These pieces were collected into two series with illustrations by George Cruikshank in 1836 and were called *Sketches by Boz*. This was the start of Dickens's rise to fame. Compare also Maria Paganoni's comments that Dickens's aesthetics 'could be likened to an impressionistic painting', *The Magic Lantern: Representations of the Double in Dickens* (London: Routledge, 2007), pp. 83–118.

[49] As was outlined in Chapter 3, *Erlebnis* is an atrophied form of modern experience where one experiences the immediate and trivialized passing moment in the city in an anxious, hyperconscious state, primarily governed by shock. Temporality appears chopped up, isolated and without depth. *Erlebnis* is a form of experience where there is a reduction of the ability to assimilate or retain the data of the world around us – thanks partly to the vigilance of consciousness in warding off the urban shock. The Franco-German coinage that Benjamin uses for the concept of the experience of the shock is '*Chockerlebnis*'.

[50] The published series of *Sketches* were divided into 'Seven Sketches from our Parish', 'Scenes', 'Characters' and 'Tales'.

As well as parallels to details like the above, there are a number of intellectual paradigms and themes which one can find in Benjamin that are applicable to urban modernity in a more general sense and which could usefully be applied to a study of Dickens, to his fiction and the role of the city of London within it. This is a rich area of study, and space dictates that only some of these can be discussed in this section; 'the flâneur' and, by extension, 'the crowd' will be uppermost among them.

Of importance to an understanding of these themes and generally to the nature of urban experience in Benjamin, is Charles Baudelaire (1821–1867). Benjamin had translated Baudelaire in 1923; and the French poet – the first to utter the term 'modernity' (modernité) – became the basis upon which many constellations and ideas about modern experience were opened up in *The Arcades Project*.[51] In the first Arcades exposé (condensed exposition) of 1935, Benjamin drew up provisional chapter headings: chapter 5 was titled 'Baudelaire or The Streets of Paris'. Around 1937, Benjamin began marshaling some of *The Arcades Project*'s convolute J material on Baudelaire – among others – into a more concentrated piece for publication by the Institute of Social Research (*Zeitschrift für Sozialforschung*). By autumn 1938, Benjamin had worked up three sections from his *Arcades* material entitled 'The Paris of the Second Empire in Baudelaire'. After consultation with Adorno, he revised the middle section, 'The Flâneur', finally producing 'On Some Motifs in Baudelaire' in 1939. There are a number of smaller essays, then, which were either synoptic versions of *The Arcades Project*, or which could be viewed as supplements of it. And this chapter involves strategic raids upon many of those texts as well as upon *The Arcades Project* itself for ideas on urban modernism. Susan Buck-Morss suggests Benjamin planned a separate book on Baudelaire which may have absorbed or superseded *The Arcades Project*.[52]

How far can it be suggested that Dickens's work opens up similar areas of interest vis-à-vis urban modernism to those Benjamin found so evocative in Dickens's contemporary, Baudelaire? What light would a convincing reading of this sort throw upon the popular interpretation of Dickens as the exemplary 'Victorian'? Could Benjamin, were he not limiting his study to Paris and its arcades, have entitled one of his chapters, 'Dickens, or The Streets of London'? Could Benjamin's concern with modern urban culture be as cogently served by a study of Dickens as it was by examining the compelling Baudelaire?

One response to this last question is, absolutely. And much of this section concerns itself with exploring Dickens in terms of themes and ideas Benjamin invoked by his Baudelairean studies in *The Arcades Project*. Besides, Benjamin's project is already served by the work of Dickens. As stated, there are no less than 15 fragments

---

[51] 'By "modernity" I mean the ephemeral, the fugitive, the contingent, the half of art whose other half is the eternal and the immutable', Charles Baudelaire, 'The Painter of Modern Life', in Lawrence Calhoone, *From Modernism to Postmodernism* (Oxford: Blackwell, 1996), p. 142. This text will hereafter be referred to as 'Painter' followed by the reference.

[52] See *The Dialectics of Seeing* (Cambridge, MA; London: MIT Press, 1999), pp. 205–15.

(quotations from Dickens's work and letters and excerpts from writers on Dickens) in *The Arcades Project*. Convolute M titled 'The Flâneur' includes six entries on Dickens. One citation, lifted from G.K. Chesterton's *Dickens*, *Lives of Illustrious Men*, states unequivocally: 'Dickens [...] had [...] the key to the street' [M11,1].[53]

Two other citations, one from the journalist Franz Mehring and another from Chesterton (again from his *Dickens*), describe the extent of Dickens's need to have London's streets around him to enable him to write [M4a,4] and [M11a,1]. Other citations include two in convolute J, 'Baudelaire' [J3,2] and [J3,3]; a citation under the remit of 'Arcades, Magasins de Nouveautés, sales clerks' (convolute A) [A11,3]; two excerpts – one from *The Old Curiosity Shop*, one from Adorno's essay on that novel – in the section on 'The Collector' (convolute H), [H2a,4] and [H2a,5]; one in the section entitled 'Panorama' (convolute Q), [Q2a,2]; and another under convolute d 'Literary History, Hugo' [d13a,3].

Dickens was, as Benjamin's inclusions suggest, an urban artist whose work discloses crucial truths about modern existence and experience – and even contributes (given its inclusion in the 'Baudelaire' convolute) to an understanding of Baudelaire's rôle in urban modernity.

## *The Flâneur*

What concept of 'the flâneur' emerges from Benjamin's writings on Baudelaire and how can Dickens be related to it? The strolling spectator who perceives, controls and defines the urban environment has an interesting status: he is both a specific historical figure and a generic literary motif. The French verb 'flâner' – meaning 'to walk without haste, aimlessly, abandoning oneself to impression and to the spectacle of the moment' – and the historical figure himself, came to prominence with the rise of city culture in the Paris of the early nineteenth century.[54] From the earliest moment, the flâneur is associated with the city and with art. Benjamin describes a waxing and waning, a 'cult' of the flâneur in Paris: in 1840 'it was briefly fashionable to take turtles for a walk in the arcades'. By 1857, the flâneur was being condemned as 'a rubberneck'.[55] For Baudelaire, who seizes upon the Parisian flâneur of the 1830s and 1840s, he *is* the artist, 'The Painter of Modern Life'. And it is at this point, when Baudelaire most eulogizes the specific identity of the nineteenth-century Parisian flâneur, that the flâneur evolves from a specific historical figure into a generic symbol or emblem of the modern artistic process. With Baudelaire's focus upon the flâneur – represented in the *Arcades* and in Benjamin's other Baudelaire material – the flâneur's spatio-temporal specificity is highlighted, but undermined at the same time. And there

53 See Catherine Waters, *Commodity Culture in Dickens's Household Words* (referenced above), ch. 4, pp. 65–81.

54 Definition of 'flâneur' from Michael Hollington, 'Dickens the Flâneur', *The Dickensian* 77.2 (Summer 1981): p. 72.

55 Both quotations, 'Second Empire', p. 31.

is a genuine ambiguity about this point. The difficulty of whether the flâneur can be reasonably understood to be trans-geographical (applicable to cities other than Paris) is not resolved in Benjamin: this is perhaps well illustrated by Benjamin's reading of Baudelaire reading Poe's 'The Man of the Crowd'.[56] Poe's short story features a character installed in a London coffee shop who then becomes a flâneur amid the London crowd.[57] But on closer inspection, Benjamin comments of the milieu of the flâneur:

> If London ever provided it for him, it was certainly not the setting described by Poe.[58]

Benjamin's 'if' does not appear to give a clear verdict on this problem, then. The international and trans-historical phenomenon of the city and of strolling spectators/ detectives, however, was something that Baudelaire hints an acknowledgment of, and that Benjamin quotes.[59] But whether this allows one to examine Dickens and Dickens's fiction in the name of a Benjaminian elaboration of flânerie is a question that, if Benjamin leaves ambiguously open, is answered in the affirmative for the purposes of this study.[60]

The Parisian 'cult' of flânerie, meanwhile, had corresponded to the rise and fall of the Parisian arcades (c.1820–1840), a brief period when that architectural innovation allowed customers to promenade and admire fantastic displays of commodities within the phantasmagoric and controlled setting of glass roofs and gas-lit walkways. But what is so special about 'the city' for the flâneur and why did he walk there? Why was his activity so 'modern' for Baudelaire?

The city is the site of 'a thousand natural shocks',[61] where one experiences the urban as *Chockerlebnis*. The flâneur's walking in the city involves his encountering ephemeral sensations, bumping up against abrupt events, immersing himself in the unstable transience of the crowd in the metropolis, just like every other pedestrian. But the flâneur attempts to master this by looking with penetrating eyes, registering every detail. He is the embodiment of the self-consciousness of visuality, of the optical encounter in the city. He strolls the streets, focusing and refocusing, assimilating and reorganizing the myriad surfaces on offer. Baudelaire claims the swift and actively defining gaze of the flâneur resembles a kaleidoscope;

---

56 See 'Motifs', pp. 168–70.

57 See section VII of 'Motifs' where Benjamin questions whether Poe's man of the crowd is a 'flâneur' (p. 168).

58 Ibid.

59 'Strolling – something that nations with imagination love' (Benjamin quoting Baudelaire in 'Second Empire', p. 28).

60 Of course, Dickens himself stayed in Paris many times and knew it well; and one of his novels, *A Tale of Two Cities*, is set in Paris as well as in London. As will be touched upon toward the end of this chapter, the cities of London and Paris in that novel are intriguingly similar if not identical.

61 Benjamin, 'Second Empire', p. 35.

it has the efficiency and power of a mechanized optical device.[62] His look is one of instant comprehension. The flâneur develops reactions that are in keeping with the tempo of a big city.[63] The flâneur enjoys *Chockerlebnis* then – as well as falling victim to it. He can allow himself to succumb to it, because to see is to know. He is not wont to be overcome like the shopper or the badaud (a gaper), for he is a self-contained, self-aware walker and a consummate observer.[64] The very raison d'étre and jouissance of the poet/flâneur is to give voice to the flood of phenomena, in a sense to reconstitute and reconfigure experience in the face of the city's transience and disintegration. As one critic puts it, the flâneur/artist collects 'fragments' of evanescent urban experience, even though familiarity can conceal the particularity of the everyday.[65] His unplanned route and the random events and fragments of life he uncovers are echoed in the text he writes. This means he has a sensitivity to the aesthetics of 'modernité', he gives form to the aesthetics of the fleeting/transient which, for Baudelaire, is the flip side of eternity.[66]

Significantly, it is in the public space that the flâneur's being is actualized. And the waking life of the flâneur is devoted to reading the complex text which is the city. This can even be phrased in existential terms: the flâneur is driven out of the private into the public sphere in a search for meaning. As Keith Tester puts it: the poet/flâneur is one 'who can reap aesthetic meaning and an individual kind of existential security from the spectacle of the teeming crowds'.[67] But this is exactly where the paradoxical status of the flâneur comes into play. In the street, he finds himself amid the crowd, occupying the unstable, unpredictable, even threatening space of the urban, where his subjectivity can easily be overwhelmed. Yet, Baudelaire claims, 'the crowd is his element' just as 'the air is the bird's'.[68] How does this work? The flâneur has a self-consciousness about being within the metropolitan realm; he is the thinking center who orders the chaos, and he knows that he is, giving him a certain 'distance' from the crowd. Baudelaire phrases this in terms of 'sovereignty' and 'princeliness'.[69] The fact that the flâneur may look like every other facc in the crowd makes his position all the more compelling: he is aware that others see him as 'just another stroller', another anonymous pedestrian to be jostled by. This interesting dialectic – to garner meaning and actualize his

62 'Painter', p. 140.

63 Benjamin, 'Second Empire', p. 22.

64 'Despite the superficial analogies between badauderie and flânerie, the former is essentially passive and affective while the latter is active and intellectual' (Richard D.E. Burton, *The Flâneur in His City: Patterns of Daily Life in Paris 1815–1851* [Brighton: University of Sussex, 1984], p. 1). Hereafter referred to as 'Burton'.

65 Kevin McLaughlin, *Writing in Parts: Imitation and Exchange in Nineteenth-Century Literature* (Stanford, CA: Stanford University Press, 1995), p. 90.

66 'Painter', p. 142.

67 *The Flâneur* (London; New York: Routledge, 1994), p. 2.

68 'Painter', p. 140.

69 Ibid.

existence, the flâneur needs to be bathing in the multitude: by being aware of his status as organizer or definer, he distances himself from the crowd – is the paradox at the heart of the flâneur. This is an infinite process that can never be resolved. As Benjamin puts it, 'Baudelaire loved solitude, but he wanted it in a crowd'.[70] Baudelaire, too, sets out the dialectic clearly:

> Multitude, solitude: identical terms and interchangeable by the active and fertile poet. The man who is unable to people his solitude is equally unable to be alone in the bustling crowd.[71]

If the flâneur's speculations upon objective reality simultaneously involve a distancing from it, his anonymity involves him in another difficulty which he shares with the detective:

> The flâneur [...] stands apart from the city even as he appears to 'fuse' with it; he interprets each of its component parts in isolation in order, subsequently, to attain to an intellectual understanding of the whole as a complex system of meaning.[72]

But no matter how many disparate clues he apprehends or comprehends, or even manages to connect, the attempt to master the whole cityscape is doomed to failure. The city is in a state of flux, experience of anything is fleeting and ephemeral. The flâneur's very entry into the space is itself a negation of his grasp upon the whole, as is every other unexpected pedestrian, event and movement. Even if little other equivalence between city dwellers exists, then, this is certainly one area in which there is total democracy between individuals: no one can grasp the inexhaustible meaning of the city as a whole.

The flâneur, at this point, can start to emerge as a man in despair. Benjamin puts it simply: Poe's flâneur is 'someone who does not feel comfortable in his own company',[73] and immersion in the multitude can only bring temporary relief before the whole process must begin again. His infinite search for meaning, his endless flânerie, begins to look like a curse which can lead to eccentricity, absurd obsolescence and melancholy.

## *Dickens the Flâneur*

While a definition of 'the flâneur' has been attempted, it must be acknowledged that the concept is a slippery one. And Benjamin's characteristic presentation of it in no way brings exactitude to the matter. But for the present purposes, how does Dickens come out in relation to what has been gleaned so far?

---

70 'Second Empire', p. 28.

71 *Paris Spleen*, trans. L. Varèse (New York: New Directions Books, 1970), p. 20.

72 'Burton', p. 2.

73 'Second Empire', p. 27

Dickens's obsession with walking in the city and his own understanding of its importance to his production, surely makes him a flâneur in the mould of Benjamin's Baudelairean writings. Dickens is certainly recognizable in the description above and most of the discussion will be conducted around bearing this statement out.

Dickens knew what flânerie was, uses the word of his own activities during a trip to Paris with Wilkie Collins in 1855, and edited material about flânerie for *Household Words*.[74] He was a great admirer of Balzac – and Balzac's *Physiologie du Mariage* (1826) was possibly one of the first treatments that placed flânerie within the artistic context. And as Hollington puts it, *Sketches by Boz* was an 'early counterpart to Balzac's flâneurial writings'.[75]

The two fragments in *The Arcades Project*'s convolute M about Dickens's need to be in the city to write – M4a,4 and M11a,1 – pertain to Dickens's 1846 trip to Switzerland when, for the first time, he experienced difficulties in writing. Surrounded by a lake and mountains, the author himself put his writer's block down to the absence of people, crowds and city streets.[76]

Ironically, considering fears about pollution in both the nineteenth century and now, Dickens even went as far as blaming his physical illness upon being away from the city.[77] Like Baudelaire, his work required him to be inside/outside, to be a part of the city as an artist/flâneur, observer/writer, to function: 'To be away from home and yet to feel oneself everywhere at home: to see the world, to be at the centre of the world, and yet to remain hidden from the world.'[78]

In this sense, the street was Dickens's study, his interior, as it was for Baudelaire's flâneur and for Baudelaire himself: 'The familiar city beckons to the flâneur as phantasmagoria – now a landscape, now a room.'[79] Benjamin, referring to the flâneur, could be talking of Dickens, here: 'Buildings' walls are the desk against which he presses his notebooks; news-stands are his libraries'[80] – while for Dickens/Copperfield: 'Each stone was a boy's book to me.'[81]

---

74 One of Dickens's own walking companions, George Augustus Sala, wrote about 'the flâneurs of Paris' for *Household Words* in 1853. And journalist Edmund Yates, another of Dickens's colleagues, wrote a series of personal columns for *The Morning Star* entitled 'The Flâneur' in the 1860s. Also, see Hollington, 'Dickens, *Household Words* and the Paris Boulevards' (as referenced above).

75 'Dickens, Sala and the London Arcades', *Dickens Quarterly* 284 (December 2011): pp. 273–84.

76 *Life*, bk. 5, ch. 5, p. 423.

77 Ibid., p. 430.

78 'Painter', p. 140. As many feminist scholars have pointed out, flânerie was very much a male preserve. Dickens's own strolling and depictions of flânerie in his novels remain firmly within this somewhat phallocentric tradition. See Appendix 1.

79 Benjamin, 'Paris, Capital', in *SW*, III, p. 40.

80 'Second Empire', p. 19.

81 *DC*, Narrator, ch. 60, p. 717.

Dickens's very creativity – as the author himself acknowledged – was wired up to the energy of the city, being fed by it and feeding back into it: 'I can't express how much I want these [streets]. It seems as if they supplied something to my brain which I cannot bear, when busy, to lose.'[82] Baudelaire similarly identifies the quintessence of the modern artist in terms of a palpable physical attachment to the city: 'the lover of universal life enters into the crowd as though it were an immense reservoir of electrical energy'.[83] He connects artistic endeavor directly to 'the shock' of urban existence, or *Chockerlebnis*:

> I [...] assert that inspiration has something in common with a convulsion, and that every sublime thought is accompanied by a more or less violent nervous shock which has its repercussion in the very core of the brain.[84]

Taking into consideration Dickens's productive procedures, his incessant walking habits, his headaches and other symptoms of nerves and anxiety – 'an extraordinary nervousness it would be hardly possible to describe',[85] – plus his avowed need for streets and crowds, it is difficult not to view him within this framework: he is the modern urban artist whose artistic production thrives upon and is even propelled by *Chockerlebnis*. And, as was argued in Chapter 3, while Benjamin claims of Proust that he retrospectively creates *Erfahrung* out of *Erlebnis*, Dickens, on the other hand (at least in the writings analyzed), creates narratives and scenes that express the fragmentariness and transitoriness of urban existence experienced as *Erlebnis*. Yet he is still doing the job of the artist: 'distilling the eternal from the transitory'.[86]

In a letter to Forster of August 30, 1846, Dickens calls London his 'magic lantern', conjuring up all the joy of epistemological ambiguity and scopophilia attached to Benjamin's use of the term 'phantasmagoria' in describing city experience.[87] (If London is for Dickens a magic lantern, Dickens's fictions of London were adapted innumerable times into magic lantern slides, as well as into narrative images on panoramas and dioramas.)[88] Dickens's walking partner George Sala, emphasizes the city's kaleidoscopic quality when they walk in it

[82] Dickens to Forster, *Life*, bk. 5, ch. 5, p. 423; also quoted by Benjamin in 'Second Empire', p. 29.

[83] 'Painter', p. 140. Benjamin highlights this Baudelairean notion in section 8 of 'Motifs', p. 171.

[84] 'Painter', p. 139.

[85] Dickens to Forster, *Life*, bk. 5, ch. 3, p. 404.

[86] See Baudelaire, 'Painter', p. 142.

[87] '*Life*' bk. 5, ch. 5, p. 423, and 'Second Empire', p. 28. The term 'phantasmagoria' comes from the French 'phantasmagorie', meaning the art of creating supernatural illusions.

[88] Grahame Smith, *Dickens and the Dream of Cinema* (Manchester; New York: Manchester University Press, 2003), p. 7. Hereafter referred to as 'Smith'.

and observe together.[89] As a concept, 'phantasmagoria' derives from the name of a public illusion show – an optical device similar to a magic lantern – which was popular in Paris in the 1790s and appeared in London in 1802. Images painted on glass were projected onto a screen, but, unlike other magic lantern shows, the phantasmagoria took place in darkness, concealing its apparatus from the audience. Semantically, and this is where Dickens's insistence upon using the term 'magic lantern' is significant, the concept broadens out to take in the more general concern with epistemology, the nature of truth/illusion, reason/deception, reality/fantasy. It can denote a constantly shifting, complex succession of things real or imagined; a fantastic sequence of haphazardly associated imagery as seen in dreams or fever; but the implication is also that the viewer is self-conscious about and enjoys the element of illusion/deception involved.[90]

This is arguably Dickens's meaning when he claims London is like a tantalizing optical spectacle, the magic lantern. And it is where Dickens's creativity comes close to the definition of 'the flâneur'. To prevent being overwhelmed and swept away by the city, like the flâneur, Dickens holds it at a distance, 'reducing' it to a 'spectacle'. But not to 'a spectacle' that opens everything up, that clarifies. The magic lantern's spectacle is quite another way of relating to the world. The city is not an object that is somehow fully available, and in any case, it is in a state of flux. Experience of it involves a gothic quality, it discloses itself as ephemeral, fragmentary, transitory; it is unpredictable and un-totalizable. Like the magic lantern patterns, its images are shifting, mutable, contingent. And memory of it adds to it a further layer of intangibility. It is just this quality that opens up the notion of the collapse of the subject/object divide – that requires the flâneur's use of his imagination in relation to the experience. The contingent, accidental fragments of the city generate the flâneur's inexhaustible speculations.

This is an important point. It is tempting to attribute, as Grahame Smith does, metaphors like 'the panorama' to evoke the visual qualities of Dickens's evocation of the city in writings, in Smith's case using it of Dickens's Paris.[91] This is understandable considering the dominance of the optical experience in the city, and the important role such leisure activities as the panorama played in urban popular culture of nineteenth-century Paris and London. Unsurprisingly, Benjamin dedicates an entire convolute to it in *The Arcades Project*

[89] 'Looking seemingly neither to the right nor the left, but of a surety looking at and into everything – now at the myriad aspects of London life, the ever-changing raree-show, the endless round-about, the infinite kaleidoscope of wealth and pauperism, of happiness and misery, of good and evil in this Babylon' (George Augustus Sala speaking of Dickens's 'flânerie' in Philip Collins, *Interviews and Recollections*, 2 vols [London: Macmillan, 1981], vol. 2, pp. 197–8).

[90] Definition of 'phantasmagoria': a paraphrase of a section of a paper entitled 'The Birth of Cinema' by Dr Thomas Gunning (University of Chicago) at the University of Sussex, February 2, 2005, at which Gunning identified the phantasmagoria as an early precursor of film.

[91] 'Smith', ch. 4, pp. 62–81. Dickens himself uses the term 'panorama' about Paris.

(convolute Q – 'Panorama'). But, as it has been argued in Chapter 3 and will be further argued here, the notion of the panorama, if by using it Smith implies a totalizable or mastering grasp over a city scene, is not one that adequately describes Dickens's relationship to the city and his fictional expression of that experience of it; whether the city concerned is Paris or London.

Dickens's, Baudelaire's and indeed David Copperfield's repetitive return to city spaces is a symptom of the evanescence of the flâneur's hold upon the world's presence (and upon the self), the partial or sometimes irrecoverable loss that such experience and memory of world and self involves. And their incessant revisitations signify, at some level, an awareness of the conditions under which such experience and memory take place.

Biographically – and, as is always the case for the flâneur, autobiographically – it seems that Dickens was to be a flâneur from boyhood. As is well documented by biographers from Forster to Ackroyd, Dickens wandered the city streets as a boy, often to escape the misery of his plight, stimulating his imagination and garnering manna and content for it. This is significant in view of Benjamin's claim that 'Only those for whom poverty or vice turns the city into a landscape in which they stray from dark till dawn know it'.[92]

And, as discussed, Dickens dramatized his intimate mental and emotional connection with urban space through his fictional double, David Copperfield, with the monadic statement: 'I came into the quiet streets, where every stone was a boy's book to me' (*DC*, Narrator, ch. 60, p. 717). The novel relates how the reading of those memories, and the retelling/rewriting of such activity is often a painful and difficult experience. One should not forget the Freudian resonances that this state of affairs implies. And, as was suggested in Chapter 3, even in terms of his 'real life', Dickens would find the retelling of his early experiences painful.[93] Dickens's life and creativity, then, exhibits an unclear distinction between fiction and 'fact'.[94]

The post-Copperfield 'Gone Astray' (*HW*, August 13, 1853) is another production of Dickens the flâneur. He famously revisits, recreates and rewrites the scene of his getting lost as a child: 'Thus I wandered about the City, like a child in a dream.'[95] The dream he inhabits is powered by a fascinating reciprocity between, and interweaving of, his own reading of popular culture and the intractable, concrete form of the city:

---

[92] 'A Berlin Chronicle', *SW*, II, p. 612.

[93] As suggested, there are a number of discernible discrepancies, including one possibility that he exaggerated the duration of the blacking factory experience. See F.S. Schwarzbach, *Dickens and the City*, p. 23.

[94] Dickens himself says of *David Copperfield*: 'I have done it very ingeniously, and with a very complicated interweaving of fact and fiction' (quoted in John Lucas's *The Melancholy Man*, p. 166). See *Life*, bk. 6, ch. 7, pp. 547–58.

[95] 'Gone Astray' reproduced in Michael Slater and John Drew (eds.), *Dickens' Journalism*, 4 vols (London: J.M. Dent, 2000), III, pp. 155–65 (p. 160). These volumes will hereafter be referred to as 'Slater' followed by the volume number and reference.

> When I started up after a long nap, I thought the giants were roaring, but it was only the City. The place was just the same as when I fell asleep: no beanstalk, no fairy, no princess, no dragon, no opening in life of any kind. So being hungry, I thought I would buy something to eat, and bring it in there and eat it, before going forth to seek my fortune on the Whittington plan.[96]

The 'giants' Dickens refers to are architectural designs decorating Guildhall, which serve as concrete manifestations of his 'Jack and the Beanstalk' fantasy. But their efficacy as fantastical props is ambiguous, since the young Dickens stops short at asking passersby directions 'to the giants' for fear of ridicule. Hence, he is aware he inhabits a space of questionable truth claims, he knows he is in the phantasmagoric space. Yet it is precisely from this that his enjoyment stems. He believes and disbelieves at the same time. He is amused and entertained by his own terrorized and confused reaction to the city and the productivity it elicits in him.

While the adult world scoffs at fantasy, almost too purposive in its activities to engage with the city's stimuli, the city itself, in contrast, simultaneously indulges fantasy and cuts it off. In urban space, the distinction between fantasy and 'reality' is not a clear one. Hence, when young Dickens hears a roar, his initial fear that it is the giants is soon replaced by the resignation that it is 'only the City' (that word 'only' registering both relief and disappointment simultaneously). Moreover, he expresses regret that there exists 'no beanstalk, no fairy, no dragon': yet the city is still haunted by them through its interaction with the 'Astray' Dickens. It is the city's incredible nature – its ability to shock, its crowded spaces and noise, its speed, its traffic, buildings and variety – that elicits and sustains fantastic possibilities in the boy. Its stimulation offers more than enough intensity for the average commuter; how much more so for the lost young dreamer who will absorb, regenerate and multiply meanings? In popular myth, London is the city where one 'seeks one's fortune'; hence, Dick Whittington's adventures are modified from 'fairy tale' to practical plan by the young Dickens. London is integral to this fantasy, and to the permeable reality/fantasy distinction that governs it. While the young Dickens mediates his route via his wealth of reading and imagination, the cityscape itself conversely provides a concrete 'otherness' for fantasy to feast upon:

> I remember how immensely broad the streets seemed now I was alone, how high the houses, how grand and mysterious everything. When I came to Temple Bar, it took me half-an-hour to stare at it, and I left it unfinished even then.[97]

The 'astray' Dickens must, like all flâneurs, give voice to the flood of phenomena which 'assaults' his young consciousness. And as Master Dickens is cut adrift 'in a series of shocks and collisions'[98] and attempts to integrate the disorderly,

---

[96] Slater, III, p. 158.

[97] Slater, III, pp. 157–8.

[98] 'Motifs', p. 171.

disparate particles of experience at the time ('it's only the city'), the older narrator of 'Gone Astray' (Dickens the adult author) returns to the experience and space with just as much glee to finish the job off. It is tempting to see this in terms of Baudelaire's announcement that 'genius is nothing more nor less than *childhood recovered* at will – a childhood now equipped for self-expression with manhood's capacities and a power of analysis which enables it to order the mass of raw material which it has involuntarily accumulated'.[99] What it certainly can be viewed as is the activity of the flâneur. Yet, it is at the same time crucial to acknowledge the role the imagination of the 'Astray' Dickens plays in his experience of the city: and this considerable input has a bearing upon the sort of 'flâneur' he can be understood to be.

### *Thinking and Flânerie*

Baudelaire, meanwhile, describes his relationship to the city, thus:

> I go, alone, to practise my curious fencing,
> In every corner smelling out the dodges of rhyme;
> Stumbling over words as over cobblestones,
> Colliding now and then with long-dreamed-of verses.[100]

Here Baudelaire's walking is not only a simile for thinking: 'Stumbling over words as over cobblestones'; the work itself takes the poetic trope of metaphor, which sets up the equivalence of walking/thinking/writing, as a subject in the poem itself, self-reflexively delineating the activity of creating poetry in its inextricability from walking in the city, as in: 'In every corner smelling out the dodges of rhyme.'[101] His suggestion of an identity between the staccato nature of flânerie (stumbling, colliding) in the 'risk-filled' city, and thought processes dominated by *Chockerlebnis* is particularly convincing – and bears a comparison with the analysis of the Dickens material in terms of *Erlebnis* in Chapter 3. Baudelaire is perhaps most Dickensian in the final line: 'colliding now and then with long-dreamed-of verses', assuming the reciprocity between city space and memory and writing/rewriting as does Dickens: 'Every stone was a boy's book to me.'

---

[99] 'Painter', p. 139.

[100] 'The Sun', in *Flowers of Evil*, quoted by Benjamin in 'Motifs', p. 160; trans. George Dillon and Edna St Vincent Millay, 1st ed. (New York; London: Harper & Brothers, 1936), pp. 178–9.

[101] This interpretation of Baudelaire comes close to Julian Wolfreys: 'Baudelaire locates the very idea of an implicitly *modern* poetic prose not in the artist but rising out of the experience of the life of cities. The cities transform the artist as s/he becomes the creative conduit' (Julian Wolfreys, *Writing London* [Basingstoke; New York: Palgrave, 1998], p. 4).

For both Baudelaire and Dickens, walking in the city has an identity with thinking, dreaming, creating fictions.[102] Dickens plainly avows this identity of walking, thinking and writing with respect to his own working methods, in correspondence with Forster. To produce an autobiographical reflection on his blacking factory days, Dickens – in exactly the way described of the character David Copperfield in Chapter 3 – revisits the space physically and therefore mentally: 'In my night walks I have walked there often, since then, and by degrees, I have come to write this.'[103] As already mentioned, this autobiographical piece was abandoned and replaced by *DC*. Walking literally exorcised/exercised Dickens's ideas for a novel, the physical activity engorging them with the energy to materialize and haunt the author: 'The first conceiving of a new book was always a restless time [...] the characters that were growing in his mind would persistently intrude themselves into his night-wanderings.'[104] And in his fiction, as if making conscious his own mysterious creative processes, Dickens depicts how the stroller's steps hammer out his thought processes upon the fabric of the city. Of Sidney Carton, the narrator says, 'From being irresolute and purposeless, his feet became animated by an intention, and, in the working out of that intention, they took him to the Doctor's door' (*TTC*, bk. 2, ch. 13, p. 179).

Walking in the city for both Dickens and Baudelaire is a form of 'synaesthesia', the experience of such a heightening of the senses and such a fluency of imagination while strolling in the city, that it amounts to a collapse of the Subject/object divide.[105] Both artists drew strength from and fed back into material they saw in the city space, dreamed up their own versions of the city, revisited, recreated and rewrote old spaces and memories and dreams. Theirs was an addictive, vampiric relationship with the urban; their production, a continual palimpsestic process of revisitation and revision. Benjamin compares such a relentless and repetitive relationship with space, the past and creativity – in Freudian vein – to an archaeological dig: 'they must not be afraid to return again and again to the same matter [...] to turn it over as one turns over soil', and he reminds the reader that 'Fruitless searching is as much a part of this as succeeding'.[106]

[102] See also Grahame Smith, 'The Travelling Lanternist and the Uncommercial Traveller: An Experiment in Correspondences', in David Seed (ed.), *Literature and the Visual Media* (Cambridge: D.S. Brewer, 2005), where Smith discusses how, in his urban wanderings, Dickens was recording what he saw in relation to what he thought, pp. 34–5.

[103] *Life*, bk. 1, ch. 2, p. 35.

[104] Ibid., bk. 5, ch. 1, p. 388.

[105] In 'Motifs', p. 177, Benjamin claims that in reading Baudelaire, Proust understood part of Baudelaire's poetic effect to involve 'synaesthesia'.

[106] Both quotations, 'A Berlin Chronicle' [Benjamin's own search for his past], *SW*, II, p. 611. The importance of Freud is clear, especially with respect to the notions of the city as mnemonic, and the identity of thinking, walking and writing. In one essay, Freud brings out the palimpsestic nature of memory by 'imagining' the city of Rome as 'not a human habitation but a psychical entity' (*Civilization and Its Discontents* [London: Penguin, 2002], p. 8).

Both Dickens's and Baudelaire's repetitive and rather obsessive returning to and re-creation of urban space, the element of 'eternal return' in their flânerie, their thinking and their writing, resembles the processes of writing, reading and thought that Benjamin outlines as ideal in *OGTD*. There he champions a mode of writing which opposes the notion that reading and the thought it generates in the reader should involve a seamless progression toward an author's meaningful intention. Rather, he demands a form of writing characterized by interruption and digression: a method that demands a thoughtful response in readers. This mode of writing, which he compares to a movement of thought (and which is here compared to Dickens's and Baudelaire's productive flânerie), allows for a type of contemplation which recognizes the many layers of meaning revealed by cultural and historical artifacts:

> Tirelessly thought begins continually from new things, laboriously returning to the same object. This continual pausing for breath is the mode most proper to the process of contemplation.[107]

Thought itself starts to take on the spatial dimensions of flânerie in the city, then. It is as fleeting and epiphanic as, say, the soon to be defunct coaching inns it records. This entirely coalesces with Baudelaire's understanding of urban experience when he describes Poe's character in 'The Man of the Crowd' as 'pleasurably absorbed in gazing at the crowd, and mingling, through the medium of thought, in the turmoil of thought that surrounds him'.[108] This notion of a kind of psycho-geo-biography, if one can so describe it, is what Benjamin's theory of experience – the issue of self, memory and city space, discussed in Chapter 3 – is about. One can also see Benjamin's attempt to redeem a collective memory in *The Arcades Project* in this light. Both projects demand a 'capacity for endless interpolations into what has been'.[109]

The other aspect of thinking and flânerie to be touched upon is the use of poetic prose by both Baudelaire and Dickens. According to Benjamin, only such poetic language, heightened and palpable as it is, could adequately express the intensity and infinite variety of the city, and the insatiability of the flâneur to interact with it. Language should express: 'an idée fixe, (which) will grip especially those who are at home in the giant cities and the web of their numberless interconnecting relationships'.[110]

The obsessive hallucinatory, even surreal, quality of some of Dickens's descriptions and scenes could be viewed within this context. As Baudelaire terms it, the artist creates fictions 'in energies more vivid than life itself'.[111]

[107] *OGTD*, p. 28.

[108] 'Painter', p. 138.

[109] 'A Berlin Chronicle', *SW*, II, p. 603.

[110] 'Motifs', p. 161.

[111] 'Painter', p. 141.

The revelatory vision of a changing world sometimes presented by Dickens – and often commented upon by critics – can be linked to the 'intensity of perception'[112] practiced by the flâneur, as well as to an intensity of imagination with which Dickens has been blessed in his textual creativity.

Pursuing this theme of the correspondence of thinking and flânerie, it is clear that digression – or the experience (or knowledge) one attains by default or chance, by being lost or en route elsewhere in the city – is an important issue in Benjamin. In 'Unpacking My Library' (1931), he notes with satisfaction, 'How many cities have revealed themselves to me in the marches I undertook in the pursuit of books!' – and presumably vice versa.[113] Such 'default discoveries' can be a perk for the flâneur-writer, the stroller who can, of course, be either purposeful and directed or contemplative and ambling.

The point is, the flâneur is the man whose life is 'spatialized'. As was mentioned, Benjamin set his life out topographically on a map, marking 'the houses of my friends and girlfriends, the assembly halls [...] the hotel and brothel rooms that I knew for one night, the [...] benches in the Tiergarten [...] the sites of prestigious cafés whose long-forgotten names daily crossed our lips'.[114]

He later records that reading in a newspaper that a forgotten café, 'an important strategic base' in his younger days, had closed down, triggered a flood of memory. In both 'A Berlin Chronicle' and in *One-Way Street* (written 1923–1926, published 1928) the kernel of life, memory, contains months and years in just a tiny moment of recollection. Within that moment – which opposes the continuous flow of time – people, streets, objects, weather, ideas and dreams enter into mysterious relations with each other. As in the discussion of the many layers of memory involved in David Copperfield's remembrance of his mother (Chapter 3) consciousness can be viewed as a graphic three-dimensional space, a labyrinth of memories and moments that color the city one finds oneself in.

Dickens describes a similar relationship to city space and memory:

> When I had money enough, I used to go to a coffee-shop, and have half-a-pint of coffee, and a slice of bread and butter. When I had no money, I took a turn in Covent garden market and stared at the pineapples. The coffee-shops to which I most resorted were one in Maiden-lane; one in a court (non-existent now) close to Hungerford-market; and one in St Martin's lane, of which I only recollect that it stood near the church, and that in the door there was an oval glass-plate, with COFFEE-ROOM painted on it, addressed towards to the street. If I ever find myself in a very different kind of coffee-room now, but where there is such an inscription on glass, and read it backward on the wrong side MOOR-EEFFOC (as I often used to do then, in a dismal reverie), a shock goes through my blood.[115]

---

[112] Smith, 'Dickens and the City of Light', p. 3.

[113] *Illuminations*, p. 64.

[114] 'A Berlin Chronicle', in *SW*, II, pp. 596–7.

[115] Dickens to Forster, *Life*, bk. 1, ch. 2, p. 28.

Here, in another Proustian moment, Dickens describes how the city's physical structure is the mnemonic for painful feelings. This moment demonstrates the monadic importance of the trivial in the everyday, how the extraordinary can suddenly burst in upon the ordinary. The moment also shows that 'the shock' of the urban is not always attributable to the city's physical movement: one's own labyrinthine mental life can similarly be the cause of *Chockerlebnis*. In a bizarre reflection of this reflection, suggesting Benjamin had come across this moment in Dickens's life but had then forgotten it, Benjamin includes in convolute R – 'Mirrors' what he calls a story 'of the man who could not bear to have, in the interior of his shop or bistro, the legend on the outer windowpane incessantly before his eyes'.[116]

The antics of the comic character Dick Swiveller similarly represent how the city's space has a simultaneous effect upon the urban dweller's physical and mental movements – again expressing the identity of flânerie and thinking. In *OCS*, his unpaid debts and the need to avoid them are beginning to limit his outlook:

> I enter in this little book the names of the streets that I can't go down while the shops are open. This dinner today closes Long Acre. I bought a pair of boots in Great Queen Street last week, and made that no thoroughfare too. There's only one avenue to the Strand left open now, and I shall have to stop up that tonight with a pair of gloves. The roads are closing so fast in every direction, that in about a month's time, unless my aunt sends me a remittance, I shall have to go three or four miles out of town to get over the way. (Dick Swiveller, *OCS*, ch. 8, p. 68)

Like Benjamin's topographical delineation of his life, Swiveller's is entirely spatially defined. Swiveller's decisions, his very life options, are determined by his relationship to the city. In an endless process of interdependence, his calculations, his needs govern his experience of the city (he must go here for food, but cannot go there); conversely, his thoughts/calculations are entirely determined by the city's coercions. Moreover, his fluent trains of thought reproduce or mime the physical movements he needs to make to get around the city unscathed. His situation also echoes Freud's mind as city analogy, with the city organized in a hierarchical manner, some parts accessible and others parts sealed off: and of course, despite the ego's struggle to be master of his mental space, the uncanny mind/city is rarely a setting in which one lives comfortably. One's needs and drives cannot but cause trouble to one's serenity.[117] And for Engels, too, 'people's lives became mediated by the negativity of their surroundings'.[118] Swiveller's taking a particular 'route' bears upon both the physical and the mental connotations of that concept.

---

116 *Arcades*, R1,2.

117 *Civilization and Its Discontents*. See note 106, p. 166, above.

118 Quoted in Marc Eli Blanchard, *In Search of the City: Engels, Baudelaire and Rimbaud* (Saratoga, CA: ANMA Libra, 1985), p. 74. Benjamin quotes Engels's *The Condition of the Working Class in England in 1844* in 'Motifs', claiming Engels's horror of the London crowd combines critical integrity with 'an old fashioned attitude', pp. 162–3.

The more debt he gets into, the less room, literally, he has in which to maneuver – and the more limited his potential experience of life/the city becomes. Like Freud's city, Swiveller's is full of unwelcome/alien guests (his creditors). 'People knew one another as debtors and creditors, salesmen and customers, employers and employees, and above all as competitors.'[119] But the more he avoids them, the less direct any route to solving his mental/financial crisis becomes. Soon he will have 'no thoroughfare' to progressing in his life, ending in total sclerosis.[120] Incidentally, Swiveller's shambolic financial arrangements and his comic insistence upon opposing bourgeois morality through petty criminality is akin to Baudelaire.[121] As Benjamin puts it, 'In his later years, Baudelaire did not often have the opportunity to stroll through the streets of Paris. His creditors were pursuing him'.[122]

Rather than being neurotic or depressed, though, Dick Swiveller is sanguine and even self-possessed. This may be because, while his engagement with the city is becoming more and more limited, a new network of streets open up under the auspices of his financial mismanagement. Going along thoroughfares he would otherwise never have used, or going three or four miles out of town may, ironically, open up entirely unpredictable opportunities to him, which are new physical and mental experiences.

### *Is Dickens a Flâneur?*

> In his book on Dickens, Chesterton has masterfully captured the man who roams the big city lost in thought. Charles Dickens' peregrinations began in his childhood. 'Whenever he had done drudging, he had no other resource but drifting, and he drifted over half London. He was a dreamy child, thinking mostly of his own dreary prospects [...] He walked in darkness under the lamps of Holborn, and was crucified at Charing Cross [...] He did not go in for "observation", a priggish habit; he did not look at Charing Cross to improve his

[119] Benjamin, 'Second Empire', *SW*, IV, p. 20.

[120] *No Thoroughfare* – a five-act melodrama by Dickens and Wilkie Collins – first performed in 1867. A wise character warns the impetuous hero off searching for his missing namesake, with 'you will find it no thoroughfare, sir, no thoroughfare' (*Complete Plays and Selected Poems of Charles Dickens* [London: Vision Press, 1970], p. 186).

[121] One stops short of the suggestion that Dick Swiveller could be a portrait of Baudelaire, since there is no evidence that Dickens read or was even aware of the French poet, particularly as early as 1840. There was no contact between Baudelaire and Dickens – even though the writers had a mutual literary contact, Edgar Allen Poe. But there is evidence that Baudelaire was aware of Dickens. He jovially accuses Champfleury of being jealous of Dickens (letter, January 14, 1854) in *Baudelaire: Correspondance, texte établi, présenté et annoté par Claude Pichois* (Paris: Editions Gallimard, 1973), 2 vols, I, pp. 255–6. Translation in *Selected Letters of Charles Baudelaire: The Conquest of Solitude*, trans. and ed. Rosemary Lloyd (London: Weidenfeld & Nicolson, 1986), pp. 60–61.

[122] 'Second Empire', in *SW*, IV, p. 41. See Appendix 1.

> mind or count the lamp-posts in Holborn to practise his arithmetic […] Dickens did not stamp these places on his mind; he stamped his mind on these places.'[123]

This quotation raises the question of whether there are ways in which Dickens does not exactly coalesce with the Baudelairean flâneur; or at least, where Dickens's version of flânerie tends to stretch the meaning of the activity considerably.[124]

For instance, at times, as is suggested by Benjamin's citation from Chesterton, here, Dickens has a tendency to use the city as a set upon which to paint his imagination. For example, in one of the 'Uncommercial Traveller' pieces, a series celebrating the activity of walking/observing and producing, Dickens claims he can sleep and dream while he is walking:

> I fell asleep to the monotonous sound of my own feet […] mile after mile I walked, without the slightest sense of exertion, dozing heavily and dreaming constantly. (*SN*, p. 118)[125]

This is surely at odds with flânerie, with what Hollington terms the flâneur's 'immanent speculation' – a reciprocal gathering up and a feeding off of the fragments of city life at the moment of looking/walking/thinking.[126] Dickens's activity here is a little more akin to the dreaming flâneur Benjamin describes in the *Arcades*: 'he [the flâneur] composes his reverie as text to accompany the images'.[127]

---

[123] Benjamin quoting G.K. Chesterton's *Dickens* (Paris 1927), in 'Second Empire', in *SW*, IV, p. 41. Benjamin's German passage was translated from the French. The *SW* editors cite from Chesterton's English *Charles Dickens* (1906; repr. New York: Schocken, 1965, pp. 45–6).

[124] Professor Andrew Sanders raised the question of whether Dickens should be interpreted as a flâneur at Dickens Day in London, October 25, 2011, coming down against the interpretation because 'Dickens's walking is purposive', and the novelist cannot accurately be viewed as an idle, privileged or disinterested observer. But this assumes a narrow definition of the concept, one that comes close to the historical figure of the early nineteenth century. The suggestion here is that a close reading of Benjamin allows for a much wider definition. As Hollington, in 'Dickens the Flâneur', in *The Dickensian* 77 (1981): pp. 71–87, finds, and is suggested here, the concept of 'The Flâneur' which comes out of *The Arcades* places the urban stroller/modern artist anywhere on a spectrum between the emotional gaping 'Badaud' and the self-obsessed commuter. This leaves much room for speculation and its flexibility means it could be applied to a walker/artist in Paris or London, despite their differing physical environments. Admittedly this is ambiguous, and hardly settles the matter.

[125] 'Shy Neighbourhoods', part of the 'The Uncommercial Traveller' series, in Slater, IV, pp. 117–26.

[126] 'immanent speculation', 'Dickens the Flâneur', p. 79. But Hollington elsewhere claims that 'Benjamin describes how the flâneur reaches oblivion through pacing the streets', 'Nickleby, Flanerie, Reverie: The View from the Cheerybles', *Dickens Studies Annual* 35 (2005): p. 23.

[127] *Arcades*, M2,2, p. 419. This interpretation contrasts with Martina Lauster's mistaken belief that 'the observer's speculative faculty, which seems at least as important as the activity of the eye, is totally left out of [Benjamin's] account' of the flâneur. See *Sketches of*

But rather than needing the immediate 'images' of the city upon which to build, the dreaming Dickens in *SN* describes a production that exists entirely within his own internal mind's eye, one which conducts little immediate interaction with the stimulation of the world around him except as a setting in which to exercise physically or an insubstantial canvas upon which to paint. The implication, again, is that physical walking and thinking/dreaming have become so inextricably connected that Dickens needs to be physically walking in order for thought/dreaming to follow. This is a definition of the flâneur without scopophilia; he is someone who 'collects' city fragments, keeping them and combining them with fantasy for later reveries undertaken during sleeping/walking/somnambulism.[128] On this particular journey, the sleeping Dickens imagines himself to be hiking in an alpine landscape, possibly the memory of his Swiss trips or fragments of a panorama or diorama Dickens had seen.

Another example to be considered in this context is Dickens's fictional flâneur in *OCS*, Master Humphrey. His preference is for approaching the city at night:

> Night is generally my time for walking [...] I seldom go out until after dark [...] it affords me greater opportunity of speculating on the characters and occupations of those who fill the streets. The flare and hurry of broad noon are not adapted to idle pursuits like mine; a glimpse of passing faces caught by the light of a street lamp or a shop window is often better for my purpose than their full revelation in the daylight, and, if I must add the truth, night is kinder in this respect than day, which too often destroys an air-built castle at the moment of its completion, without the smallest ceremony. (Master Humphrey, *OCS*, ch. 1, pp. 5–6)

When one reads Master Humphrey's explanation of why he prefers a setting where his imagination can have free rein, it is worth remembering that Dickens thrived upon nocturnal walking. Master Humphrey positively favors elliptical glimpses, fragments and partial revelations over the brighter perspectives available in full light: this is a particular form of flânerie as one usually understands it. In fact, light and actively looking, Master Humphrey implies, stymies his imagination. His interest is in cryptic clues, mystery, castles in the air, not 'knowledge'. And one cannot call this activity 'passive' or 'non-purposive' even though he terms the process 'idle'.[129]

---

*the Nineteenth Century: European Journalism and its Physiologies, 1830–50* (Basingstoke: Palgrave Macmillan, 2007), p. 10. There are a number of narrow interpretations of Benjamin in Lauster's interesting book on nineteenth-century sketches, which at times seeks to slay the master (Benjamin) that underpins and opens up the study.

[128] 'Scopophilia', literally the love of looking. A term used in feminist art and film criticism, analyzing the emphasis upon 'the look' or gaze upon the object within epistemology and aesthetics as phallocentric, an element within culture which 'masters' the object, often woman, rendering it powerless and without subjectivity (influenced by both Freudian and Lacanian psychoanalysis).

[129] One of Michael Hollington's assertions is that flânerie holds a mediating position between the continuum of 'purposive and non-purposive' activity on the street: 'Dickens the Flâneur', *The Dickensian* 77.2 (Summer 1981): pp. 71–87.

Presumably gaslight, which Benjamin claims helped make crowds feel safe and at home in the nighttime city, was an added dramatic aid to Master Humphrey's urban dreaming, with its creation of chiaroscuro and shadows.[130] The eloquence of Master Humphrey's musings, together with the importance of nocturnal wandering to Dickens – some of which went on for miles and hours at a time – makes it tempting to attribute Master Humphrey's explanations to Dickens himself.

The onus Dickens puts upon the work of imagination in flânerie was something Benjamin again recorded in the broader context of the definition of the flâneur in convolute M ('The Flâneur') of the *Arcades*:

> On the psychology of the flaneur: 'The undying scenes we can all see if we shut our eyes are not the scenes that we have stared at under the direction of guide-books; the scenes we see are the scenes at which we did not look at all – the scenes in which we walked when we were thinking about something else – about a sin, or a love affair, or some childish sorrow. We can see the background now because we did not see it then. So Dickens did not stamp these places on his mind; he stamped his mind on these places.'[131]

Here Benjamin opens up 'the flâneur' as the dreamer, with exactly Dickens in mind.[132] His depiction of a preoccupied walker puts one in mind not only of Dickens himself as a hungry boy wandering the streets, but of the fictional Sydney Carton's amorous flânerie in *TTC*. Carton's urge to make love to Lucie Manette takes the form of his physically and mentally traversing her byways:

> he did care something for the streets that environed that house, and for the senseless stones that made their pavements. Many a night he vaguely and unhappily wandered there. (*TTC*, bk. 2, ch. 13, p. 179)

There is another aspect in which Dickens is not quite a flâneur: he was not sufficiently aloof. As early as 1808, there is a disapproving nuance to the concept of the flâneur; he was seen as the leisured, dandy outsider: 'lazybones, the insufferable idler',[133] perhaps bourgeois, certainly of a superior class. 'The flâneur

[130] Discussion of gaslight: Benjamin, 'Second Empire', p. 28.

[131] *The Arcades Project*, M11,3: excerpt from G.K. Chesterton, *Dickens*, series entitled *Vie des homes illustres*, vol. 9, translated from the English by Laurent and Martin-DuPont (Paris: Gallimard, 1927), p. 31.

[132] John Tullock claims Dickens's journalistic career consists of the journey from flâneurial observation early on to mid-century social criticism. I work with a broader definition of 'the flâneur' than Tullock, one which involves more than merely the ironic, detached observer. See 'Charles Dickens and the Voices of Journalism', in Richard Keeble and Sharon Wheeler (eds.), *The Journalistic Imagination: Literary Journalists from Defoe to Capote and Carter* (Oxford; New York: Routledge, 2007), p. 63.

[133] Priscilla Parkhurst Ferguson, 'The flâneur on and off the streets of Paris' in Keith Tester (ed.), *The Flâneur* (London: Routledge, 1994), p. 24. Hereafter, Ferguson's essay will be referred to as 'Ferguson'.

is in society as he is in the city, suspended from social obligation, disengaged, disinterested, dispassionate.'[134]

When Victor Hugo claims in *Les Misérables* that 'To wander is human, flânerie is Parisian', one assumes this idea of the urbane flâneur, the moneyed, bored, leisurely outsider is certainly one aspect he was conjuring up. Even Benjamin claims flâneurs 'demanded elbow room and [were] unwilling to forgo the life of a gentleman of leisure', and they 'liked to have the turtle set the pace for them'.[135] In another passage, Benjamin suggests the flâneur regards the crowd with aristocratic 'contempt'.[136]

It is not the case that Dickens's flânerie – whether he depicts himself as a boy ('Gone Astray'), or in his 'Sketches by Boz' or in 'The Uncommercial Traveller' pieces, can be understood very effectively on these terms. One could go as far as claiming that on no occasion is he a leisurely, privileged idler. He tells the reader in *SN*,

> My walking is of two kinds; one, straight on end to a definitive goal at a round pace; one, objectless, loitering, and purely vagabond. In the latter state, no gypsy on earth is a greater vagabond than myself.[137]

Even when Dickens is 'sauntering' – which he at one point claims is the 'core' of his 'uncommercial pursuits' – his relationship to the city is not one of mastery and detachment, but is, at least at times, of powerlessness and dependence. Forster spends much wordage on Dickens's blacking warehouse experiences (*Life*, bk. 1, ch. 2, pp. 25–9), and he quotes Dickens: 'I know I have lounged about the streets insufficiently and unsatisfactorily fed.'[138] As opposed to the upper-class stroller who struts around wanting to be seen observing, when Dickens was hungry, he often lounged around the streets, staring longingly into shop windows, charting his way via the city's pudding shops. With such experience under his belt, it is hardly surprising that Dickens can rarely be found to cultivate the detachment, neutrality and objectivity toward the city which would apply to the flâneur of this privileged sort.

Look at this passage from 'Wapping Workhouse':

> It made my heart ache to think of this miserable trifling, in the streets of a city where every stone seemed to call to me, as I walked along, 'Turn this way, man, and see what waits to be done!' So I decoyed myself into another train of thought to ease my heart. But I don't know that I did it, for I was so full of paupers.[139]

---

[134] 'Ferguson', p. 26.

[135] Both quotations, 'Second Empire', p. 30.

[136] 'Motifs', section VI, p. 168.

[137] 'Slater', IV, p. 119.

[138] *Life*, bk. 1, ch. 2, p. 28.

[139] 'Slater', IV, p. 51.

This relationship to the city is fairly far away from:

> He (the flâneur) consumes the city at one remove, savouring the display without expenditure, financial or emotional.[140]

The emotional Dickens, here, comes closer on the spectrum to the 'badaud', who is 'affective', rather than the intellectual flâneur.[141] But the badaud is also passive, and it is never satisfactory to attribute this quality to Dickens, even when he is sleepwalking or loitering.

Taking this point about the empathetic, engaged side of Dickens further, a clear comparison between Dickens's stance toward the world and Baudelaire's can be achieved if we look at a segment of Baudelaire's definition of the artist/flaneur in 'The Painter of Modern Life'. In that text, Baudelaire claims that 'The artist lives very little, if at all, in the world of morals and politics', and he goes on, 'it must be admitted that the majority of artists are no more than highly skilled animals, pure artisans, village intellects, cottage brains'.[142] While it is perhaps unfair to pull sentences out of Baudelaire's piece and discuss them in isolation, it is difficult to resist the temptation here because of the difference it announces between Dickens and Baudelaire. But it is a difference that has already been noted. Baudelaire is claiming 'the artist' is not the scholar or the politician with a trained mind who theorizes about abstractions like morals or political frameworks. His is the improvised response to the concrete. He is the passionate spectator, seeing the world and painting it in vivid colors in all its fleeting immediacy. Such a description fits Dickens; as argued, he is a flâneur with an important reciprocal relationship with the concrete, with the city – and the city's variety, pace and dynamism, and the process by which it is experienced, makes its way into his writings. But the other dimension to Dickens is his engagement in morals and politics, 'abstractions' with which he became inured through his concrete experience as a journalist. Moreover, there is no better catalyst than poverty – which Dickens suffered as a boy – to trigger an interest in society's arrangements (politics) as well as in how such arrangements affect human behavior (morality). His novels are full of moral prescription and political satire – and, as was mentioned in Chapter 3, Baudelaire and others attempted to distinguished themselves from this approach. Here, then, Dickens departs from Baudelaire's definition. Dickens is as far from this particular Baudelairean definition of the 'privileged', disinterested flâneur as it is possible to be.

140 'Ferguson', p. 28.

141 Burton's distinction between the badaud and the flâneur, in 'Burton', p. 1.

142 Both quotations 'Painter', p. 138.

Fig. 4.2 'The Sea Rises' by Hablot Knight Browne, an engraving for *A Tale of Two Cities*, Book Two, Chapter 22. The image appeared in *All the Year Round* in October 1859. Reproduced by courtesy of the Charles Dickens Museum, London.

## The Crowd

> The crowd – no subject was more entitled to the attention of nineteenth century writers. ('On Some Motifs in Baudelaire', p. 162)
>
> My figures seem disposed to stagnate without crowds about them. (Dickens to Forster, *Life*, bk. 5, ch. 5, p. 423)
>
> … the life and crowd of that extraordinary place [London] will come vividly to my assistance in writing. (The Pilgrim edition of the *Letters of Charles Dickens*, ed. M. House, G. Storey and K. Tillotson [Oxford: Clarendon Press, 1965], vol. IV, p. 569)

As discussed in Chapter 3, for Benjamin, the rapid economic and social processes of urban modernity involved a change in experience. Any understanding of the changing nature of urban experience – comprised as it is by accelerated speeds and fragmented space – must involve a discussion of 'the crowd'.[143]

---

[143] The most fruitful of Benjamin's passages on 'the crowd' can be found in the *The Arcades Project* itself, especially in the convolute J on Baudelaire, in convolute K on Dream City and Dream House and in convolute M on The Flâneur. Predictably, it also appears as a theme in the smaller studies Benjamin prepared upon the basis of the *Arcades*: in the two

The presence of the crowd in the city space was an integral part of the experience of flânerie, of experience as dominated by 'the shock' (*Chockerlebnis*). If one accepts the assumption Benjamin's work on Baudelaire implies – that the urban space is a correlative of consciousness, that the city's physical geography has an effect upon how one experiences and represents the world[144] – then questions about the crowd's effect upon the individual psyche must come into play. The city, then, is a setting for the experimentation of ideas about identity – and, indeed, with its welter of sudden transitions, interminglings and improvisations, the site of the interrogation of the subject/object divide and the crisis of the Subject. One critic understands Benjamin to be claiming that the city's impermanence, movement and complexity replaces the notions of substance and the Subject with 'transitivity', 'porosity' and 'fluidity'; a state of affairs where the old Kantian categories somehow no longer hold.[145] Baudelaire's reading of Poe's 'The Man of the Crowd' certainly depicts the eponymous man as overwhelmed by the crowd, yet gaining a jouissance in his own dissolution into it.[146]

The deeply felt 'threat' the crowd posed to the Subject led to a growth in attempts to classify, control and throw light upon the city, including the numbering of houses, and the use of photography to help identify criminals.[147] There was also a short-lived fad for classifying the passerby through the lens of certain external types and city codes of behavior: the 'physiologies'[148] – born out of a need to combat the fear of crowdedness in the city.[149] While Benjamin condemns this phenomenon of instant categorization as lightweight, there is, at the same time, something of an attachment to such dilettantism: 'The phantasmagoria of the flâneur: to read from faces the profession, the ancestry, the character.'[150] Boz's job, as has been suggested, was to look, instantly classify and move on. His sketches of city life, an attempt to organize the concatenations of impressions, people and events in the city, could be understood to prefigure or reflect the cult of physiologies across the Channel.

versions of 'Paris – the Capital of the 19th Century' (1935, 1939), 'The Paris of the Second Empire in Baudelaire' (1938) and in 'On Some Motifs in Baudelaire' (1939). (These essays are abbreviated in this book as 'Paris, Capital'; 'Second Empire' and 'Motifs', respectively.)

[144] As has been mentioned, this assumption is reliant upon the work of sociologist Georg Simmel, especially his 'The Metropolis and Mental Life' (1902–1903). See section XI of 'Motifs', p. 187. There are 11 fragments concerning Simmel in *The Arcades Project*, including two in convolute M, 'The Flâneur'.

[145] This is Howard Caygill's argument in *Walter Benjamin, The Colour of Experience* (London; New York: Routledge, 1998). He reads Benjamin's theory of experience as primarily an engagement with neo-Kantianism.

[146] 'Painter', p. 138.

[147] 'Second Empire', pp. 26–9. The most extreme example of this attempt to 'control' was, of course, in Paris, where the fear of the barricade 'mobs' took the form of the Haussmannisation of large swathes of labyrinthine streets and poverty-stricken hamlets.

[148] 'Second Empire', p. 18. In 1841, there were 76 new physiologies.

[149] *Arcades*, M16a,2.

[150] *Arcades*, M6,6.

*The Threatening Physical Presence of the Crowd*

Dickens's depictions of the urban crowd show evidence of the kind of anxiety associated with the overwhelming of the faculties Benjamin describes in his Baudelaire writings. The fear of the palpable physical dominance of the crowd is evoked by Dickens's habit of spatially counterposing the crowd to a fixed nodal point, a single entity, person or quality. The novelist, at times, seems unable to conceive of a crowd unless it is through the concept of a multitude in contrast to singularity.

In the first court scene of *TTC*, Dickens's image is of hundreds of eyes fixed on one point, Charles Darnay, conjuring a sickeningly surreal, vertiginous side to the multiplication of numbers the crowd represents:

> Everybody present [...] stared at him. All the human breath in the place, rolled at him, like a sea, or a wind, or a fire. Eager faces strained round pillars and corners, to get a sight of him; spectators in back rows stood up, not to miss a hair of him; people on the floor of the court laid their hands on the shoulders of the people before them. (*TTC*, bk. 2, ch. 2, p. 92)

And once again, in a later passage:

> The people closed round, and looked at Monsieur the Marquis. There was nothing revealed by the many eyes that looked at him but watchfulness and eagerness. (The Marquis runs over a child in his carriage, *TTC*, bk. 2, ch. 7, p. 141)[151]

In both excerpts, the overbearing presence of the crowd is emphasized – all eyes focused upon the same target, the one is 'trapped' by the many. Suddenly, Darnay and the Marquis are reduced: they are petrified objects to be scrutinized and judged. In the first excerpt, the many-eyed monster is unfathomable with its stillness, its blank staring eyes, anonymity and unanimity. The mindless, persecutory nature of all its attention being directed toward one is Dickens's paranoia in the face of the crowd at its most nightmarish. Dickens's repetition of this depiction of the crowd as brutalized persecutor in *TTC* seems to deny the possibility that the crowd could be a collection of individuals, whose movement and attention is unorchestrated and dissipated. Here, the crowd's energy and power is unified and it overwhelms. Its predatory intentions are emphasized by public space; pillars are obstacles the

[151] The representation of a vehicle crushing a child and the gathering of an accusing crowd also features in King Vidor's 1928 silent film, *The Crowd*. As has already been indicated, one filmmaker and one Dickens scholar make a link between Dickens's fictional techniques and tendencies in early cinema: Eisenstein in *Film Form* and Grahame Smith, *Dickens and the Dream of Cinema* (Manchester and New York: Manchester University Press, 2003). Other scholars make the link between urban experience and film, including Miriam Hansen, 'The Mass Production of the Senses: Classical Cinema as Vernacular Modernism', *Modernism/Modernity* 6.2 (April 1999): pp. 59–77; and Howard R. Weiner, 'The Cinema and the City', *Journal of Popular Culture* 3.4 (Spring 1970): p. 825.

crowd can peer around. The weight of the crowd's unspoken intention threatens and challenges.

In the second excerpt, the eyes are upon the higher-status Marquis. Uncannily, these eyes are speaking, they radiate reproach, they accuse in their silent intentness. These bodies and sets of eyes represent a reminder to the Marquis of his responsibilities; their watchfulness and eagerness indicate his remoteness, neglect and cruelty. This crowd's multitude signifies their powerlessness in relation to the powerful 'one', yet the sheer numbers of eyes is still an uncanny and horrifying threat. This crowd is the poor as dependent, a burden; but in closing around and focusing upon the Marquis, they demand an explanation. One of the sights the city affords is that of the eyes of the poor upon the rich.[152] Eyes are not a passive surface of reflection, yet Dickens claims these eyes reveal nothing. Again, this is uncanny. Watching the poor's eyes upon the rich would involve witnessing a refraction of that object through conditions of suffering and poverty endured; here, the eyes revealing nothing indicates repression, fear and resignation felt in the presence of the only 'one' that matters – the master. This is a frightening and ambiguous depiction of the crowd, then, whose sheer numbers represent a threat to the one (the Marquis), yet whose habitual subservience both reveals and conceals their deeper feelings of anger and resentment toward him.

In chapter 5 of *TTC*, the crowd is juxtaposed with the fixed points of hunger, the mill and, of course, the wine:

> All the people within reach had suspended their business, or their idleness, to run to the spot and drink the wine [...] each by its own jostling group or crowd, according to its size.

and

> Samples of a people that had undergone a terrible grinding and re-grinding in the mill [...] the mill that grinds young people old; [...] and upon the grown faces, and ploughed into every furrow of age and coming up afresh, was the sign, Hunger. (*TTC*, bk. 1, ch. 5, p. 59 and p. 60, respectively)

Both passages again augment the idea of a great number by its contrast with a single quality. In both excerpts, the single quality is the source of the crowd's awareness of their own powerlessness. In the wine scene, the sheer numbers wanting to quench their thirst forces individuals into a kind of mock celebration of their crowdedness, as they laugh at their jostling and competitive efforts, and stem the flow of the wine together. This depiction of jovial crowdedness can be seen as evidence of the crowd's passive mentality or lack of intelligence. Such a

[152] Baudelaire acknowledges this urban experience in 'Les Petites Vieilles' ('Little Old Ladies'), part of the 'Tableaux Parisiens', in *Charles Baudelaire: Selected Poems*, p. 97.

conservative eye upon a depiction of this sort would be the critic, Le Bon 'In a crowd, every sentiment and act is contagious'.[153]

Benjamin himself is not immune to this imperious gaze upon the crowd. One observation compares the economic, abrupt movements of a crowd to the mechanistic jerkiness of 'the repertoire of clowns',[154] (gesturing toward early film's crowd scenes or even the Keystone Kops).[155]

For Dickens, though, this crowd's crowdedness is not to be mocked, even if they are jovial. He places the wine scene within the context of the people's poverty, having already described their vile social conditions. Their sharing and helping one another to wine therefore is an index of some dignity, while yet the description of their lascivious and uncouth dalliances (*TTC*, bk. 1, ch. 5, p. 60) has a slightly haughty tone. The terms in which Dickens frames the novel – the tale of two cities – and his use of the term 'samples of a people' in the second excerpt suggests this crowd is a metonymic representation of 'the poor' of France per se, the French poor who participated in revolution. Since the narrative claims the mill grinds them down like so many valueless pieces of clay, their ability to make the most of their situation is brave, admirable. This is an empathetic attempt to understand the conditions that go into the making of revolutionary action, although the crowd's overt physicality and uncivilized behavior, their willingness to band together in the poverty, is still a threatening phenomenon.

The second excerpt registers the difficulty of conceiving of the crowd in the very depiction of them. The crowd is, literally, innumerable. Dickens presents, he specifies, only 'a sample' and that 'token' of the crowds of poor lives an emblematic lifetime in an instant, laboring from cradle to grave in one image. As has been suggested, in the city, one cannot grasp the whole, experience can only ever be fragmentary, and here, the narrative reflects that urban dilemma. If the crowd's vastness causes an awareness in the passing onlooker that their faculties cannot encompass it, and hence anxiety, the narrative assumes that perspective.[156] The crowd's size is also the heart of the problem for the individual member of the crowd. A multitude of hungry people reduces the individual's visibility and any prospect of relief – as the outsider backs away, overwhelmed. Dickens's close up, horrified gaze at the hunger that molds the wrinkles of their faces, illustrates how a crowd of paupers would cause the flight of an onlooker. The sight of so

[153] Gustave Le Bon, *The Crowd: A Study of the Popular Mind* (New York: Viking Press, 1960), p. 29.

[154] 'Second Empire', p. 30.

[155] The Keystone Kops were the subject of a series of silent film comedies featuring an incompetent group of policemen. The films included *Hoffmeyer's Legacy* (1912) and *The Bangville Police* (1913).

[156] Dickens does, rarely, describe a scene from a position within the crowd. See Appendix 2, 'The Political Meaning of the Crowd in Dickens', where the crowd at elections in *BR* is discussed.

many needy people amounts to an overwhelming assault upon the senses. Crowd members must hate and fear their own crowdedness.

Again, the hungry 'sample' is a metonym for what happened to an entire class in France before the Revolution. Its presence on the street voices the people's suffering in public, but it differs from the organized demonstrations of, say, the Chartist movement of the 1840s, with its insistence upon being heard and entering into public discourse. This crowd signifies the tired, vulnerable, helpless mass. While suffering, its presence on the street is a sign which can be and is ignored by those in power, with the possibility of starvation in a public space. The problem of the poor's having a voice that is taken seriously is hinted at in *BR*: Lord George Gordon claims members of his organization 'are the only men who regard the mass out of doors, and are regarded by them' (*BR*, ch. 35, p. 340). Dickens's narrative is Janus-faced in this excerpt. He angrily disapproves of the suffering they undergo, emphasizing their human qualities by focusing upon a small number, and dramatically evincing their lives as a 'grinding' by poverty and labor. Yet the narrative still demonstrates the anxiety and repulsion felt in the face of a suffering crowd through its horrified, fascinated close-up gaze.

Dickens's treatment of Gordon's crowd on the move in *BR* crystallizes the fearful physical power of the crowd. The parameters of city space are pushed to the limit by the crowd. Crammed with bodies, the city becomes a claustrophobic site which determines the movement of individuals as they are physically driven by the intention of the crowd. Caught up in the demonstration, 'The whole field was in motion; Barnaby was whirled away into the heart of a dense mass of men' (*BR*, ch. 48, p. 449), while, of the convergence of the crowds upon Westminster, Dickens claims the individual is unable to retreat, 'borne as on a great wave', and claims a boy must 'walk upon the heads of others' to assert his intention upon space. Hence the anxiety of the Subject is one of being trampled by the crowd. Dickens claims this crowd is chaotic and disorganized, yet while its maneuvers are not military, it has a unity of energy that differs from, say, the crowd of individuals Engels describes as obsessively pursuing their own aims.[157] Waves of energy, often from an unidentified source, affect crowds. Dickens tends to resort to natural metaphors like the sea, the wind or a field of crop, an accurate visual reference that captures the surging and swaying effect a large number of discreet individuals undergo and dissipate through their physical movement in a dense crowd. It expresses too the crowd as mindless and impervious, an urban hydra that can crush, whose activity is as uncontrollable as the movements of nature.

In *TTC* and *BR*, the harrowing vision of the unstable, dangerous and violent urban crowd is presented. The crowd as a chaotic mob bent on destruction, once stirred, reflects the viewpoint, brought up in *The Arcades Project*, that the mob was seen as a major threat to social order and is capable of bringing down structures of political power.[158] As Humphry House put it, between 1834–1848, 'the possibility

[157] Engels quoted in 'Motifs', pp. 162–3.

[158] 'Second Empire', p. 26.

of revolution was rarely far from men's minds'.[159] In several scenes, Dickens adopts this voice of the threatened, authoritarian middle-class gentleman, who finds the crowd loathsome and dangerous. The crowd gathered outside the House of Commons in *BR*, then, is 'composed for the most part of the very scum and refuse of London' (*BR*, ch. 49, p.453).

And in scenes of a rioting mob, the narrative voice is barely calm. The crowd is objectified as wild and monstrous:

> These, the people tore to pieces and scattered far and wide with great enjoyment, while the tradesmen hurriedly shut up their shops; for a crowd in those times stopped at nothing and was a monster much dreaded. (Cly's mock funeral scene, *TTC*, bk. 2, ch. 14, p. 186)

This anxious tone is repeated in the most famous crowd scene in *TTC*, when the narrator speaks the unashamed discourse of disgust. A fast-paced, tense rhythm – the rhythm of gathering anxiety – governs the flow of the narrative. Again, a horrified, close up gaze amplifies the fear of and revulsion at the distorted faces, smells, and sounds of the grotesque carnival:

> The grindstone had a double handle, and, turning at it madly were two men, whose faces […] were more horrible and cruel than the visages of the wildest savages in their most barbarous disguise. False eyebrows and false moustaches were stuck upon them, and their hideous countenances were all bloody and sweaty, and all awry with howling, and all staring and glaring with beastly excitement and want of sleep […] and what with dropping blood, and what with dropping wine, and what with the stream of sparks struck out of the stone, all their wicked atmosphere seemed gore and fire. (*TTC*, bk. 3, ch. 2, p. 291)

The frightening, even surreal nature of the crowd extends to the mob's own awareness of its ability to arouse terror – indexed through their donning of melodramatic villains' mustaches and through their howling. Dickens revels in his survey of the appalling scene, conjuring a tone of wildness with his use of extreme, emotional vocabulary, breathlessly elongated sentences, and close-up, detailed description. Again, he has both a horror and fascination, exhibiting the 'attraction of repulsion' scenes of poverty always had for him.[160]

The narrative shifts from this myth-inflected image of a hellish frenzy, from the fantasized danger the crowd poses to the vulnerable self (indeed, to the Narrator), to a shocking scene where this anxiety is realized. Dicken's treatment of the battering and crushing of Foulon by the crowd is shockingly matter of fact:

> the long-gathering rain of stabs and blows fell heavy […] he dropped down dead under it [and] suddenly animated, she put her foot upon his neck and with her cruel knife – long ready – hacked off his head. (*TTC*, bk. 2, ch. 21, p. 249)

[159] *The Dickens World*, 2nd ed. (Oxford: Oxford University Press, 1942), p. 49.

[160] *Life*, bk. 1, ch. 1, p. 11.

Dickens – conjuring up all the rawness and brutality of the act in a play upon its rhythm with four simple one-syllable words: 'hacked of his head' – is so appalled at this turn of events he immediately offers an explanation on behalf of the mob. He claims their 'faces hardened in the furnaces of suffering' have endured so much that the 'touch of pity could make no mark on them' (both, *TTC*, bk. 2, ch. 21, p. 249). Yet the vision of the frenzied killing and destruction indulged in by the mob is too terrible to assuage Dickens's terror:

> any unbrutalised beholder would have given twenty years of life, to petrify with a well-directed gun. (*TTC*, bk. 3, ch. 2, p. 292)

Dickens shows in no uncertain terms how the crowd's terrifying physical presence can have a deeply disorientating effect upon the Subject's psyche. In *LD*, Dickens depicts how the anxious Clennam's vertiginous thought processes – a result of the shocks, noise and confusion of city life – reflect and are exacerbated by the crowd's presence:

> The crowd in the street jostling the crowd in his mind, and the two crowds making a confusion, he avoided London Bridge. (*LD*, ch. 22, p. 253)

Baudelaire sets up an image of the flâneur as 'a mirror as vast as the crowd itself; a […] kaleidoscope gifted with consciousness',[161] and Dickens appears to ratify this view of the stroller's activity of reflecting, mirror-like, the crowd's excess and unpredictability, calling Arthur Clennam's confusion of thoughts, his mental activity, 'a crowd'.[162] Clennam struggles to orientate himself, resisting the breakdown of the subject/object divide that city experience can involve. He is a kind of walking monad in the city. The *Chockerlebnis*-like quality of his strolling, the anxiety-generated accumulation of thoughts and the physical jostling by the crowd is brought together in an image, again suggesting an identity of strolling and thinking. But while Clennam's crowd of thoughts and the urban crowd may bump against each other's 'realm', a binary separation of internal and external 'crowds' is still maintained. Here, Dickens depicts that dreamlike urban state of mind where both internal and external 'crowds' are intangible and elusive: one can neither concentrate upon one nor the other, both vie for attention, while the other is a distraction.

Another uncanny and horrifying vision that Dickens conjures up of crowds is in their suffocating proximity, and yet their mindless, zombie-like unawareness of the Subject's existence. It is, indeed, a general anxiety that one might lose a

[161] 'Painter', p. 140.

[162] Another example of this is in the already cited 'Wapping Workhouse' when Dickens declares, 'I was so full of paupers', see above, p. 174, note 139. The novelist was by no means the first author to enlist the image of 'the crowd' to evoke the effect urban hustle and bustle has upon the thought processes. Thomas De Quincey (1785–1859) implies as much in his 1822 *The Confessions of an English Opium Eater* (London: J.M. Dent; New York: E.P. Dutton, n.d.), when a crowd of phantoms haunt his brain (p. 176).

loved one in the crowd, virtually jostle them, yet miss them and be unaware of the fact, cut off by the city's phantasmagoric qualities, by space and the crowd. In one of his *SB*, 'A Visit to Newgate', Dickens depicts crowds of oblivious people passing within feet of the crowd of condemned men in Newgate: 'day by day, and hour by hour, pass and repass this gloomy depository of the guilt and misery of London, in one perpetual stream of life and bustle, utterly unmindful of the throng of wretched creatures pent up within' (*SB*, Scenes: ch. 25, p. 234).[163] As Benjamin claims of the flâneur's conflictual relationship to the crowd: 'he was nevertheless unable to rid himself of a sense of their essentially inhuman make-up'.[164]

The flâneur, establishing a stable sense of self, distances himself from the crowd, but this raises a problem: loneliness. As Benjamin puts it, in parrying the shocks of the city, Baudelaire becomes isolated, abandoned in the crowd.[165] Engels, quoted by Benjamin as was mentioned above, is horrified at the apparent isolation in which individuals exist amid the London crowd, individuals who hurry past one another as if they had nothing in common.[166] Dickens treats this theme: and he especially emphasizes the disaster that this state of affairs represents for the urban poor – the point being made by Engels. For instance, as was outlined in chapter 1, Nell and Grandfather suffer the hard end of isolation in the crowd in Wolverhampton. The harsh treatment meted out to the homeless wanderers as they beg along the road to destruction comes to a climax in this scene, as if Dickens is claiming that the propounded doctrine of laissez-faire toward the poor found its ultimate expression in the busy city streets. Interestingly, while Benjamin includes Engels's lamentations about the behavior of the London crowd, he also suggests Engels's view is an 'old fashioned' fear of the phenomenon. One could suggest, then, Dickens appears to be more politically nuanced than the 'Marxist-influenced' Benjamin. Moreover, the political meaning of how Dickens treats the crowd in a number of scenes amounts to a dramatic contrast with Baudelaire's use of the figure of the crowd, which Benjamin claims 'conspicuously lacks any social or political significance as a class'.[167]

David Copperfield articulates a shamefulness in public solitariness, as well as the cruel indifference on the part of others to the alone:

> More solitary than Robinson Crusoe, who had nobody to look at him and see that he was solitary. (*DC*, ch. 5, p. 62)

---

[163] This depiction of a crowd of mindless, gazing people treading in an endless stream, as if on a treadmill, conjures up the image of the downtrodden workers in the underworld in Fritz Lang's 1927 silent film *Metropolis*.

[164] 'Motifs', p. 168.

[165] 'Second Empire', p. 31.

[166] 'Motifs', pp. 162–3.

[167] Quoted in Tomoko Masuzawa, 'Tracing the Figure of Redemption: Walter Benjamin's Physiognomy of Modernity', *Modern Language Notes* 100.3 (April 1985): pp. 514–36 (p. 525). See Appendix 2 for a lengthy discussion of the political meaning in Dickens's treatment of the crowd in his fiction.

The implication here is that the suffering of loneliness is augmented by the crowd's witnessing of it. The presence of the many brings it home all the more starkly to 'the one' that he/she is alone, a single speck within infinite variety. The crowd's looking at, yet being indifferent to, one's solitariness makes one more self-conscious of, even ashamed of, that state; as well as being mournful that no kindly hand is proffered even among a vast number of individuals available to do so. Hence, here, the one feels fundamentally, even existentially cut off from the world. And, flâneur-like, the loner in the crowd is desperate to bathe and forget himself in it, to have human contact.

If Dickens is fond of emphasizing the multitude of the crowd by setting it against 'the one', his tendency to weirdly absorb the multitude into the one, must also be mentioned. In *TTC*, Dickens depicts the uncanny relationship between the crowd and 'the one' as that of mirror images of each other:

> Any strongly marked expression of face on the part of a chief actor in a scene of great interest to whom many eyes are directed, will be unconsciously imitated by the spectators [...] a great majority of the foreheads there might have been mirrors reflecting the witness. (bk. 2, ch. 3, p. 102)

Again, this comes close to Benjamin's Keystone Kops image of the crowd's jerky urban movements resembling the 'repertoire of clowns'.

In *BR*, Dickens goes further. Grip, Barnaby's raven, 'sounded like the murmurs of a crowd of people' (ch. 17, p. 188). This is, obviously, an intensely perceptive evocation of the amazing vocal range and eerie strangeness of such birds. But one can also view this image as Dickens expressing the ultimate multitude/one model – in one literary stroke erecting a boundary around the infinite multitude.[168] The notion of a bounded infinite is for Dickens the author perhaps, a much more comfortable thought than the unmasterable infinitude of the crowd. However, it still presents a frightening image of an unstable 'self'.

### *The 'Gothic' Crowd in Space and Time*

As well as the terrifying threat of the crowd's physical presence, Dickens also evinces the experience of the urban crowd as evanescent, as haunting the city. It is as if the crowd's effect goes far beyond its physical manifestation – terrifying as that is – and becomes part of the phantasmagoria of the city. Chapter 3 explored the fact that Benjaminian urban theory suggests that time (memories, the past) constitutes an integral part of urban space. Within that framework, the memories, dreams, consciousness of the character David Copperfield, for example, were seen to be reworked and rewritten upon the labyrinthine surfaces of Dickens's fictional cityscape. In *TTC*, Dickens again conjures up this notion of the past haunting a

[168] Interestingly, Dickens's friend, Leigh Hunt claims of Dickens's face: 'it has the life and soul in it of fifty human beings', *Life*, bk. 2, ch. 1, p. 84.

space – in one image. In the first court scene, the crowd is represented not only in space on the surface of a mirror but also through time:

> Over the prisoner's head there was a mirror, to throw the light down upon him. Crowds of the wicked and the wretched had been reflected in it, and had passed from its surface and the earth's together. Haunted in a most ghastly manner that abominable place would have been, if the glass could ever have rendered back its reflections, as the ocean is one day to give up its dead. (*TTC*, bk. 2, ch. 2, p. 94)[169]

It could also be suggested that this image is a fictional equivalent of Benjamin's 'dialectical image' where past and present are brought together in a temporal montage. What this image does do, interestingly, is represent in graphic terms how the city crowd has a haunting quality: it can be experienced as either absent or present or both at once. And Dickens uses a time lapse in the reading process to demonstrate the effect of this 'gothic' experience. First Dickens presents the reader with a mirror reflection of the prisoner – which appears in the present moment. He then evokes the reflection of the past; the mirror reflection of the crowd appears once the reader has paused over the full stop and read the sentence: 'Crowds of the wicked and the wretched had been reflected in it.' The graduated, montaged temporality of the image is enacted in the act of reading.

As argued, Benjamin characterizes the city as an ambiguous space where one is condemned to endlessly revisit the same places, to pound the pavements, either lost in thought, or as a more positive agency looking, watching, observing. In the discussion on the character David Copperfield, the city is the place where fragments of dreams and memories exist, recur, interrelate and never resolve themselves. Ultimately, Benjamin suggests, the nature of the city is that one will never get to the heart of the matter. The haunting absence/presence of the crowd in the city space is an important part of this understanding of urban experience as gothic or phantasmagoric. The crowd can obfuscate and hide, or suddenly become the source of, what one seeks in the city. The crowd can either be tangibly present or elusively absent. Benjamin expresses the crowd's evanescent quality in the city space in terms of the opacity of fabric: 'The mass was the agitated veil; through it Baudelaire saw Paris.'[170] The experience of the crowd as a spectral entity is one that happens while walking dreamily in the city as well as during an elliptical memory of that urban experience.[171] Dickens represents the crowd's illusory semi-absence, in the excerpt, in the shimmering gothic lighting or chiaroscuro of a mirror's surface. Dickens's mirror is a good metaphor for the evanescence of the urban crowd: captured reflections of crowds, and reflections of reflections,

[169] I suggest Dickens lifted this image from Ann Radcliffe's *The Mysteries of Udolpho* (1794), which Dickens would have undoubtedly read. See *The Mysteries of Udolpho*, ed. Binamy Dobrée (Oxford and New York: Oxford World Classics, 1998), ch. VI, p. 547.

[170] 'Motifs', p. 164.

[171] John Plotz makes this point: *The Crowd: British Literature and Public Politics* (Berkeley; Los Angeles: University of California Press, 2000), p. 78.

or watching a crowd through a shop window, is all part of the experience of the plate-glass furniture of the street.[172] His mirror is evocative of memory, too: with its tendency to suggest something palpable is present when it offers only an insubstantial, intangible reflection. The mirror image conjures up the dialectical nature of memory: is it something one has or something one has lost?

Further evidence of Dickens's evocation of the gothic absense/presence of the crowd, of its haunting of the city, is in his use of sound to evoke the crowd.

In *TTC*, in the chapter 'Hundreds of People', the Manette family sit in their fixed nodal point, the corner house, listening to and dreaming about the crowds outside:

> There was a great hurry in the streets, of people speeding away to get shelter before the storm broke; the wonderful corner for echoes resounded with the echoes of footsteps coming and going, yet not a footstep was there. (bk. 2, ch. 6, p. 132)[173]

Dickens dramatizes an urban crowd as ghostly and uncannily ambiguous through the evocation of the sounds and the echoes of the city. While the echoes exist, Dickens claims, 'yet not a footstep was there', refusing to disclose whether the 'echoes' of footsteps are echoes of the mind or genuine city sounds. For the purposes of dramatic effect, Dickens refuses the unreality/reality distinction. The spectrality of this crowd is also evoked by Dickens's play upon time and space:

> The footsteps were incessant, and the hurry of them became more and more rapid. The corner echoed and re-echoed with the tread of feet; some, as it seemed, under the windows; some, as it seemed, in the room; some coming, some going, some breaking off, some stopping altogether; all in the distant streets and not one within sight. (*TTC*, bk. 2, ch. 6, p. 133)

The fast-paced, irregular and seemingly unending rhythm of sounds of footsteps evoke the city crowd. In addition, the speeding up of this rhythm suggests an intention among a multitude, the jostling, urban hurry and hustle and bustle. But there is no clarity in the soundscape, no footstep can be isolated, listened for or identified with certainty. The 'original' sounds of footsteps merge with the echoing and re-echoing of the former sounds of tread. Each moment for the family, then, is a repetitive blend of second-wave echoes and new sounds. This dreamy mix of past and present sounds within each dense moment, displaces the family's sequential experience of temporality, a confusion only augmented by the uncertainty of

[172] In a letter to Forster (July 29, 1841) concerning *BR*, Dickens asks, 'seen no 71? I thought there was a good glimpse of a crowd from a window, eh?' *Life*, bk. 2, ch. 9, p. 169.

[173] The setting of 'the corner house' is significant in the Gothic and detective genres. The panoramic optics and receptivity to noise and echoes such a house affords makes it the perfect haunt for the fictional urban detective. Stevenson's *Dr Jekyll and Mr Hyde* features such a setting. In a discussion on Baudelaire's reading of Poe's 'The Man of the Crowd', Benjamin mentions E.T.A. Hoffman's short story 'The Cousin's Corner Window' as an interesting representation of how a leisured man watches the crowd: 'Motifs', p. 169.

where exactly the sounds are emanating from. The crowd is simultaneously under the window, in distant streets and within the room but cannot be seen. Undermining not only the conventional understanding of time but the category of space, then, Dickens delineates here the fearful, Gothic experience of the city. This is a scary haunting, with its presentiments of mob violence and aggression indexed in the confusion of the footsteps, the incessant but variable rhythm, and in the powerlessness of the Manettes to effect any control over the strange haunting. This is the crowd as unreachable, impervious to reason or modification by outside forces or rational individuals: the sort of crowd that will later play out the scenes of revolutionary violence in the novel.

This Dickensian play upon the absence/presence of the crowd is also evoked through the idea of the crowd's affect upon the fabric of the city and its inhabitants. For instance, Dickens depicts the noise of an approaching crowd – in a play, once again, upon space and time. There is the disturbing anticipation of an approaching crowd that has not yet arrived:

> Hark! Something very faint and distant, not unlike the murmuring in a sea-shell. Now it grew louder, fainter now, and now it altogether died away. Presently, it came again, subsided, came once more, grew louder, fainter – swelled into a roar. It was on the road, and varied with its windings. All at once it burst into a distinct sound – the voices, and the tramping feet of many men. (*BR*, ch. 54, p. 494)

Even when the crowd is not physically present in time and space, then, it pervades, it haunts the city space, in this instance through sound waves. But Dickens also delineates its haunting via the mental after-effects of riots – the crowd's rumored antics among the townsfolk are rife once they are geographically elsewhere (*BR*, ch. 54, p. 492). The crowd as rumor is both omnipresent and absent at the same time.

The crowd's centrality to urban space and time even manifests itself in the form of premonitions in the minds of Dickens's characters. Never having set eyes upon a crowd before and ahead of becoming a rioter himself, Barnaby Rudge asks the blind man, 'Do you see great crowds of faces?' (*BR*, ch. 45, p. 421). Barnaby attributes his own talent for second sight to the blind man, here, and when he gets to London, he will have an experience of déjà vu, finding that the city, as well as his own mind, is haunted by the crowd. In *TTC*, the crowd similarly appears as a presentiment of the future:

> I have sometimes sat alone here of an evening, listening, until I have made the echoes out to be the echoes of all the footsteps that are coming by-and-by into our lives. 'There is a great crowd coming one day into our lives, if that be so', Sidney Carton struck in. (Bk. 2, ch. 6, p. 133)

Of course, a great crowd, the revolutionary mob, does soon enter the lives of the characters, having an indelible effect upon them.

Dickens can either represent the crowd as palpably and threateningly present (as in the rioting scenes in *TTC* discussed above) or as evanescently present/absent and ghostly, then. This echoes the pattern of material in Benjamin's Baudelaire studies. Just taking a couple of passages from 'Motifs' as evidence, Benjamin says that, for Baudelaire, 'The masses had become so much a part of Baudelaire that it is rare to find a description of them in his works [...] In *Tableaux parisiens* the secret presence of a crowd is demonstrable almost everywhere'.[174]

Yet, a little later, in a description of Poe's 'The Man of the Crowd', Benjamin concedes that for Poe, 'there was something menacing in the spectacle they [the crowd] presented'.[175]

Since one is obliged in reading Benjamin to feed both suggestions (fragments) into an understanding of the city crowd, one can conclude that Dickens's ambivalent presentation of the crowd echoes what can be gleaned from the contours of Benjamin's work on this point.

Dickens's delineation also resonates with the psychological ambivalence of the flâneur toward the crowd. The flâneur's is a paradoxical need to bathe in the crowd which at the same time involves battling to maintain a stable sense of self. 'If he [Baudelaire] succumbed to the force by which he was drawn to them and, as a flâneur, was made one of them, he was nevertheless unable to rid himself of a sense of their essentially inhuman make-up.'[176] This is the source of the flâneur's anxiety and of his 'heroism'.

## *The Crowd and Coincidence*

A coincidence of a certain time and a certain space is at the heart of how the crowd affects the individual flâneur or urban dweller in the city. Benjamin notes how often, 'Far from experiencing the crowd as an opposed, antagonistic element, this very crowd brings the city dweller the figure that fascinates'.[177] Here Benjamin, like Dickens, expresses the model which picks out 'the one' from among the multitude. What this passage opens up is the idea that the crowd is what provides and what withholds moments of revelation in the city. Baudelaire's version of this phenomenon in his poetry takes the form of the tantalizing love affair: 'The delight of the urban poet is love – not at first sight, but at last.'[178] And Baudelaire's 'A une passante' (To a Passer-by) in *Les Fleurs du Mal* reads:

> Too late! Perhaps never! / For where you're off to I'll never know, nor do you know where I'm going- / O you whom I could have loved, O you who knew it too![179]

---

[174] Section V, p. 164.

[175] Ibid., p. 168.

[176] 'Motifs', p. 168

[177] Ibid., pp. 165–6.

[178] Ibid., p. 166.

[179] Benjamin quoting Baudelaire in 'Second Empire', in *SW*, IV, p. 25.

The crowd is the source of eroticism: it provides the flash of sexual desire and takes it away. Without the crowd, the excitement of the love affair could not exist. Benjamin's idea of the crowd as 'veil' makes sense under this analysis. Dickens's notion of the intimacy, or even the identity of the crowd and 'the one' is also interesting in this light. The crowd could be thought of as having a connection to, or even being a determinant of, the lover's consciousness. If the city is a labyrinth, the crowd is identical with the city. The crowd is, moreover, the moving labyrinth: it embodies the flux, the contingency and the fleeting nature of the urban experience par excellence.[180] The crowd provides moments (or shocks) where one individual can be picked out, and is delivered over to the flâneur, like a stone washed onto the beach, only to be covered over again by the next wave. It is reasonable to suggest that, considering what has already been argued about the nature of urban experience as *Erlebnis* and the theory of the shock (*Chockerlebnis*), there are few other ways one can imagine one could experience the crowd on Benjaminian terms. The crowd must at times be an insubstantial blur that jostles one, whose shocks one's consciousness does its best to ward off, and which has little real impression upon one's mind while strolling in the city. But this state of mind is then punctuated by particular accented moments, moments of revelation, when the attention is fully drawn to some event, thing or person. Coincidences of this spatio-temporal sort are the quintessence of modern experience, for Benjamin. Remember, for him, modern existence only offers experiences of this evanescent sort; there are no presentations for representing the totality of what there is. This was the challenge Benjamin took up in forging his new literary style, literary montage: such a structure articulates the breaking up of totalized ways of seeing.[181] These precious moments in the crowd, then, celebrated by Baudelaire as erotic love affairs, are jewels at the heart of Benjamin's theory of modern experience. And urban experience, in this sense, emerges as the quintessence of modern experience as Benjamin understands it.

This is an important point to bear in mind, since a coincidence of a certain time and a certain space in the city is an extremely regular occurrence in the novels of Dickens. So many coincidences are depicted by him, in fact, that this is almost too obvious a point to make about the novelist's delineation of the city; and there are almost too many instances from which to select possible examples. In what can perhaps be viewed as a piece of meta-commentary by Dickens, the character Tim Linkinwater comments, 'Why I don't believe now [...] that there's such a place in all the world for coincidences as London is!' (*NN*, bk. 14, ch. 43, p. 649).

The novels give ample space to this phenomenon. The fleeting, contingent nature of a coincidence makes it *the* monadic event in urban modernity. The Dickensian coincidence of time and space, though, goes beyond Baudelaire's fixation on love in the city – although Dickens also includes love on these space/

[180] This point is made by J. Hillis Miller in *Charles Dickens: The World of his Novels* (Cambridge, MA: Harvard University Press, 1958), ch. 2, p. 65.

[181] See 'The Modernism of Benjamin's Methodology' above, p. 89.

time coincidental terms. The episode already cited when Arthur Clennam tries to escape the confusion of his two 'crowds' ends, inevitably, with a chance meeting with his beloved near London Bridge, the 'figure of fascination' of whom he had been already been thinking, Amy Dorrit (*LD*, ch. 22, p. 253).

Here, going further than Baudelaire, Dickens seems to suggest that the mental attachment, or the emotional yearning involved in loving someone, could somehow will connection in urban space and time to take place. He wills the crowd to present him with the lover, and it obliges. Presumably this is the kind of connection Sidney Carton hopes for in his aimless wandering in Lucie Manette's street (*TTC*, bk. 2, ch. 13, p. 179) and is Benjamin's purpose in his 'Moscow Diary' entry: 'As I was walking around during the day, I entered the church of Our Lady of Kazan, which Asja had told me was one of her favourites.'[182] Both lovers (Carton and Benjamin) here have a sort of spatial connection but not the temporal coincidence they desire. Benjamin claims that even in the physical absence of the beloved, the city space can be haunted by the beloved's presence:

> For two hours I walked the streets in solitude. Never again have I seen them so. From every gate a flame darted; each cornerstone sprayed sparks, and every streetcar came toward me like a fire engine.[183]

Dickens's use of a 'willed' coincidence between lovers shows that Dickens longs, at times, for a system behind the urban randomness – although there is no doubt he makes ample use of 'random' coincidence too. The notion of willed coincidence moreover adds another layer of complexity and fear to the phantasmagoric city – can one really will the lover into presence?

A planned 'coincidence' in *TTC* is when Charles Darnay arranges that his wife, Lucie Manette, stand at a certain spot in the city at a certain time so he can see her from his remote Parisian prison cell. Lucie meanwhile cannot see him but knows that he can see her (*TTC*, bk. 3, ch. 5, p. 305). This intimate congruence at a distance takes place, movingly and importantly, in the public space, amid the crowd and the hustle and bustle of the city. Again, this is the depiction of a precious and precarious moment snatched from the general melée of thoughts and shocks the city dweller experiences on an average day in the metropolis. The city's unpredictability and the almost mercurial quality of the crowd's giving and snatching away is central to this set up. The status of the singular moment is made higher, and its contents, more revelatory, because a slight variation in time or space, an unforeseen event or distraction, the activity of the crowd, can scupper it forever.

Coincidental urban meetings do not only pertain to lovers in Dickens. They also occur between friends: Copperfield's meeting with Micawber while he's taking tea with Uriah Heep (*DC*, ch. 17, p. 224) is a case in point. A piece of Copperfield's past explodes into the present when Micawber suddenly walks by

---

182 Benjamin being spatially close to his lover, Asja Lacis, 'Moscow Diary', ibid., p. 51.

183 *One-Way Street*, *SW*, I, p. 461.

Heep's house, a part of town not usually frequented by David. When Copperfield chases after Micawber, needing to believe the family's fortunes have improved, he spots them on top of an omnibus looking happy. Notice here, again, Dickens insists that there is a coincidence (Micawber walks by) followed by a willed coincidence – the city provides what Copperfield needs to see (the Micawbers looking fairly happy). The layers of this coincidence give Dickens's delineation of the machinations of the city the 'double condition' that Raymond Williams argues is so idiosyncratically Dickensian.[184] For Williams, Dickens evokes the city as both random and yet systematic, involving elements that are both visible and obscured. In this coincidence, the city is full of distractions, dislocations, chance and shock and yet seems to provide just what David psychologically needs at a particular moment, evidencing Williams's point.

In one moment in *DC*, David passes a face in the crowd that looks familiar: his recognition takes place only afterwards, when he realizes it is the face of the prostitute, Martha Endell (*DC*, ch. 40, p. 497). This delayed recognition must be the quintessential urban experience and makes Benjamin's notion of the 'dream city' so potent (convolute K of *The Arcades Project* is entitled 'Dream City and Dream House'). In the case of Copperfield and Martha Endell, a face floats into David's purview on the wave of a crowd – and then, is gone. The face haunts his memory of the momentary encounter, it plays in his consciousness. It intermingles with the transitions, shocks and multifarious images of the city everyone experiences as he continues strolling, deep in thought, trying to remember to whom the face belongs. Suddenly, he is able to place the fleeting image of the face within the context of yet another memory – and recognition takes place. Such is the city's role in consciousness, memory and experience: it is indeed a 'dream city' or a city which absorbs, creates, augments memories and dreams.

Coincidence can also involve the crowd bringing a character's unwanted enemy to them. While the depiction of coincidence is always a furthering of Dickens's plot, it is when the villain coincidentally appears that the novelist's strategy becomes most obvious, most enjoyable for the reader. Such novelistic sleights of hand appear both melodramatic/staged and come across as a realist depiction of city life, at the same time. While Nell is on the run, she crosses paths with Quilp (*OCS*, ch. 27, pp. 214–15). She manages to avoid him by hiding in the shadows of a gothic archway, and this moment is illustrated in the novel (*OCS*, ch. 27, p. 215). Oliver Twist mistakenly takes the wrong turning, and his decision to see where it leads means he bumps into Nancy, who spirits him back to Fagin (*OT*, ch. 15, pp. 95–6). Martin Chuzzlewit chooses one pawn shop out of the many in London and recognizes the voice of the 'villainous' Montague Tigg negotiating in the next booth (*MC*, ch. 19, pp. 219–24). He hopes to avoid him but Tigg spots him and makes fun of his financial embarrassment. In *LD*, the significant stranger in the city is literally carried to Arthur Clennam by the crowd (*LD*, ch. 13, pp. 155–6). John Baptist Cavaletto, Blandois's co-prisoner has been run over by a coach, and

---

[184] *The Country and the City*, p. 154.

the crowd, like some machine with many components, or a creature with many heads and hands, provide a stretcher and water and proceeds with the injured man toward hospital. Arthur witnesses the approach of the crowd, satisfies his curiosity as to what is going on and ends by joining the procession. But Cavaletto's identity remains a secret to all but the reader. It is only through his use of the habitual phrase 'altro!' that we recognize, unlike Clennam, that this foreigner is a colleague of the novel's villain. Here Dickens stages the drama of recognition in the city, allowing the reader to know more than the protagonist via a special linguistic signal – a speech pattern we recognize. The coincidence, then, is one in which Clennam takes part, without knowing it as a coincidence at all. The coincidence – and the revelation that the villain has escaped to London with his cohort – is part of a literary strategy to drop clues to the reader about the novel's central mystery. It is, as it were, a meta-literary coincidence, an incident of déjà vu for the reader. Dickens's delineation says, 'here is Arthur Clennam walking in the city, and here, by accident, we have come across another character in the novel: remember him from the novel's opening?' And in this sense the form of the novel starts to take on the unpredictable and labyrinthine nature of the city itself. The little shock delivered to the reader by 'altro!', the little pang of recognition we undergo, is like a meta-literary version of *Chockerlebnis* in the city.

Coincidences are a literary sleight of hand which foregrounds the constructive element of Dickens's text. It is surely Dickens's tendency to produce this self conscious, explicitly wrought literary form, which is simultaneously an expression of realism, that makes his work such a curious and fascinating phenomenon. It can be argued that part of the reason Dickens manages to make this combination of 'artifice' and 'realism' work so well is that he is drawing attention to what often appears to be the strangely constructed or theatrical element to reality itself.

## The Gothic City

The motifs of the flâneur and the crowd, then, are integral to the 'magic lantern' (to use Dickens's phrase), to the emotionally charged, the epistemologically uncertain, indeed, to the gothic nature of the city. The city's shifting, fast-paced, complex nature overwhelms the Subject, and 'The more alien a big city becomes – the more knowledge of human nature [...] one needs to operate in it'.[185]

As indicated above, a network of controls were introduced in Paris to attempt to master the city, to apprehend the criminal in the crowd, photography preserving permanent and unmistakable human traces for the first time.[186]

The detective novel, for Benjamin, developed out of this conscious probing of the city's mystery. Flânerie, with its identity of looking with knowledge, gives the

[185] 'Second Empire', p. 26.

[186] Ibid.

best 'prospects of playing detective', a dovetailing of detective with flâneur.[187] The detective 'develops reactions that are in keeping with the tempo of a big city', the 'glance' encompassing the urban flux with the penetration and intensity suggested in the discussion above.[188] So, as has already been suggested, if Dickens can be seen as a flâneur, he can also be seen as a 'detective' – the photographic plate recording pictures, the allegorist collecting metonymic fragments, reading the surfaces, searching for clues, in the city.[189] And then he writes about it.

Dickens exemplifies Benjamin's dovetailing of the flâneur with the detective in the processes and the results of his production. Since, as has been argued, thinking, flânerie and writing have an identity in Dickens (and in Baudelaire), it makes sense that Dickens's works should express his (the flâneur's/detective's) experience of the city, including the experience of not being able to 'master' the fragmentary nature of the urban world but aiming to read the clues and fragments available. In other words, it makes sense that much of Dickens's fiction is pitched in the gothic mode[190] and has the format of detective fiction.[191] It would not be going too far to claim that the urban experience described by Benjamin with its *Chockerlebnis*, epistemological uncertainty and fragmentariness almost adds up to the literary form of gothic sensation and mystery, fragmentary clues and detection – in both form and content. Moreover, a depiction, in the case of *DC*, of attempting to gather up and order/reorder the content of experience of the city and of the self in a continual process, as well as the article 'Gone Astray', which explicitly celebrates the reflexive, creative, imaginative relationship between the city and self; and Dickens's indulgence in and comments about his own flânerie, suggests a level of self-consciousness about this process in Dickens. The infinite reflection Benjamin

[187] Both quotations, 'Second Empire', p. 21.

[188] 'Second Empire', p. 23.

[189] Forster describes Dickens production as being a question of photographing the world around him (*Life*, bk. 3, ch. 5, p. 246).

[190] Much scholarly discussion exists as to what, exactly, constitutes Gothic fiction. Here the term 'Gothic mode' is used loosely to designate certain conventions identifiable in texts usually grouped under that heading: a central secret or mystery; a tense tone that stokes it up; the appearance of mysterious or disguised figures; mistaken identity/ambiguity about identity; haunting; the featuring of death, corpses, graveyards; the possible existence of a supernatural realm; a vulnerable heroine, perhaps pursued or entrapped by a cruel distant male/villain; a large house/property and questions of identity relating thereto; depictions of feelings of terror in characters; multiple narratives, unreliable narrators, a narrative voice that is not omniscient; sensational events or revelations, melodramatic scenes, scenes in the dead of night; events interpretable in ambiguous ways. The list could go on.

[191] In terms of detective fiction, *Bleak House* featuring Inspector Bucket (1852–1853) is usually seen as Dickens's blueprint. But there is an even earlier version of the detective in Dickens: Mr Nadgett in *Martin Chuzzlewit* (1843–1845). And if Benjamin claims the first detective stories in Paris were Baudelaire's translations of Poe's 'The Murders in the Rue Morgue' (1841) and 'The Purloined Letter' (1845) ('The Paris of the Second Empire in Baudelaire', p. 23), Dickens is one of the pioneers of this genre in Europe.

associates with the monadic fragment is analogous to the infinite reciprocity and reflexivity of the flâneur's urban activity, of his gathering up and reconstitution of the fragmentary city.[192] The shock of the modern, of the havoc technology wreaks upon the senses, and the vertiginous terror that can result, comes together most obviously in gothic form in Dickens's 1866 ghost story, 'The Signalman', the text that transmutes the fear of new technology into supernatural terror.[193]

But before it is claimed that Benjaminian insights into the flâneur and urban experience provides a theory of Dicken's fictions, his use of the gothic mode or the formulae of mystery and detection, it must be remembered that the source from which Benjamin's later materialist 'theory' of experience grew were innumerable fragments of literary (as well as other) citations, including material concerning Baudelaire and Dickens himself. Any search for the original blueprint of urban experience would surely fall into a 'chicken and egg' impasse about the nature of cultural discourses and urban texts. What can be said with confidence is that Dickens and Benjamin both described and contributed to a cultural understanding of urban experience.

### *Gothic, Fallen City*

Dickens's gothic, mysterious fictional world has an affinity to the 'fallen' world of Benjamin's early theology and language theory. For example, take the following passage in *TTC*:

> A wonderful fact to reflect upon, that every human creature is constituted to be that profound secret and mystery to every other. A solemn consideration, when I enter a great city by night, that every one of those darkly clustered houses encloses its own secret; that every room in every one of them encloses its own secret; that every beating heart in the hundreds of thousands of breasts there, is, in some of its imaginings, a secret to the heart nearest it! [...] No more can I turn the leaves of this dear book that I loved, and vainly hope in time to read it all. No more can I look into the depths of this unfathomable water, wherein, as momentary lights glanced into it, I have had glimpses of buried treasure and other things submerged. It was appointed that the book should be shut with a spring, forever and forever, when I had read but a page. It was appointed that the water should be locked in an eternal frost, when the light was playing on its surface, and I stood in ignorance on the shore. (Narrator, bk. 1, ch. 3, p. 44)

The unknown narrator announces that knowledge in this fictional world, like the description Benjamin gives of the fallen world in his early theology, is apprehended in partial, fragmented ways: truth, meaning expresses itself in, as

[192] Benjamin's understanding of this theory of the fragment can be gleaned from his reading of the German Romantics in 'The Concept of Criticism in German Romanticism', in *SW*, I, pp. 116–200.

[193] Published in the Christmas edition of *Household Words*.

it were, a veiled way.[194] From Benjamin's point of view, Dickens's delineation of his fictional world, here, is an uncanny act of mimesis. Dickens's text makes conscious the nature of 'real' modern experience through his evocation of a gothic city – whose elliptical, fragmentary nature necessitates the reading and rereading of the allegorist/detective/reader.

Dickens's treatment of character, particularly in *TTC*, where he presents characters from the outside as cryptic signs to be read, bears out this epistemological point. Sidney Carton, for instance, has a tendency to self-destruction, but the cause is a mystery that is not solved in the novel. It is a haunting partially exorcised in, and signified by, his habit of restless flânerie in the city: 'Many a night he vaguely and unhappily wandered there.'[195] Like a passerby in the crowd to be swiftly judged on the basis of external appearances, the narrative presents an external sketch of him – the urban experience of him. But is it an index to what is within? On first meeting, the reader is directed to observe Carton's slovenly posture. When the reader looks at him, his eyes are fixed on the ceiling, giving away little, he conceals as much as he reveals. The narrative, in other words, requires the reader to become a detective.

Carton's uncanny doubling with Darnay is a further complication in the interpretative process. The two look alike but are different people: apparently qualifying the notion that the external is an index to the internal. It is certainly a complication of the relationship between signifier and signified (again Dickens's gothic world resembles Benjamin's allegorical one, where the signifier/signified relationship is problematic). The characters' differences of opinion and attitude jar with their physical samenesses: an uncanny shock Dickens emphasizes by repeatedly doubling them in a series of graphic tableaux. The novelist presents Carton and Darnay face to face, and delineates a reflection of that image in a mirror above; he puts them side by side in the street: 'This must be a strange night to you, standing alone here with your counterpart on these street stones';[196] intersects them (they discuss their differences and samenesses); as a symmetrical image, face to face, they resign themselves before the opaqueness of subjectivity, 'Looking his companion full in the face'.[197] Dickens turns the image of the double round and round, upside down and inside out, a series of stills presented side by side, but 'the inexorable consolidation and perpetuation of the secret that was always in that individuality' remains.[198]

Finally, Carton scrutinizes the mystery of his own face:

---

[194] This use of the term 'veil' to describe the elliptical expression of meaning and transcendence in the fallen world of Benjamin's early vision is found, for instance, his essay 'Goethe's Elective Affinities', in *SW*, 1, pp. 297–360 (p. 351).

[195] *TTC*, bk. 2, ch. 13, p. 179.

[196] Ibid., bk. 2, ch. 4, p. 113.

[197] Ibid., bk. 2, ch. 4, p. 114.

[198] Ibid., bk. 1, ch. 3, p. 44.

> When he was left alone [...] (he) went to a glass [...] and surveyed himself minutely in it. 'Do you particularly like the man?' he muttered at his own image: 'why should you particularly like a man who resembles you? [...] There is nothing in you to like; you know that [...] Come on, and have it out in plain words! You hate the fellow'.[199]

Carton stages how singular character is, and how it reveals and conceals itself. Closely scrutinizing his own mysterious 'sign' (the surface of his face), he questions whether he likes 'the man' – this 'man', a reference to either himself or Darnay. It is in fact to both, since the succeeding remarks seamlessly switch from a reference to Darnay's appearance and back to his own again, as if fragments of character are revealed or refracted via a facsimile of the self. Part of the uncanniness of doubling involves the idea that even the most closely identified have a singularity, offset and disclosed by one another.

Dickens allows us glimpses into character that then help interpret further actions. Again, this involves the reader in a process of divination or detective work. When Carton dons the mask of indifference toward Lucie, for instance, we guess that he is insincere – putting his extreme reaction to Darnay down to sexual jealousy. A later revelation confirms that we are right. When he dons the garments of his döppleganger, Darnay, to suffer death in his place, his sincerity is obvious for the reader (we know of his promise to Lucie to go to any lengths to keep her happy) – but not for the crowds of Paris. But we do not really know why he sacrifices himself. His unhappiness in the city is not solely attributable to doomed love. There is something unfathomable at the heart of the character which he himself cannot penetrate – much like the labyrinthine city he traverses, whose entrances and alleyways he keeps pounding, but whose heart he can never enter:

> he threw himself down in his clothes on a neglected bed, and its pillow was wet with wasted tears.
> Sadly, sadly, the sun rose; it rose upon no sadder sight than the man of good abilities and good emotions, incapable of their directed exercise, incapable of his own help and his own happiness, sensible of the blight on him.[200]

His elusiveness even extends to his doubling with the reader as detective. Carton's nocturnal wanderings, his urban flânerie have – like Dickens – rendered him adept at reading cryptic signs, he has the skills of a detective,too. In Paris these qualities come into their own; he spies on, tails and outwits John Barsad. But he cannot solve the mystery of himself.

---

199 Ibid., bk. 2, ch. 4, p. 116.
200 Ibid., bk. 2, ch. 5, p. 122.

*The Prominence of Looking*

If the fictional world is mysterious and cryptic, and interpretation is all, getting 'knowledge' through looking becomes the primary source of experience – compounding the phantasmagoria and scopophilia of the urban experience. Dickens's characters try to read identity, to crack the mystery of character through inspection. In *TTC*, Lucie, en route to Paris, scrutinizes Jarvis Lorry and says, '"Are you quite a stranger to me, sir?" He replies, "Am I not?"'[201] In meeting his daughter, Dr Manette, 'stared at her with a fearful look'; 'he turned her full to the light and looked at her'; 'took Lucie's face in his hands and looked at it', and he complements it with: 'Was it you?'[202] Lucie's subjectivity is not totally wrested into view in the surface of her face. Dr Manette can only 'look', exploring how subjectivity veils as much as reveals itself to him. Similarly, in court, witnesses are called upon to identify potential spies through looking:

> Miss Manette, look upon the prisoner […] Miss Manette, have you seen the prisoner before?

But while Lucie sees/knows one man, the court sees/knows another:

> 'When the gentleman came on board …'
> 'Do you mean the prisoner?' inquired the Judge.
> 'Yes, my Lord.'
> 'Then say the prisoner.'[203]

Lucie's fragmentary experience of Darnay – she glimpsed him briefly one night on a crossing from France – is that he is a gentleman. To the court, he signifies 'the condemned man', he is a prisoner. Again, this is the mystery of subjectivity whose elliptical quality bears these interpretations and so many more.

Since the urban character can melt away in the anonymity of the crowd, intelligence gathering, watching people and following them becomes essential. There are two types of spy in *TTC*. The professional spy is represented by Barsad and Roger Cly, Miss Pross's brother, the Defarges, and professional revolutionary spies and state spies. The amateur spy is a role taken on by a number of characters. For instance Darnay travels under an assumed name. His real name is D'Aulnais, the reader later learns from a spy. Jarvis Lorry is introduced as a man with a secret, who speaks the language of the spy. Carton spies on Barsad in Paris. Even Miss Pross 'watches' Dr Manette and his daughter.

The prevalence of spies is further dramatization of how things are hardly ever what they 'seem'. The trope of the mask is a leitmotif in the novel. It is present in the stone gargoyles that change; in the self-conscious mimicry of the road-mender;

[201] Ibid., bk. 1, ch. 4, p. 53.

[202] Ibid., bk. 1, ch. 6, p. 74, and three quotes on p. 75, respectively.

[203] Both quotations, ibid., bk. 2, ch. 3, pp. 100–101.

in the mask of indifference donned by Madame Defarge and by Carton in court; and by the mask, which never falls away, of the Marquis:

> It portended that there was one stone face too many up at the chateau. The Gorgon had surveyed the building again in the night, and had added the one stone face wanting; the stone face for which it had waited through about two hundred years. It lay back on the pillow of Monsieur the Marquis. It was like a fine mask, suddenly startled, made angry, and petrified.[204]

The paranoia surrounding the need to avoid surveillance necessitates the use of coded means of communication – again compounding the mysterious nature of the city's fragments for the urban onlooker. In *BR*, Dickens describes how leaflets are 'delivered' to people, but no one knows from where they appear. Messages are passed from man to man: 'some man would come and stand beside [another man] in the throng […] would say a word […] Then they part, like strangers' (*BR*, ch. 38, p. 361 [my alteration]).

In *TTC*, the crowd also has a secret means of communication. Coded phrases or slight gestures by the Defarges prompt specific reactions from followers. Madame Defarge enciphers the injustices of the regime in a knitted, coded account that will be settled later.[205] Revolutionaries plotting against the state use their position amid the crowd: it is their hiding place and it enables their anonymity. They camouflage themselves in sameness, calling themselves 'Jacques One, two, three'. Benjamin touches upon the crowd as hiding place: 'individuals no longer blush in the crowd'.[206]

## *Gothic Eyes*

Eyes are prevalent in the gothic urban context where watching and looking at the labyrinthine surfaces is the norm. Eyes as a trope feature in much of Baudelaire's poetry and in Modernist aesthetics too.[207] They feature heavily in *TTC*. Dickens uses them as signifiers which can either be read or which can speak.

Through the depiction of eyes, a crowd is metonymically evoked:

> Depressed and slinking though they were, eyes of fire were not wanting among them.[208]

---

[204] The murder of the Marquis, ibid., bk. 2, ch. 9, p. 159.

[205] Dickens's depiction of Madame Defarge's use of coded communications has a direct literary descendent in spy novels, such as those of John le Carré.

[206] 'Second Empire', p. 21.

[207] Eyes are a leitmotif in Baudelaire's 'The Dancing Snake', 'The Living Torch', 'Her Poison', 'The Cat', 'A Parisian Dream', 'The Voyage', among others. In T.S. Eliot's 'Prufock', 'The Preludes' and 'The Wasteland', the prevalence of the trope of eyes too is obvious.

[208] *TTC*, bk. 1, ch. 5, p. 62.

Eyes here express a collective feeling of torment. They can also shout an aggressive intention: 'Darnay saw a rush in the eyes of the crowd' and 'The same hue was red in their frenzied eyes'.[209]

Eyes can project a violent fantasy onto the object of the gaze: 'The accused [...] was (and who knew he was) being mentally hanged, beheaded and quartered by everybody there.'[210]

Eyes can exhibit defiance and a secret presentiment of vengeance: 'But the woman who stood knitting looked up steadily, and looked the Marquis in the face.'[211]

Eyes can also express sympathetic encouragement to the object of the gaze:

> 'Miss Manette, look upon the prisoner.' To be confronted with such pity and such earnest youth and beauty, was far more trying to the accused than to be confronted with all the crowd.[212]

Dickens here emphasizes the effect of a look by describing the response in the character and, simultaneously, encouraging it in the reader.

At the level of the individual, eyes can be insincere in what they express. They can be masklike, a guise for the character, a contraindication. Carton's eyes in court are on the ceiling – he strikes a pose, an attitude of superior indifference – yet he is extremely interested and knows/sees much. This gives him an advantage over his legal opponents, who might falsely assume his indifference. In fact, the reader learns later that he suffers from self-hatred, not a superiority complex.

Madame Defarge's eyes perform the ultimate trick – they allow her the guise of sightlessness or lack of knowledge:

> One soul was to be seen, and that was Madame Defarge – who leaned against the door-post, knitting, and saw nothing.[213]

Of course, this is the mask of the spy – since, as the reader knows, she knows and sees much.

### *Narrative Design*

A lack of narrative omniscience is a crucial ingredient in the evocation of the gothic city – in casting the reader as detective – and this is the case in *TTC*. Passages describing the night journey of the Dover mail are a good example. The narrator conjures up fog, darkness and fear of attack to limit the vision and knowledge of not only the passengers but the reader, too. No names are given, merely a detailed

209 The Terror begins, ibid., bk. 3, ch. 1, p. 278, and the grindstone scene, bk. 3, ch. 2, p. 292, respectively.

210 Ibid., bk. 2, ch. 2, p. 93.

211 Mde Defarge marks out the Marquis for death, ibid. ch. 7, p. 143.

212 Ibid., bk. 2, ch. 3, p. 100.

213 Ibid., bk. 1, ch. 6, p. 80.

description of the elliptical environment.[214] An interlocking of the categories of sight and knowledge again is implied:

> Not one of the three could have said, from anything he saw, what either of the other two was like; and each was hidden under almost as many wrappers from the eyes of the mind, as from the eyes of the body, of his two companions.[215]

At every moment, the passengers pulses are 'quickened by expectation' – a kind of *Chockerlebnis* – as their eyes of the mind predict or imaginatively develop the fragments they see with their bodily eyes.

The narrator stokes up mystery with respect to characters. The narrative in *TTC* is recounting a history, a tale that takes place in the past, so the narrator should be well informed. Yet he only offers up 'clues' concerning Jerry Cruncher (the body snatcher's) nocturnal activities. The comic gothic drama of the gravedigging scene is designed for dramatic effect – the narrator 'knows' what the denouement is but withholds it from the reader until the last moment. And the moment itself is played for all it is worth. The narrator follows Young Jerry to the grave scene, and takes on his childlike sensibility. The 'truth' of what Cruncher is up to – grave-robbing – is only evanescently evoked, refracted through the interpretation of a child – Cruncher had told his son he was going fishing. The narrator, with a wink at the reader, persists in this 'fishing' metaphor (miming the credulousness of Young Jerry).[216]

The narrative also proves to be inconsistent. It can and does change its interpretation of the fictional world. For example, at one point it asks the reader to accept a fantastical framework for an event, claiming that, in this fictional world, stone faces can 'change':

> The stone faces on the outer walls stared blindly [...] Then the grey water [...] began to be ghostly in the light, and the eyes of the stone faces of the chateau were opened.[217]

But later it announces that the idea that the stone faces 'change' is a matter of irrational rumor or fancy:

> the few village scarecrows who [...] strayed within sight of the great stone court-yard and terrace staircase, had it borne in upon their starved fancy that the expression of the faces was altered. A rumour just lived in the village [...] that when the knife struck home, the faces changed, from faces of pride to faces of anger and pain.[218]

---

214 See ibid., bk. 1, ch. 2, p. 38.

215 Narrator, ibid.

216 Ibid., bk. 2, ch. 14, p. 192.

217 Ibid., bk. 2, ch. 9, p. 157.

218 Ibid., bk. 3, ch. 11, p. 205.

This wrong-foots the reader in a play on ambiguity which is both deliberate and effective.

There are moments when the narrator's omniscience is explicitly punctuated, and the reader, as detective, is required to pick up the clues. In a conspiratorial scene between Defarge, his wife and the road mender, a clue is dropped which will prove important for the momentum of the plot:

> 'The tall man is lost, and he is sought – how many months?'
> 'No matter the number', said Defarge. 'He is well hidden, but at last he is unluckily found.'[219]

Why does the character Defarge disclose the capture of Gaspard instead of the narrator here? Because, as is suggested, Dickens's fictional world is cryptic and elliptical; one where certainty and knowledge are problematic. The author dramatizes this by punctuating the omniscience of the narrator.

### *City of Glass*

As the title *The Arcades Project* implies, an important part of the city as phantasmagoric in Benjamin is the optical seduction of commodity display, and the technology that glamorizes it, glass. The arcades with their play of reflected light upon glass became central to Benjamin's historical project because they represented a reification of history and economy.[220] Glass interrogated 'inside/ outside', it dispensed with thresholds. The arcades displayed interiors outdoors; once inside, they brought the street-scene in. Strolling in gas-lit arcades, one inhabited a giant aquarium that eclipsed the stars, it was a world in itself. Glass was the technology out of which the world's biggest shop window, the Crystal Palace, would be constructed in 1851. Chesterton believed Dickens responded to this tantalizing side of the city's character, claiming his title 'The Old Curiosity Shop' was 'a key to the whole' of Dickens, that 'Every shop [...] was to Dickens the door of romance'. Locating his imagination firmly in the street scene among crowds, vendors, shop signs and commodities, Chesterton speculates that Dickens could have written an 'endless periodical' called 'the street', each number of which could have been named after a shop.[221] Such a Dickensian serialization would have been a literary version of the dazzling arcades.

Dickens himself was not immune from understanding his creativity in terms of the optical quality of the city. Rather than creating his characters from scratch, Dickens merely needed to look in the arcades-like shop-window of his own mind

[219] Ibid., bk. 2, ch. 15, p. 197.

[220] See section *The Arcades Project*, pp. 143–51, above.

[221] Benjamin quoting Chesterton, *Dickens*, in *Arcades*, convolute A, 'Arcades, novelty shops, sales clerks', A11,3.

to 'see' the display that would become his work: 'I am at work, and see the story in a wonderful glass.'[222]

Yet there is an obverse side to the phantasmagoric city: uncanniness and the anxiety of *Chockerlebnis*. And Dickens, it is suggested, was more ambiguous toward the bright, gas-lit city and its fairy grottos of commodity display than Chesterton allows. Rather than dazzling, for him: 'London is shabby by daylight, and shabbier by gaslight.'[223] Displaying the shock-fatigue of the city dweller, in Geneva, Dickens admits to feeling nervous of the gas lighting and noise of the streets.[224] Similarly, during three months in Paris in 1846–1847, 'he took a colossal walk about the city of which the brilliancy and brightness almost frightened him'.[225] The quantity of commodities and the spectacle of the displays of the Great Exhibition made Dickens vertiginous, in his words it was 'bewildering' and 'too much'.[226] Dickens even recorded his experience of the uncanny in the city – he disliked 'the multiplication of my countenance in the shop windows';[227] and the reverse reflection of 'coffee shop' gave him 'a shock' of déjà vu, as mentioned above.[228]

These arresting, uncanny moments in the city when 'something was breaking through the familiar',[229] are reproduced innumerable times in Dickens's fiction.[230] One example of the uncanny multiplication of images is in *TTC* with the doubling of Carton and Darnay, who face each other in court, and are then reflected again in the mirror above. Carton will later check his 'countenance' in a shop window ahead of substituting himself for Darnay at the guillotine.

Despite his telling a Pittsburgh citizen that 'the notion of London being so dark a place was a popular mistake',[231] then, it is becoming clear that London as a dark, labyrinthine space – one he invariably chose to walk in at night – is what dominated Dickens's experience of London in his flânerie, in his imagination and in his writing. If Dickens as flâneur here differs from the leisured, self-possessed stroller among the bright lights and commodity displays of Paris, this distinction has already been noted above.[232] The dark London, rather than the bright, seductive one, was the London that he was most attuned to.[233] Delineated as elliptical and

222 Dickens talking about writing *TTC*, Ackroyd, *Dickens*, p. 867.

223 'The Uncommercial', Slater, IV, p. 279.

224 *Life*, bk. 5, ch. 5, p. 428

225 Ibid., bk. 5, ch. 7, p. 443.

226 See Appendix 1, pp. 218–19, below.

227 Nonesuch *Letters*, II, p. 819.

228 Cited by Benjamin, *Arcades*, J3,2.

229 Benjamin, *Berlin Childhood around 1900*, p. 356.

230 See D.S. Racadio, *The Comic, the Grotesque and the Uncanny in Dickens*, PhD thesis, University of East Anglia Press, 1990.

231 *Life*, bk. 3, ch. 5, p. 252

232 See p. 172, above.

233 As also suggested above, in 'Dreaming Dickens', p. 102.

cryptic in some of the most famous scenes, like the opening of *BH*, this is the recognizable Dickensian London that is such a leitmotif in his writing.

It seems fair to speculate that the unmasterable, frightening and mysterious London – as opposed to the bright, sparkling, seductive one – perhaps dominated Dickens's psyche because, as a poor, often hungry boy, his window-shopping was of a very serious kind:

> When I had money enough, I used to get half a pint of ready made coffee and a slice of bread and butter. When I had none, I used to look at a venison shop in Fleet Street; or I [...] strolled, at such a time, as far as Covent Garden Market, and stared at the pineapples.[234]

This is a conflictual, melancholy relationship to the phantasmagoric plethora of goods in the shop window; a world away from that commodity fetishism the mesmerized Boffins indulge in in *OMF*.[235] Under the circumstances of poverty – and in contrast to the moneyed, middle classes – phantasmagoric London becomes not so much the 'dream city' as the nightmare one.[236] Dicken's haunting urban London – his gothic city – in this sense is an evocation of the city as the urban poor experience it. While Dickens was only poor as a boy and was soon to become successful and wealthy, that boyhood experience obviously haunted him for the rest of his life. It is a small step from here to the suggestion that the subject matter – working-class life, poverty, crime, murder, mystery – and the sensational effects of detective fiction and the Sensation Novel genre grew out of this more troubled, sad side of urban reflexivity and creativity. But Dickens is a great storyteller and entertainer. The fearful, gothic city did not dominate his drive for life and laughter. His cities pulse with a rhythm that is both a celebration of the urban as well as emphasizing the dark side of metropolitan life.

## Concluding Remarks

This chapter, it has hopefully become clear, has been more than a mere juxtaposition of Benjamin's and Dickens's vision of the city and modern urban experience. Since Dickens's life and work itself, or at least commentary upon it, was part of the source from which Benjamin's 'formulation' of urban modernity emerged (fragments on Dickens are present in the *Arcades*), it is hardly surprising that the authors' models of the city coalesce in many respects and are closely related.

What can be drawn out of Dickens's use of the gothic mode? It has been suggested that Dickens's gothic city is not merely an aesthetic choice that came out of nothing – but is possibly a phenomenon that grew out of his particular

234 The autobiographical *DC*, p. 141.

235 *OMF*, bk. 3, ch. 5, pp. 527–9.

236 'Dream City', part of the title of convolute K, *The Arcades Project*.

style of production. As a flâneur, he faced the same epistemological problem of all flâneurs, the fearful unmasterability of the city. The phantasmagoria, speed, *Erlebnis* and *Chockerlebnis* of urban life was further cause for fear and anxiety. Dickens's gothic city, then, it was suggested, rather than being a distortion of 'reality' is, more accurately understood, a form of mimesis. Furthermore, Dickens's own peculiar form of flânerie, dominated by his 'stamping his mind' upon the cityscape, may have effected an even more personal, psychological delineation of urban life. Dickens's city space was traced through with the dark, frightening experience of the poor, abandoned boy, Dickens. This is a similar point to that made by Mark Spilka (albeit talking about the grotesque):

> In modern times, the world itself accommodates the [gothic]. Our squalid, crowded urban mazes, our under-privileged classes reduced to something like subhuman status and our personalities shattered by disruptive tensions, suggest the point of correspondence.[237] (my substitution)

Moreover, as was stated previously, such gothic settings have a metaphysical significance, too. They come back to an understanding of the modern world that echoes Benjamin's messianic worldview or his antinomy of allegory, whereby there is a hidden element or concealed meaning that constantly requires interpretation. Dickens is an allegorist who delineates the experience of modern urban life in all its epistemological partiality and fragmentariness through the gothic mode. He holds the fragments together within the narrative of his novels – sometimes, even while vividly depicting, as is the case in *DC*, the difficulty of capturing evanescent experience in a linear narrative. Dickens's status as an allegorist goes beyond the self-consciously allegorical work, *OCS*, and can be understood in relation to his use of the gothic mode, which is an aesthetic expression of how truth is a problem in the modern urban world.

Other aspects of urban poetics (the flâneur, the crowd) gleaned from Benjamin's extensive Baudelaire material – located both in *The Arcades Project* and the essays Benjamin developed from it – were also discussed in relation to Dickens's writings. This Baudelaire/Dickens comparison proved useful in two ways: it allowed for a fuller reflection upon and expansion of the possible meanings of the Dickens fragments in the *Arcades* – fragments which burst into life in an intellectual constellation with the Baudelaire material. The comparison of Baudelaire with Dickens also showed that, if Benjamin produced what could be called a 'grammar' of the city in the *Arcades* and his other works, Dickens was very much part of that grammar. Indeed, the efficaciousness with which one can produce a reading of Dickens in terms of the flâneur and the crowd suggests that, had Benjamin been working in London, Dickens would have been the obvious figure to focus upon in the investigation of urban modernity – in the way that Baudelaire was in Benjamin's Parisian researches.

---

[237] *Dickens and Kafka*, p. 64.

The notion that the *Arcades* and other writings generate an arsenal of ideas and ways of seeing urban experience that amounts to a grammar is interesting. It might even point to a problem. It seems to claim that self-consciously getting to know one city intimately is to have a way of knowing all cities. The danger, in terms of literary study, is that juxtaposing Benjamin's paradigms with Dickens's fictional cities (paradigms which drew upon Dickens's life and works) could result in the collapsing of all Dickens's depictions of the city into one city. And this, it is suggested, is a very real drawback. While scenes and delineations from a number of Dickens's novels have successfully been analyzed in relation to Benjamin's formulations of urban experience, one wonders what specificities beyond the paradigms applied – and there are many more Benjaminian ideas and paradigms to be concerned with than just the flâneur, the crowd and the gothic city – might be glossed over or buried in the process. Of course, the fragmentary nature of Benjamin's *Arcades Project* means the volume of ideas generated is inexhaustible. And, since Dickens is in *The Arcades Project*, all areas of the Dickensian city are, presumably, to be included in any extensive reflection upon it. One just has to have the time and space to look for them.[238]

Dickens himself demonstrates this difficulty of how to conceive of and represent the city's infinite variety and specificity. In *TTC*, he presents Paris and London as symmetrical; he alternates scenes in the cities, refracting the textual experience of one city through the memory of the textual image of the other city. One city haunts the other. The same events happen in Paris and London, the same characters attend the same events in both cities, the cities are uncanny doubles, they are reduced, in a sense, to each other. As Schwarzbach puts it, here, at least: 'Dickens [uses] London not so much as a city, but as a general type for the city.'[239] But unlike Dickens's approach in *TTC*, where the reflexive structure of the presentation of Paris and London emphasizes the cities' samenesses, rather than their differences – a strategy based in the didactic desire to warn that revolution could happen in London as easily as it does in Paris – Benjamin's grammar of city experience is intended, like any grammar, to provide the structure from which new or different concepts, as well as familiar ones, can be accessed. In *OT*, Dickens suggests just such an offsetting of one 'city' (the London of the gentry) with another 'city' (the London of the criminal underworld). Oliver's crossing of the threshold between the two 'cities' provides the counterfactuals with which one can begin to view London in that novel as two cities in one.

---

[238] An example of this process in the course of this project was in coming across Benjamin's comment that Baudelaire did not deal with the political meaning of the crowd. This prompted an investigation into Dickens's approach to the crowd's political meaning: see Appendix 2.

[239] *Dickens and the City*, p. 101.

Having acknowledged the possible problems with this reading of Dickens, one cannot help but be taken with it. The notion that the quintessential Victorian and 'the man who invented Christmas'[240] was a proto-Modernist who was alive to the impact technology and urbanization had upon experience is too striking to be ignored. Moreover, it is a view of the city and literary production that has influenced generations of urban artists and thinkers right up to the present moment. And Dickens's tendency to show both an extraordinary excitement and welcoming of modernity as well as his regret and fear about the loss it involved, is also to be noted. Again, this is echoed in Benjamin, who ostensibly laments the changes wrought upon experience in 'The Storyteller' yet celebrates modern fragmentary experience in all its aesthetic and actual forms in essays like 'The Work of Art in the Age of Mechanical Reproduction'.

[240] Philip V. Allingham, *The Victorian Web*, quoting the *Sunday Telegraph*, December 18, 1988, p. 1, <http://www.victorianweb.org/authors/dickens/pva/pav63.html>.

# Conclusion

What has been learned in the process of this project?

This book attempted to assess the significance of the literary connection between the nineteenth-century novelist Charles Dickens and the twentieth-century writer-philosopher Walter Benjamin. It began with the intertextual moments, 15 fragments concerning Dickens in Benjamin's *Arcades Project*, but has burgeoned into an account of shared visions and responses to modernity that have proved far more wide-ranging than one would have expected between two such historically and geographically disparate figures.

This may be because Benjamin's modernity owes much to the past. This is hardly surprising when his understanding of historiography is taken into account. The past is not a fixed absolute, for Benjamin, it is in constant negotiation with, it presses insistently upon, the present moment. His melancholy vision of the modern world devastated by its loss of the absolute or meaning was inspired by his engagement with the seventeenth-century *Trauerspiel* playwrights as well as by the Jewish Kabbalah. His dark view of Baudelaire as an allegorist piecing together fragments of modern existence in a vain bid to attain transcendence points again to his *Trauerspiel* studies; an effect that fed through into his own methodology, whereby a montaging of fragments provided access to truth. And his theory of the monadic fragment was heavily influenced by the German Romantics, by Fichte and Schlegel, for whom absolute reality consisted of subjects infinitely reflecting reflection. The German Romantics, themselves fascinated by, and taking a cue in their metaphysics from the Kabbalah, would provide the natural route for Benjamin to follow toward his theological concerns. Of course, Benjamin's understanding of his urban present was also heavily indebted to his nineteenth-century studies. And this is where Dickens most obviously comes into Benjamin's formulation of modernity, although, as has been argued, Dickens can be viewed in relation to Benjamin in the other areas of his interests as well.

Against the received wisdom of most Benjamin scholarship, it can be suggested that there is a unity of purpose to be found in Benjamin's writings.[1] From Benjamin's early essay 'On Language as Such and On the Language of Man' (1916) and his Theological-Political Fragment (1920–1921), right through *The Origin of German Tragic Drama* (1925) to his later works, *The Arcades Project* (1927–1940), 'The Image of Proust' (1929), 'The Storyteller' (1936) or 'On Some Motifs in Baudelaire' (1939), Benjamin's concern is to understand how a fullness of experience can be maintained in the face of a modern existence that seems to determine a reduction in it. In his early years, this concern was framed within a theological language, rooted as it was in the Kabbalah's notion that the absolute, God or divine meaning, could no longer express itself fully in the fallen language of the historical world.

---

1 As stated earlier, Caygill in *The Colour of Experience* argues this position.

The result was that the everyday was, for Benjamin, virtually devoid of experience of the absolute or truth; the world was a hollow place in need of messianic redemption. Later, through an engagement with Marxism and Surrealism, Benjamin takes on a more materialist inflection in his treatment of experience, formulating a theory that, with the physical, spatio-temporal changes governed by urban and industrialized life, the integrity of experience was falling away: one was cut off, as it were, from experiencing fully. But, in both of these intellectual 'phases' Benjamin treats the same subject: the nature of modern experience. In both phases, the notion of the present as a site of loss, the fragmented nature of access to truth or knowledge, the importance of remembrance, of collecting fragments as a form of redemption,[2] will prove to be the focus. And of importance to him in both phases was the formulation of a concept of experience wherein totality or truth, religious experience, is conceivable and possible in the everyday. As Benjamin puts it plainly: 'the eternal [...] is far more the ruffle on a dress than some idea'.[3]

This book has argued that Dickens, in the texts analyzed, expresses an imaginative response to modernity comparable to Benjamin's description of the religious and epistemological atrophy that modern existence, for Benjamin, necessitates. In *OCS*, Dickens sets out the vision of an unforgiving world devoid of religious transcendence except for tiny sparks of revelation; the autobiographical *DC* depicts Dickens's form of production in the creative, reflexive and retrospective gathering up of memories and fragments of experience in the city; 'A Flight' suggests that Dickens sensed that experience had a new depthlessness, repetitiveness and shock about it; the gothic *TTC* depicts the urban world as cryptic and mysterious, the natural environment of the flâneur and the crowd. Dickens also has a tendency to handle objects or ordinary events, acts of kindness between characters, as if there were a magic about them – as if the absolute, a religious dimension, were breaking through into the mundane world. As has been suggested, these aspects of modern experience all feature in Benjamin's writings.

What needs to be addressed is whether the passages that have been analyzed can be understood to point to a persistent set of attitudes and qualities in Dickens's oeuvre more generally. If the question, then, is whether the absence or presence of a living religious sphere is a pervasive issue in Dickens's novels; or whether urban experience, urban characters, events and settings are a fixed feature; or whether the gothic atmospheres of mystery and epistemological uncertainty can be considered a constant in his works, the answer to all of these questions must be in the affirmative. Furthermore, there may be something in Chesterton's claim that *OCS* is 'a key to the whole Dickens romance'.[4] *OCS* is an allegory of the human world as a curiosity

---

[2] The 'redemption' of Dickensian fragments, of objects traceable to Dickens, persists more than ever today. Two buttons made by Rivière and Co, with a letter from Georgina Hogarth verifying that they had belonged to Dickens, were said to be worth £2,000 on the collectors' market (*Antiques Roadshow*, BBC1, November 13, 2005).

[3] *Arcades*, N3,2.

[4] Benjamin quoting Chesterton's *Dickens*, *Arcades*, A11,3, p. 57.

shop with God as its merchant (Männling's reading suggests as much). And London, Dickens's most important character, is the biggest shop of all, with the most varied merchandise and phantasmagoric displays one could ever imagine. As Wordsworth puts it, London is 'the great emporium',[5] and Dickens, as flâneur, and we as readers, are window shoppers at what had become the most densely populated and technologically advanced bazaar the world had so far seen – the city. Benjamin's and Dickens's stance toward modernity, industrial capitalism and urbanization, was Janus-faced. It exhibits both a regret at what was lost (a sense of transcendence and meaning) and, yet, a celebration of the potential gains involved (new sensations and ways of seeing).

What does this ostensible anticipation of Benjamin's formulated response to modernity tell us about Dickens in his historical context, that of the mid-nineteenth century? Afterall, as Laurence Lerner puts it, 'our [...] mythic sense of what Victorian England was like has been importantly shaped by his works, which themselves have been abstracted into myths'.[6]

It tells us that Dickens was perhaps a more forward-thinking, modern man than we usually give him credit for, a creative artist whose innovations in form and content would prove to be a significant prefiguring of the Modernist impulse and of urban art more generally. While Dickens is usually roughly understood to be working within the realist tradition, he can also be understood to interrogate it. As has been argued, he leaves behind the old Enlightenment idea that one can and must tell the truth, the whole truth about anything; taking up, in his gothic mode, the arrestingly modern idea that we cannot tell each other the truth about anything. The fragmentary nature of his urban cityscapes was apparently so radical that Walter Bagehot (1826–1877) lambasted his 'detective ingenuity in microscopic detail' excluding him from the pantheon of great artists because he failed to 'stamp the mark of unity' upon them.[7] This book suggests, in contrast, that it is this very fact that makes Dickens such an astonishingly modern urban artist.

If Dickens is the exemplary Victorian, the term 'Victorian' needs to be urgently investigated, since its connotations are not neutral and certainly do not easily admit of notions such as 'modern' or 'modernity'. The concept 'Victorian' was only conceived of late in the century: the Victorians themselves did not conceive of themselves as 'Victorian' at all.[8] Perhaps, in Benjaminian vein, fragments of that subdivision of the past, 'the Victorian' period, are ready to be redeemed and opened up in the present, creating the image of a new truth?

---

[5] Prelude, bk. VIII, vol. 3 (1850 version), l. 594, <http://www.gutenberg.org/files/12383/12383-h/Wordsworth3c.html#24b8>; also quoted in Schwarzbach, *Dickens and the City*, p. 104.

[6] *The Context of English Literature: The Victorians*, ed. Laurence Lerner (London: Methuen and Co. 1978), p. 4.

[7] *The Collected Works of Walter Bagehot*, ed. Norman St John-Stevas, 2 vols (London: The Economist, 1965), vol. II (p. 84).

[8] Rudolph Glitz in a paper entitled 'The Formation of the Concept 'Victorian' 1837–39' at the conference, 'The Twentieth Century and the Victorians', referenced above.

# Appendix 1

## Part 1: Exquisite Agony: Elements of Messianism and the Baroque in Benjamin and Dickens

*Chapter 1*

***Note 14, page 13***

In his essay, 'On the Programme of the Coming Philosophy' ('Uber das Programm der kommenden Philosophie') of 1918, Benjamin suggests no less than a restructuring of Kant's theory of experience. For Benjamin, the idea that Kant's 'subject' was not able to experience 'thing thing itself' or the absolute was a reductive, anaemic concept of knowledge traceable to his roots in the Enlightenment. If that illustrious project had sought to banish superstition and ignorance from human life, it had, at times, succeeded in driving metaphysics and religion into ambiguous intellectual spaces due to their 'unknowable' and 'scientifically unproven' epistemic status. As Benjamin avers of Kant's epistemology, 'that theory of knowledge, which was not yet able to determine sufficiently the logical place of metaphysical research' (*SW*, I, pp. 102–3).

According to Kant's transcendental model of the human soul, cognition was divided into the entirely separate theoretical faculty of 'the understanding' and the practical sphere of 'reason'. Understanding dealt with the objects of the world given to the mind in sensory experience. Forms of intuition, within the understanding, locate objects in time and space, dealing with sense experience from a visual/geometric perspective; while 12 categories organize impressions into concepts through which objects are thought. This is the linguistic/discursive side of theoretical experience. Within the totally distinct sphere of 'reason', however, regulative ideas attempt to grasp such notions as the absolute, totality, God, world. These regulative ideas correspond to no object given in sense experience. The separate faculties (the understanding and reason) provide an entirely distinct contribution to experience. Hence, for instance, no object in the world could furnish any material that would 'aid' an idea of totality or the absolute, for Kant: the absolute is excluded from all but moral ideas.

But for Benjamin, this was a totally inadequate formulation of experience. He felt the Enlightenment project had stripped away the unfathomable heart of human affairs in its ruthless reorientation of knowledge and truth along scientific lines. Benjamin had a vision of a much fuller theory of experience:

> the task of the coming philosophy can be conceived as the discovery or creation of the concept of knowledge which [...] makes not only mechanical but also religious experience logically possible. This should definitely be taken to mean not that knowledge makes God possible but that it definitely does make the experience and doctrine of Him possible. (*SW*, I, p. 105)

What Benjamin proposed was a total breaking down of the distinction between the Kantian faculties, allowing space for the appearance of totality and the absolute within intuitions and concepts; even entertaining the possibility of an instance of infinity within spatio-temporal experience. This involves the complex idea of a 'bounded infinity' – a notion that crops up several times in Benjamin's writings, particularly in his work on color. Benjamin's was a radical repositioning, then, of the absolute and religion within the bounds of the knowable – suggesting that the absolute was part and parcel of a metaphysics of everyday life. As Caygill puts it,

> This recasts the distinction between intuition/understanding and reason into an avowed metaphysics of experience in which the absolute manifests itself in spatio-temporal experience, but indirectly in complex, tortuous and even violent forms. (Howard Caygill, *The Colour of Experience* [London and New York: Routledge, 1998], p. 2)

Moreover, such occurrences would be rare. The task of the critic, when approaching artworks – granting that Benjamin later states that art must be politicized – is to redeem such moments from their hiding places within works of art: making them the focus of present hope. As for the historian, she too must locate immanent moments of transcendence in the past. And we are all, in this sense, historians. As Benjamin will state in the 'Theses':

> The past carries with it a temporal index by which it is referred to redemption. There is a secret agreement between past generations and the present one. Our coming was expected on earth. Like every generation that preceded us, we have been endowed with a weak Messianic power. (Thesis II, 'Theses on the Philosophy of History', in *Illuminations* [London: Pimlico, 1999], p. 245)

***Note 50, page 45***

The translators Edmund Jephott and Howard Eiland in *SW*, III, translate this passage with intriguing differences: 'just as a force, by virtue of the path it is moving along, can augment another force on the opposite path, so the secular order – because of its nature as secular – promotes the coming of the Messianic Kingdom. The secular, therefore, though not itself a category of this kingdom, is a decisive category of its most unobtrusive approach' (p. 305). The differences in the use of 'profane' and 'secular' is of significance. Jacobson, a scholar specializing in Jewish theology and trained in Israel, uses the concept that expresses the theological context within which he works.

*Chapter 2*

***Note 38, page 69***

Quilp is mostly labeled a 'dwarf' but is also an 'elderly man' and a 'creature': his physical description is closer to a grotesque fairy-tale dwarf than to the presumably 'realistic' freak-show dwarfs who crop up along Nell's journey. His eating of metal and drinking of boiling brews; his ability to pop up at the most unexpected and private moments as if by magic, all point to a theatrically inflected and fantastically unstable identity. This is further nuanced through the idea of his resemblance to the puppet, Punch. He physically resembles him:

> so low in stature as to be quite a dwarf, though his head and face were large enough for the body of a giant. His black eyes were restless, sly, and cunning; his mouth and chin bristly with the stubble of a coarse hard beard; and his complexion was one of that kind which never looks clean or wholesome. But what added most to the grotesque expression of his face, was a ghastly smile, which, appearing to be the mere result of habit and to have no connexion with any mirthful or complacent feeling … gave him the aspect of a panting dog. (Description of Quilp, *OCS*, ch. 3, pp. 26–7)

According to Cohen, Quilp can also be read as a study in sexuality and embodiment.[1] And Katherine Inglis believes him to involve an 'automatous simulation of humanity', labeling him a 'clockwork villain'.[2]

## Part 2: Dickens, Benjamin and the City

*Chapter 3*

***Note 3, page 83***

Entrepreneurs and officials are evidently so confident of the indelible grasp Dickens's London has upon the public imagination, huge sums of money have been risked to build 'Dickens World', a £62 million theme park in Chatham, Kent. It opened on May 27, 2007. Its attractions include reproductions of 'Victorian architecture, cobbled streets and specialist lighting' – all of which gives the effect of being on a stage set. Rides and other entertainment, including interaction with actors and automated characters, take place. At the center of it is a replica of London street scenes 'based on the life, times and books of Dickens'. The complex also includes an impressive theater in which, alas, automated figures, rather than live performances can be seen. It is hoped 'Dickens World' will help 'regenerate' the Chatham and Rochester areas, although in October 2010, according to a local reporter, the theme park was experiencing financial difficulties and recruitment freezes. Managers attributed poor attendance figures to the overall economic downturn.

---

1 William A Cohen, 'Interiors: Sex and the Body in Dickens', *Critical Survey* 17.2 (May 2005).

2 Katherine Inglis, 'Becoming Automatous: Automata in *The Old Curiosity Shop* and *Our Mutual Friend*', 19, *Interdisciplinary Studies in the Long Nineteenth Century* 6 (2008), <http://www.19.bbk.ac.uk>, both quotations, p. 14.

***Note 9, page 89***

Approaching a work of art before the historical onset of reproducibility meant coming into contact with the work's 'aura', for Benjamin. He claims the 'aura' is something akin to the work's 'distance' from the viewer, an ontological phenomenon dependent partly upon the traditional production and cultural reception of works. Benjamin claims that the unique presence of the auratic work allows it to raise its eyes and 'look back at' the viewer – it imposes itself on the viewer, who subjugates her own concerns to attend to the work's possible meaning. In the modern age of mechanical reproduction, claims Benjamin, the original work loses its aura. With reproducibility comes the loss of traditional contexts and references of meaning, together with a development of forms of production which do not lead to auratic works. It is being suggested here, then, that Benjamin's concern with the attenuation of experience (discussed fully in this chapter) – and understood by him as a loss – has an analogous relationship to the loss of aura described in his 'Work of Art' essay. Hence the fuller, epiphanic experience which Benjamin wants to 'redeem' might be termed 'auratic'. See Jennifer Todd's essay, 'Production, Reception, Criticism: Walter Benjamin and the Problem of Meaning in Art', in *Benjamin: Philosophy, Aesthetics, History*, ed. Gary Smith (London; Chicago, University of Chicago, 1989), pp. 102–25.

***Note 54, page 100***

For his farewell reading tour in October 1868, Dickens devised a new item, 'Sikes and Nancy', the enactment of Nancy's murder from *Oliver Twist*. He tried it out at a gala performance (November 14) before a specially invited audience. Edmund Yates claimed listeners were astonished at 'the volcanic activity and restlessness, the feverish excitability of genius' (E. Yates, *Recollections and Experiences*, [London, 1884] p. 126). Dickens himself noted that listeners were 'pale and had horror-stricken faces'; while Dickens's reading tour manager, George Dolby, claimed in his memoirs, 'One visitor, a celebrated critic, expressed an opinion as to the danger of giving the reading before a mixed audience, as he had an irresistible desire to scream. A celebrated physician, concurring with this, declared that if 'only one woman cries out when you murder the girl, there will be a contagion of hysteria all over the place' (*Charles Dickens as I knew him: The Story of the Reading Tours in Great Britain and America 1866–1870*, p. 351). Despite advice from friends against doing so, Dickens added 'Sikes and Nancy' to his repertoire. He became obsessed with the scene's almost mythical sensationalism, and it took such a toll on his health that doctors forced him to abandon the tour in April 1869.

***Note 57, page 101***

Playwrights J.B. Buckstone, W.T. Moncrieff and Edward Stirling as well as actors like W.J. Hammond (who played Sam Weller) and Mrs Keeley (who played Oliver, Smike, Little Nell and Barnaby Rudge) all cashed in on the popularity of Boz. Dickens was irritated that stage adaptations often anticipated his plots or simplified his characters; and were mounted before novels were complete. Before 1840, *The Pickwick Papers, Oliver Twist* and *Nicholas Nickleby* had been staged at least 60 times. By 1850, Dickens's work had been dramatized in at least 240 productions. But dramatizations declined in the following decade. And in the 1860s, Dickens attempted to clamp down on productions legally. When Dickens died (June 8, 1870), there was a huge resurgence of interest in Dickens dramatizations, and a whole generation learned their Dickens through the medium of theater. See Paul Schlicke (ed.), *The Oxford Reader's Companion to Dickens* (Oxford University Press, 1999), pp. 198–202.

***Note 90, page 110***
Film scholar Jay Leyda, translator and editor of Eisenstein's *Film Form*, was so impressed by Benjamin's 'Work of Art' essay on its first appearance in French in 1935, he approached Horkheimer for the job of translating it into English. He was turned down.

***Note 122, page 128***
Simply speaking, a number of qualities contribute to an original work's aura: its presence in time and space; its institutionalized presentation and criticism; the way it demands the viewer concentrate before it and attend to its meaning in such a setting. Reproducibility takes the image out of its 'sacred' context into the world of the consumer, it loses its singularity and aura and takes on a disposable, object quality, to which new meanings can be attributed.

*Chapter 4*

***Note 1, page 144***
Benjamin fled France ahead of the advancing German army in September 1940, having managed to obtain Spanish transit papers to escape via Spain. After taking a boat from Marseilles to Port Vendres, he traveled on foot, together with a number of other escapees, along a remote mountain track over the Pyrenees. The steep climb lasted nine hours. When the authorities denied him permission to cross the border at Port-Bou, Benjamin took a massive overdose of morphine. The thought of being escorted back into France and ensconced in a camp was too much for him. He died the following morning, having written a last letter dated September 25 explaining himself to Theodor Adorno and Henny Gurland. Chastened officials provided his traveling companions with French exit visas after the tragic incident. An account by Lisa Fittko, who guided the escapees through the mountains, throws another important light on the fate of Benjamin's *Passagen* material. She claims Benjamin carried an important manuscript with him over the Pyrenees in a black briefcase. She maintains it might have been a version of the *Passagenwerk* (Lisa Fittko, 'The Story of Old Benjamin', *Arcades*, pp. 946–54). According to Fittko's account, the briefcase was lost in the confusion that accompanied Benjamin's suicide.

However, this account of Benjamin as a suicide has been disputed by leading figures in Benjamin scholarship. Ingrid and Konrad Scheurmann, who helped create the Internationale Walter Benjamin Gesellschaft (International Walter Benjamin Society), got hold of documents relating to Benjamin's death and suggest that it is possible that Benjamin did not kill himself in Port Bou. They argued at the Walter Benjamin Conference in Barcelona held in September 2000, that Benjamin may have died, in fact, of a cerebral hemorrhage, the cause of death recorded on the death certificate. This alternative slant on Benjamin's death can be viewed as an attempt to cut against the mythologization of Benjamin as an unlucky melancholic. See Esther Leslie's report on the Walter Benjamin Conference in Barcelona, 'Crossing Borders' on the Walter Benjamin Research Syndicate website, <http://www.wbenhamin.org/walterbenjamin.html>.

***Note 18, page 147 and note 226, page 203***

An important aspect of *The Arcades Project* was to dispel what Benjamin saw as the 'myth' of progress that was virtually synonymous with nineteenth-century industrialization. New machines and burgeoning technology became integral to the movement of history, as if, like the new railways, history surged forward with energy and speed that could only imply progress. The great expositions were national monuments to the progress industrial capitalism yielded. By tracing the waxing and waning of the physical transformation of Paris, Benjamin attempted to show, visually, how in fact rather than progressing, history had not budged an inch. While the temporality of capitalist economic history certainly implied movement and pace, Benjamin suggested that relations of production and commodities themselves proceeded according to repetition or the relentlessness of eternal return. History was not, in this sense, a narrative of progress at all.

The Parisian arcades were a case in point. The arcades' innovative iron and glass design enabled the maximum fetishization of commodities; consumers gazed at the spectacular displays and forms, enjoyed commodities within the setting of the latest technology. At their height the arcades were a home to crowds of consumers, they were dreamworlds of light and mirrors and surfaces. In this urban phantasmagoria, the middle class conspicuously spent, and idlers and flâneurs loitered and strolled. But the arcades were soon superceded. Like all fashionable products, they were abandoned for the next big thing: the department store and its greater capacities for luxury and fetishism. The arcades fell out of use and became the fossilized curiosities of Benjamin's *Arcades Project*. As soon as they were out of vogue, they were ancient history. Like an archaeological site, the passages harbored last century's fashions. Adverts of women with long hair exhibited, says Benjamin, 'fossilized hair curls'; while, 'the Passages lie in the great cities like caves containing fossils of an ur-animal presumed extinct'. For Benjamin, the creative potential in the commodity's 'fossilization' was that it disclosed the fleeting temporality of the new nature, technology. Industrial capitalism involved the relentless pursuit of novelty that brought about little that was new in history.

Dickens shows ambivalence toward the notion of progress, discernible especially in his response to the Great Exhibition. While he praised Paxton and his design many times in speeches, Dickens desisted from endorsing the exhibition itself. For instance, in a letter (July 11, 1851, to Mrs Watson), he complains that the exhibition represents an oversaturation of the senses; it exhausts him:

> I find I am 'used up' by the Exhibition. I don't say 'There is nothing in it' – there's too much. I have only been twice; so many things bewildered me. (*The Letters of Charles Dickens* [ed.], Walter Dexter, vol. II [Bloomsbury: The Nonesuch Press, 1938], pp. 325–8 [p. 327])

Abundance and excess, monumental size and expansion are all part of the constellation of the 'myth of progress'. As convolute G of *The Arcades Project* – on world expositions – makes clear, fantastic scale and variety was integral to the triumphant capitalist message exhibitions imparted to consumers and workers alike. The significance of a massive display or industrial and technological innovation is what it implies about the future. Delegations of workers were bussed in to view the utopian fantasy, a future rendered so rosy by the glossy display, it obliterated the injustices of industrial relations. As Susan Buck-Morss puts it, 'a "heaven" of class harmony and material abundance – this conceptual constellation blocked revolutionary consciousness like an astrological force' (*The Dialectics of Seeing*, p. 95).

Dickens, then, seems particularly offended by this play on excess, luxury and abundance; he is rendered vertiginous, he is disorientated by it. Even the inclusion of a statue of Little Nell by sculptor Robert Ball Hughes (1806–1868) as part of the exhibition did not soften his mind toward it. And the implication, especially when one takes account of his piece for *Household Words*, 'The Last Words of the Old Year', is that for Dickens, the Great Exhibition is a shamefully conspicuous phantasmagoria of merchandise and consumption in an age when many suffered poverty and hardship:

> Which of my children shall behold the Princes, Prelates, Nobles, Merchants, of England, equally united, for another Exhibition – for a great display of England's sins and negligences, to be, by steady contemplation of all eyes, and steady union of all hearts and hands, set right? (*Household Words*, vol. V, January 4, 1851)

Dickens disapproved of the triumphalism and complaisance implicit in an exhibition whose plethora of exhibits told a utopian tale of plenty and progress. And one cannot accuse Dickens of inconsistency on this topic. His dystopian image of what industrialization meant for many people was available at the start of the 'Hungry Forties', in a memorable scene from *The Old Curiosity Shop*:

> In a large and lofty building, supported by pillars of iron, with great black apertures in the upper walls, open to the external air; echoing to the roof with the beating of hammers and the roar of furnaces, mingled with the hissing of red-hot metal plunged in water, and a hundred strange unearthly noises never heard elsewhere; in this gloomy place, moving like demons among the flame and

> smoke, dimly and fitfully seen, flushed and tormented by the burning fires, and wielding great weapons, a faulty blow from any one of which must have crushed some workman's skull, a number of men laboured like giants. Others, reposing upon heaps of coals or ashes with their faces turned to the black vault above, slept or rested from their toil. (*OCS* ch. 44, p. 342)

Little interpretation is needed to grasp this plainly critical image of the industrial site as hell. For Dickens, it is a mythical, monstrous space where working people are reduced to little more than beasts: an image revisited many times by the French novelist Émile Zola.[3]

In 'Shops and their Tenants', a 'scene' in the collected *Sketches by Boz*, Dickens also undercuts the notion of progress, echoing instead a theme in *The Arcades* – the temporality of fashion: capitalism as eternal return. The sketch depicts the successive rise and fall of businesses on one site, from the point of view of the regular passerby. The physical signs of the shop – its plush refit, its initial grandeur, followed by its loss of confidence, evidenced in its unmended windows and reduction of staff – are read from the pavement. One failed shop is replaced by another and another. Meanwhile, the premises get more and more decrepit. Like Benjamin traces the decline of the arcades, Dickens in 'Shops and their Tenants' tells a tale of fragility and transience without progress. Rather than representing progress, capitalism's temporality implies decay:

> When we paused in front of our old friend, and observed these signs of poverty, which are not to be mistaken, we thought, as we turned away, that the house had attained its lowest pitch of degradation. We were wrong. (*SB*, Scenes: ch. 3, p. 84)

The 'mythical' temporality of eternal return is matched by the mythical efforts of the urban dweller to cope with relentless repetition. In Baudelaire's poetry, for instance, classical mythological figures roam the urban space. Modern man is heroic, like a Tantalus or a Sysiphus. Like the Danaides, shop assistants sieve water and pour it into broken vessels. In 'Shops and their Tenants', a Penelope-like heroine is similarly depicted in epic combat with the shop's fate:

> somehow we always thought, as we passed, that it looked like a poor and struggling concern. We wished the man well, but we trembled for his success. He was a widower evidently, and had employment elsewhere, for he passed us every morning on his road to the city. The business was carried on by his eldest daughter. Poor girl! She needed no assistance. We occasionally caught a glimpse of two or three children, in mourning like herself, as they sat in the little parlour behind the shop; and we never passed at night without seeing the eldest girl at work, either for them, or in making some elegant little trifle for sale. (*SB*, Scenes: ch. 3, p. 82)

---

[3] Émile Zola (1840–1902) wrote *La Bête Humaine* (The Beast in Man) in 1890. He also wrote *Au Bonheur des Dames* in 1883, about the world of the department stores which replaced the dreamworlds of the arcades. Zola features nine times in *The Arcades Project*.

In other pieces in *Sketches*, a bailiff is 'Mercury', a waitress 'Hebe' and porters are 'Atlases'. Here Dickens echoes the Baudelairean notion that the pointless relentlessness of modern life requires an heroic constitution:

> The essence of the mythic event is recurrence. Inscribed as a hidden figure in such events is the futility that furrows the brow of some of the heroic personages of the underworld. (*The Arcades Project* [D10a,4])

***Note 25, page 150***

The 36 sheaves (convolutes) of notes and research of *The Arcades Project* form a monumental ruin or torso, the basis upon which constant reflection and scholarship and attempts to reach conclusions about how to approach the material have been made. But since *The Arcades Project* is determined by a belief in a fragmented, critical presentation, any concern with its 'unfinished' status takes on an interesting meaning. Like Benjamin's understanding of the work of art in his 1919 essay 'The Concept of Criticism in German Romanticism' (Der Begriff der Kunstkritik in der deutschen Romantik), the infinite process of reflection continues within the artwork, which contains the literary absolute within itself. Any artwork is always in a process of becoming and can never be completed. Even a work considered 'complete' by the artist, is not so because it is always criticizable. On Benjamin's own theoretical ground, then, critics and scholars will continue to mine *The Arcades Project* for its secrets, ad infinitum – its form as notes collated under titles and themes only exemplifying the drama of Benjamin's philosophical and historiographical procedures.

***Note 78, page 160***

The treatment of women and femininity in urban modernity is problematic and has been the center of much productive discussion. See especially Anke Gleber, 'Women on the Screens and Streets of Modernity: In Search of the Female Flâneur', in Dudley Andrew (ed.), *The Image in Dispute: Art and Cinema in the Age of Photography* (Austin: University of Texas, 1997), pp. 55–85; Deborah Parsons, 'Flâneur or Flâneuse: Mythologies of Modernity', in *New Formations* 38 (Summer 1999): pp. 91–100; and Griselda Pollock, 'Modernity and the Spaces of Femininity', in *Vision and Difference: Feminism, Femininity and the Histories of Art* (London: Routledge, 1988), pp. 70–127.

***Note 122, page 170***

The comi-tragic notion that there are always penniless characters to be found in the city played itself out in Dickens's life, too. He caused controversy through his portrayal of the profligate Skimpole in *Bleak House* (1852–1853). Comments to Forster and speculation in the press pointed to his basing the character upon his friend, the radical journalist, James Henry Leigh Hunt (1784–1859). The parody caused Hunt pain and Dickens's apologies and 'A Remonstance' in *ATYR* (December 24, 1859) never really resolved the situation. 'A Remonstance' is reprinted in 'Slater' IV, pp. 14–19.

# Appendix 2

## The Political Meaning of the Crowd in Dickens

*Note 156, page 180*

As has been argued, passages in *The Arcades Project* threw light upon how the crowd contributed to an understanding of modern urban experience; Benjamin's methodology meant he glimpsed aspects of the crowd's effect from, as it were, street level. His treatment of the question of the political status of the masses in an increasingly urbanized and industrialized modern culture emerges, of course, out of fragments; and Benjamin devotes an entire convolute to this question, which includes copious excerpts of Marxian theory. It would be impossible to discuss an entire section here, but one of the main issues Benjamin brings out is that Baron Haussmann's renovation of Paris under Napoleon III, which included the sweeping away of narrow, labyrinthine streets and the building of wide boulevards, was motivated by a wish to prevent the erection of barricades by a revolutionary mob.[1] The crowd was threatening enough to the state in mid-nineteenth-century France to feed into French public policy:

> 'Since the French Revolution, an extensive network of controls', had been brought in, while, 'In proletarian neighbourhoods, to be sure, this simple police measure had encountered resistance'.[2]

Also worth noting is Benjamin's complaint that 'this central figure, the crowd, is actually invisible most of the time [...] Baudelaire's mass conspicuously lacks any social or political significance as a class or, for that matter, as a human collective'.[3]

In contrast to Baudelaire, the crowd's political significance is something that can be gleaned from Dickens's representations of the crowd in his fiction.[4] His positioning of the crowd within a narrative establishes a critical questioning of particular social and political arrangements of concern to the author. Dickens's crowd at times represents an expression of the tyranny of the state – for

---

1 Convolute E of *The Arcades Project* is entitled 'Haussmannization, Barricade Fighting'. Section V of the Expose of 1935 and E of the Expose of 1939 was entitled 'Haussmann, or the Barricades', *Arcades*, pp. 120–49 and p. 11 and p. 23, respectively.

2 Both quotations, 'Second Empire', p. 26.

3 Quoted from Tomoko Masuzawa, 'Tracing the Figure of Redemption: Walter Benjamin's Physiognomy of Modernity', *Modern Language Notes* 100.3 (April 1985): pp. 514–36 (p. 525).

4 See Mark Willis, 'Charles Dickens and Fictions of the Crowd', *Dickens Quarterly* 23.2 (June 2006): p. 85

instance, when he depicts a crowd at a public hanging or as a manipulated mob. Elsewhere, the crowd can become the state's independent or critical interlocutor or conscience – such as at an election. And, in the most dramatic of crowd scenes, the revolutionary mob plays the role of the state's possible and perhaps desirable nemesis.

### *The Crowd as a Malleable Entity or Energy*

As was touched upon, one of Dickens's presentations of the crowd involves its becoming one entity – almost one creature comprising a concerted multitude.[5] Within this framework, it is something to be manipulated or at least thought of on those terms by characters.

In a passage recounting how he stirred up and moved a Suffolk crowd, Lord George Gordon says of rival politicians: 'which of them can raise this human sea and make it swell and roar at pleasure?' (Gordon, *BR*, ch. 35, p. 340). Gordon has such 'control' over this entity that it becomes a giant mouthpiece for him. Its language is the language of public gesture:

> My lord has thoughts of our walking in procession through the streets – just as an innocent display of strength. (*BR*, ch. 37, p. 356)

Such a procession says one thing, loudly: that Gordon's views should be taken seriously or else 'the creature' becomes destructive, 'a monster' – Dickens uses this term for rioters (*TTC*, Cly's mock funeral scene, bk. 2, ch. 14, p. 186). At one point, Dickens even suggests the crowd is such a useful threat against political opponents, if it did not exist, Gordon would need to invent it to lever the political elite into taking note of him (*BR*, ch. 37, p. 348).

In *BR*, Dickens seems genuinely convinced that crowds are a lumpen, rather gullible mass that are goaded into action by irresponsible leaders. The crowd is 'an ignorant and excited throng' and 'idlers of the lowest grade' (*BR*, ch. 43, pp. 406 and 400, respectively) who cannot resist the mystery of 'False priests, false prophets, false doctors, false patriots, false prodigies of every kind' (*BR*, ch. 37, p. 347). The criminal Gashford, who has become Gordon's adviser, incites Hugh and Dennis to lead a crowd in razing Haredale's house to the ground, and hence, claims the novelist, 'The worst passions of the worst men were working thus' (*BR*, ch. 44, p. 414).

In this sense, Dickens comes close to Le Bon's view that 'In crowds, it is stupidity and not mother-wit that is accumulated'.[6]

---

[5] One scholar argues that in failing to distinguish between individual and collective psychology, Dickens has 'a pre-modern perception of the crowd'. See R.C.M. Maia, PhD thesis, 'Crowd theory in some modern fiction: Dickens, Zola and Canetti, 1842–1960', Nottingham University, 42-5177 (1992), introductory abstract.

[6] Excerpt from Gustave Le Bon, *The Crowd: A Study of the Popular Mind* (New York: Viking Press, 1960), p. 29.

But rather than a sneering mockery of the crowd in *BR*, Dickens's focus is corrupt authority, which manipulates those in misery. This is one of the main differences in the presentations of the rioting crowd of *BR* and the revolutionary mob of *TTC*. Dickens spends much time in the latter novel depicting the appalling poverty and suffering of the French poor, as well as playing up the arrogant indifference and decadence of the *ancien régime*. This enables the revolution almost to seem inevitable – its explosion is not a question of manipulation by ambitious and corrupt leaders, but the natural and violent consequence of an unfolding of smaller violent events and continual injustice. In the case of *BR*, Dickens describes a number of scenes where riot leaders plan their next move. The crowd, here, are instigated into marching on parliament and later into rioting. Perhaps despite himself, then, Dickens displays a sensitive understanding of how the Gordon rioters get to the stage of mindlessly destroying property. While not painting their social conditions in detail, Dickens states that they are 'stimulated by their own headlong passions, by poverty, by ignorance' (*BR*, ch. 53, pp. 483–4) and once they have taken part – committing actions over which individuals may have little control amid the multitude's intentions – they fear they have gone too far to be let off. Their action then becomes spontaneous: 'new leaders sprang up as they were wanted, disappeared when the necessity was over' and 'Each tumult took shape and form from the circumstances of the moment'. Even sober workmen, claims Dickens, down tools to riot. Rioting becomes 'an attraction they had no firmness to resist' and 'a moral plague ran through the city' (all quotations, *BR*, ch. 53, pp. 483–4). Dickens, then, shows an imaginative and sympathetic understanding of the processes that go into becoming a rioter. While he situates rioting as morally unjustifiable in the phrase 'a moral plague', he is not prepared to condemn the rioters as much as he is the corrupt leaders who instigate them.

The notion that the crowd is a gullible and dull composite entity is especially powerful when it takes on the appearance of a very slow computer or a mind in the throes of a decision-making process. At one point, the crowd's 'cells' are not unified in intention, causing a state of confusion:

> the crowd faltered and stared at each other with irresolute and timid looks. Many tried to turn towards the door; some of the faintest-hearted cried they had best go back, and called to those behind to give way; and the panic and confusion were increasing rapidly. (*BR*, ch. 49, p. 457)

Afterwards, having entertained different suggestions, when ideas are voiced aloud by members of the crowd, and either accepted or rejected, the 'decision' to stone Haredale is arrived at (*BR*, ch. 43, pp. 407–9), but this takes time and is a matter of chance and of the crowd's mood. It is a highly volatile affair and it is in this sense that individuals who might be at variance with the crowd can exert little control over its actions.

This is a depiction of the crowd, then, as a physical entity or body whose cells are sometimes at variance, but which receives transmitted signals, and, absorbing them, becomes an identifiable or more unified force. While there may be division or confusion at first, with the crowd '[driving] on in a very disorderly way [...] as a crowd is wont to do' (*BR*, ch. 43, p. 404), the more suggestions and intentions are heard and rehearsed in a blunt, confrontational and public way, the more a sense of palpable 'energy' that can either be released, blocked or directed at each moment, becomes apparent. For instance, when a suggestion is shouted out by a member of the crowd, the moment before an acceptance or rejection of it takes place is one filled with density, tension and electricity. For it can go either way, and can be coaxed or directed to do so, if timed correctly. The riot leaders in *BR* claim 'we had a spurt today', 'we broke the ice' (*BR*, ch. 45, p. 421). Their understanding of the crowd here is entirely in concert with its being an energy to be directed and controlled. In the crowd's energy having already been released in a 'spurt' and dammed up, the resulting breaking of the dam could be all the more destructive, so the leaders hope. Baudelaire himself describes crowds in such terms: 'plunging into the crowd is like plunging into a reservoir of electric energy'.[7]

The 'energy' associated with crowds is felt even by those who are leading, who are attempting to manipulate from the outside, from a distance. Just the recounting of a speech he gave and the remembrance of the effect it had upon the crowd, stirs up Lord Gordon again (*BR*, ch. 35, p. 339). Men standing near the riotous burning down of Newgate Prison cannot but become infected by the destructive energy of the rioters: 'rather than do nothing, [they] tore up the pavement of the street, and did so with a haste and fury they could not have surpassed [...] Not a living creature in the throng was for an instant still' (*BR*, ch. 64, p. 583).

### *The Crowd at a Public Execution*

A number of public execution scenes take place in Dickens's fiction, from that of Sidney Carton's in *TTC*, and Hugh's in *BR* to Bill Sikes's (accidental hanging) in *OT* and even Jonas Chuzzlewit's dream of being apprehended by a crowd in *MC*. What these scenes have in common is that the crowd is viewed from the outside, objectively: they come across as either an extension of the barbarism already partaken in by characters (as in the case of Sikes and Chuzzlewit), or a limb of the unjust establishment that Dickens is attacking, or both.

It is worth noting that Dickens was extremely concerned about the phenomenon of public executions. It is believed he attended a number of public hangings and the behavior of the crowd was an issue that exercised him greatly.[8] Early on in his career, he was an abolitionist; later his position was to support executions behind closed doors.[9] It was not so much the punishment of death that exercised Dickens, as its status as an urban spectacle.

Hence, the disquiet he feels at what happens to consciousness at executions makes its way into his treatment of a fictional crowd at a public execution.

7 'Painter', p. 140.

8 Collins, *Dickens and Crime*, pp. 220–55.

9 See Dickens's 1864 letter to this effect, *Dickens and Crime*, p. 245.

In *TTC*, Charles Darnay is on trial for spying, but the bellicose multitude assumes Darnay's guilt in anticipation of witnessing his gory demise: this is the 'tainted' crowd, imagining itself at a public execution. The crowd's only fear is that the prisoner might get off, and, in reassuring each other that 'Oh! They'll find him guilty [...] Don't you be afraid of that', Dickens exposes how they invert moral and legal propriety (both quotations, *TTC*, bk. 2, ch. 2, p. 91). The crowd is in fact like a set of vultures (Dickens uses the image of swarming flies) devouring a piece of carrion:

> Had he stood in peril of a less horrible sentence – had there been a chance of any one of its savage details being spared – by just so much would he have lost in his fascination. The form that was to be doomed to be so shamefully mangled, was the sight; the immortal creature that was to be so butchered and torn asunder, yielded the sensation.[10]

This is an arrestingly modern take on exposure to violence, crowd psychology and desensitization. The excerpt makes clear that witnessing an execution involves a stimulation of the senses – it is literally sensational. This is significant in view of what has been argued in Chapter 3, where Dickens noted that urban dwellers had evolved an enjoyment of, or even an addition to, heightened stimulation.[11] The relish with which the crowd as audience anticipates a bloody execution, their blood lust for the spectacle of 'shameful' torture is so unreasonable, it immediately draws attention to Dickens's point that public executions brutalize and desensitize public consciousness. Complex, sensitive responses are nowhere to be found. As blundering as the crowd that 'made up its mind' in *BR*, this is a blunt, desensitized crowd response – that would not result if one witnessed execution alone.

There are two aspects to this. Firstly, the regularity of executions – gleanable from conversations held among the court crowd – will have helped naturalize proceedings and acclimatize this crowd to macabre rituals to some extent. It is fair to assume Dickens is claiming that regular exposure to the shock of the violence of execution blunts the reaction, making the crowd blasé:

> it agitates the nerves to their strongest reactivity for such a long time that they finally cease to react at all.[12]

Benjamin, too, notes how the reactions of crowds have become 'dehumanized':

> The people [...] behave as if they can no longer express themselves through anything but reflex actions.[13]

10 *TTC*, bk. 2, ch. 2, p. 93

11 See 'Dickens and Benjamin's theory of experience', above, p. 178.

12 As already cited above, Georg Simmel, 'The Metropolis', p. 414.

13 'Second Empire', p. 30.

Executions at the point Dickens wrote were staged like a piece of theater, encouraging 'the audience' to consume the event on these terms. Hence, taking pleasure in the group response ensues. The heightened sadism of the images of violence adds to the experience's 'unreal' or theatrical quality: suggesting the 'attraction of repulsion' one feels at a Webster drama.[14] Dickens seems to know that some violent acts are so difficult to assimilate, laughter is the only response: his comic yet dark tone in this scene underscores this response. The process of law and the resulting violence, then, becomes a lurid piece of theater toward which the crowd is distanced as audience – hence, the crowd's inappropriately jovial reactions to events. They relate to Darnay and the judge as if they were leading actors in a popular show. They also clamor for 'tickets'.

Secondly, public executions and their concomitant macabre representations of suffering are attempts at deterrence – they are the ultimate expression of a tyrannous regime warning its citizens to tow the line. Hence, the bloodthirsty, vengeful judge who fronts a cruel, corrupt penal system which, like the crowd, assumes guilt. Here, then, the crowd emerges as another version of the obtuse, manipulated crowd. Watching a public execution involves the secret relief that one is a member of the crowd, one's level of hysterical support for the execution can be an index to the amount of relief felt. The crowd in this sense is the limb of the establishment, warning off all dissenting voices.

> 'A multitude of people, and yet a solitude!' said Darnay. (*TTC*, bk. 2, ch. 6, p. 132)

Of course, Sidney Carton suffers the ultimate persecution at the hands of a predatory crowd – who are willing spectators at his demise on the guillotine. Again, his singleness to the crowd is an 'Otherness', and they witness a solitary life being extinguished, and distance themselves from it as entertainment. Dickens's most potent criticism here is in the fact that any sense the crowd has as to the justness of their cause – their revolutionary cause – and any sense of a right to revenge is utterly undermined by the irony of Carton's innocence. The reader knows this, but the crowd, of course, does not. The crowd is the reflection of the brutalized, cruel world from which it has emerged. Dickens dramatizes the loneliness of going to death amid the crowd as a religious internal monologue conducted by Carton with himself, in a similar vein to the depiction of Christ's death in the Bible. This thoughtful, introverted stance by the condemned man is a final acceptance of what one's singleness amounts to: a metaphysical severance from the crowd. Death, public or otherwise, is a process that is solely one's own, a road one must take alone, and along which others cannot follow. And it is this that holds the clue to Dickens's rejection of public execution. The gravity of what is at stake and the complexities of an individual's thoughts and feelings at such a moment can hardly be appreciated by an outsider let alone a multitude reacting en masse.

---

[14] Dickens's relationship to the London slum, St Giles, as described by Forster, *Life*, bk. 1, ch. 1, p. 11.

Dickens firmly obviates any notion that death should be on display for an audience to witness and react to as spectacle. This is Dickens's critique of the barbarian crowd that forms a blurry backdrop to the final revelatory moment.

*The Crowd as Independent Entity*

In contrast to Dickens's depiction of crowds as malleable and dull-witted is his presentation of them as not being in thrall to authority or leaders at all. The crowd in *PP* could be understood on these terms: it is the crowd as a boisterous audience or a Hogarth-inspired satirical chorus.[15] Dickens also enables the reader to feel what it is like to be one of the crowd.

In *PP*, the crowd's crude and raucous heckling in the election scene (*PP*, ch. 13, pp. 191–7) serves to send up the pomposity of the Blues and the Buffs, the corrupt political parties attempting to get reelected. Here the power dynamic between 'the many' and 'the one' described in the accident scene in *TTC* is entirely overturned: this is the Dickensian version of the carnivalesque.[16] The comedy mileage in the Pickwick election comes out of the fact that while the politicians think they are cleverly manipulating, and indeed are bribing the crowd – the crowd (unbeknown to the politicians) know they are doing it and milk it for everything they can get. The crowd is in jovial mood since the need for their votes gives them a temporary level of power which they intend to enjoy fully. The posturing and self-importance of the politicians becomes a source of ridicule and fun for the crowd, then, who take pleasure in the politicians' ignorance as to the situation they find themselves in. This is a knowing crowd.[17] Hogarth highlights one voter, among the 'manipulated' crowd, capitalizing upon his situation by taking bribes from both parties (Canvassing for Votes). While Dickens does not go quite that far, he positively presents the politicians as corrupt: in one scene, party workers ply voters with drink so they are too inebriated to vote. Dickensian politicians, like those in Hogarth, then, are presented entirely without redeeming qualities; too arrogant to see when they are being laughed at, they lack integrity and lord it over a system creaking with corruption. Such a depiction positions the reader among the crowd in relation to the politicians. They are exposed on a public scene, as if upon a stage. The reader stands among the crowd during an address; and the crowd is the choric voice – airing not only the opinion of Dickens who was notoriously scathing of parliament and politicians – but also those feelings of the reader. Part of the pleasure of the reader's standing amid the crowd in this instance is the fact that the quips are quick, coruscating and comic. They, as it were, gazump anything

[15] Here I refer to William Hogarth's 1754 series of oils, *An Election Entertainment; Canvassing for Votes; The Polling and Chairing Member*, John Soane Museum, London.

[16] Of course, the great theorist of the carnivalesque is Mikhail Bakhtin (1895–1975).

[17] The crowd's position of power over the erstwhile powerful is presumably the state of affairs which so galls Shakespeare's Coriolanus who, unlike the Dickensian politicians, knows the crowd knows it is in control of his fate.

the reader can come up with in the moment of reading, or, at least, are a kind of fully formulated and instant version of how the reader might like to respond.

### *The Crowd as Rioters or as a Mob*

Dickens presents the crowd in *TTC* and *BR* as always on the cusp of potential or actual instability. Unbearable social conditions or unscrupulous or ambitious leaders help flip that state of affairs over into destruction. This evocation of the crowd as tantamount to chaos, violence and disorder would normally be seen as Dickens's fear of the masses, a political aversion to what they might do, perhaps inspired by Thomas Carlyle's position in *Chartism* (1839) and in *History of the French Revolution* (1837) which, simply put, warned the ruling classes to attend to the problems of the poor or else suffer the consequences. As Humphry House puts it, between 1839 and 1848, 'the possibility of revolution was rarely far from men's minds' in England; while the Carlyle of *Chartism* and *Past and Present* was 'not only an angry but a frightened man'.[18] Carlyle's was not an intervention on behalf of the poor but a championing of a new kind of hierarchical political order in which the needs of the poor, and their anger, could be assuaged. It is, rather, a staving off of revolution, closer to Le Bon's reactionary and essentialist view: 'Crowds are only powerful for destruction. Their rule is always tantamount to a barbarian phase.'[19] And at times, Dickens's fear of disorder and crime saw him advocating a stronger expression of authority in the shape of a better police force or harsher prison conditions. Of the rioters gathered outside the Houses of Commons in *BR*, the novelist says they are 'composed for the most part of the very scum and refuse of London, whose growth was fostered by bad criminal laws, bad prison regulations, and the worst conceivable police'.[20]

As Philip Collins argues, Dickens often appears to have respected authority and order. His avowed support for the retributive role of punishment – as well as his complaint that public executions encouraged onlookers to sympathize with the criminal – make a reading of him as fairly hawkish on law and order tempting.[21]

The anxiety associated with this position expresses itself in Dickens's fiction particularly when he represents the rioting crowd. As was discussed in the main text, in these scenes, the crowd is a frightening 'mob' (Cly's mock funeral scene, *TTC*, bk. 2, ch. 14, p. 186, and the Grindstone scene, bk. 3, ch. 2, p. 291). On the other hand, there is another way of considering Dickens's delineation of the crowd – in *TTC* and in *BR* – in a light that takes him far away from Le Bon's or Carlyle's positions. As John Carey points out, the lucidity and relish with which Dickens describes the above cited and other scenes in

---

18 *The Dickens World* (Oxford: Oxford University Press, 2nd ed., 1942), p. 49.

19 *The Crowd: A Study in the Popular Mind* (New York: Viking Press, 1960), p. 18.

20 *BR*, ed. Gordon Spence (Harmondsworth: Penguin 1997), ch. 49, p. 453.

21 See *Dickens and Crime* (London: Indiana University Press, 1962), ch. X, pp. 220–55.

*TTC*, as well as in the burning down of Newgate scene in *BR*, must point to his being imaginatively on the side of the mob, even if his tone is one of disgust and fear.[22] Such scenes have a 'hypersensitivity' pointing to an ability to see and delineate the scene from the perspective of the rioters. This point is further enhanced, as already argued, in Dickens's insistence that the reader comprehend what has gone into the explosive state of affairs, a comprehension which at least qualifies any harsh judgment one might make of the mob. For instance, the *TTC*, the hysterical mob ruthlessly murder the vile old Foulon (a grocer who scorned and ridiculed desperate pleas for food and credit). This and other acts the crowd indulge in are hideous and disturbing and are luridly delineated, but Dickens has already made space to consider why things might have come to this. Dickens's treatment of the battering and crushing of Foulon by the crowd is shockingly matter of fact:

> the long-gathering rain of stabs and blows fell heavy [...] he dropped down dead under it [and] suddenly animated, she put her foot upon his neck and with her cruel knife – long ready – hacked off his head.[23]

But he follows this passage up immediately with a reminder to the reader that the harsh cruelties of the past, plenty of which have been brought to life dramatically in the narrative leading up to this climactic point, directly feed into the present moment:

> The remorseless sea of turbulent swaying shapes, voices of vengeance, and faces hardened in the furnaces of suffering until the touch of pity could make no mark on them.[24]

Dickens depicts the slaughter of Foulon as well as the storming of the Bastille only after having carefully built the case against the Marquis and the *ancien régime*. He presents one grotesque injustice or abhorrent piece of behavior after another and even juxtaposes scenes of starvation in St Antoine, with one of gargantuan displays of plenty and decadence at the Marquis's Paris and country residences – a strategy the radical novelist Émile Zola will use to create emotional impact in his fiction.[25] The effect of this is that the rising up of the revolutionaries and the resulting violence is an undoubtedly grotesque climactic moment based firmly within a linear, causally driven continuum. Dickens depicts history as an unfolding of catastrophic events, an evocation of time given structure through the

22 *The Violent Effigy* (London: Faber and Faber, 1973), pp. 13–14.

23 *TTC*, bk. 2, ch. 21, p. 249.

24 Ibid.

25 In *Germinal* (1885), Zola depicts the landowner's daughter, Cécile Grégoire, luxuriating in chocolate and brioche in a chapter that immediately follows a delineation of dire poverty and near starvation of 10,000 miners, trans. Leonard Tancock (Harmondsworth: Penguin, 1954), p. 81.

forward movement of the narratological process.[26] One could even suggest that Dickens deliberately builds as much melodrama and lurid height and color into the account of the crowd's outrageous actions by design, like a composer would build up a crescendo. The operatic scale of the hysteria of Foulon's attackers is so convincingly drawn and so emotionally shattering, it can almost move one to pity for the murderers. Such horror-laden scenes, which evoke mixed reactions of horror and empathy within the reader, are overwrought and frankly incoherent if taken in isolation. They force the reader back onto the unfolding narrative; the reader has to reconsider the linear chain of events and historical time that led up to that point to arrive at some explanation in the face of what would otherwise be unbearably mindless atrocity.

Moreover, the London and Paris of *TTC*, as well as in the London of *BR*, are transient, lawless, precarious worlds – where social outcomes are left to fate, the poor are left to their own devices: 'in this matter, as in all others, the common wretches were left to get out of their difficulties as they could'.[27] Dickens depicts a number of events which clearly express this state of affairs: the mob parody a funeral, taking the law into their own hands in London and no authority intervenes; in Paris, the crowd spontaneously drink spilt wine and no one tries to stop them; a child is accidentally run over and no legal redress is either possible or sought. Murder is the only available route to justice. Similarly, in *BR*, one cannot help asking the question as to why the crowd is so open to the suggestions and manipulations of its leaders. Dickens's straightforward answer is ignorance and poverty.[28] Once stirred up, this crowd meets with very little restraint from authorities conspicuous by their absence for at least two-thirds of the novel. Without other channels for their grievances and with a little encouragement from their leaders, then, they destroy Catholic property as well as the symbols of state repression (prisons). One needs little imagination to conclude that Dickens is suggesting that within the nihilistic contexts of the lawless cities of both novels, within a state of affairs where the poor have no voice at all, their suffering will find a way of forcing itself into public discourse.

What can one make of Dickens's fictional delineation of the crowd, in view of what, all too briefly, has been outlined here? Even T.A. Jackson, the Marxist critic intent upon reading Dickens as bordering on radicalism which 'with a little outside aid might easily have emerged as positive Socialism or Communism', resigns himself to judging Dickens's depiction of rioting crowds in *BR* as his

26 The subject of Dickens's depiction of history as an unfolding and catastrophic chain of causal events is treated in an article by John Rignall, 'Dickens and the Catastrophic Continuum of History in A Tale of Two Cities', *English Literary History* 51 (1984): pp. 575–87. See also Daniel Siegel's 'Griffith, Dickens and the Politics of Composure', *PMLA* 124.2 (March 2009), where it is argued that *TTC*'s resistance to the onslaught of historical time is a deliberate and productive one.

27 *TTC*, bk. 2, ch. 7, p. 140.

28 *BR*, ch. 53, pp. 483–4.

being against 'physical force' Chartism.[29] However, it can be argued that this is too definitive a statement. Dickens's treatment of some scenes of crowd violence may initially seem to 'repudiate the sentiments and methods of physical-force Chartism'[30]; but it can be posited that he equally demonstrates a deeply felt imaginative understanding and appreciation of why revolutions or rioting occur even in the midst of depicting their most abhorrent and brutal consequences.[31] It is an understanding that pertains perhaps in spite of the anxiety of his tone in such scenes. This 'understanding' may be more to do with Dickens's skills as a novelist, his ability to enter fully into the world of all characters, institutions or points of view whether 'villainous' or 'moral'; it may be Dickens's boundless and effortless ability to create great drama that accounts for his 'understanding' of the crowd, rather than any conscious or well-thought-through political tendency. But it is worth noting that, even at as significant a date as 1844, when the Chartist movement was in the throes of developing and gathering strength, Dickens, during a trip to Italy, was writing to Forster the following sentiments. Having referred to the American slaves, whom he predicted would rise up in revolt, he continues:

> Heaven help us, too, from explosions nearer home! I declare, I never go into what is called 'society' that I am not aweary of it, despise it, hate it, and reject it. The more I see of its extraordinary conceit, and its stupendous ignorance of what is passing out of doors, the more certain I am that it is approaching the period when, being incapable of reforming itself, it will have to submit to being reformed by others off the face of the earth.

Of course, it could be added that these early years were Dickens's radical 'phase', a temporary state of affairs, and Forster implies as much with his comment: 'Thus we see that the old radical leanings were again rather strong in him at present.'[32] But the point being argued here is that the treatment of the crowd in both *BR* (written in that early phase in 1841) as well as in *TTC* (written much later, in 1859) both express the notion that physical force by the crowd is necessary or even inevitable in some social contexts where there is no way out of injustice. While Dickens 'repudiates' the violence and death such revolts result in, imaginatively he understands all too well what goes into their making. If one thing can be said with certainty, it is that Dickens's fiction shows that he repudiates poverty, ignorance, grim social conditions and the injustice of a laissez-faire reaction to these states of affairs. What emerges from his treatment of the crowd in his two historical novels is not so much an expression of fear and hatred of the mob, as a desire for social change.

---

[29] T.A. Jackson, *Charles Dickens: The Progress of a Radical* (London: Lawrence and Wishart, 1937; repr. International Publishers Co. Inc., 1987), p. 7 and p. 16, respectively.

[30] Phrasing used by Jackson, p. 16.

[31] Mangum has a similar reading of Dickens's delineation of the revolutionaries, in 'Dickens and the Female Terrorist: The Long Shadow of Madame Defarge', *19th Century Contexts* 31.2 (June 2009): p. 145.

[32] Both quotations, *Life*, bk. 4, ch. 3, p. 324.

*Dickens, Benjamin and Revolution*

What more does Dickens's treatment of the revolutionary mob tell us about his imaginative sympathies? Benjamin's *Arcades* includes a fragment that suggests that one can read Dickens as a political revolutionary: 'There was a great deal of the actual and unbroken tradition of the Revolution itself in his early radical indictments; in his denunciations of the Fleet Prison there was a great deal of the capture of the Bastille,' as Benjamin quotes from G.K. Chesterton, *Dickens*.[33] But is such a reading reasonable? Dickens, in *TTC*, as has been argued, depicts historical time as a causally determined continuum. Within that framework, he presents the violence meted out later in response to an original injustice – often sympathetically depicted by him – as just as horrifying. Hence, the guillotine is 'terrible in history', and the depiction of the grindstone scene and the Terror itself is hardly anything other than a disgusted narrator depicting a violent event generated by an earlier violent event:

> And the frantic wielders of these weapons snatched them from the stream of sparks and tore away into the streets, the same red hue was red in their frenzied eyes; – eyes which any unbrutalised beholder would have given twenty years of life, to petrify with a well-directed gun.[34]

This seems a pretty clear turning away from revolution as any solution to the catastrophic events he describes. Revolution, then, is not Dickens's idea of justice in the future.

This is some way away from Benjamin's Marxist sympathies, from his understanding of what redemption is and from his theory of historical time as interruption. For him, in contrast, redemption is a positive and necessary righting of a wrong – and he would see revolution as the messianic event that halts the ongoing march of end-determined time. Like the messianic arrival, the revolution is an event that blasts the whole state of affairs apart; an event that should be looked for and worked toward at every moment:

> we shall clearly realize that it is our task to bring about a real state of emergency [revolution], and this will improve our position in the struggle against Fascism.[35]

But there is a further fact worth considering. While historical time in *TTC* is depicted as a continuum of unfolding violent events, there is a counter-tendency. At the start of the novel, the narrator outlines the extravagant cruelties of the state penal system in France in 1775, before making the following comment:

33 *Arcades*, D16,4.

34 The grindstone scene, *TTC*, bk. 3, ch. 2, p. 292.

35 'Theses', VIII, p. 28.

> It is likely enough that, rooted in the woods in France and Norway, there were growing trees, when that sufferer was put to death, already marked by the woodman, Fate, to come down and be sawn into boards, to make a certain movable framework with a sack knife in it, terrible in history. (Narrator, *TTC*, bk. 1, ch. 1, p. 36)

This is a tone of vengeance; the language is apocalyptic. A similar tone pervades in the depiction of the starving poor in St Antoine: 'eyes of fire were not wanting among them'; 'For the time was to come when the gaunt scarecrows of that region'; 'But, the time was not come yet; and every wind that blew over France shook the rags of the scarecrows in vain' (all quotes, *TTC*, bk. 1, ch. 5, p. 62).

The narrator, recounting the past, ensures what Benjamin calls 'the silent stranger', the future, is always already present in the (past) moment. This has a dramatic effect, putting into relief the suffering being depicted. But there is surely also a yearning for justice in the language used. Is Dickens claiming a fated resolution, or even a redemptive force in the unfolding of time? The past is certainly for Dickens, as it is for Benjamin, incomplete in the use of this tone of voice.[36]

This contrapuntal urge to break the continuum of history in the novel is a fictional questioning of history as progress. It is an urge that yearns for an explosive end to it all, that comes close to utopianism or messianiam. It was argued in chapter 1 that messianism is an element in *OCS*. This element again shows itself, it is suggested, in *TTC*, where Dickens's yearning for redemption in the future is quite explicitly present. Moreover, it is present in Dickens's historical novels generally, identifiable in the treatment of the burning down of Newgate Prison in *BR* and in the revolutionary scenes in *TTC*. The relish with which Dickens describes those events shows a taste for total destruction, the kind of destruction that many revolutionaries (of whatever label, anarchist, socialist) in the mid nineteenth century believed was necessary before a just world could be instated in its place. While one acknowledges, then, that Dickens was an avowed and unstinting reformer, areas of his imaginative creativity exhibit the tendencies of the radical revolutionary.

---

[36] See 'Theses', II, p. 245.

# Bibliography


**Unpublished Works**

Maia, R.C.M., PhD thesis, 'Crowd theory in some modern fiction: Dickens, Zola and Canetti, 1842–1960', Nottingham University, 42-5177, 1992, A8a.

Racadio, D.S., PhD thesis, '*The Comic, the Grotesque and the Uncanny in Dickens*', University of East Anglia Press, 008471392, 1990.

**Published Works**

*Primary Sources – Walter Benjamin*

*Letters*

Adorno, Theodor and Gerhard Scholem (eds.), *Briefe*, 2 vols (Frankfurt a.M: Suhrkamp Verlag, 1966); trans. Manfred R. Jacobson and Evelyn M. Jacobson as *The Complete Correspondence of Walter Benjamin*, ed. and annotated Gershom Scholem and Theodor W. Adorno (Chicago; London: Chicago University Press, 1994).

Adorno, Theodor W. and Walter Benjamin, *Briefwechsel 1928–1940* (Suhrkamp Verlag, 1994); trans. Nicholas Walker as *Adorno-Benjamin: The Complete Correspondence 1928–1940*, ed. Henri Lonitz (Oxford; Cambridge: Polity Press, with Blackwell, 1999).

*Collected Works*

Adorno, Theodor (ed.), *Schriften*, 2 vols (Frankfurt a.M: Suhrkamp Verlag, 1955).

Adorno, Theodor and Walter Benjamin, *Aesthetics and Politics*, trans. and ed. Ronald Taylor (London; New York: Verso 1977).

Arendt, Hannah (ed.), *Walter Benjamin: Illuminations*, trans. Harry Zohn (London: Pimlico, 1999). Reference to this work is given as 'Illuminations'.

Jennings, Michael W. and others (eds.), *Walter Benjamin: Selected Writings*, 4 vols (Cambridge, MA; London: The Belknap Press of Harvard University Press, 1996–2003). Reference to these volumes is given as *SW*.

Tiedemann, Rolf and Hermann Schweppenhäuser (eds.), *Gesammelte Schriften*, 7 vols, with the assistance of Theodor W. Adorno and Gershom Scholem (Frankfurt a.M: Suhrkamp Verlag, 1972–1989). Reference to these volumes is given as *GS*.

*Works Mentioned: Arranged Chronologically*

'Das Leben der Studenten', in *GS*, II, 1, pp. 75–87; trans. Rodney Livingstone as 'The Life of Students', in *SW*, I, pp. 37–47.

'Über die Sprache überhaupt und über die Sprache des Menschen', in *GS*, II, 1, pp. 140–57; trans. Edmund Jephcott as 'On Language as Such and On the Language of Man', in *SW*, I, pp. 62–74.
'Über das Programm der kommenden Philosophie', in *GS*, II, 1, pp. 157–71; trans. Mark Ritter as 'On the Program of the Coming Philosophy', in *SW*, I, pp. 100–110.
'Der Begriff der Kunstkritik in der deutschen Romantik', in *GS*, I, 1, pp. 7–122; trans. David Lachterman and others as 'The Concept of Criticism in German Romanticism', in *SW*, I, pp. 116–200.
'Goethes Wahlverwandtschaften', in *GS*, I, 1, pp. 125–201; trans. Stanley Corngold as 'Goethe's Elective Affinities', in *SW*, I, pp. 297–360.
'Alte vergessene Kinderbücher', in *GS*, III, pp. 14–22; trans. Rodney Livingstone as 'Old Forgotten Children's Books', in *SW*, I, pp. 406–13.
'Neapel' (mit Asja Lacis), in *GS*, IV, 1, pp. 307–16; trans. Edmund Jephcott as 'Naples', in *SW*, I, pp. 414–21.
'Aussicht ins Kinderbuch', in *GS*, IV, 2, pp. 609–15; trans. Rodney Livingstone as 'A Glimpse into the World of Children's Books', in *SW*, I, pp. 435–43.
'Gespräch über dem Corso', in *GS*, IV, 2, pp. 763–71; trans. Edmund Jephcott as 'Conversation above the Corso', in *SW*, III, pp. 25–31.
*Ursprung des deutschen Trauerspiels* revidierte ausgabe besorg von Rolf Tiedemann (Frankfurt a.M: Suhrkamp, 1963), also in *GS*, I, 1, pp. 205–430; trans. John Osborne as *The Origin of German Tragic Drama* (London: Verso, 1977).
'Einbahnstraße', in *GS*, IV, 1, pp. 83–148; trans. Edmund Jephcott as *One-Way Street*, in *SW*, I, pp. 444–88.
'Das Passagen-Werk', in *GS*, V, 1 and 2; trans. Howard Eiland and Kevin McLaughlin as *The Arcades Project* (Cambridge, MA,; London: The Belknap Press of Harvard University Press, 1999).
*Moskauer Tagebuck* (Frankfurt a.M: Suhrkamp Verlag, 1980), also in *GS*, VI, pp. 292–409; trans. Richard Sieburth as *Moscow Diary*, ed. Gary Smith (Cambridge, MA; London: Harvard University Press, 1986).
'Moskau', in *GS*, IV, pp. 316–48; trans, Edmund Jephcott as 'Moscow', in *SW*, II, pp. 22–46.
'Chaplin', in *GS*, VI, pp. 137–8; trans. Rodney Livingstone in *SW*, II, pp. 199–200.
'Der Sürrealismus', in *GS*, II, 1, pp. 295–310; trans. Edmund Jephcott as 'Surrealism', in *SW*, II, pp. 207–21.
'Marseille', in GS, IV, 1, pp. 359–64; trans. Edmund Jephcott as 'Marseilles', in *SW*, II, pp. 232–6.
'Zum Bilde Prousts', in *GS*, II, 1, pp. 310–24; trans. Harry Zohn as 'The Image of Proust', in *Illuminations*, pp. 197–210.
*Versuche über Brecht* (Frankfurt am Main: Suhrkamp Verlag, 1966); trans. Anna Bostock as *Understanding Brecht* (London: Verso, 1998).
'Rückblick auf Chaplin', in *GS*, III, pp. 157–9; trans. Rodney Livingstone as 'Chaplin in Retrospect', in SW, II, pp. 222–4.

'Ich packe meine Bibliothek aus', in *GS*, 1, pp. 388–96; trans. Harry Zohn as 'Unpacking My Library', in *Illuminations*, pp. 61–9.

'Kleine Geschichte der Photographie', in *GS*, II, 1, pp. 368–85; trans. Edmund Jephcott and Kingsley Shorter as 'Little History of Photography', in SW, II, pp. 507–30.

'Die Eisenbahnkatastrophe vom Firth of Tay', in *GS*, VII, 1, pp. 232–7; trans. Rodney Livingstone as 'The Railway Disaster at the Firth of Tay', in *SW*, II, pp. 563–8.

'Berliner Chronik', in *GS*, VI, pp. 465–519; trans. Edmund Jephcott as 'A Berlin Chronicle', in *SW*, II, pp. 595–637.

'Haschisch in Marseille', in *GS*, IV, 1, pp. 409–16; trans. Edmund Jephcott as 'Hashish in Marseilles', in *S*W, II, pp. 673–8.

'Erfahrung und Armut', in *GS*, II, 1, pp. 213–19; trans. Rodney Livingstone as 'Experience and Poverty', in *SW*, II, pp. 731–6.

'Berliner Kindheit um 1900' (two versions): 1934 version in *GS*, IV, 1, pp. 235–304; 1938 version in *GS*, VII, 1, pp. 385–433; trans. Howard Eiland as 'A Berlin Childhood around 1900', in *SW*, III, pp. 344–413.

'Der Autor als Produzent', in *GS*, II, 2, pp. 683–701; trans. Edmund Jephcott as 'The Author as Producer', in *SW*, II, pp. 768–82.

'Der Erzähler', in *GS*, II, 2, pp. 438–65; trans. Harry Zohn as 'The Storyteller', in *Illuminations*, pp. 83–107.

'Eduard Fuchs, der Sammler und der Historiker', in *GS*, II, 2, pp. 465–505; trans. Howard Eiland and Michael W. Jennings as 'Eduard Fuchs, Collector and Historian', in *SW*, III, pp. 260–302.

'Theologisch-politisches Fragment', in *GS*, II, 1, pp. 203–4; trans. Edmund Jephcott as 'Theological-Political Fragment', in *SW*, III, pp. 305–6.

'Das Paris des Second Empire bei Baudelaire', in *GS*, I, 2, pp. 511–604; trans. Harry Zohn as 'The Paris of the Second Empire in Baudelaire', in *SW*, IV, pp. 3–92.

'Kunstwerk im Zeitalter seiner technischen Reproduzierbarkeit' (three versions) in *GS*, I, 2, pp. 435–508; *GS*, VII, 1, pp. 350–84; and *GS*, I, pp. 471–508; trans. Harry Zohn as 'The Work of Art in the Age of Mechanical Reproduction', in *Illuminations*, pp. 211–44.

'Über einige Motive bei Baudelaire', in *GS*, I, 2, pp. 605–53; trans. Harry Zohn as 'On Some Motifs in Baudelaire', in *Illuminations*, pp. 152–96.

'Zentralpark', in *GS*, I, 2, pp. 655–90; trans. Lloyd Spencer with Mark Harrington as 'Central Park', *New German Critique* 34 (Winter 1985): pp. 32–58.

'über den Begriff der Geschichte (Theses)', in *GS*, I, 2, pp. 691–704; trans. Harry Zohn as 'Theses on the Philosophy of History', in *Illuminations*, pp. 245–55.

*Charles Baudelaire: Ein Lyriker im Zeitalter des Hockkapitalismus*, in *GS*, I, 2, pp. 511–690; trans. Harry Zohn and Quintin Hoare as *Charles Baudelaire: A Lyric Poet in the Era of High Capitalism* (London: N.L.B., 1973). (Contains 'The Paris of the 2nd Empire in Baudelaire', 'On Some Motifs in Baudelaire' and 'Paris – The Capital of the Nineteenth Century'.)

*Primary Sources – Charles Dickens*

*Letters*

Dexter, Walter (ed.), *The Letters of Charles Dickens*, 3 vols (Bloomsbury: Nonesuch Press, 1938); I: 1832–1846; II: 1847–1857; III: 1858–1870.

Storey, Graham and others (eds.), *The Letters of Charles Dickens*, The Pilgrim/British Academy Series, 12 vols (Oxford: Clarendon Press, 1965–2002).

*Collected Works*

*Complete Plays and Selected Poems of Charles Dickens* (London: Vision Press Ltd., 1970).

Slater, Michael and John Drew (eds.), *Dickens' Journalism*, 4 vols (London: J.M. Dent, 1994–2000).

*Works Consulted and Discussed*

Editions were either Clarendon where available or Penguin. 'Penguin' indicates place of publication as Harmondsworth, Middlesex and worldwide; 'OUP' indicates place of publication as Oxford and New York:

*Barnaby Rudge*, ed. Gordon Spence (Penguin, 1997).

*Bleak House*, ed. Norman Page (Penguin, 1983).

*Charles Dickens's Christmas Books*, ed. Ruth Glancy (OUP, 1998).

*David Copperfield*, ed. Nina Burgis (Oxford: Clarendon Press, 1981).

*Dombey and Son*, ed. Alan Horsman (Oxford: Clarendon Press, 1974).

*Hard Times*, ed. David Craig (Penguin, 1984).

*Little Dorrit*, ed. Harvey Peter Sucksmith (Oxford: Clarendon Press, 1974).

*Martin Chuzzlewit*, ed. Margaret Cardwell (Oxford: Clarendon Press, 1982).

*Nicholas Nickleby*, ed. Michael Slater (Penguin, 1983).

*The Old Curiosity Shop*, ed. Angus Calder (Penguin, 1972).

*The Old Curiosity Shop*, ed. Elizabeth M. Brennan (Oxford: Clarendon Press, 1997).

*The Old Curiosity Shop*, ed. Malcolm Andrews (Penguin, 1972).

*Oliver Twist*, ed. Kathleen Tillotson (Oxford: Clarendon Press, 1966).

*Our Mutual Friend*, ed. Stephen Gill (Penguin, 1981).

*The Pickwick Papers*, ed. James Kinsley (Oxford: Clarendon, 1986).

*Sketches by Boz*, ed. Dennis Walder (Penguin, 1995).

*A Tale of Two Cities*, ed. George Woodcock (Penguin, 1983).

*Secondary Sources – Walter Benjamin and Charles Dickens*

Abrams, Meyer Howard, *The Mirror and the Lamp: Romantic Theory and the Critical Tradition* (New York: Oxford University Press, 1953).

Ackroyd, Peter, *Dickens' London: An Imaginative Vision* (London: Headline, 1987).

———, *Dickens* (London: Sinclair-Stevenson Ltd., 1990).

———, *London, The Biography* (London: Vintage, 2001).

———, *Dickens: Public Life and Private Passion* (London: BBC Books, 2002).

———, 'The Eternal Mystery of Edwin Drood', *The Guardian*, Review Section, September 4, 2004, pp. 42–3.

Adorno, Theodor, 'Rede über den Raritätenladen von Charles Dickens', in *Gesammelte Schriften*, ed. Gretel Adorno and Rolf Tiedemann, vol. 11, pp. 515–22; trans. Michael Hollington as 'An address on Charles Dickens's *The Old Curiosity Shop*', *Dickens Quarterly* 6.3 (September 1989): pp. 95–101.

Andrew, Dudley (ed.), *The Image in Dispute: Art and Cinema in the Age of Photography* (Austin: University of Texas, 1997).

Barthes, Roland, *Camera Lucida*, trans. Richard Howard (London: Vintage, 2000).

Baudelaire, Charles, *Flowers of Evil*, trans. George Dillon and Edna St Vincent Millay, 1st ed. (New York; London: Harper & Brothers, 1936).

———, *Paris Spleen*, trans. L. Varèse (New York: New Directions Books, 1970).

———, *Baudelaire: Correspondance*, texte établi, pré senté et annoté par Claude Pichois, 2 vols (Paris: Editions Gallimard, 1973).

———, *Selected Letters of Charles Baudelaire: The Conquest of Solitude*, trans. and ed. Rosemary Lloyd (London: Weidenfeld & Nicolson, 1986).

———, *Selected Poems*; trans. Carol Clark (London: Penguin, 2004).

Benjamin, Andrew (ed.), *The Problems of Modernity: Adorno and Benjamin* (London; New York: Routledge, 1989).

———, *Present Hope: Philosophy, Architecture, Judaism* (London; New York: Routledge, 1997).

Bennett, Rachel, 'Punch vs Christian in *The Old Curiosity Shop*', *RES* 22 (1971): pp. 423–34.

Ben-Sasson, H.H. and S. Ettinger (eds.), *Jewish Society through the Ages* (London: Valentine, Mitchell, 1968).

Birch, Dinah, *Our Victorian Education* (Oxford: Blackwell, 2008).

Blanchard, Marc Eli, *In Search of the City: Engels, Baudelaire and Rimbaud* (Saratoga, CA: ANMA Libra, 1985).

Blanchot, Maurice, *The Infinite Conversation* (Minneapolis: University of Minnesota Press, 1993).

Bloom, Harold (ed.), *Romanticism and Consciousness* (New York: W.W. Norton, 1970).

Le Bon, Gustave, *The Crowd: A Study of the Popular Mind* (New York: Viking Press, 1960).

Bowen, John, *Other Dickens: Pickwick to Chuzzlewit* (Oxford; New York: Oxford University Press, 2000).

——— and Robert L. Patten, *Palgrave Advances in Charles Dickens Studies* (Basingstoke, Hampshire: Palgrave Macmillan, 2006).

Bown, Nicola, 'Introduction: Crying Over Little Nell', 19, *Interdisciplinary Studies in the Long Nineteenth Century* 4 (2007), <http://www.19.bbk.ac.uk/index.php/19/article/view/453>.

Breton, André, *Les Vases Communicants* (Paris: Editions Gallimard, 1955); trans. Mary Ann Caws and Geoffrey T. Harris as *Communicating Vessels* (Lincoln; London: University of Nebraska Press, 1990).

———, *Nadja* (Paris: Gallimard, 1972); trans. Richard Howard as *Nadja* (New York; Grove; London: Evergreen Books, 1999).

Buck-Morss, Susan, *The Dialectics of Seeing* (Cambridge, MA; London: MIT Press, 1999).

Bunyan, John, *The Pilgrim's Progress*, with annotated by Thomas Scott (London: Seeley, 1801).

Burton, Richard, D.E., *The Flâneur in his City: Patterns of Daily Life in Paris 1815–1851* (Brighton: University of Sussex, 1984).

Burton, Robert, *The Anatomy of Melancholy* (publishers: John Lichfield and James Short for Henry Cripps, Oxford, 1624).

Calhoone, Lawrence (ed.), *From Modernism to Postmodernism* (Oxford: Blackwell, 1996).

Carey, John, *The Violent Effigy* (London: Faber and Faber, 1973).

Carlyle, Thomas, *Sartor Resartus*, introduction by Alasdair Gray (Edinburgh: Canongate Classic, 2002).

Carter, Ian, *Railways and Culture in Britain: The Epitome of Modernity* (Manchester; New York: Manchester University Press, 2001).

Caygill, Howard, *The Colour of Experience* (London; New York: Routledge, 1998).

Chesterton, G.K., *Charles Dickens*, 11th ed. (London: Methuen & Co, 1917).

Cleere, Eileen, '"Implicit Faith in the Deception": Misanthropy, Natural History and *The Old Curiosity Shop*', *Dickens Studies Annual* 35 (2005).

Cobbe, Frances Power, *The Hours of Work and Play* (London: N. Trübner & Co., 1867).

Cohen, Margaret, *Profane Illumination: Walter Benjamin and the Paris of the Surrealist Revolution* (Berkeley; Los Angeles: University of California Press, 1993).

Cohen, William A., 'Interiors: Sex and the Body in Dickens', *Critical Survey* 17.2 (May 2005): pp. 5–19.

Collins, Philip, *Dickens and Crime* (Bloomington; London: Indiana University Press, 1962).

———, *Reading Aloud: A Victorian Métier* (Lincoln: Tennyson Society, 1972).

——— (ed.), *Dickens: The Critical Heritage* (London: Routledge & Kegan Paul, 1971).

——— (ed.), *Dickens: Interviews and Recollections*, 2 vols (London: Macmillan, 1981).

Colman, George, *Broad Grins* (London: T. Cadell and W. Davies, 1807).

Connor, Steven (ed.), *Charles Dickens* (London: Longman, 1996).

Darwin, Charles, *On the Origin of Species*, facsimile of the 1st ed. (London: John Murray, 1872).

Davis, Philip, *The Oxford English Literary History*, 13 vols (London: Oxford University Press, 2002).

Dolby, George, *Charles Dickens as I Knew Him: The Story of the Reading Tours in Great Britain and America (1866–1870)* (London: T. Fisher Unwin, 1885).

Eagleton, Terry, *Walter Benjamin: or, Towards a Revolutionary Criticism* (London: Verso, 1985).

Eigner, Edwin M., *The Metaphysical Novel in England and America: Dickens, Bulwer, Melville and Hawthorne* (Berkeley; London: University of California Press, 1978).

Eisenstein, Sergei, *Film Form: Essays in Film Theory*, ed. and trans. Jay Leyda (London; San Diego; New York: Harvest, Harcourt Inc., 1977).

Fanger, Donald, *Dostoevsky and Romantic Realism*, Harvard Studies in Comparative Literature, 27 (Cambridge, MA: Harvard University Press, 1965).

Ferris, David (ed.), *The Cambridge Companion to Walter Benjamin* (Cambridge; New York: Cambridge University Press, 2004).

Fields, Annie, *Memories of a Hostess: A Chronicle of Eminent Friendships, drawn chiefly from the diaries of Mrs. James T. Fields*, ed. M.A. DeWolfe Howe (Boston: Atlantic Monthly Press, 1922).

Forster, John, *The Life of Charles Dickens*, 2 vols (London: Chapman and Hall, n.d. [possibly 1873, 1874, 1876 or 1880]).

———, *The Life of Charles Dickens*, ed. and annotated with an introduction by J.W.T. Ley (London: Cecil Palmer, 1928).

Freud, Sigmund, *The Standard Edition of the Complete Psychological Works*, 24 vols (London: Hogarth Press and The Institute of Pycho-analysis, 1955), trans. under the general editorship of James Strachey in collaboration with Anna Freud.

———, *Civilization and its Discontents*, trans. David McLintock (London: Penguin, 2002).

Gissing, George, *The Immortal Dickens*, 1st ed. (London: Cecil Palmer, 1925).

Gleber, Anke, 'Women on the Screens and Streets of Modernity: In Search of the Female Flâneur', in *The Image in Dispute: Art and Cinema in the Age of Photography*, ed. Andrew Dudley (Austin: University of Texas, 1997), pp. 55–85.

Goldberg, Michael, *Carlyle and Dickens* (Athens: University of Georgia Press, 1972).

Gunning, Thomas, 'The Birth of Cinema', paper presented at the University of Sussex, February 2, 2005.

Hansen, Miriam, 'The Mass Production of the Senses: Classical Cinema as Vernacular Modernism', *Modernism/Modernity* 6.2 (April 1999): pp. 59–77.

Harrold, C.F., *Carlyle and German Thought 1819–1834* (New Haven: Yale University Press, 1934).

Hartog, D., *Dickens and Romantic Psychology* (Basingstoke: Macmillan, 1987).

Hennelly, Mark, 'Carnivalesque "Unlawful Games" in *The Old Curiosity Shop*', *Dickens Studies Annual* (1993): pp. 67–120.

Higbie, Robert, *Dickens and the Imagination* (Gainesville: University Press of Florida, 1998).

Hollington, Michael, 'Dickens the Flâneur', *The Dickensian* 77.2 (Summer 1981): pp. 71–87.

———, 'Adorno, Benjamin and *The Old Curiosity Shop*', *Dickens Quarterly* 6.3 (September 1989): pp. 87–95.

———, 'The Dance of Death in Charles Dickens' *Dombey and Son*', *Tanz und Tod in Kunst und Literatur*, Herausgegeben von Franz Link, Schriften zur Literaturwissenschaft, Band 8, (Berlin: Duncker & Humblot, 1993), pp. 201–11.

———, 'Milton, Walter Benjamin, and Baroque Allegory', *Journal of the Australasian Universities Language & Literature Association* 79 (May 1993).

———, 'Dickens, Household Words and the Paris Boulevards', parts I and II, *Dickens Quarterly* 14.3 (September 1997): pp. 154–64; and *DQ* 14.4 (December 1997): pp. 199–212, respectively.

———, 'Nickleby, Flanerie, Reverie: The View from the Cheerybles', *Dickens Studies Annual* 35 (2005): pp. 21–43.

———, 'Remaining Modern: Dickens and the 19th-Century European Novel, with special reference to Dostoevsky and Russian', lecture delivered at Exeter University, March 15, 2009.

———, 'The Voice of Objects in *The Old Curiosity Shop*', *Australasian Journal of Victorian Studies* 14.1 (2009).

———, 'Dickens, Sala and the London Arcades', *Dickens Quarterly* 28.4 (December 2011): pp. 273–84.

Hopkins, Gerard Manley, *Poems and Prose*, ed. W.H. Gardner (Penguin, 1983).

Horne, R.H., *A New Spirit of the Age*, 2 vols (London: Smith Elder & Co., 1844).

House, Humphry, *The Dickens World*, 2nd ed. (Oxford: Oxford University Press, 1942).

Huxley, Aldous, *Vulgarity in Literature* (London: Chatto & Windus, 1930).

Inglis, Katherine, 'Becoming Automatous: Automata in *The Old Curiosity Shop* and *Our Mutual Friend*', *19*, 6 (April 2008), <http://www.19.bbk.ac.uk/issue6/papers/inglisautomata.pdf7>.

Jackson, T.A., *Charles Dickens: The Progress of a Radical* (London: Lawrence and Wishart, 1937; repr.: International Publishers Co. Inc., 1987).

Jacobson, Eric, *Metaphysics of the Profane: The Political Theology of Walter Benjamin and Gershom Scholem* (New York: Columbia University Press, 2003).

John, Juliet, *Dickens's Villains: Melodrama, Character and Popular Culture* (Oxford: Oxford University Press, 2001).

Judin, H. and I. Vladislavić (eds.), *Architecture, Apartheid and After* (Rotterdam: Nai; New York: Distributor D.A.P., 1998).

Kant, Immanuel, *Kritik der Urteilskraft*; trans. J.H. Bernard as *Critique of Judgement* (London: Collier Macmillan Publishers; New York: Hafner Press, 1951).

Keeble, Richard and Wheeler, Sharon (eds.), *The Journalistic Imagination: Literary Journalists from Defoe to Capote and Carter* (Oxford; New York: Routledge, 2007).

Kincaid, James, *Dickens and the Rhetoric of Laughter* (Oxford; London: Oxford University Press, 1971).

Kotzin, Michael C., *Dickens and the Fairy Tale* (Bowling Green, OH: Bowling Green University Press, 1972).

Lary, N.M., *Dostoevsky and Dickens: A Study of Literary Influence* (London: Routledge, 1973).

Lauster, Martina, *Sketches of the Nineteenth Century: European Journalism and its Physiologies 1830–50* (Houndsmills Basingstoke: Palgrave Macmillan, 2007).

Leavis, F.R., *English Literature in Our Time and the University: The Clark Lectures (1967)* (Cambridge; London; New York: Cambridge University Press, 1979).

Lerner, Laurence (ed.), *The Context of English Literature: The Victorians* (London: Methuen & Co., 1978).

Leslie, Esther, *Walter Benjamin: Overcoming Conformism* (London; Sterling, VA: Pluto Press, 2000).

Löwy, Michael, *Redemption and Utopia: Jewish Libertarian Thought in Central Europe*, trans. Hope Heaney (London: The Athlone Press, 1992).

Lucas, John, *The Melancholy Man* (London: Methuen & Co., 1970).

Lukács, György Szegedi, *Geschichte und Klassenbewusstsein: Studien über marxistische Dialektik* (Berlin; Der Malik-Verlag, 1923); trans. Rodney Livingstone as *History and Class Consciousness: Studies in Marxist Dialectics*, 2nd ed. (London: Merlin Press, 1971).

Lyotard, Jean-François, *The Postmodern Condition: A Report on Knowledge*, trans. Geoff Bennington and Brian Massumi (Minneapolis: University of Minnesota Press, 1983).

MacPike, Loralee, *Dostoevsky's Dickens* (London: Prior, 1981).

Magnum, Teresa, 'Dickens and the Female Terrorist: The Long Shadow of Madame Defarge,' *19th Century Contexts* 31.2 (June 2009).

Masuzawa, Tomoko, 'Tracing the Figure of Redemption: Walter Benjamin's Physiognomy of Modernity', *Modern Language Notes* 100.3 (April 1985): pp. 514–36.

Matus, Jill L., 'Trauma, Memory, and Railway Disaster: The Dickensian Connection', *Victorian Studies* 43.3 (Spring 2001): pp. 413–36.

McBride, James, 'Marooned in the Realm of the Profane: Walter Benjamin's synthesis of Kabbalah and Communism', *Journal of the American Academy of Religion* 57.2 (Summer 1989): pp. 241–66.

McCracken, Scott, 'Random Patterns, Flashes of Insight: Walter Benjamin's Arcades Project', roundtable discussion, 'Walter Benjamin's Arcades Project', *Journal of Victorian Culture* 7 (Autumn 2002): pp. 263–96 (pp. 275–86).

McLaughlin, Kevin, *Writing in Parts: Imitation and Exchange in Nineteenth-Century Literature* (Stanford, CA: Stanford University Press, 1995).

Miller, J. Hillis, *Charles Dickens: The World of his Novels* (Cambridge, MA: Harvard University Press, 1958).

Moore, Grace, 'Turkish Robbers, Lumps of Delight, and the Detritus of Empire: The East Revisited in Dickens's Late Novels', *Critical Survey* 21.1 (January 2009): pp. 74–87.

Nead, Lynda, *Victorian Babylon: People, Streets and Images in Nineteenth-Century London* (New Haven; London: Yale University Press, 2000).

Newsom, Robert, *Dickens on the Romantic Side of Familiar Things: 'Bleak House' and the Novel Tradition* (New York; Guildford: Columbia University Press, 1977).

Oddie, William, *Dickens and Carlyle: The Question of Influence* (London: Centenary Press, 1972).

Oost, Regina B., '"More Like than Life": Painting, Photography, and Dickens's *Bleak House*', *Dickens Studies Annual* 30 (2001): pp. 141–58.

Ostry, Elaine, *Social Dreaming: Dickens and the Fairy Tale* (New York; London: Routledge, 2002).

Paganoni, Maria Cristina, *The Magic Lantern: Representations of the Double in Dickens* (London: Routledge, 2007).

Painter, George D., *Marcel Proust* (London: Penguin, 1990).

Parsons, Deborah, 'Flâneur or Flâneuse: Mythologies of Modernity', *New Formations* 38 (Summer 1999): pp. 91–100.

Plotz, John, *The Crowd*: *British Literature and Public Politics* (Berkeley; Los Angeles: University of California Press, 2000).

Poe, Edgar Allen, 'The Man of the Crowd', in *Tales of Mystery and Imagination* (Hertfordshire: Wordsworth Classics, 1993), pp. 255–62.

Pollock, Griselda, 'Modernity and the Spaces of Femininity', in *Vision and Difference: Femininity, Feminism and the Histories of Art* (London: Routledge, 1988), pp. 70–127.

Pound, Ezra, 'In a Station of the Metro', *Poetry Magazine* 2.1 (April 1913).

Proust, Marcel, *Á la recherché du temps perdu*, trans. C.K. Scott Moncrieff and Terence Kilmartin as *In Search of Lost Time*, 6 vols (London: Vintage, 1996–2000).

Qualls, Barry V., *The Secular Pilgrims of Victorian Fiction* (Cambridge; London: Cambridge University Press, 1981).

Quarles, Francis, *Emblemes* (Cambridge: Printed by R.D. for Francis Egleffeild [St. Paul's Churchyard] 1643).

De Quincey, Thomas, *The Confessions of an English Opium Eater*, Everyman's Library Series (London: J.M. Dent; New York: E.P. Dutton, n.d.).

Radcliffe, Ann, *The Mysteries of Udolpho*, ed. Binamy Dobrée (Oxford & New York: Oxford World Classics, 1998).

Rignall, John, 'Dickens and the Catastrophic Continuum of History in *A Tale of Two Cities*', *English Literary History* 51 (1984): pp. 575–87.

———, *Realism and the Strolling Spectator* (London: Routledge, 1992).

Robinson, David, *Chaplin: His Life and Art* (London: William Collins & Sons, 1985).

Rose, Gillian, *Judaism and Modernity: Philosophical Essays* (Oxford: Blackwell, 1993).

Schad, John (ed.), *Dickens Refigured: Bodies, Desires and Other Histories* (Manchester; New York: Manchester University Press, 1996).
Schivelbusch, Wolfgang, *The Railway Journey: Trains and Travel in the 19th Century*, trans. Anselm Hollo (Oxford: Basil Blackwell, 1980).
Schlicke, Paul, *Dickens and Popular Entertainment* (London: Allen & Unwin, 1985).
———, *Oxford Reader's Companion to Dickens* (Oxford; New York: Oxford University Press, 1999).
Scholem, Gershom, *The Messianic Idea in Judaism and Other Essays on Jewish Spirituality* (New York: Schocken Books, 1974).
———, *Walter Benjamin: The Story of a Friendship*, trans. Harry Zohn (New York: New York Review Books, 1981).
Schwarzbach, F.S., *Dickens and the City* (London: The Athlone Press, University of London, 1979).
Seed, David (ed.), *Literature and the Visual Media* (Cambridge: D.S. Brewer, 2005).
Siegel, Daniel, 'Griffiths, Dickens and the Politics of Composure', *PMLA* 124.2 (March 2009): pp. 375–89.
Simmel, Georg, *The Sociology of Georg Simmel*, ed. K.H. Wolff (New York: New York Free Press, 1950).
Slater, Michael and John Drew (eds.), *Dickens' Journalism*, 4 vols (London: J.M. Dent, 2000).
Smith, Gary (ed.), *Benjamin: Philosophy, Aesthetics, History* (London; Chicago: University of Chicago Press, 1983, 1989).
Smith, Grahame, 'Dickens and the City of Light', conference paper, Middle East Technical University, Turkey, presented March 1998, <http://www.victorianweb.org/authors/dickens/turkey/turlit10.html>.
———, *Dickens and the Dream of Cinema* (Manchester; New York: Manchester University Press, 2003).
———, 'The Travelling Lanternist and the Uncommercial Traveller: An Experiment in Correspondences', in *Literature and the Visual Media*, ed. David Seed (Cambridge, England: D.S. Brewer, 2005).
Smith, Karl, *Dickens and the Unreal City* (Basingstoke: Palgrave Macmillan, 2008).
Spilka, Mark, *Dickens and Kafka: a mutual interpretation* (London: Dennis Dobson, 1963).
St. John-Stevas, Norman (ed.), *The Collected Works of Walter Bagehot*, 2 vols (London: The Economist, 1965).
Sterne, Laurence, *The Life and Opinions of Tristram Shandy* (Aberdeen: George Clark & Son; London: W. Brittain, 1848).
Stevenson, Robert Louis, *The Strange Case of Dr Jekyll and Mr Hyde* (Oxford: Oxford World's Classics, 1998).
Stoehr, Taylor, *Dickens: The Dreamer's Stance* (Ithaca, NY: Cornell University Press, 1965).

Stone, Harry, *Dickens and the Invisible World: Fairy Tales, Fantasy and Novel-making* (London: Macmillan, 1979).

Sussman, Herbert L., *Victorians and the Machine* (Cambridge, MA: Harvard University Press, 1968).

Tambling, Jeremy, *Going Astray: Dickens and London* (Harlow, Essex: Pearson Longman, 2009).

Taylor, Jenny Bourne and Sally Shuttleworth (eds.), *Embodied Selves: An Anthology of Psychological Texts 1830–1890* (Oxford: Clarendon Press, 1998).

Taylor, Ronald, trans., *Aesthetics and Politics* (London; New York: Verso, 1977).

Tester, Keith (ed.), *The Flâneur* (London: Routledge, 1994).

Tiedemann, Rolf, *Studien zur Philosophie Walter Benjamins* (Frankfurt am Main: Suhrkamp Verlag, 1973).

Todd, Jennifer, 'Production, Reception, Criticism: Walter Benjamin and the Problem of Meaning in Art', in *Benjamin: Philosophy Aesthetics*, ed. Gary Smith (London; Chicago: University of Chicago, 1989), pp. 102–25.

Vlock, Deborah, *Dickens, Novel Reading and the Victorian Popular Theatre* (Cambridge: Cambridge University Press, 1998).

Wagner, Richard. *Der Ring des Nibelungen*, Wiener Philharmoniker, conducted by Sir Georg Solti, Decca, 1981, *Das Rheingold.* CD 2 414, 103–2. Scene 3, Sound cue 13 [3 min, 32], 'Schnell hinauf: dort ist er unser' (30 secs in).

Walder, Dennis, *Dickens and Religion* (London: Allen & Unwin, 1981).

Waters, Catherine, *Commodity Culture in Dickens's* 'Household Words': *The Social Life of Goods* (Aldershot: Ashgate, 2008).

Way, T.R. and G.R. Dennis (eds.), *The Art of James McNeill Whistler* (London: George Bell & Sons, 1903).

Weiner, Howard R., 'The Cinema and the City', *Journal of Popular Culture* 3.4 (Spring 1970): p. 825.

Welsh, Alexander, *The City of Dickens* (Oxford: Clarendon, 1971; repr. Cambridge, MA; London: Harvard University Press, 1986).

Williams, Raymond, *The Country and the City* (New York: Oxford University Press, 1973).

Willis, Mark, 'Charles Dickens and Fictions of the Crowd', *Dickens Quarterly* 23 (June 2006): pp. 85–107.

Wilson, Edmund, 'Marcel Proust', in Wilson, *Axel's Castle: A Study in the Imaginative Literature of 1870–1930*, 9th impression (London: Fontana, Flamingo, 1979).

Wolfreys, Julian, *Writing London* (Basingstoke; New York: Palgrave, 1998).

———, *Dickens to Hardy 1837–1884* (Basingstoke; New York: Palgrave, 2007).

Wolin, Richard, *Walter Benjamin: An Aesthetic of Redemption* (Berkeley; Los Angeles; London: University of California Press, 1994).

Wyndham, Violet, *The Sphinx and her Circle: A Biographical Sketch of Ada Leverson 1862–1933* (London: André Deutsch, 1963).

Yates, Edmund, *Recollections and Experiences*, 2 vols (London: Richard Bentley & Son, 1884).

Zimmerman, Virginia, *Excavating Victorians* (Albany: State University of New York Press, 2008).

Zola, Emile, *Germinal*, trans. Leonard Tancock (London: Everyman's Library, 1954).

———, *The Beast in Man*, trans. Alec Brown (London: Panther, 1956).

## Internet Sources

Allingham, Philip V., *The Victorian Web*, quoting the *Sunday Telegraph*, December 18, 1988, p. 1, <http://www.victorianweb.org/authors/dickens/pva/pav63.html>.

Leslie, Esther, 'Crossing Borders' Report on the Walter Benjamin Conference in Barcelona, September 25–27, 2000, Walter Benjamin Research Syndicate website, <http://www.wbenjamin.org/walterbenjamin.html>.

Sinclair, Iain, 'Maybe it's because he's a Londoner?', review of Peter Ackroyd's *London: The Biography*', *Guardian*, October 14, 2000, <http://books.guardian.co.uk/print/0,,4076226-99937,00.html>.

Wilson, Keith, 'London Contracting: The Internalizing of Urban Space in the Literature of Contemporary London', <http://www.literarylondon.org/london-journal/march2004/wilson.html>.

Wordsworth, William, *The Prelude*, 1850 version in 14 books, online at <http://www.gutenberg.org/files/12383/12383-h/Wordsworth3c.html#24b8>.

## Illustrations and Visual Works

Browne, Hablot Knight (1815–1882), 'The Sea Rises', September 3, 1859, the Victorian Web, <http://www.victorianweb.org/art/illustration/phiz/5b.html>.

Buss, Robert W. (1804–1875), 'Dickens's Dream', 1872, uncompleted watercolor in the Dickens House Museum, 48 Doughty Street, WC1, <http://www.dickensmuseum.com/vtour/firstfloor/study/dickensdream.php>.

Dürer, Albrecht (1471–1528), 'Melancholia I', 1514 woodcut, <http://www.alchemylab.com/melancholia.htm>.

Hogarth, William (1697–1764), 1754 series of oils on canvas, *An Election Entertainment; Canvassing for Votes; The Polling* and *Chairing the Member*, John Soane Museum, London. Engravings of these scenes are in the British Museum.

Millais, John Everett (1829–1896), 'Christ in the House of His Parents', 1849–1850, oil on canvas (34x55in), Tate Britain, London, and <http://www.victorianweb.org/painting/millais/paintings/house.html>.

Murillo, Bartolemé Esteban (1617–1682), 'The Immaculate Conception', 1678, oil on canvas in the Metropolitan Museum of Art, New York.

Whistler, James Abbott McNeill (1834–1903), 'Nocturne in Blue and Gold – Old Battersea Bridge', 1872–1875, oil on canvas, Tate Britain, London.

———, 'Old Westminster Bridge', 1859, etching on laid paper, in S.P. Avery Collection, New York Library.
———, 'Westminster Bridge in Progress', 1861, etching in black ink on creamy antique laid paper, S.P. Avery Collection, New York Library.
Williams, Samuel (1788–1853), 'The Child Asleep in her Bed', 1840, wood-engraving, <http://www.fidnet.com/~dap1955/dickens/curiosityshop.html>.

# Index